SWEDEN AND EUROPEAN INTEGRATION

Dedicated to my precious daughter, Anna

Sweden and European Integration

LEE MILES
Centre For European Union Studies (CEUS)
University of Hull

Ashgate

Aldershot • Brookfield USA • Singapore • Sydney

© Lee Miles 1997

Published by
Ashgate Publishing Limited
Gower House
Croft Road
Aldershot
Hants GU11 3HR
England

Ashgate Publishing Company
Old Post Road
Brookfield
Vermont 05036
USA

British Library Cataloguing in Publication Data
Miles, Lee
    Sweden and European integration
    1.Europe - Economic integration 2.Sweden - Politics and
    government - 1973 -
    I.Title
    327.4'85'04

Library of Congress Cataloging-in-Publication Data
Miles, Lee, 1969-
    Sweden and European integration / Lee Miles.
        p.   cm.
    ISBN 1-85521-629-9 (hardcover)
    1. European Union–Sweden. 2. Sweden–Economic policy.
I. Title.
HC241.25.S8M55   1997
337.48504–dc21   97-13479
                                                                                CIP

ISBN 1 85521 629 9

Printed and bound by Athenaeum Press, Ltd.,
Gateshead, Tyne & Wear.

Contents

List of Tables

List of Abbreviations

C	Centre Party (*Centrepartiet*)
CAP	Common Agricultural Policy
CFP	Common Fisheries Policy
CFSP	Common Foreign and Security Policy
EC	European Community
ECSC	European Coal and Steel Community
EDC	European Defence Community
EEC	European Economic Community
EFTA	European Free Trade Association
EMU	Economic and Monetary Union
EURATOM	European Atomic Energy Community
EU	European Union
FP	Liberal Party (*Folkpartiet Liberalerna*)
JHA	Justice and Home Affairs
KD	Christian Democratic Party (*Kristdemokraterna*)
LO	Swedish Confederation of Trade Unions (*Landsorganisationen*)
M	Moderate Party (*Moderata Samlingspartiet*)
MP	Green Party (*Miljöpartiet de Gröna*)
NORDEK	Nordic Economic Community
OECD	Organisation of Economic Cooperation and Development
OEEC	Organisation of European Economic Cooperation
PTK	Federation of Salaried Employees (*Privattjänstemannakartellen*)
SAF	Swedish Employers Confederation *(Svenska Arbetsgivareföreningen)*
SAP	Social Democratic Party (*Socialdemokratriska Arbetarepartiet*)
SACO	Swedish Central Organisation of Academics (*Sveriges akademikers centralorganisation*)
TCO	Swedish Central Organisation of Salaried Employees (*Tjänstemännens centralorganisation*)
TEU	Treaty on European Union
V	Left Party (*Vänsterpartiet*)

Foreword by Björn von Sydow

It is always gratifying when eminent academics from other countries take an interest in Sweden, particularly in a field which is of special interest to me. Over the decades, the international academic community has shown interest in Sweden, above all in our way of tackling welfare and income distribution issues. Well known examples include John Kenneth Galbraith and Marquis Childs who wrote about the 'Swedish model'. However, it is important that modern-day Sweden also becomes the object of academic analysis. Events in Sweden after 1989 need to be subjected to international scrutiny and interpretation.

Sweden's membership of the EU was a revolutionary event for the whole of our society. We shed our outside identity and joined the Community. Sweden had previously had the best solution to all problems, but now suddenly we were experiencing concrete cooperation with others who considered *their* solutions to be the best - cooperation of an intensity we had not previously experienced. All changes of identity involve not only new opportunities but also problems and difficulties in adapting. Foreign policy became domestic policy. Domestic policy became foreign policy. Constitutional and administrative changes followed. To be effective in Brussels, we had to speak with one voice while, at the same time, democracy required that many voices were heard. And all this took place at a time when legitimate demands for a sound economy led to the most extensive programme of budgetary reorganisation in the history of our country. The changes and deterioration were attributed to the EU by many Swedes.

Personally, I believe in progress and remain an ardent supporter of European cooperation. I have been, and continue to be, deeply committed to the process. I served in the Prime Minister's Office for several years in the 1980s and 1990s and was responsible for research. Thanks to the EU's framework programmes on research in which we participated in our capacity as members of EFTA, I learned a great deal about the functioning of the EU. As a Member of Parliament I worked to promote Sweden's EU membership. In my capacity as chairman of the Parliamentary IGC 96 Committee I led the work of informing the general public and stimulating the debate on the issues to be included in a new treaty. As Minister for Foreign Trade I saw in practical terms what a difference EU membership makes to a country's ability to exert influence, when I took part in the first World Trade Organisation (WTO) intergovernmental conference in Singapore. Sweden was able to exert much greater influence than would have been the case if we had not been a member of the EU, something which some other non-EU countries discovered. In the Social Democratic Party, to which I belòng, I am responsible for EU issues, including both Nordic and European assignments.

Lee Miles is launching the concept of the 'Swedish Diamond'. His main thesis is that the tension between Sweden's political and economic relationship with Europe determines the link to the European Union. The four main points of the 'Swedish Diamond' are consensual democracy, the country's corporate model, the high levels of economic interdependence and the pressures emanating from the external strategic environment. In terms of political science methodology, Miles' work is gifted and at the same time concrete. He captures the historical train of events leading to EU membership and demonstrates how and why primarily the Swedish establishment changed its attitude to membership.

He also convincingly describes how Sweden's economic dependence on foreign trade grew steadily during the period, and we sought to find ways of participating in arenas affecting us and our economy. This should, however, be accomplished without disrupting the other points of the 'Swedish Diamond'.

Miles' line of reasoning with regard to our relationship with the other Nordic countries is very interesting. He points out that, for the Swedes, the Nordic context has always been not a path *per se* but rather a path to something else. The picture of NORDEK is relevant, as it shows that Sweden was too strong for the others to venture to commit themselves to cooperation. On the other hand, the analysis shows that Sweden never really dared subscribe to any supranational solutions, not even at the Nordic level.

The Nordic way was not the answer to the need for more established cooperation to promote above all, economic interests in Western Europe. It was not until we joined EFTA that we made *any* progress. Through membership of the EEA, Sweden then ventured to take a step which it had not been bold enough to take before - integration into the EU's First Pillar, including the Single Market. We were not able to take any further steps to secure control over decisions affecting our foreign-trade-based economy until 1989 when the Cold War came to an end. Then it became possible for the Swedish establishment to agree that membership of the EU was both desirable and necessary, and a membership application was submitted. At this point in time, the majority of Swedish people were positive to the EU.

Lee Miles shows that when the non-socialist government took office in 1991, there was a swing in public opinion with people becoming more sceptical. The consensus that existed then and still exists today among members of the establishment is not to be found among the general public. This presents a great challenge to the people of Sweden and their representatives.

Finally, I would like to express my satisfaction that an international audience is becoming aware of the Swedish way of working through the Parliament's Advisory Committee on European Affairs and the Parliamentary IGC 96 Committee. I am convinced that these aspects of Swedish tradition represent deepened democracy and popular participation, which are preconditions for a living democracy in European cooperation.

Björn von Sydow 1997.

Acknowledgments

As an Englishman (or 'non-Swede') interested in both Sweden and the European Union, writing a book of this kind seems something of a lonely (and often misunderstood) endeavour. Any declaration of such an unusual combination of research interests is usually greeted by either silent incomprehension, amusement or simply a raised eyebrow anywhere outside the Nordic region. Swedish politics - like a well-mannered elder statesmen or gentlemen - seems to be the focus of attention for a small and measured few. In contrast, the subject of European integration endures the opposite extreme. Like an immature, emotional adolescent teenager - always receiving attention, the subject of some controversy and the source of much misinformation.

Therefore, to some extent, the decision to write this book is in response to the lack of general appreciation (certainly outside Scandinavia) of the significant contribution Sweden (and its practitioners and academics) have made to political science and to the study of European integration. The country, after all, was for a long time labelled as one of original and leading 'reluctant Europeans' and a champion of those wary of building a supranational European Community and Union. Moreover, the application for (1991) and achievement of (1995) full EU membership status reveals a deeper shift in Swedish society and attitudes towards European integration, which is in many ways endemic in most of the European liberal democracies. If this book (in some small way) provides a source of enlightenment (especially to 'non-Swedes') of the important role this small country has made and will make to the future of the European Union, then the author has, at least in part, fulfilled his fundamental objective.

Yet, a book of this kind is never entirely the product of one person. In particular, the author would like to take the opportunity to acknowledge the advice and contributions of others. Sincere thanks to Björn von Sydow for finding the time to write the Foreword and to Christopher Dent, Anna-Carin Johansson, Corinne Schurmann, Amanda Smith and Darren Sugden for their 'technical' expertise. The author was also grateful to Gabrielle Sjöstedt and the staff of the Swedish Institute, Stockholm and the Embassy of Sweden, London for their consistent patience in dealing with his (sometimes obscure) requests. In addition, the contributions, interviews and information provided by officials of the

Ministries of Foreign Affairs, Commerce and Finance during my various research trips to Sweden proved critical to the insights incorporated within this book.

Finally, and most of all, the author would like to thank his long-suffering wife, Lesa, for enduring the usual deprivations of anyone married to an academic and the hours and evenings spent alone downstairs whilst the author 'entertained' his word processor; and to my grandfather, Samuel Bernard Smith for providing the author with the inspiration and self-confidence that has culminated in the production of this book. This of course, does not detract from the fact that the views and any errors contained within this work can and must be placed at the door of Lee Miles.

Lee Miles
Deputy Director
Centre for European Union Studies (CEUS)
University of Hull

1 Introduction

To many outside observers, Sweden represents something of an enigma. This, to a large degree, derives from contrasting the country's political profile with its geographical size. As one commentator once noted, Sweden 'thinks the world of itself, yet the world thinks little of Sweden'.[1] The country appears also to have a dual reputation - being seen on the one hand, as a rather cold small state perched on the northern periphery of Europe and on the other, as the epicentre of Scandinavia due to its status as the largest of the Nordic countries. In geographical terms, Sweden is the fifth largest country in Europe - covering 977 miles from North to South, and sharing long land borders with Norway (in the North and West) and with Finland (in the North East) and a two thousand miles-long coastline that stretches from the North Sea (in the South West) to the Baltic Sea (in the East). Sweden is also rich in natural resources, having large amounts of forestry (covering over half the country), iron ore and water reserves. These attributes have, at least partly, secured the country's wealth[2] and contributed to its other notable characteristics in the eyes of external observers - that of being an affluent and environmentally conscious nation.

Despite the country's geographic expanse, the reason why Sweden is perceived as a small state relates to her size of population (see Table 1.1), which only amounts to around 8.8 million and gives the country an exceedingly low population density of 21 inhabitants per square kilometre (or 52 inhabitants per square mile). Moreover, the demographic trends within the Swedish population, such as an increasingly ageing populace, also highlights the country's status as one of Europe's advanced industrialised democracies. In the last 20 years, population growth has been slow as a result of simultaneous declining birth and death rates. In 1994, there were 1.6 million people under the age of 15 and as many pensioners over the age of 65. In reflection of its industrialised status, the three largest cities of Stockholm, Malmö and Göteborg dominate the demographic location of the population with, for example, 1.7 million Swedes living within the county of Stockholm (the Malmö county accounts for a further 0.8 million, with the Göteborg and Bohus counties adding another 0.8 million residents). In contrast, the northern province of Norrland, which comprises over half of Sweden

1

(in terms of square kilometres) has a total population of a mere 1.2 million people. However, from a political perspective, Sweden's relationship to Europe has centred around, amongst other things, four major influences.

Table 1.1   Facts About Sweden

Area	449,964 square kilometres
	173,731 square miles
Population	8.8 million (10 percent immigrants)
Population Density	21 inhabitants per square kilometre
	52 inhabitants per square mile
Capital	Stockholm
Highest Mountain	Kebnekaise 2,111 metres (6,926 feet)
Longest River	Klarälven-Gotä älv, 720 kilometres (446 miles)
Largest Lake	Vänern 5,585 square kilometres (3,470 square miles)
Religion	88 percent Church of Sweden (Lutheran)
Main Exports	Wood, paper pulp, paper, paperboard, cars, trucks, aircraft, machinery, electrics/telecommunications, chemical products, iron and steel
Main Imports	Oil, cars, machinery and clothes

Source: Swedish Institute, Stockholm (1996).

Constant Trading Relations With the Rest of Europe

The political stability and economic prosperity of Sweden has been directly related to the country's constant focus on closer ties and trading opportunities with the rest of Europe. Even in the early days of its history, Sweden never remained aloof from wider Nordic and European influences and the country's development was intrinsically linked to her foreign trade with Europe. Stockholm which was established in 1250, expanded quickly as the result of exports (of iron, copper, butter, furs and hides) mainly to Germany.

Sweden's economic power has been reliant upon its ties with its Nordic and European neighbours and its territorial borders have shifted over time in relation to its degree of influence in Europe. Swedish power was, for instance, extended into Finland as long ago as the 14th century after a border agreement with Novgorod in 1323. Later and after continual armed conflict in the region, the Danish Queen Margereta united Sweden, Denmark and Norway as one large kingdom known as the Kalmar Union, after the place in southern Sweden where it was first agreed in 1397. Sweden remained subsumed into the wider Kalmar

Union until the re-emergence of the Swedish state under the reign of Gustav Vasa and the Vasa Monarchy of 1523-1611.

The intrinsic link between Sweden's prosperity and trade with Europe was no more evident than during the reign of Gustav II Adolf (1611-32), when the country rose from the ranks of the peripheral minor powers to become, if only for a short time, a European Great Power. The political leadership and administrative skills of the king[3] and his chancellor, Axel Oxenstierna, were chiefly responsible for this meteoric rise, especially in securing foreign capital and military supplies from overseas. The Swedish Empire built between 1560-1660 (although mainly from 1611 onwards) was primarily driven by the need to secure greater revenues abroad, especially as the population at this time was only around 1.5 million (of which 300,000 lived in the Swedish controlled territories in Finland). During these years, the Swedish Empire grew at the expense of Denmark, Russia and Poland and came to cover parts of Estonia (1561; taken from Russia), the provinces of Älvsborg (1613), Gotland, Skåne, Halland and Blekinge (from Denmark), as well as the acquisition of Jämtlands, Härjedalen and Bohuslän (from Norway, 1645) and Livonie (from Poland). After the Treaty of Westphalia in 1648, Sweden even gained a foothold in present-day Germany, gaining large areas of Pomerania, the city of Wismar, Bremen and Verden.

Given Sweden's small size and weak economy, the extent of the Empire at its zenith in 1660 was nothing short of breathtaking, and yet it was always destined to be a brief encounter. Sweden's superiority derived from its participation in the Thirty Years War, the utilisation of military innovation and from the outstanding military and political leadership of its rulers - a devastating cocktail that was far from permanent. Hence, after 1660, Sweden 'was not only a saturated power, but an over extended one'[4] and by the time of the Great Northern War with Russia (1700-1721), the external pressures upon the Empire were simply too great. One lesson that can be drawn from the Imperial experience was that the country's prosperity could only be maintained if substantial political and economic ties with Europe were secured. It was the loss of these ties as a result of military defeat that sealed the Empire's fate.

Constitutional Engineering

The second important influence was that Sweden was intermittently at the forefront of constitutional design in Europe. Elements that first appeared within the Swedish political system can be found all over Europe. Although there has been some controversy over the date of the birth of the Swedish Parliament, the Riksdag,[5] and that the Empire appeared to be 'no more than a ripple in a backwater'[6] leaving no permanent mark on European history, Sweden has, at various times, included some notable political characteristics. The 1634

Instrument of Government, which reorganised central government is regarded as being one of the most advanced models of its time and created a bureaucratic system that was effective in governing a rather disparate Empire.

Again, during the relatively short-lived 'Age of Liberty' (1719-1772), Sweden was at the spearhead of European constitutional design. In this era, early variants of parliamentary government, a party system and freedom of expression were all experimented with. The 1719 Instrument of Government, for instance, weakened royal power whilst that of the Riksdag increased. In effect, the Parliament's business was conducted through the Four Estates - the nobility, clergy, burghers and peasants - all of which became increasingly powerful and basically governed the country, although sometimes far from democratically. There were however, important accompanying and longer lasting breakthroughs during the 'Age of Liberty'. Sweden, for example, was one of the first to pass a Freedom of the Press Act (in 1766) allowing for the principle of publicity (*offentlighetsprincipen*) and improved control over the country's bureaucracy. Unfortunately, the Age of Liberty was quickly superseded by another equally brief Gustavian autocracy (1772-1809).

However, the strength of Swedish political traditions also reinforced stability within the country and allowed its polity to absorb seismic shocks, which in other nations would have resulted in civil unrest and even war. As a consequence of, for instance, the country's defeat in another disastrous war with Russia, the Kingdom of Sweden experienced the loss of Finland and a huge political crisis (which led to the abdication of Gustav IV Adolf after a coup d'état) in 1809; yet policy-makers managed to politically negotiate a new constitution that was to prove to be an unqualified success.

The 1809 Instrument of Government was to serve the country until 1975 (with numerous amendments). In practice, the constitutional drafters struck a fine balance between the unrestrained powers of the Estates in the Age of Liberty and the absolutism of previous monarchical regimes. It was mainly for this reason that the 1809 Instrument has been referred to as 'Swedish history translated into legal paragraphs'.[7] The Instrument included notable constitutional elements, including an elaborate system encompassing the separation of powers. It was a careful mix of modernising features - legislative power being split between the Crown and the Riksdag, with each able to initiate and veto legislation - and conservative measures reflecting the social and economic structures of the country's pre-industrial society; for example, the Riksdag of the Four Estates was retained.

The Swedish political system was further modernised by another path-breaking constitutional reform embodied in the 1866 Riksdag Act, which allowed for the dissolution of the Four-Estates Parliament and its replacement by a new bi-cameral Riksdag. However, despite Sweden being at the forefront of constitutional modernisation, the pace was much slower as regards the mass democratisation of its political system. Even with the 1866 Riksdag Act, for instance, the new Upper House was indirectly elected and appointed by a very small minority of elite Swedes. Its members were appointed by town and county councils, whilst companies and businesses were also enfranchised as corporate bodies. Although the new Lower House was directly elected, it was not until 1921 that elections were conducted by a universal and equal suffrage. Ironically, despite Sweden's constitutional progressiveness 'a government by the people for the people came late to Sweden, even later than to any of its Nordic neighbours'.[8]

The durability of these constitutional arrangements was most of all illustrated during the years of 1905-20. At a time when the rest of Europe suffered from continual bouts of political instability, Swedish policy-makers engineered relatively major constitutional changes without resorting to civil war or the undermining of the political system. In 1905, the Conservative Prime Minister Arvid Lindman brought about a peaceful dissolution of Sweden's Union with Norway and went on to propose reforms introducing universal male suffrage in 1907 with widespread party support. In March 1920, the world's first peacefully elected socialist government came to power in Sweden illustrating the country's progressiveness and the strength of its parliamentary democracy.[9]

An Affluent and Leading Industrialised Nation-State

The third major characteristic in relation to European integration was that Sweden came to be regarded (in conjunction with her highly sophisticated polity), as one of Europe's most stable, industrialised and affluent countries within the space of a century. Yet, the country's status as an advanced industrialised democracy is still comparatively recent. In the mid-19th century, the Swedish economy was still dominated by agriculture and related occupations and in 1850, a mere 10 percent of the population lived in cities and towns. Industrialisation only became more intense after 1850, with the share of the workforce engaged in industry and crafts rising from 10 percent in 1850 to over 30 percent in 1910. Once again, this industrialisation was linked, to a limited degree, to levels of European cooperation as the introduction of new technology, such as steam powered saw-mills, led to a significant increase in productivity in Swedish forestry, paper and pulp industries, which combined with rising demand from key markets, such as from Great Britain, allowed for a significant growth in exports.

During the late 19th and early 20th century, Sweden was transformed from a primarily agricultural country into a modern industrialised nation-state. Her large natural resources, especially iron ore and forestry, proved to be critical in fuelling this growth as they became more efficiently used as new technologies became available. At least in part, the economy benefited greatly from the growth of international trade and substantial exports to other European markets.

According to Hadenius, Sweden's dramatic transformation can be attributed to three main reasons.[10] First, its industrialisation was accompanied by a gradual internationalisation of commerce. The fact that Sweden is a small state reliant upon overseas trade and revenues for its prosperity remained as applicable in the early 20th century as it did during the days of the Empire. The increase in demand for Swedish goods was primarily export-driven. Second, the expansion of the railroad network (starting with the 1864 Göteborg-Stockholm line) provided Sweden with a low cost transport infrastructure and acted as an integral part of *de facto* regional development policy, linking together regions which had hitherto been neglected.

Third, the industrialisation was also aided by population growth - rising from 3.5 million in 1850 to 5.9 million in 1920 - and providing the new factories and mills with a good supply of labour. Swedish governments were also relatively quick to promote an educated work force. From as early as 1842 a system of publicly operated primary schools was created. Ironically, this growth in population was also in spite of mass emigration from the mainly rural parts of southern and western Sweden to North America, which amounted to around 850,000 between 1850-1900. This emigration ensured that the majority of remaining Swedish labour was always in work.

In many ways, international influences again helped to ensure that Swedish industrialisation was sustained for almost 70 years and that the country had an industrial base capable of fully utilising raw materials for both domestic and foreign markets by the end of the 19th century. Textiles, paper pulp and engineering products came to represent almost half of Swedish exports in 1890, whilst the other 50 percent consisted of raw materials, such as iron, grain, metal ores and timber.[11] Indeed, this emphasis on key materials and foreign markets led to the establishment of key Swedish firms, which have since become household names, such as Ericsson, and of course, Sweden's best known industrialist, Alfred Nobel (1833-96).

The country's industrialisation and urbanisation continued throughout the inter-war period, although in 1920, agriculture and forestry still accounted for 43.5 percent of the entire Swedish workforce. However, there was substantial growth in the distributive and communications sectors and in general, Swedish industrial production leapt by around 35 percent from 1925-29.[12] The expansion of the economy was especially striking during the 1913-45 period, when it grew on average by 2.5 percent per year - a rate unequalled by any other country. In the post-war period, the structural trends continued unabated until 1974. Agriculture fell from a 15 percent share of GNP in 1945 to just over 6 percent in 1970 and industrial production peaked in the boom period of the 1960s climbing on average 6 percent a year.[13]

As Samuelsson notes, it was during the 1960s that Sweden 'fully matured' as an industrial society and allowed it to be regarded (sometimes absurdly) as 'a country of near-exotic qualities' with high standards of living, advanced welfare policies and a harmonious labour market.[14] Certainly, the country's privileged position influenced 'Sweden's view of herself and of the world around her, producing a feeling of isolation and self-sufficiency' - manifested in the country's neutrality policy. The sound industrial structure provided a firm foundation for even stronger economic growth in the latter part of the 20th century and secured the country's mantle as one of the most affluent countries in Europe (until 1990).[15] Although the severe recession in the early 1990s led to substantial economic problems and saw the country fall to 19th in the OECD's 1995 GDP per capita league table (of advanced industrialised nations), Sweden is still generally regarded as one of Europe's most prosperous states.

A Social Democratic and Corporate Polity

The country's long period of sustained prosperity reinforced the fourth main characteristic of Sweden as regards its wider European profile - namely that of being one of the leading social democratic and corporate countries. Many political scientists argued, albeit to various degrees, that from 1930-90, the country could be attributed with its own 'Swedish model' of social democratic, corporate and consensus policy-making, representing a 'middle way' between capitalism and communism (see Chapter Two).[16]

The rudiments of this claim derive from the development of a relatively unusual style of industrial relations developing within the country. A natural tendency towards consensus was identifiable even in the early days. In 1898, the Swedish Confederation of Trade Unions (*Landsorganisationen, LO*) was formed to negotiate wage increases on behalf of member unions and in response, the Swedish Employers' Confederation (*Svenska Arbetsgivareföreningen, SAF*) was created - representing the beginning of organised industrial relations.

However, it was during the 1930s that the first major traces of the now widely regarded consensual and corporate style of Swedish decision-making became obvious. From 1920-33, Sweden experienced a period of unstable minority and coalition governments, primarily as a result of grappling with the wider phenomenon of severe recession and greater domestic demands for economic solutions from governments. Nine different Cabinets held office during 1920-33, making it virtually impossible to implement a consistent and stable economic policy. Unemployment reached record breaking levels during the early 1930s - for example, some 20 percent of the country's trade union members were out of work in 1930 - and following closely upon the heels of substantial industrial unrest in the 1920s. Sweden endured a series of economic crises - including the 1931-32 Kreuger crash and the 1931 Ådalen riots - which came to symbolise the rising confrontation between Swedish business and employees at the workplace.

Yet, unlike in many other European countries where similar economic and political problems led to either ineffective coalition government, (for instance, in France's Third Republic) and/or increased the popularity of extreme political ideologies, (such as Fascism in Italy and Spain and Nazism in Germany), what was noticeable in Sweden was the emergence of a moderate, yet highly successful solution by government to deal with the enveloping economic recession of the 1930s. Although it is fair to say that the depression within Sweden was not as harsh as that in say Germany, a moderate approach was possible as democracy became quickly entrenched in the Swedish political system with political parties and the trade union movement better equipped to deal with economic crisis. As early as 1930, the Social Democratic Party (SAP) presented proposals to the Riksdag calling for expansive economic measures and a strong commitment to full employment aimed at combating the depression.

In 1932, a new Social Democratic government came to power under the leadership of Per Albin Hansson, which enjoyed strong parliamentary support after reaching broad agreement with the Agrarians (later known as the Centre Party) in 1933.[17] During the 1930s, this 'red-green' coalition became more permanent and successive governments under Hansson followed an economic strategy that was to mould Swedish politics for over 50 years. Hansson was to be the architect of the so-called 'People's Home' (*Folkhemmet*). As well as following a primarily Keynesian approach to solving unemployment and the first foundations of the expansive welfare state being laid, (for example, a special unemployment insurance scheme was established in 1934 and in 1935 basic pensions to retired people were raised), the government also secured a path-breaking agreement between the two arms of Swedish industrial relations.

The so-called 'spirit of Saltsjöbaden' emerged from the 1938 Basic Agreement (otherwise known as the Saltsjöbaden Agreement) between the two major interest organisations in the labour market - the LO and the SAF. Saltsjöbaden not only secured industrial peace, but laid the foundation for the development of what became known as the 'Swedish Model' (see Chapter Two). This 'historic compromise' established the base for a system of collective bargaining between business and labour, which although revised at various times, maintained the 'spirit' of the Agreement. The labour movement signalled to the owners of private industry that they would not have to fear the threat of large-scale nationalisation and that the labour movement accepted that trade and industry must remain in private hands. In turn, these promises would remain as long as the employers ensured that industry was efficiently run and that private industry would accept the fact that the labour movement would use its influence in the Riksdag to implement social welfare policies.

The Basic Agreement incorporated two notable features. First, that collective bargaining would be centralised and second, it did not foresee government interference. Both sides effectively guaranteed that their respective rank and files would abide by any deals reached by the two main organisations' elite. This highly centralised system of collective bargaining included numerous checks and balances aimed at reducing the chances of conflict and with state-appointed arbitrators only being called in if industrial action was taken by either side. This agreement or rather the 'spirit' emanating from it was to govern Swedish industrial relations for the next 50 years and 'ushered in an age of unprecedented labour peace in Sweden'.[18] As Gustaf Söderlund, President of the SAF in the 1930s once commented, 'it was absolutely necessary to create an atmosphere that concentrates on practical and reasonable solutions. ...We grew together out there'.[19] In sum, the Agreement marked the turning-point in the development of corporate and consensual approaches to decision-making and facilitated the expansion of the welfare state, which were to become the other main Swedish characteristics of the post-war era (see Chapter Two).

As a result of this new and relatively peaceful era of industrial relations, combined with the fact that the country avoided being drawn into the Second World War at any cost, Sweden enjoyed almost continual economic growth from the 1940s until the early 1970s. This bolstered political scientists' claims that Sweden represented a practical example of the viability of social democratic and generous welfare polices, although in reality, the country's prosperity was always reliant upon her success in (mainly European) export markets. Her economic growth was again primarily export-driven with all the major export-orientated industries being very successful.[20] These high rates of growth provided the economic foundation for industrial modernisation, allowed for an accompanying increase in service sector employment and public services and for a continuation of centralised and collectively bargained agreements between capital and labour. According to Fullerton and Knowles, the combined strength of the employers and trade union organisations actually reinforced each other.[21] Employers and trade unions both sought higher productivity and were prepared to settle for wage levels that did not price their products out of foreign markets. The country's reliance on foreign markets acted as an external pressure and ensured Sweden remained competitive, prosperous and allowed for the expansion of welfare state provision.

In many ways then, the historical development of Sweden has been intertwined with that of the European continent. However, since the evolution of the ambitious European integration process, the challenges confronting her have become progressively larger.

The Objectives of the Book

In the author's view, the relationship between Sweden and European integration is of specific and increasing interest. From a Swedish perspective, the country's prosperity has been and is related to the wider relationship with Europe. Sweden provides a good practical example of the challenges confronting a peripheral state in dealing with the emerging challenge of an integrating Europe. Second, Sweden's sound economic performance in the past must, at least in part, be related to her ability to succeed politically and economically in Europe and act as an indicator of how small states operate in the European context. Third, Sweden has, at various times, been at the forefront of constitutional development and it can be argued is worthy of attention on political grounds alone. More importantly, the development of a specific 'Swedish model' has relied upon continued economic growth induced from foreign trade. Ironically, the country's domestic model of an advanced consensual, corporate, social democratic welfare state was, albeit to a limited extent, reliant upon external European considerations.

Yet, to most outside observers, Sweden's relations with Western Europe were an enigma for most of the post-war period. On the one hand, a country heavily reliant upon its economic links with Europe and thus one that cannot afford to be isolated from its main earnings potential, and yet, its governments continued to resist the European integration process for political reasons. This has been referred to elsewhere as the 'Swedish Paradox' which authors such as James Waite have articulated since the 1970s. Waite argued that events by the early 1970s had forced Sweden 'to come to terms with a politically loaded economic situation which threatens the very premise of neutrality, i.e. independence of action'.[22] He suggested that Swedish perspectives on European integration encompassed two dimensions - one economic and one political.[23] On the one hand, Swedish policy-makers deemed it necessary to maintain very close trading relations with the rest of Europe in order that the country could guarantee its exports access to European markets and consequently, fund its own policy and welfare outcomes. For economic reasons, Sweden needed to find some type of close relationship with the expanding EEC.

However, the political dimension was 'another matter' and rested on the problems of reconciling any close economic alliance with Swedish principles of independence and neutrality. Swedish governments remained deeply suspicious of any external framework of which membership would require a substantial transfer of national sovereignty and thereby infringe its neutrality doctrine. Any international organisation that would require a transfer of national sovereignty and which would, at best, inhibit, or at worst, discredit, Sweden's traditional foreign policy of 'non-alignment in peacetime and neutrality in wartime' was resisted.[24] This 'Paradox' of reconciling economic interdependence with, and the need for political independence from, Europe provided one of the central themes governing foreign policy towards Western Europe and European integration.[25]

The 'Swedish Paradox' continued, albeit to a lessening degree, to govern Swedish relations with the European Community up until the late 1980s. Membership of European organisations of a primarily intergovernmental nature, such as the Nordic Council and the European Free Trade Association (EFTA) helped to square this circle. It is not surprising therefore, that Sweden earned the reputation for being a 'reluctant European'. Swedish governments sought to reconcile pre-conceptions of national sovereignty and neutrality with the country's historical reliance on Europe for economic prosperity.[26] However, the emergence of a successful and expanding European Community (EC) called for more sophisticated Swedish policies dealing with European integration. Swedish relations with the EC underwent relatively dramatic changes during the late 1980s and eventually the country went on to become a full member in January 1995. None the less, very few recent attempts have been made at trying to make sense of the longer term changes in Swedish perspectives towards European integration covering the whole era of the EC's development from 1958-96.

Therefore, the achievement of Swedish full membership of the (now) expanded European Union (EU) provides both a timely and viable opportunity for attempting such a task. A more extensive study of Sweden and European integration is appropriate now that the country has completed her transition from an EFTA neutral to a full EU member. Furthermore, as Sweden represents one-third of Nordic representation in the European Union and combined with its traditional role as the largest and to some extent, most influential nation in Scandinavia, Swedish governments will play an active role in promoting Nordic interests within the EU and in defending wider Nordic interests in EU decision-making. Indeed, given the fact that since 1995, the majority of the Nordic countries are now part of the EU, Sweden will also seek to ensure that the interests of other Nordic non-member states are considered. To what extent the country will act as a Nordic champion and defender of the region remains to be seen. Yet, it is perhaps fair to say that Swedish governments do perceive that they have a useful contribution to make to the EU's development as the Union seeks to expand to include more members and 'deepen' as the 21st century approaches.

This book is therefore one of the first recent attempts at such an extensive study. It is aimed at the non-specialist in Swedish politics and those who may be interested in European integration in general. With this in mind, this book introduces the conceptual framework of the 'Swedish Diamond' to explain the development of Swedish perspectives on European integration, before finally arguing that since the country has become a full member of the EU a revised 'Membership Diamond' is now useful in explaining present and future Swedish policies towards the European Union. The intention, whilst in no way suggesting that the author has developed a new theory of integration, is not merely to provide a chronological assessment, but also to propose a conceptual framework in which to examine Swedish perspectives on the European Union. The book by introducing the 'Membership Diamond' should therefore in its final sections provide an indication of the problems facing future governments in reconciling the challenges of membership obligations, the new agendas of the Union and the caution of a mostly hostile domestic population.

Notes

[1] Mosey, C. (1991) *Cruel Awakening: Sweden and the Killing of Olof Palme*, Hurst & Co., London, p. 1.

[2] Forestry products still account for 17 percent of the country's total export value. For a detailed assessment of export patterns - see Ministry of Foreign Affairs, (1996) *Annual Report Sweden 1995*, Ministry of Foreign Affairs, Stockholm, p. 9.

[3] For a comprehensive appraisal of Gustav II Adolf see Roberts, M. (1992) *Gustavus Adolphus*, Longman, London.

[4] Rystad, G. (1987) The Estates of the Realm, the Monarchy, and Empire, 1611-1718 in Metcalf, M. *The Riksdag: A History of the Swedish Parliament*, St. Martins Press, New York, p. 64.

[5] The Arboga Assembly of 1435 was for a long time considered to be the most likely starting date of the Riksdag, although Schück has argued that the traditional Four-Estate parliament did not emerge until the 1520s and the term 'Riksdag' did not appear until 1561. - Schück, H. (1987) Sweden's Early Parliamentary Institutions From the Thirteenth Century and 1611 in Metcalf, M. *The Riksdag: A History of the Swedish Parliament*, St. Martins Press, New York, pp. 5-58.

[6] Roberts, M. (1979) *Sweden's Imperial Experience 1560-1718*, Cambridge University Press, Cambridge, p. 1.

[7] Fahlbeck, P. (1910) *Regeringsformen i historisk belysning*, Stockholm, p. 29.

[8] Fleischer, F. (1967) *The New Sweden: The Challenge of a Disciplined Democracy*, McKay, New York, p. 145.

[9] Scott, F. D. (1977) *Sweden - The Nation's History*, University of Minnesota Press, Minneapolis, pp. 484-5.

[10] Hadenius, S. (1990) *Swedish Politics During the 20th Century*, Swedish Institute, Stockholm, p. 8.

[11] Op. cit., Hadenius (1990) p. 9.

[12] The 1920s, the decade when Swedish industry made its most notable breakthroughs, has rightly been called 'Sweden's Second Great Age' - see Weibull, J. (1993) *Swedish History in Outline*, Swedish Institute, Stockholm, pp. 117-8.

[13] Hallvarsson, M. (1981) *Swedish Industry in the 1980s*, Swedish Institute, Stockholm, p. 22.

[14] Samuelsson, K. (1968) *From Great Power to Welfare State*, Allen & Unwin, London, pp. 223-4.

[15] This version of Swedish success has been challenged by others. Most notably, Roland Huntford argued that Sweden's comprehensive social welfare provision, neutrality and corporate efficiency are 'products not of enlightenment but of a profound insecurity and uniformity in the Swedish character'. Huntford suggested that Sweden was the nearest practical example of Aldous Huxley's *Brave New World* - Huntford, R. (1971) *The New Totalitarians,* Allen Lane, London, pp.7-13.

[16] See Childs, M. W. (1980) *The Middle Way on Trial,* Yale University Press, New Haven.

[17] A useful summary of this critical period is provided in Söderpalm, S. A. (1975) The Crisis Agreement and the Social Democratic Road to Power in Koblik, S. *Sweden's Development from Poverty to Affluence 1750-1970,* University of Minnesota Press, Minneapolis, pp. 258-78.

[18] Campbell, C., Feigenbaum, H., Linden, R. & Norpoth, H. (1995) *Politics and Government in Europe Today,* Houghton, Boston, p. 588.

[19] Op. cit., Fleischer (1967) pp. 80-1.

[20] Assar Lindbeck for instance has estimated that despite Sweden being 'a latecomer to the process of modern economic growth', the growth rate in Sweden from 1870-1970 was second only to that of Japan and that this was 'basically an export-led, or export-biased process, closely connected with the expansion of international demand for Swedish exports' - see Lindbeck, A. (1975) *Swedish Economic Policy,* Macmillan, London, pp. 1-3.

[21] Fullerton, B. & Knowles, R. (1991) *Scandinavia,* Paul Chapman, London, p. 22.

[22] Waite, J. L. (1973) The Swedish Paradox: EEC and Neutrality, *Journal of Common Market Studies,* 12, pp. 319-36.

[23] Op. cit., Fullerton & Knowles (1991) p. 16.

[24] For a discussion of Swedish neutrality - see for example, Hakovirta, H. (1988) *East-West Conflict and European Neutrality,* Clarendon, Oxford, or Sundelius, B. (ed.) (1987) *The Committed Neutral: Sweden's Foreign Policy,* Westview, Boulder.

[25] Miles, L. (1994) Sweden and Finland - From EFTA Neutrals to EU Members in Redmond, J. (ed.) *Prospective Europeans,* Harvester-Wheatsheaf, London, pp. 59-85.

[26] The phrase became synonymous with a detailed study of Nordic attitudes towards European integration by Miljan, T. (1977) *The Reluctant Europeans,* Hurst & Co., London.

2 Decision-Making and the 'Swedish Diamond'

If Swedish attitudes towards European integration are to be fully understood then an appreciation of domestic policy-making is essential. The country's decision-making process, and the perceptions that derive from it, have without doubt influenced its overall policy on European integration. This is further reinforced by the fact that Sweden has, in the past, been regarded from the outside as maintaining a successful organisational model for governing the political and economic functioning of the state. Consequently, this status also influenced governmental policy on European supranational organisations.

The objective of the chapter is to introduce the reader to Swedish domestic politics and its role in defining elite attitudes towards European integration. In particular, the chapter will argue that Swedish resistance to full membership of the European Community (EC) can be broadly understood through the conceptual framework of the 'Swedish Diamond'. The Diamond advocates that there were four main variables (or 'points') that determined whether full membership was a viable option between 1958-90 and that it was changes to the balance and nature of these four points that eventually enabled Swedish policy-makers to lodge a full membership application (1 July 1991).

The chapter will outline the four points of the 'Swedish Diamond' - an integrative and consensual democracy, the country's corporate model, the high levels of economic interdependence and the pressures emanating from the external strategic environment. The intention is to provide the reader with an introduction to the main aspects of Swedish politics/political economy and emanating from this, the Diamond's conceptual framework. By taking this approach and through the Diamond, the main considerations that have historically dominated governmental perspectives regarding European integration will be obvious and will underpin the assessment of Swedish-EC relations of the later chapters.

The 'Swedish Diamond'

The objective of the chapter is not to deliberate on the debate surrounding the merits of a 'Swedish model',[1] but rather to stress those aspects that are important for the country's relationship to European integration. Sweden has none the less, been of intense interest to political scientists and has been labelled in different ways. Tilton, for example, argued that Sweden represents the best Nordic type of an 'integrative' democracy, whereby all the main political actors are consulted and there is an excellent synthesis between political decision-making and economic policy.[2] In contrast, Korpi argued that Sweden represented a prime example for explaining the constant balance of power between labour and capitalist forces within an economy and that the development of a substantial 'Swedish model' (see later section) marked a victory for the labour movement.[3] To some extent, Esping-Andersen[4] and Pontusson[5] also recognise that the country illustrates the importance of political forces in shaping the organisation of a state's economy, although Pontusson goes on to suggest that the development of the 'Swedish model' was as a result of 'production politics' between those involved in economic activity. However, in this context, the problem with the existing debate is that the model was essentially aimed at addressing the conduct of domestic politics and consequently, either ignored or underestimated the growing role of European integration in shaping economic forces. To a limited extent, this book begins to address this deficiency.

Whilst not ruling out or rejecting the validity of previous analysis of Swedish politics, there has also been a tendency to examine Sweden as an isolated national case, almost devoid of, and immune from, outside political pressures. Clearly, there is a place for a coherent conceptual approach explaining Sweden's transformation into a full EU member. In reality, there is a direct link between the organisation and conduct of the domestic polity and governmental positions on European integration as, for the most part, any Swedish European policy must accommodate domestic political attitudes and constellations if it is to maintain credibility. Consequently, the interface between domestic perceptions and external influences is one of the central assumptions surrounding the concept of the 'Swedish Diamond'.

In short, the interrelationship between the domestic polity and European integration is incorporated within the Diamond's four points. The Diamond does not provide a comprehensive appraisal of all domestic factors operating within Sweden, for this is done in greater detail elsewhere, yet it does provide a conceptual framework for considering those aspects that are most important in determining Swedish elite attitudes towards European integration. In general, these notable characteristics fall into four broad categories or points:

- *An Integrative and Consensual Democracy.* Sweden has a mature parliamentary democracy characterised by traditions of decision-making by consensus and a low degree of opposition to the existing political system. This has also been translated into meaning open government and a large degree of public access to government documents. These traditions have encouraged strong attachments to national sovereignty, a domestic self-confidence in the strength of Swedish democracy and elite resistance to any elements of the European integration process that were perceived to undermine them.

- *A Limited Acceptance of and Attachment to the 'Swedish Model'.* Sweden has developed elaborate corporate procedures for economic policy-making, a long association with the usage of collective bargaining, generous welfare provision and comprehensive social and environmental standards. Corporate actors, for the most part, believed that the strength and long-standing success of the country's economy derived from their structured type of industrial relations and policy-making and in similar vein, remained wary that the European integration process could undermine it.

- *A Small Export-Reliant Nation-State.* Policy-makers have nevertheless, been constantly aware of the country's economic interdependence with the rest of Europe and her vulnerability as a small state. In general, they have shown a strong preference for a free trade, (preferably) global economy and the fullest possible access to European markets for Swedish exports. Governmental priorities as regards European integration have therefore reflected concerns surrounding international trade.

- *A Neutral and Non-Aligned Power.* The country, for various reasons, has remained neutral voluntarily since 1814 and developed a domestic consensus amongst the main political parties in favour of a security policy based upon 'non-alignment in peacetime leading to neutrality in the event of war'. The established doctrine of neutrality policy was consequently a primary influence on domestic policies and above all, on elite attitudes towards European integration.[6]

The Diamond's four points (see Table 2.1) in effect governed Swedish governmental policy towards the EC until 1990 and ensured that the country could not become a full member. Moreover, as later chapters will discuss, it was substantial changes to at least three of the four points that led to the reversal of Swedish policy towards the EC and the lodging of a full membership application (1 July 1991). With these considerations in mind, this chapter will now evaluate the Diamond's four points in greater detail.

Table 2.1 **The 'Swedish Diamond'**

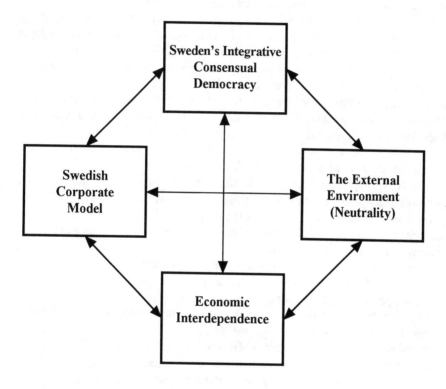

a) Point 1: An Integrative and Consensual Democracy

It has been generally recognised amongst political scientists that aspects of Swedish decision-making, whilst not being completely distinct from other models or nations, suggested that Swedish politics were different in spirit, if not always in terms of constitutional maxims, rules or laws. Most notably, many have identified that the country's decision-making process incorporates a commitment at all levels to governing though consensus. Elder, Thomas and Arter, for instance, have argued that the Nordic countries (of which Sweden provides the best example) can be regarded as 'consensual democracies'.[7] According to them, Swedish decision-making adheres to three fundamental rules (and thus qualifies as a consensual democracy). First, a consensual democracy must be a liberal democratic state characterised by a minimal level of opposition to the political framework designed to deal with the resolution of political conflict. Second, it also includes an equally low degree of domestic conflict over the actual exercise of power within the state. Third, a consensual democracy also encompasses 'a high degree of concertation in the gestation of public policy'.[8]

When the main mechanisms of decision-making are examined, then the country does, even now, seem to fit the bill laid down by Elder, Thomas and Arter. A strong identification with the 1974 Instrument of Government's constitutional arrangements still exists. The Instrument established the relationship between the Riksdag, the Head of State, the government, legislation, the power of appropriation, relations with other states, justice, administration and the right of scrutiny. The country retained its constitutional monarchy, although the sovereign's powers as regards decision-making were all but removed. The responsibility for the formation of Swedish governments, for instance, now lies with the Speaker and the Riksdag.

The Instrument also included several important principles - that all public power derives from the people and that Sweden will have 'a representative and parliamentary polity' (Instrument of Government, paragraph 2). Consequently, the constitution incorporates a commitment to the principle of open government (*offenlighetsprincipen*) and public accountability. Free public access to official records and the protection of those giving information to the media (*meddalarfriheten*) are covered by the 1949 Freedom of the Press Act and the 1991 Freedom of Expression Act, which whilst not giving an absolute right of public access to official documents, is widely regarded as being one of the most progressive of the Western European democracies.

This balanced constitution is popular and domestic loyalty to it remains high. Although there have been some changes, the strong level of public support has, in fact, been reflected within domestic perspectives towards European integration. Both politicians and public alike remain defensive and resistant to any aspects of European integration that will undermine Swedish constitutional principles, especially those of open government and public accountability. To a limited extent, the fact that Sweden has a successful constitution neutralised one of the main arguments for joining the Community prevalent in other countries (such as Spain, Portugal and Greece in the 1970s-80s) - namely as a way of bolstering their parliamentary democracies. Rather, it reinforced the (rather condescending) view within the elite that Sweden's democracy was, in many ways, superior to its continental counterparts and that the Community would have more to learn from Sweden than vice-versa.

i) Introducing the Swedish Political System - The Riksdag and Parliamentary Sovereignty

More importantly, the Riksdag maintains parliamentary sovereignty under the Instrument and the main political parties and interest groups remain committed to the central role of the Riksdag within decision-making. The modern Parliament (and incidentally a new electoral procedure) were introduced in time for the 1970 general election and the revised unicameral Riksdag was inaugurated in 1971, with a membership of 350. As an outcome of the tied result in the 1973 election (where the socialists and non-socialist each controlled 175 seats and the new government had to be decided by lottery), the number of representatives in the Riksdag was reduced to 349 in the 1974 Instrument.[9] Crucially, for this context, the Riksdag is central to Swedish decision-making and remains, at least officially, the sovereign institution in terms of political power. Moreover, its long history of evolution - dating back in various forms from 1435 - has facilitated a strong public and party attachment to the Riksdag and parliamentary sovereignty. To many Swedes, the Riksdag is the embodiment of democracy and the nation-state.

It is not surprising then that one of the constant features of the domestic debate on European integration since 1958 has surrounded the implication of integration for the Riksdag's parliamentary sovereignty and provided one of the main reasons for resisting full membership. The fact that the life of each session of the Parliament is also comparatively short - with only three years between general elections during 1970-94[10] - fostered domestic loyalty to the 1974 Instrument of Government. Indeed, turnout in Swedish national elections has consistently been high averaging around 89 percent between 1973-94.[11]

Furthermore, as Petersson notes, Sweden has a disproportionately large parliament when compared to her relatively small size of population and her continental or British counterparts.[12] The large number of seats in proportion to population size is, in part, designed to ensure that the sparsely populated areas of Northern Sweden are not inadequately represented. The Riksdag serves, amongst others, a dual function. On the one hand, as publicity for the good health of the country's democratic institutions and on the other, as an acknowledgement of the differences between the cosmopolitan areas of southern Sweden and the more sparse and rural North. The 349 Riksdag seats consist of 310 fixed constituency seats and 39 additional members or supplementary seats. These supplementary seats reflect the party list system used in Swedish elections and are allocated so that the parliamentary seats for the entire country are in proportion to the votes cast for each party nation-wide. In general, the supplementary seats favour small parties who have managed to jump the national 4 percent rule, as these are the parties that generally do well across the country, but fail to win seats in individual fixed constituencies.

Political parties rather than individual members are the dominant actors in the Riksdag, especially as members of the House are elected according to a party list system in which the members may be elected to individual seats, but the parties control the nomination of candidates on the ballot. Consequently, the whip system in the Riksdag is very strong and defections are rare. Historically, this has meant that MPs' dissension on EU issues in the Riksdag were less noticeable than say in other comparable legislatures, even when they nevertheless existed politically. Yet, since the 1994 municipal elections and the September 1995 direct elections to the European Parliament, voters were also able to indicate their preference for individual candidates - with voters ticking the candidate's name that should be placed at the head of the party list. However, for the most part, the electoral system, whilst sturdy enough to withstand modernisation has also acted as an enforcer of party discipline inside the Riksdag.

According to the 1974 Instrument, the Riksdag is central to the Swedish constitution and enjoys four roles - which are not dissimilar from those enjoyed by most Western European legislatures. The first three roles are those fundamental to any legislature - that of passing legislation, exercising financial control and supervising the executive. Yet, unlike other European legislatures, the slippage of power to the executive has been less noticeable as the limited three year life span of most governments constrained their ability to dominate the initiation of legislation. As Larsson notes, 'important changes in current policy must be supported by the legislating of the Riksdag. In fact, there are no limitations in the rights of the Riksdag to make decisions on any issue it considers interesting, be it important or trivial'.[13] Arter goes further. He argues that the Riksdag is an unusually strong policy-influencing assembly in so far as it is able to effectively participate at all three stages of the policy cycle - formulation, deliberation and implementation.[14]

There are several features associated with the Riksdag's procedures which are of relevance to the later discussion on European integration. The first, ironically, is that any government bill has already been subject to a rather elaborate referral process in which any prospective legislative proposals are circulated amongst interested parties and pressure groups in order that legislation takes account of their views. As Larsson comments, 'traditionally, the Swedish decision-making process is also characterised by openness, rationality and consensus-seeking. Almost all important Swedish political decisions are preceded by a rather extensive investigation'.[15]

In fact, government bills are in part, initiated as an information gathering exercise. On key issues, the government usually appoints an *ad hoc* commission of inquiry - although they vary in size and composition - with the remit to investigate the aspect in question. Once a commission has submitted its report, then the referral process is enacted - signalling the consensual nature of Swedish decision-making - although the government retains the right to postpone any decision. The referral process is unusual in that it aims to incorporate the views of all interested parties both inside and outside government. All administrative authorities and organisations considered relevant to the proposal may be invited and have the right to submit comments on the results of the commission's report. When the referral process has been completed, the government will usually either suspend the process of inquiry or proceed to drafting a parliamentary bill for presentation to the Riksdag. Of course, once the bill is presented to the Parliament, then one of the parliamentary committees takes over the examination of the bill. Yet, the open and lengthy referral system is a central feature of decision-making. In practice, all proposals of a commission of inquiry that may lead to a major change in policy are perceived as virtually constitutionally binding. In addition, the government can set up parliamentary *ad hoc* commissions/committees, which are usually given a written mandate and are appointed to consider important or politically controversial areas. Consequently, they invariably consist of representatives of the parliamentary parties and in effect, a mini Riksdag is created in which consensus can be more easily reached.[16]

Although the referral process may actually slow down decision-making and make it somewhat pedantic, it is nevertheless, open and rational, especially given that all interested parties have the right to contribute to any decision. It also has two extra advantages, First, there is a much wider dispersal of information and debate in Sweden than in other comparable states. Second, once a decision is reached, all interested parties are broadly in agreement and the implementation of the decision is considerably easier. Yet, this 'pre-cooking' is not without its critics. Given the increasingly wide portfolios of the commissions and the referral process, a larger number of reservations are now prevalent within reports and governments have become disposed towards simply springing decisions on the political arena.

Another feature is the central role of the 16 parliamentary committees within the Riksdag, which examine government proposed legislation and either contain or can hear specialists in key policy areas. The majority of the Riksdag's business is channelled through these committees. It is within them that the negotiations between the parties on policy takes place, especially as the negotiations in the committees are usually held behind closed doors.[17] This aspect was particularly important as regards the position of the parties within Sweden on European integration. It was in this forum that many of the merits of the full membership were debated and alliances developed. This book will pay particular attention to the views of key parliamentary committees (and *ad-hoc* commissions) on European integration as they, albeit to a limited extent, had a disproportionate influence on Swedish attitudes on full membership. As a case in point, the Committee on Foreign Affairs was influential in determining the longer-term objectives of Swedish security policy,[18] perspectives towards the EU and indeed, the maintenance of consensus to support these policies.

The final aspects of the Riksdag, which indirectly affect attitudes towards European integration were the Parliament's control on government finances and its formal role in ratifying international agreements signed by the Swedish government, such as the European Economic Area (EEA) agreement. As regards the former, the Riksdag was increasingly at loggerheads with successive governments over economic policy as they failed to gain working majorities in the Parliament, voter allegiances became more fluid and the country encountered structural difficulties in its economy. Ironically from the 1980s, it has been the Parliament that has campaigned for rises in public expenditure, and since the early 1990s, has, at least, lobbied to try and maintain existing high levels in the face of economic recession and successive governmental attempts at budgetary cuts. Furthermore, as a parliamentary democracy, the Riksdag is able to determine the configuration of Swedish governments and move motions of 'no confidence' in order to have them removed. Overall, parliamentary interest in European integration intensified during the 1980s as parliamentarians looked for wider solutions to Swedish economic problems.

As regards the latter feature, the role of the Riksdag in ratifying such agreements was always an area of governmental concern as the possibilities of closer Swedish ties with the evolving EC became more realistic. Swedish governments have become preoccupied with the demands of gaining parliamentary majorities in support of governmental initiatives towards further European integration. This book will pay attention to parliamentary developments on European integration as befits the Riksdag's role as the champion of parliamentary democracy and a primary influence on the Swedish political debate.

ii) Cabinet Government

As in the case of most Western democracies, the influence of the executive has become more pronounced in Sweden in the post-war period. Indeed, the growing presence of the executive in dictating the parameters of policy is incorporated within the assumptions of Swedish policy-making in this book. However, there are a number of additional trends that are worth special mention. First, whilst the executive became more powerful in terms of policy-making, the role of Cabinet government is still a major aspect in Swedish politics. This may in part be due to the fact that parliamentary government founded upon universal and equal suffrage appeared rather late in comparison to many other European states - not until the years immediately after the end of the First World War. Thus, some of the trends prevalent in other states have not yet made their mark in Sweden.[19]

Cabinet government derives from the standing of the political parties within the Riksdag, although the role and influence of successive governments has depended on the central figure (and personality) of the Prime Minister (*statsminister*). During the long years of Tage Erlander's premiership (1946-69) for example, governments operated mainly on consensus, with decisions taken collectively and all major parties consulted - the so-called *Harpsund democracy*.[20] In contrast, Olof Palme's terms in office (1969-76, 1982-86) were noted for their ideological zeal (especially in terms of international affairs) and the dominance of the Prime Minister in determining policy.[21] Yet, in general, personality questions have been less central and despite the Prime Minister's key role within domestic politics, they have tended to be less well-known internationally. Second, Sweden has been characterised in the 20th century by the dominance of the Social Democratic Party (SAP) in government. Between the years 1932-76, the Social Democrats remained the permanent and dominant party within Swedish governments. From 1932-96, for example, the Social Democrats were in government for 55 of the 64 years. Hence, this had important implications for the Swedish debate on European integration. The permanent presence of the SAP in government for most of the period encompassing the EC's early development ensured that:

- The views of the Prime Minister on European integration were critical in determining governmental perspectives as he tended to lead the government for long periods of time. In Tage Erlander's case, for example, it was for 23 years.

- The central concern of successive SAP governments during the 1930-70s was the development of a social democratic welfare state.[22] Most kinds of supranational integration were either treated with scepticism or resisted on the grounds of undermining the sovereignty of social democratic economic policy and the 'People's Home'. The SAP's continuity in government facilitated the development of a specific political and economic model, which was tolerated by the opposing non-socialist parties.

- The lengthy era of SAP tenure also ensured that most of the prevailing views and arguments against full EC membership derived from social democratic perspectives and ideology. In essence, Social Democratic hegemony fostered a consensus about, for instance, the nature and role of the Swedish public sector.

Yet, the large degree of continuity and prominence of the Social Democrats within domestic politics has, since the 1980s, been less evident, with non-socialist governments holding power twice for a total of 9 years (from 1976-82 and from 1991-94) in the last two decades. Consequently, the debate on European integration became more pluralist.

Third, the governments displayed an overt commitment to consensual policy making and included elaborate mechanisms for delivering coherent and mutually supporting domestic policies. The legislative process is lengthy, passing through key and clearly defined stages - from the appointment and deliberations of the commissions of inquiry, the publication of its conclusions, the referral process, the formulation and presentation of a bill to the Riksdag, its examination by the standing committees through to the Parliament's final decision. However, in practice, the government does maintain considerable influence over the commission of inquiry. Not only is the government influential in deciding its composition, mandate and bureaucratic support, but the chairmen of these commissions find it virtually essential to maintain close liaisons with the respective government ministries. As the *ad hoc* commissions are also responsible for considering new policy and reforms - which usually have implications for government finances and expenditure - these bodies have found that determining the financing of such reforms is difficult and thus government advice is vital.

iii) The Swedish Party System

For a long time, Sweden was regarded as having one of the most stable party systems in Europe. From the introduction of universal and equal suffrage in 1921, the political scene was dominated by five main parties in the Riksdag, roughly divided into two blocs of socialists and non-socialists. On the Left, were the Euro-communist Left Party and the much larger and politically dominant Social Democrats. Moving from the Centre to the Right were the agrarian-based Centre

Party, the Liberals and the conservative Moderates. However, since 1988, this stable five-party system was replaced by a more fluid seven-party one due to the emergence of new parliamentary forces.[23] The Greens have appeared as another anti-EC force of the Swedish parliamentary Left. In 1988, the Green Party was first elected to the Riksdag, only to fall away in the 1991 general election before returning with seats in the 1994 general election. In contrast, in the 1991 general election, the Greens were supplanted by the centrist Christian Democrats, which has been the other new force in Swedish politics. In addition, 1991 also saw the emergence of the Right-wing (and now defunct) New Democracy - yet, this proved to be a temporary phenomenon as the party lost all their seats in the 1994 general election and effectively imploded.

Yet, it has been the division of the political parties into two blocs - socialist and non-socialist - that has been the most influential aspect for government formation since the present Instrument came into operation in 1975. With only a few exceptions, one or other of the blocs has maintained a slender majority in the Riksdag and dictated the configuration of the government. Ironically, the multi-party system, which is a result of the proportional election system has been at least partially, counteracted by the adherence of the political parties in the Riksdag to one of the two blocs. The only major exceptions to these rules was of course, the Green Party (from 1988-91) and to some extent, New Democracy (1991-94). Surprisingly, this did not lead to many years of majority government, but promoted a practical consensus between the main political parties to ensure the stability of government. Since the inauguration of the unicameral Riksdag (1970), the country enjoyed a majority government for approximately four of the 26 years (until 1996). Minority governments (consisting of one party) have been in power for 17 of those 26 years - the Social Democrats for 16 of those 17 years.[24]

Despite Sweden's image as a solid party system with very stable government, the recent past has been less persuasive. Since 1976, the general trend has been towards less stable government with new parties emerging and for the most part, leading to a weaker basis for forming governments. Coalition governments have found it difficult to remain in power, leading to a flurry of non-socialist governments particularly in the 1970s. The non-socialist governments formed in the 1970s (1976 and 1979 respectively) fell prematurely as a result of internal divisions, whilst the Bildt government of 1991-94 tentatively stayed in power, enduring numerous internal problems during its tenure. Even the Social Democrats have faced similar, if less dramatic challenges. The Carlsson government was forced to resign in 1990 after its changes to economic policy were rejected by the Riksdag.

The implications for the debate on European integration has been four-fold. First, the original stability of the Swedish political system meant that a consensus against full membership was easily achieved and prevented the EC issue from becoming especially divisive during the early years of the EC's development. Second and in contrast, the European integration issue re-entered Swedish politics in the late 1980s when the domestic political scene was itself in a state of flux. Third, internal party cohesion and alliances between the parties on the EC issue have been difficult due to the fragility of the political coalitions. Fourth, the views of smaller parties, such as the Centre Party (which provided parliamentary support for the post-1994 Social Democratic governments), and the anti-EC Left Party and Greens, have become important as parliamentary majorities have been more difficult to find and the EC debate has become politicised. Without doubt, pre-conceptions of Sweden's integrative and consensual democracy are changing and with them, domestic attitudes on the merits of European integration.

b) Point 2: The 'Swedish Model'

Sweden has not only been labelled as having a rather elaborate type of consensual democracy, but it has also been argued that the country has developed a rather specific 'Swedish model' for organising the economy. As long ago as 1932, Marquis Childs suggested that the country had developed a 'middle way' between fascism and communism.[25] To some extent, this 'middle way' has to be placed in context of the 1930s, when ideological attractions were strong in Europe - 'the world seemed to face a choice between fascism and communism, and Sweden as a laboratory of social and rational democratic decision-making could conceivably offer an alternative to the two extremes'.[26] Childs further argued that Sweden represented a stable country and virtually the only state to have effectively dealt with the widespread depression in the 1930s. According to Childs, this was due to a number of factors.

First, the flexibility of the Swedish political system to adapt to change and compromise as 'they have not been bound by a 'system' nor have they been committed to a dogma'.[27] Second, the emergence of the Social Democrats with their commitment to 'cautious gradualism, advancing step by step with the approval of the voters'[28] - in practice, a successful social democracy. The SAP after all, entered government in 1932 after winning over 40 percent of the vote. The strength of popular support, the high level of unionisation and party membership and the fragmentation of the Right-wing parties moulded a society committed to the welfare of all its citizens and the prosperity of its industries.[29] In short, social democracy and the 'Swedish model' were mutually supportive - viewing the goals of efficiency and equality as complimentary rather than contradictory.[30] Third, Sweden's primary interest in lower prices and better quality products rather than profitability of firms; fourth, the development of cooperatives, so that ultimately, 'the state has competed so efficiently in many fields that private enterprise has been prevented from establishing extortionate monopolies'.[31] Finally, the adoption of a Keynesian strategy with the goal of achieving full employment. In his later work (1980), Childs further suggested that the 'middle way' was still of relevance, but now was reflected in the development of social democracy (via governmental initiatives and the labour movement) as an alternative to fully fledged *laissez-faire* capitalism and/or communism. In short, the 'Swedish model' was based upon consensual reformism.[32]

Most importantly for this context, Lane has suggested that the 'Swedish model' is 'best understood as a mode of regulation' and as a practical, rather than theoretical model.[33] In fact, there is no international consensus within the existing literature as to how Swedish politics should be interpreted. Rustow, for example, argued that the country is best described by as a so-called 'compromise model',[34] whereas this is contradicted by Heclo and Madsen's 'hegemony' perspective of Sweden.[35] Yet, regardless of the interpretation, the 'Swedish model' comprises of a set of assumptions regarding the nature of 'good government' and in particular, how the public sector is structured and what roles it plays in national society.

If Lane's perspective is taken as accurate then the 'Swedish model' can be more broadly interpreted using the views of Petersson - that it incorporates, on the one hand, 'a specific type of polity' (in which capitalism, parliamentary democracy and the welfare state were integrated through powerful state machinery and interest groups and operated on the principles of consensus); and on the other, 'a specific type of public policy' (in which welfare provision was, at least in principle, comprehensive, universal and institutionalised).[36] Swedish welfare provision was not, for the most part, based upon levels of income[37] and intended to create solidarity between influential social groups.[38] Yet, as Petersson concedes, these traits were undermined by the dual threats of increased individualism in Swedish society and the impact of severe recession during the early 1990s.[39]

Without doubt then, Sweden can be identified as the 'land of big government'. By the mid 1980s, Sweden was probably the first modern state in the western world to have a majority of its voters dependent on public funds for their livelihood.[40] Public expenditure figures for all levels of government were regularly quoted as amounting to approximately two-thirds of the country's Gross National Product (GNP), whilst the public sector employed more than one in three workers and was roughly equivalent in size to the entire manufacturing segment of the economy. In many ways, Sweden came the closest yet to a 'People's Home' (the old conservative term that Swedish Social Democrats popularised during the 1930s) - in other words, a social democratic welfare state. As Heclo and Madsen argue the 'Swedish model' was 'corporate in terms of group-based political expression, communitarian in terms of aspiring to social equality, and progressive in terms of promoting economic growth and change'.[41]

Of course, much of the development of this 'People's Home' and adaptive reformism was associated with the fact that the Social Democratic Party (SAP), allied with a powerful and well-organised trade union movement, retained government power for 44 years (from 1932-76). Both the Social Democratic Party (formed in 1889) and the Trade Union Confederation (the LO and founded in 1898) came into existence concurrently and have maintained a durable relationship ever since. After a string of electoral setbacks in the 1920s, the labour movement turned away from radical claims of socialising wealth and nationalising industry and towards a moderate, incremental approach to transforming society. Once the Social Democrats gained power in the 1930s, their reforms were repaid by a long-string of electoral victories - 'all of which cemented the mutual identification of the labour movement, reformist government and Swedish nationhood'.[42] Sweden experienced a long period in which a dominant, reforming SAP held such a cast-iron grip on the state apparatus and policy initiation that it became part of the national political culture.[43]

Furthermore, the aforementioned referral (or remiss) procedure also provided an opportunity for collective interests to determine the style of Swedish decision-making. The heavy usage of commissions of inquiry and/or parliamentary committees provided the rationale and opportunity for the country's interest groups to gear their own internal structures towards influencing the referral process, especially as the process requires a high degree of aggregation of social and economic interests if it is to work effectively. In effect, this reinforced the perception that the party system reflected not just the ideological divide between Left and Right, but also between employees and employers. There are strong links between highly structured interest groups representation, and at least four of the main political parties. The largest and longest connection of course, has been between the working class/trade unions and the Social Democrats. Yet, equally strong is the identification of the three non-socialist parties as the 'bourgeois party bloc' and for example, farming interests have traditionally been represented by the Centre Party (known until the late-1950s as the *Bondeförbundet* - the peasants' association).[44]

Part of the 'Swedish model' assumes and requires a structured and high profile role for interest groups within decision-making.[45] It is not surprising then that Sweden has enjoyed one of the highest rates of union membership in the world and easily exceeds the combined membership of all mainstream political parties. In 1980, for example, 89 percent of total dependent employees were trade union members, and this had risen to 96.2 percent by 1991, although only around 79.9 percent were actually active trade union members. Thus, Swedish interest groups are more than just pressure groups, 'they are powerful social actors whose scope of concern and influence has become almost as broad as that of any political party'.[46] In fact, the organisation of wage earners still reflects the now, in many ways, obsolete distinction between blue-collar and white collar workers. The blue-collar trade union federation - LO - consists of twenty-three national trade unions covering around 90 percent of blue-collar workers and about half of the entire Swedish work force. It still remains the largest wage earner voice in Sweden, although its primacy has been contested with greater frequency by the rapid rise of white-collar unions outside the LO. Yet, the 'Swedish model' is essentially a 'Social Democratic hegemony'. The SAP and the LO have enjoyed superior organisational power in bringing pressure to bear on the referral process.[47]

In contrast, white-collar unionism dates from the early 1920s, but has made substantial inroads as the service and public sectors have grown as a proportion of the country's infrastructure. The Federation of Salaried Employees in Industry and Services (PTK - *Privattjänstemannakartellen*) negotiate for the white collar workers in the private sector. Other private sector workers, together with salaried employees in the public sector, are organised into two central organisations, the Swedish Central Organisation of Salaried Employees (TCO - *Tjänstemännens centralorganisation*) and the Swedish Central Organisation of Academics (SACO - *Sveriges akademikers centralorganisation*). In contrast, employers in the private sector are organised into the 35 member federation - the SAF - which along with the LO, were the two main institutions for collective bargaining purposes. The SAF still has considerable influence for in spite of not being the only private employers' organisation, its membership includes Sweden's largest companies and at the same time, incorporates the majority of the small business sector.[48]

Although the 'Swedish model' was expanded to cover many aspects of decision-making, its ·roots lie in a specific method of regulating industrial relations. In short, both the trade unions and employers came together to negotiate on the basis of their common interest for resolving industrial conflicts in a structured fashion.[49] United by the desire to ensure that government intervention in wage negotiations was avoided, both management and the trade unions agreed to establish an independent system of collective bargaining for determining wages and working conditions embodied in a series of agreements - (the most famous is the 1938 Saltsjöbaden Agreement - see Chapter One). In the 1950s, centralised collective bargaining became the norm, with wage settlement in reality, being decided by the leaderships of the LO and the SAF. These centrally negotiated agreements determined wage levels for the whole of the Swedish labour market and wage policy was more easily implemented as a result of this centralisation. Whilst these wage bargaining rounds were eventually not as independent as first seems - as state intervention was frequent in the post-war period due to the huge expansion of the public sector - the 'spirit of Saltsjöbaden' lived on.

The 'Swedish model' was also expanded to accommodate more than just the regulatory system and power structure of the labour market and came to reflect a culture of consensus between the two main classes of society. This 'historic compromise' between labour and capital became an integral part of national political culture. On the one hand, Swedish business, for the most part, recognised the need for and was tolerant of welfare reforms and on the other, the labour movement refrained from pushing for the nationalisation of industry. Hence, governmental attitudes acknowledged that although governmental regulation of the economy is beneficial, there has equally been 'no arbitrary rule of state ownership *per se*'.[50] Unlike other comparable Western European states, a strong role for government in economic affairs has not been equated with widespread nationalisation and state ownership. Hence, the Swedish example represents a more complex form of public control than orthodox interpretations of state ownership would have us first believe. As Visser has argued elsewhere, the 'Swedish model' represents a core example of 'bargained corporatism' and can be seen as,

> 'a political attempt to attain a particular set of social objectives within a market economy, or perhaps more accurately, as a market economy based on, and co-ordinated through, large and comprehensive interest groups. Its intellectual belief system - contrary to current neo-liberal creed - is that markets are not efficient, but need the help of powerful institutions to become efficient. ... In short, the state supports and encourages associational policies which remove the need for statutory income policies'.[51]

Pontusson has further argued that the 'Swedish model' was governed by 'production politics' and that the role of an organised labour movement was responsible for three main aspects (principally between 1968-76).[52] First, the labour movement was responsible for the introduction of an active industrial policy, proposing institutional reforms to extend the state's capacity to intervene selectively in industrial restructuring. Second, co-determination and/or an industrial democracy was fostered by proposing legislation designed to help employee representation influence corporate decision-making.[53] Finally, the popularising of collective share ownership by endorsing the build-up of 'wage earner funds' through collective profit sharing. Whilst this third part proved controversial and was effectively toned down,[54] all three aspects, for the most part, were integrated into economic policy as a result of the tolerance of Swedish business and the model's emphasis on political compromise.

There are two further elements of the 'Swedish model' worth mentioning in this context. To a large extent, the organisational and corporate features of the model were bound up with the popularity of social democracy. Thus, one of the assumptions of the model was the goal of full employment and the introduction of universal welfare provision. In practice, what made Sweden seem unusual to outside observers was its solidaristic wage policy, a generous welfare state and that successive governments equated the overall goal of full employment with low inflation, high growth and a more equitable distribution of income.

The intellectual foundations of Swedish economic policy until the end of the 1970s lay within the so-called Rehn-Meidner model (developed by two labour union economists of the LO) - the goal of which was to beat inflation without causing unemployment.[55] Rehn and Meidner 'were aware of the existence of a trade-off between unemployment and inflation long before Phillips published his famous article in 1958'.[56] The objective of Rehn-Meidner was to ensure inflation was controlled without resorting to either an incomes policy which would deprive the trade unions of their main function, nor increasing unemployment, which would also reduce their political power. Gösta Rehn and Rudolf Meidner advocated that in order to ensure full employment, the government introduced an active labour market policy, including re-training programmes and initiatives aiming at increased mobility of labour. Inflation would be averted by high indirect taxes 'dampening down demand and financing a high level of social provision'.[57] In the meantime, 'solidaristic bargaining' would ensure that all workers received commensurate wage increases. In reality, the Rehn-Meidner model operated through a combination of restrictive demand policy, an interventionist labour market policy and a wages policy based on solidarity and centralised bargaining.

The purpose of the restrictive demand policy was to prevent general demand exceeding the point where inflationary effects would occur, which ironically may actually increase unemployment. To offset any chances of unemployment rising, Swedish governments also developed an active labour market policy. It was built around on the one hand, mobility stimulating measures, (such as public employment services, retraining and geographical mobility grants), which encouraged workers to move to areas of the labour market that had shortages and on the other, selective job creation schemes, which would help to generally reduce unemployment in poorer areas or where workers were unable to move. Ironically, the additional solidaristic and centralised bargained wage policy did not originate from Rehn or Meidner, but were accepted by the trade unions on the grounds that the norm of equal pay for equal work ought to guide wage policy and by employers on the basis that the policy should assume a level of co-ordination of wage bargaining between different sectors of the economy. The trade unions favoured the principle of equality as any move to reduce large wage differentials would also allow the national wage structure to move in a fairer direction. Employers saw centralised wage bargaining as means of preventing accelerating and inflationary wage increases within the overheated Swedish economy of the 1950s and in allowing for a better allocation of labour.

Although the institutional foundations for centralised bargaining were already in existence, it was in the 1950s that the Rehn-Meidner model was developed. The first central agreement was reached in 1952 (19 more would follow in the next 40 years). It was with the development of the Labour Market Board (from 1957) that the solidaristic and centralised bargaining system became organised and labour market policy became active. Except for cyclical fluctuations, expenditures on the active labour market policy grew from about 1 percent of GDP in the beginning of the 1960s to over 3 percent at the end of the 1980s, which was an especially high figure given Sweden's low unemployment and in comparison to other Western European countries.[58]

In general, this combination of policies were regarded as a huge success at the time.[59] Despite being open to debate,[60] Sweden enjoyed very low levels of unemployment from the 1960-80s in comparison to other European countries and without major wage increasing effects - suggesting that the active labour market policy was beneficial.[61] Wage differentials between the high and low paid narrowed.[62] Strikes became exceedingly rare especially during the 1960-70s.[63] However, to some extent, the low levels of unemployment enjoyed by Sweden in the 1970s in particular, must be accounted for by the expansion of the public sector which counter-balanced the decline of the private sector during the recessional periods.[64]

Yet, by the mid-1970s the country had developed structural difficulties within her economy.[65] In 1975, Sweden, for example, encountered the beginning of a cost crisis. In that year, negotiated wage increases were extremely high - amounting to 22 percent in the manufacturing sector - whilst the expansion of the public sector and governmental responsibilities, led to large budgetary deficits, reaching 13 percent of GDP in the early 1980s. In practice, both the public and private sectors were agreeing annual wage rises that were larger than increases in productivity could support - thereby fuelling inflation and concerns over international competitiveness. The debate over the economy's organisation was by the 1970-80s increasingly politicised. Attempts at introducing 'wage-earner funds', despite eventually leading to a 1983 Law setting up five regional employee funds, fostered tension between the LO and SAP leaderships over their configuration and opposition from Swedish business[66] which viewed them as 'an attempt to introduce a socialist economy by the back door'.[67]

Moreover, the traditional norms of centralised collective-bargaining was also affected by the drift away from consensus approaches and from 1983, the structure of these negotiations - and the centre-point of the 'Swedish model' changed. As Visser notes, 'the history of centralised bargaining after 1980 is one of fragmentation, distributional competition and increased state interference'.[68] Centralised bilateral bargaining between the trade union movement and the employers' federation reached the point of breakdown when the SAF refused to negotiate centrally.[69] By the early 1980s the SAF felt that it was time to concentrate its efforts on three major objectives: economic growth, political pluralism and a wage structure more favourable to private business.[70] Yet, the break with over two decades of centralised bargaining officially occurred in 1983 when the SAF's most powerful affiliate, the Engineering Employers' Association (VF) allied itself with the Union of Metal Workers (Metall) and concluded separate agreements outside the usual LO and SAF bargaining channels. In the following bargaining round, all negotiations were relegated to the industry and sector level.[71] In short, this revised age of 'neo-corporatism' was spurred, in part by what Pontusson and Swenson label 'a Swedish Employer Offensive'.[72]

In addition, the growing strength of white collar unions continue to challenge the centrality of the LO in collective negotiations. This greater pluralism of actors reinforced the trend within Sweden towards neo-liberal values supporting market solutions, rather than the principle of securing equal pay rises during the early 1980s. Consequently, from 1983, the principle of a solidaristic and centrally bargained wage policy was replaced by localised wage bargaining at the sectoral and firm level. Although some central agreements were signed (1983, 1985, 1986-87 and 1989-90), most of these agreements were more restrictive than before. In addition, the government adopted a more active incomes policy, with formal meetings between government and interest groups on levels of wage demands commonplace and the government using its role as an large employer (given the expanded size of the public sector) to restrict wage increases. However, the usage of incomes policy was not successful. Between 1984-90, annual wage increases exceeded government declared levels by around 3 percent. This led to growing concerns regarding Swedish levels of inflation which remained stubbornly higher than the OECD average (by 1-2 percent) during the 1980s.[73]

In effect, the decentralisation of wage setting that Sweden's powerful employers had pushed for in the early 1980s was all but achieved by the early 1990s even if it was through 'a fitful and conflictual process'.[74] In practice, collective negotiations became more pluralistic (as the number of trade unions representing the public sector increased), less centralised or homogenous, as a system of negotiations based on individual unions was established. As Petersson identifies the importance of local, rather than nationally-set targets and deals rose - 'Instead of a single centralised bargaining round, pay deals are nowadays a complicated game. ... The implementation of a wage policy based on solidarity - while at the same time exercising restraint and maintaining low inflation and international competitiveness - has become much more difficult'.[75] Indeed, after 1991, the SAF's declaration that it would no longer participate in central agreements with the LO or PTK (after the Rhenberg measures had expired) effectively meant that industrial relations were in a transitional period.[76]

Yet, for the most part, it has been the experience of severe recession (1990-93), that deepened the uncertainty about the economy's future and the continued relevance of any kind of 'Swedish model'. A survey of the performance of the economy during the period says it all. From 1990-93, Sweden endured a negative growth rate of about 1.5-2 percent per annum; real GDP shrank by between 5-6 percent and -2.2 percent alone in 1993.[77] Unemployment dramatically increased to around 15 percent;[78] the manufacturing sector lost, for example, 22 percent of its jobs. In addition, the recession led to corresponding increased demands on welfare provision, which combined with governmental support to the collapsed banking sector (after its disastrous deregulation in the late 1980s) prompted a substantial rise in the budgetary deficit. By 1993, public spending averaged 73 percent of GDP and drove up the budgetary deficit to an enormous SEK 217 billion (around 15 percent of GDP) in same year.

In reality, the Swedish government financed these growing deficits through increased borrowing and national debt. The interest payments alone on national debt in the fiscal year 1993-94 reached a staggering SEK 95 billion or roughly equivalent to 17 percent of government expenditure. The interest on foreign debt alone was estimated to have increased the total debt by about SEK 60 billion by 1994. By the end of the fiscal year 1994-95, the national debt was estimated to be a massive SEK 1,400 billion - equivalent to SEK 160,000 per inhabitant in Sweden. Indeed, some economists highlighted that just as Europe suffered from 'Euro-sclerosis' in the late 1970s-80s, Sweden may now be suffering from a more vicious strain of 'Suedosclerosis'.[79] The costs of key elements of the model were no longer sustainable and forced successive governments to implement austerity packages in order to bring government finances under control.

Since the late 1980s then, the 'Swedish model' has been in transition. It is unclear at this point whether it is effectively dead or if the ingrained elements of it within society will enable it to be re-configured to face the challenges for the 1990s. Certainly, it has already moved substantially away from some of its original preconceptions. Ultimately, concerns surrounding the model's ability to reconcile unemployment and inflation have been raised. The competitiveness of Swedish industry was continuously damaged by rising labour costs and the long-standing governmental strategy of intermittent devaluation of the Krona as a means of restoring international competitiveness proved to be ineffective in the long-term by clouding the more pressing problem of declining productivity. Consequently, the priority of controlling inflation and government fiscal balances are now dominant - to the point of replacing the solidaristic wage policy, centralised bargaining and generous welfare provision.[80]

Yet, the 'Swedish model', by providing on the one hand, a set of maxims that nearly all of the main interest groups adhered to, and on the other, being perceived as a long-running success until the 1980s, substantially influenced elite attitudes towards European integration. Until the 1980s, the model acted as one of the main reasons for not joining the Community as successive governments highlighted its good performance and the need to maintain essential economic sovereignty as rationales for rejecting full membership. Ironically, the model entered its transitional period at the same time as the EC issue once again appeared on the Swedish political agenda as a result of the 'Luxembourg Process' and thereby allowed greater flexibility regarding policy on the EC. Yet, without doubt, the overarching political dominance of the model also affected the performance of the economy - which represents the Diamond's third point.

c) Point 3: Swedish Economic Interdependence With Europe

A number of unusual characteristics of the Swedish economy derive from two dominating influences upon it. First, the economy is influenced by its peripheral position in northern Europe, the country's highly industrialised base and its relatively large natural resources in a few key raw materials, such as iron ore and forestry. In effect, Sweden's industrial/manufacturing and raw material-based sectors have been pre-occupied by their reliance upon foreign markets and international trade to guarantee economic growth. Consequently, successive governments have been constantly pressured to maintain access to foreign markets for exports and to pay attention to the country's international competitiveness through economic and monetary policy. Second, the country developed a fragile domestic economy dominated by the implications of the 'Swedish model'. The creation of a specific type of social democratic economic policy and a large public sector, had a disproportionately large influence on the configuration of the domestic economy.[81] In short, Sweden has maintained a 'dual economy' with a large segment of its industries, on the one hand, pressing government for an active international trade policy - embodying market access for, and ensuring the competitiveness of, Swedish exports in foreign markets - and on the other, a small domestic economy dominated by a large public sector, where open competition was limited and firms were fearful of greater penetration by foreign imports.

i) The Significance of International Trade and Competitiveness

The importance of international trade has in fact led to several notable tendencies affecting Sweden's trade patterns. Its status as an industrialised nation with a large manufacturing sector, specialising in the production of mainly finished goods is reflected in the configuration of exports and imports. Traditional exports, such as iron, steel and forestry products, although remaining significant aspects of international trade have declined in relative importance over the past decades. Wood and paper products for example, have fallen from 21 percent of total export value in 1970 to around 14 percent in 1993, whilst metals have similarly fallen from 10 percent in 1970 to 7 percent in 1993 respectively. It has instead been products from the chemical and above all from the engineering industry that have increased their relative share of total exports. In 1993, engineering products represented some 51 percent of the total value of exports, amounting to SEK 198 billion out of a total value for exports of SEK 388 billion.[82] As a percentage of the total value of imports in 1993, engineering products accounted for no less than 45 percent of the country's total imports. Private cars comprised around 3 percent of total imports denoting Sweden's status as an advanced consumer society with mature and sophisticated markets.

The country's principal export markets also illustrate her advanced industrialised status as the majority of international trade occurs with other industrialised countries. Sweden's principal export markets are in descending order of importance - Germany (13.3 percent), the UK (10.2 percent), Norway (8.1 percent) and the USA (8.0 percent) - with 10 countries (the tenth being Italy) comprising some three-quarters of total exports in 1995 (SEK 331,892 million out of a total of SEK 471,000 million). In terms of continental trade then the other dominant feature has been the growing concentration of trade with mainland Europe and in particular, with the EU. In 1994, the year before Sweden became a full EU member, for instance, trade with the EU (SEK 250,476 million) was almost 3.5 times that of with the rest of the EFTA states (SEK 77,392 million) and five times the size of the trade with the NAFTA states (SEK 44,714 million) and the Far East (SEK 47,165 million) respectively.

However, Sweden's policy-makers have been particularly concerned with the decline in its international competitiveness. In the late 1970s, Swedish competitiveness declined significantly as a consequence of the rapid increase in costs of production and leading to a simultaneous fall in the volume of exports. Between 1975-80, for instance, Swedish exports lost 16 percent of their share of foreign markets. These losses were caused, amongst other things, by the cost inflation of the 1970s when unit costs rose much more rapidly than elsewhere in Europe. Sweden experienced a progressive rise in relative unit labour costs from 1970 onwards, highlighting that the economy suffered from structural deficiencies. During the period of rapid cost inflation in the mid-1970s, unit labour costs increased more rapidly in Sweden than in other countries. Since the early 1970s, Swedish unit labour costs for example, increased by 32 percent more than in competitor countries. This directly affected industrial productivity - for example, industrial output which rose by more than 6 percent per annum during the 1960s, declined after 1973 to 1 percent per annum (compared to an OECD average of 1.9 percent).

Consequently, during the 1970s, Sweden's balance of trade deteriorated sharply and export competitiveness was only maintained, for the most part, by drastic exchange rate policy measures and the intermittent devaluation of the Krona. The five devaluations between 1976-82 improved international competitiveness and unit labour costs declined markedly. In particular, the major devaluations of the 1980s did at least, partially enhance export competitiveness and led to an improvement in the real balance of trade. Yet, in spite of sizeable devaluations in 1981 and 1982 respectively (the two amounting to 26 percent), Sweden still only recovered a small proportion of its lost market share.[83] In effect, this artificial enhancement was only short-lived since it was also not accompanied by any domestic restraint on costs.

Throughout the post-war period, policy-makers have been sensitive to concerns regarding the country's international competitiveness as a direct result of its dependence on foreign trade, the direction of its trade patterns and the negative structural dynamics operating on Swedish productivity back home. The country's continual problems with its international competitiveness and its causal relationship to the country's high production and unit labour costs was, for example, universally recognised in the government's high profile 1980 Medium Term Survey of the Swedish Economy. In the survey, the Ministry of Economic Affairs recognised that it was in the latter parts of the 1960s that the economy's positive picture 'started to crack' and that the 1970s represented 'a decade of thwarted expectations'.[84] Although the government retained its overall economic objectives of 'full employment, stable prices, good growth, fair distribution of incomes and regional balance',[85] the survey outlined two alternative scenarios for the future of the economy - one positive and one pessimistic. Whilst both alternatives acknowledged that the imbalances in the economy were 'the central problems of economic policy', Alternative One stipulated that these imbalances would be reduced, leading to a gradual improvement and Alternative Two illustrated that the country's structural problems would worsen if the economy continued to follow the same track as in the 1970s.[86] As part of the solution, the survey outlined three strategies - a reduction in current account deficits, an increase in real capital formation and a strengthening of the industrial sector.

Unfortunately, Swedish governments, for the most part, continued to prefer the strategy of securing artificial international competitiveness through exchange rate policy rather than any attempts at controlling costs or improving the productivity of firms.[87] Overall, the government failed to meet its targets set out in the survey, with public expenditure standing at 66 percent of GDP in 1982 and a government deficit of 13 percent of GDP (instead of the survey's targets of 60 percent and 6.7 percent respectively).[88] None the less, the picture was obscured by the return to a positive balance of trade at current prices enjoyed in the late 1980s and gave a false sense of security to the Swedes. It was in fact, a favourable movement in the country's terms of trade as export prices rose rapidly and oil prices declined. Yet, by the late 1980s, unit labour costs had risen substantially again, reviving concerns over international competitiveness. Swedish productivity for example, stagnated from an output per man hour average of 5 percent per annum during the 1960s-early 1970s to an average of no more than 1.7 percent per annum in the late 1980s. The implications for international competitiveness were at least, temporarily reversed by yet another devaluation of the Krona (when it left its pegging arrangement with the ECU in November 1992).[89] Indeed, during the early 1990s, the balance of trade moved into surplus largely as a result of the substantial fall in imports brought about by domestic recession and the rapid increase in exports following the depreciation of the Krona in 1992-93.[90] The depreciation of the Krona facilitated lower prices for Swedish goods abroad and the country's share of foreign markets increased from 1992 onwards.

Overall, concerns over international competitiveness have also been accentuated by the changes in Sweden's trade patterns and most notably, Sweden's increasing reliance upon EC, rather than Pan-European or Nordic markets. Swedish exports to the EC, for instance, increased by 70 percent between 1973-78, mainly as a result of Sweden's Free Trade Agreement (FTA) with the EC. By 1991 - the year of the full membership application - EC markets received some 55 percent of Swedish exports and EC goods made up some 55 percent of imports to Sweden. These figures have remained more or less constant since 1991. Yet, in reality, interdependence with the EU was constantly expanding. Indeed, as Stålvant and Hamilton have commented this interdependence is also asymmetrical. In 1985, for example, the EC supplied approximately 25 percent of the Swedish home demand for manufactures. Yet, in the same year, Sweden supplied barely 1 percent of the EC home demand due to the huge size of the Community's domestic market in relation to its imports.[91] Thus, the country's growing concentration of international trade with a few, essentially EU partners has, albeit to a limited extent, highlighted the need for, and the fragility of, international competitiveness, especially as Swedish business operated in even more competitive markets as a result of the EC's trade liberalisation programmes.

As regards international trade then the competitiveness of the private sector has remained of critical importance to Swedish policy-makers, which has at least in part been shaped by the configuration of the country's industrial structure. Sweden for example, has the largest number of multinationals per head of population. Seventeen of the world's largest industrial companies are Swedish, which per unit of GDP is twice as many as in Japan and four times as many as in the United States.[92] The large preponderance of flagship essentially export-orientated firms, such as Volvo, IKEA, Saab, Scania, Ericsson, increased pressure on government policy to address issues such as market access to EC markets and measures to improve levels of international competitiveness.

These factors had major implications for government policy on European integration. Trade policy was, for most of the early years, directed at the first objective of securing continued access for Swedish business to the main export markets of the EC. Once this was achieved, it was the issue of international competitiveness that was important. On both counts, continued pressure on Sweden's European policy came squarely from her large multinationals. To a large degree, it was pressure from these economic lobbies that kept the issue of European integration and full membership intermittently on the domestic political agenda.[93] However, with the evolution of the SEM programme in the late 1980s, especially as, by this time, the traditional Swedish mechanisms for maintaining international competitiveness were under criticism, both market access and international competitiveness were severely affected. For the most part, the industrial lobbies through the SAF were constant promoters of Swedish full membership.

ii) A Fragile Domestic Economy

The large size and number of Swedish multinationals has also affected the state of the domestic economy. The three biggest corporations in the Swedish construction industry, for instance, (which rank among the 20 largest building corporations in Europe) account for half of all domestic building activity. In practice, the domestic market has suffered from significant market concentration limiting levels of competition. From the domestic competition policy perspective, there were two major reasons for the country's poor growth rates in the 1980-90s - the rapid expansion of the public sector[94] and a corresponding governmental tendency to regulate the private sectors of the economy; both of which restricted levels of competition.[95] In particular, the Swedish public sector was especially important. Its size (the largest in the OECD area, accounting for roughly one-third of total employment) and operational principles which aimed at providing quality public services rather than any pretext of commercial viability ensured that it was relatively immune from competitive pressures.

Furthermore, many sectors of the economy, such as the food and beverage industry and housing, were strictly regulated in order to stifle competition, resulting for the most part in relatively higher prices and greater inefficiency. Regulation, for example, in the food industry resulted in food prices rising 130 percent more than non-regulated prices throughout the 1980s. Successive governments also provided comprehensive support measures for industry amounting to 11 percent of industrial value-added in 1983. The bulk of state aids were used to bail out state enterprises (representing around 12 percent of business sector employment) mainly in the northern regions and to preserve jobs in ailing firms and industries, such as mining (LKAB) and iron and steel (SSAB).

In addition, there was also widespread legal usage of cartel arrangements and restrictive practices. In 1992, for instance, there were some 1250 formal competition-restraining agreements on the Swedish cartel register, affecting some 10-13 percent of the total sales of goods and services. Crucially, Swedish competition policy (until 1993) was designed to only promote competition in the business sector which is desirable in the 'public interest', rather than to enhance competition *per se*.[96] Thus, for the most part, Swedish domestic markets experienced low levels of efficiency and competition, with poor allocation of resources. This was reinforced by the fact that the domestic economy lacks a critical mass of medium-sized firms able to undermine the power of multinationals in the domestic marketplace. In effect, the home market is numerically dominated by small companies, which operate exclusively in the domestic marketplace and yet are unable to prevent the market concentration of the larger firms.[97]

Ironically then at the same time as successive governments have been confronted by the growing challenges of economic interdependence and the need for greater trade liberalisation with the country's European partners, they have also been conscious of the ability of the domestic economy to endure major increases in competition from foreign companies.[98] The solution to this dilemma lay in measures taken by successive governments to improve levels of competition within Sweden. The pace of implementing these measures, however, increased once Swedish governments participated in the 'Luxembourg Process' and the SEM programme was launched (see Chapter Six). Most importantly, the liberalisation and deregulation of the economy was accelerated once the non-socialist government was in office (1991-94) as it introduced a commitment to neo-liberal values and a stronger adherence to the principles of the market. Non-socialist measures aimed at injecting greater efficiency into Swedish industry and the domestic economy, included, amongst others, reductions in the expenditure of the public sector and the introduction of market pressures into public services; the establishment of a new competition regime in 1993 based primarily on EC competition rules; a substantial reduction in levels of state aids so that by 1993 they were comparable to OECD averages; the deregulation of many of the private sectors and the enactment of a cautious, incremental programme of privatisation between 1991-94.[99] Of course, the measures are relatively new and their overall effects are still difficult to quantify, especially as the 1990-93 recession brought with it special problems, such as a banking sector crisis, which destroyed governmental attempts at financial deregulation and forced the government to increase support measures in key areas.[100]

Yet, without doubt, international trade and the strength of Sweden's growing economic interdependence with the EC, provided one of the main points of the 'Swedish Diamond' and shaped elite attitudes towards European integration. For the most part, the third point brought constant pressure in favour of closer ties with the EC and in contrast to the other three points of the Diamond has not dramatically changed. The influence of the third point became progressively larger (and eventually prevailed over the other three) and provided the most consistent and credible basis of argument for those elements of Swedish society pushing for full membership.

d) Point 4: Swedish Neutrality

The Diamond's final point emanates from Sweden's traditional security policy. Until 1991, security policy was narrowly defined as 'non-alignment in peace time in order to retain neutrality in the event of war'.[101] More specifically it was built around the concept of 'active neutrality' in which the country voluntarily chose to remain neutral and articulated policies designed to reinforce and re-affirm her neutral status. However, the intention here is not to evaluate the nature of Swedish neutrality policy[102] but rather to stress its importance in shaping elite attitudes and governmental policy on European integration.

Suffice to say, Swedish neutrality was a relatively old and deep-seated concept, originating from 1814 and lasting in its most complicated form until 1991. Most importantly for this discussion, it provided the primary rationale for not joining the European Community (until 1991) and acted as the counter-lever to the economic interdependence pressures of the Diamond's third point. According to Goldmann, the Swedish model of security policy was two-dimensional - namely that emphasis should be placed on the country neutral status and its international orientation.[103] However, for the most part, it was the former - its neutral status - that acted as the main brake on any overtures towards full EC membership. As Hakovirta argued, Swedish neutrality revolved around the two basic tenets of constant credibility and predictability.[104] It was essential for Sweden that her neutrality was consistent and clearly exposed. All foreign policy decisions needed to be compatible with the country's declared neutrality so that her actions were predictable and would build confidence in her ability to remain neutral abroad. The key challenge for Swedish governments was to constantly show to outside powers that the country was 'a committed neutral', especially as the status was maintained voluntarily.[105] Swedish neutrality was in fact not guaranteed by any international treaty and was not part of international law.

Hence from this perspective, the doctrine of neutrality incorporated a number of important principles relevant to later discussion on European integration. First, Sweden officially pursued an 'unflinching' policy of neutrality (*orubblight*) under which and according to official doctrine, the credibility of Swedish neutrality required complete public support and indeed, there was a very high degree of consensus between domestic political parties regarding security policy and neutrality.[106] Second, neutrality policy included both domestic and international concerns and influenced all areas of Swedish decision-making.[107] All major domestic as well as foreign policy decisions needed to accommodate the requirement that they must be compatible with the parameters of neutrality. Swedish governments followed a dual strategy of, on the one hand, constantly reiterating her neutrality in the international arena, and on the other, ensuring that domestic as well as foreign policies took account of and sought to reinforce Swedish neutrality. Hence, for a long time, full membership was rejected on the grounds that Sweden's economic sovereignty could not be compromised as the EC included supranational features and a Common Commercial Policy (CCP). Neither the government's foreign or domestic policies could afford to be undermined by the obligations of full membership or be secondary to any decisions of the supranational EC institutions as this was deemed by the Swedish elite as incompatible with the requirements of neutrality.[108]

Third, the credibility of the country's neutrality was also reinforced by her government's commitment to 'Total Defence', which incorporated the maintenance of large armed forces and exclusive support for indigenous technological and military industries.[109] In the post-war period, Sweden's defence spending was consistently one of the highest of the Western European countries and the size of her forces were disproportionately large when compared to her overall size of population. Sweden also supplied some 70 percent of defence requirements from domestic sources and built up several of the world's leading arms manufacturers.[110] In particular, successive governments were suspicious of any initiatives within the Community towards closer supranational defence co-operation as this once again had negative consequences for the traditional doctrine of 'armed neutrality'.

Fourth, Swedish neutrality was also combined with Goldmann's second dimension - internationalism. Successive governments argued that the country should remain aloof from the EC in order to maintain an active independent role in international politics and as an integral part of the credibility of neutrality policy. In practice then, the country's neutrality and internationalism were mutually supportive. At times, Swedish policy-makers tried to illustrate the country's independence from the (then) two blocs in Europe by criticising the superpowers over their actions. During the early Palme years, for example, the Prime Minister heavily criticised the United States intervention in Vietnam causing a strain in Swedish-US relations for most of that decade.[111] The commitment to internationalism remains even today in the post-1989 period. Sweden has played a very active role in international organisations, such as the United Nations, provided large amounts of foreign aid and contributed to UN peace-keeping activities.[112] Swedish troops for example have been deployed as part of UN commands in Macedonia in 1993 and in Bosnia since 1994 as part of a Nordic battalion.[113] In effect, the Swedish version of neutrality was more active and more deeply associated with internationalism than say either the Austrian, Swiss or Finnish variants.

Thus, for many years, Swedish neutrality provided one of the main obstacles to full EC membership. It was only in the 1980s that cracks started to appear in the hegemony of the neutrality doctrine and full membership began to be considered much more seriously. In particular and as Chapter Seven will testify it was only really in this decade that the first serious inklings that neutrality was no longer an effective policy emerged and even then, it remained important. It took the cataclysmic post-1989 political changes in Eastern Europe to finally break the grip of the doctrine of neutrality on Swedish security policy and governmental attitudes towards deeper European integration. In essence, the rationales for neutrality itself declined as Europe and its bloc arrangements were also revised.

Once it became apparent that the changes away from bloc arrangement were to be more permanent, Prime Minister Carlsson felt confident enough to announce that Swedish EC membership was 'compatible with the requirement of our policy of neutrality'. Yet, it took a change of government in October 1991 to facilitate more ambitious changes to security policy. In his first speech as Prime Minister (4 October 1991), Carl Bildt introduced a revised 'foreign and security policy with a European identity' and the arguments over the compatibility of neutrality and full membership slowly disappeared from the mainstay political debate. In theory, Sweden's security policy was reduced to merely an explicit reference to 'non-participation in military alliances' and thus the long-standing friction between the (economic) third and (neutrality) fourth points of the 'Swedish Diamond' was effectively removed.

Conclusion

The aim of this chapter has been to introduce the four points of the 'Swedish Diamond' as a conceptual framework for evaluating Swedish attitudes towards European integration. This potent cocktail of domestic and international influences help to differentiate the variables affecting the interrelationship between Sweden and the emerging European Community. What should be obvious from the discussion in this chapter is that whilst all four points were indeed, important, their degree of influence on governmental policy-making varied in ascendancy and over time. When the overall time period is examined. it will be clear that there was a tension between the first (consensual democracy), second ('Swedish model') and fourth (neutrality) points - which tended to reinforce the government's traditional resistance to full membership on the one side - and the third point (economic interdependence), which acted as continual catalyst pushing Swedish accession on the other. In addition, the fourth point of the Diamond tended to dominate Swedish thinking in the 1960s and 1970s, whilst the third point became progressively more influential from the 1980s onwards. Ultimately, it was due to this shift in emphasis, with the influence of the second and fourth points declining, the first becoming more fluid and third point achieving ascendancy, that allowed Sweden to eventually attain full membership of the European Union in 1995. It is to such a discussion that the following chapters address.

Notes

[1] For a detailed examination of the 'Swedish model' see Lane, J.-E. (1991) *Understanding the Swedish Model,* Frank Cass, London.
[2] Tilton, T. (1991) *The Political Theory of Swedish Social Democracy,* Clarendon, Oxford.
[3] Korpi, W. (1978) *The Working Class in Welfare Capitalism: Work, Unions and Politics in Sweden,* Routledge, London.
[4] Esping-Andersen, G. (1985) *Politics Against Markets: The Social Democratic Road To Power,* Princeton University Press, Princeton, and (1990) *The Three Worlds of Capitalism,* Princeton University Press, Princeton.
[5] Pontusson, J. (1992) *The Limits of Social Democracy,* Cornell University Press, Cornell.
[6] See for instance, Andrén, N. (1984) Sweden: Neutrality, Defence and Disarmament in Neuhold, H. & Thalberg, H. (eds.) *The European Neutrals in International Affairs,* Austrian Institute of International Affairs, Laxenburg, pp. 39-58.
[7] Elder, N., Thomas, A. & Arter, D. (1988) *The Consensual Democracies?,* Blackwells, Oxford, revised edition.
[8] Ibid., (1988) p. 11.
[9] According to Arter, the primary consequence of the move to a unicameral system (from a party-political standpoint) has been that the Social Democrats, although remaining comfortably the single largest political force, have lost their absolute majority in the legislature. Since the adoption of a single-chamber assembly there has been a marked trend towards stable minority governments as the dominant mode of government - Arter, D. (1984) *The Nordic Parliaments: A Comparative Analysis,* Hurst & Co., London.
[10] Constitutional revisions now allow for general elections to be held every four years starting from 1998.

[11] The September 1995 European Parliamentary Election is taken to be a recent exception to the rule as turnout at this election proved to be only 41.63 percent - see Miles, L. & Kintis A. (1996) The New Members: Sweden, Austria and Finland in Lodge, J. (ed.) *The 1994 Elections To The European Parliament*, Pinter, London, pp. 227-36.

[12] Ibid., (1996) p. 60.

[13] Larsson, T. (1995) *Governing Sweden*, Statskontoret, Stockholm, p. 30.

[14] Arter, D. (1990) The Swedish Riksdag: A Strong Assembly in Norton P. (ed.) *Parliaments in Western Europe*, Frank Cass, London, pp. 120-42.

[15] Ibid., Larsson (1995) p. 80.

[16] In particular, Arter argues that it is the high level of participation by Swedish parliamentarians on these pre-legislative commissions that makes this procedure 'a singularity of legislative practice in Western Europe'. It also has major advantages. Not only is cross-party consensus on government policy easier, but parliamentarians also have greater access to specialist information to make informed decisions - op. cit., Arter (1990) pp. 125-8.

[17] Ibid., Larsson (1995) p. 32.

[18] Jerneck, M., Sannerstedt, A. & Sjölin, M. (1988) Internationalisation and Parliamentary Decision-Making: the Case of Sweden 1970-1985, *Scandinavian Political Studies*, 11, pp. 169-94.

[19] Ruin, O. (1991) Three Swedish Prime Ministers: Tage Erlander, Olof Palme and Ingvar Carlsson in Lane, J.-E. *Understanding the Swedish Model*, Frank Cass, London, p. 58.

[20] Harpsund is the official residence of the Swedish Prime Minister. It was used by Tage Erlander as a meeting place of influential businessmen, labour leaders and politicians in frank discussions of Swedish economic policy. The 'spirit of Harpsund' is an expression commonly used to imply a desire to compromise and to build a broad consensus - Ruin, O. (1990) *Tage Erlander. Serving the Welfare State, 1946-1969*, University of Pittsburgh Press, Pittsburgh.

[21] See for instance, Elmbrant, B. (1969) *Palme*, Författarförlaget, Stockholm.

[22] A good appraisal of the rise, development and ideology of the SAP is provided by Misgeld, K., Molin, K. & Åmark, K. (1992) *Creating Social Democracy - A Century of the Social Democratic Labour Party in Sweden*, Pennsylvania State University Press, Pennsylvania.

[23] If New Democracy are included then Sweden could have an eight-party system.

[24] Op. cit., Larsson (1995) p. 41.

[25] Childs, M. (1932) *Sweden: The Middle Way*, Yale University Press, New Haven.

[26] Childs, M. (1980) *Sweden: The Middle Way on Trial*, Yale University Press, New Haven, p. 19.

[27] Op. cit., Childs (1932) p. 161.

[28] Op. cit., Childs (1932) p. 164.

[29] Wilde, L. (1994) *Modern European Socialism*, Dartmouth, Aldershot, p. 55.

[30] Milner, H. (1989) *Sweden - Social Democracy in Practice*, Oxford University Press, Oxford, pp. 60-1.

[31] Op. cit., Childs (1932) p. xv.

[32] Op. cit., Wilde (1994) p. 55.

[33] Lane, J.-E. (1991) Interpretations of the Swedish Model in Lane, J.-E. *Understanding the Swedish Model*, Frank Cass, London, p. 1.

[34] Rustow, D. (1955) *The Politics of Compromise: A Study of Parties and Cabinet Governments in Sweden*, Princeton University Press, Princeton.

[35] Heclo, H. & Madsen H. (1987) *Politics and Policy in Sweden: Principled Pragmatism*, Temple University Press, Philadelphia.

[36] A good defence of the principle of a universal welfare state is provided in Rothstein, B. (1996) The Moral Logic of the Universal Welfare State in Eriksen, E. O. & Loftager, J. (eds.) *The Rationality of the Welfare State*, Scandinavian University Press, Oslo, pp. 98-119.

[37] In other words, social protection was established as a universal right of citizenship - Olsson, S. E. (1990) *Social Policy and Welfare State in Sweden*, Arkiv, Lund.

[38] Taken and adapted from Petersson, O. (1994) *The Government and Politics of the Nordic Countries*, Publica, Stockholm, p. 34.

[39] Taken from Petersson, O. (1994) *Swedish Government and Politics*, Publica, Stockholm, pp. 50-8.

[40] Op. cit., Heclo & Madsen (1987) p. 4.

[41] Op. cit., Heclo & Madsen (1987) p. 6.

[42] Op. cit., Heclo & Madsen (1987) p. 7.

[43] The limitations of this view have been illustrated by Bo Rothstein. He argues that no matter how dominant the SAP may be or how wisely a reformist policy is designed, if the administrative arrangements are faulty then Social Democratic policy will fail at the stage of implementation - Rothstein, B. (1996) *The Social Democratic State - The Swedish Model and the Bureaucratic Problem of Social Reforms*, University of Pittsburgh Press, Pittsburgh.

[44] Micheletti, M. (1990) *The Swedish Farmers' Movement and Government Agricultural Policy*, Praeger, New York.

[45] See for instance, Rothstein, B. (1989) State and Capital: The Importance of Corporatist Arrangements, *Scandinavian Political Studies*, 11, pp. 235-60.

[46] Op. cit., Heclo & Madsen (1987) p. 19.

[47] The SAF became more active in agitating for reform of the 'Swedish model' and the welfare state since the early 1980s and has led to greater tension between the two arms of Swedish industrial relations - Micheletti, M. (1991) Swedish Corporatism at a Crossroads: The Impact of New Politics and New Social Movements in Lane J.-E. *Understanding the Swedish Model*, Frank Cass, London, pp. 144-65.

[48] De Geer, H. (1992) *The Rise and Fall of the Swedish Model*, Carden, London.

[49] According to Swenson, the centralisation of the Swedish industrial relations system came about as a result of a cross-class alliance between groups of workers and employers which imposed norms and institutions of peak-level bargaining on other groups - Swenson, P. (1989) *Fair Shares: Unions, Pay and Politics in Sweden and West Germany*, Cornell University Press, Cornell.

[50] Op. cit., Childs (1932) p. 71.

[51] Visser, J. (1996) Corporatism Beyond Repair? Industrial Relations in Sweden in Ruysseveldt, J. V. & Visser, J. (eds.) *Industrial Relations in Europe*, Sage, London, p. 176.

[52] Op. cit., Pontusson (1992) p. 2.

[53] Hadenius has argued that 'spirit of Saltsjöbaden' was replaced by the introduction of labour and employment laws in the 1970s. At the 1971 LO Congress, the Trade Union Confederation asked the government to limit the powers of employers and led to a bout of strike action during that year. The eventual outcome was legislation, such as the Security of Employment Act (operational 1974) and the Act on Employee Participation in Decision-making (the Co-Determination Act - operational 1977) - Hadenius, S. (1997) *Swedish Politics in the 20th Century*, 4th edition, Swedish Institute, Stockholm.

[54] A good summary of the 'Wage Earner Funds' episode is provided by Lewin, L. (1988) *Ideology and Strategy - A Century of Swedish Politics*, Cambridge University Press, Cambridge.

[55] Rehn, G. (1957) Hata inflationen *Tiden*, 49.

[56] Åberg, R. (1994) Wage Control and Cost-Push Inflation in Sweden since 1960 in Dore, R., Boyer R. & Mars, Z. (eds.) *The Return of Incomes Policy*, Pinter, London, p. 73.

[57] Op. cit., Wilde (1994) p. 56.

[58] Op. cit., Åberg (1994) p. 76.

[59] See studies by Korpi - op. cit., (1978); Lundberg, E. (1985) The Rise and Fall of the Swedish Model, *Journal of Scandinavian Literature*, 23, 1, pp. 1-36.

[60] For example, Calmfors has argued that an active labour market policy may have impacted negatively upon employment - Calmfors, L. (1992) *Lessons From the Macroeconomic Experience of Sweden*, Institute of International Economic Studies, Stockholm University, Stockholm.

[61] Layard, R. (1992)Varför överge den svenska modellen? in L. Calmfors (ed.) *Löner och sysselsättning*, SNS Förlag, Stockholm.

[62] Hibbs, D. A. Jnr. (1991) Market Forces, Trade Union Ideology and Trends in Swedish Wage Dispersal, *Acta Sociologica*, 34, 2, pp. 89-102 and Nilsson, C. (1993) The Swedish Model: Labour Institutions and Contracts in Hartog, J. & Theeuwes, J. (eds.) *Labour Market Contracts and Institutions: A Cross-National Comparison*, North-Holland, Amsterdam.

[63] Shalev, M. (1992) The Resurgence of Labour Quiescence in Reginin M. (ed.) *The Future of Labour Movements*, Sage, London.

[64] The Rehn-Meidner Model has been extensively criticised in some quarters. J. Magnus Ryner, for example, has argued that the model became an obstacle to progressive and essential economic reforms during the late 1980s and in part, accentuated the impact of the 1990-93 recession - Ryner, J. M. (1993) *The Economic 'Success' and Political 'Failure' of Swedish Social Democracy in the 1980s*, Research Report No. 1., Swedish Centre For Working Life, Stockholm.

[65] This view is not shared by all Swedish economists and there has been a considerable amount of debate regarding the under-performance of the Swedish economy. In particular, Walter Korpi has refuted this contention and argued that the measurements

used by the majority of economists to gauge the weakness of the Swedish economy is based almost exclusively on comparative macro-economic growth data and therefore 'careless analysis'. Korpi argued that Sweden's economy according to a full set of OECD figures was stable between 1977-90 - Korpi, W. (1992) *Halkar Sverige efter? Sveriges ekonomiska tillväxt 1870-90 i jämförande belysning,* Carlsson, Stockholm or Korpi, W. (1996) Eurosclerosis and the Sclerosis of Objectivity: On the Role of Values Among Economic Policy Experts, *The Economic Journal,* 106, November, pp. 1727-46.
[66] In fact, the employee investment funds were at the centre of political debate since the launch of the idea in the 1970s. Despite being established in the early 1980s, the non-socialist parties pledged repeatedly that the funds would be abolished if the Social Democrats lost power. This task began in the autumn 1991, when Parliament approved the dismantling of the five employee fund boards. During spring 1992, the Riksdag passed a further law specifying that the fund assets would be used for such purposes as promoting research and supporting the development of small and medium sized enterprises.
[67] A view expressed by the former Volvo President and 1991 SAF Chairman, Gunnar Johansson in a letter on 3 October 1991 - Taken from op. cit., Wilde (1994) p. 60.
[68] Op. cit., Visser (1994) p. 196.
[69] In effect, the VF, the employers' association in metal engineering decided 'to go it alone' and secured the support of the LO's 'Metall' union to defect from the central agreement. In addition, three white-collar unions (SIF, SALF and CF) representing 400,000 workers also negotiated separate deals.
[70] Op. cit., Micheletti (1991) p. 152.
[71] For an assessment of a new model of Swedish industrial relations see Iversen, T. (1996) Power, Flexibility, and the Breakdown of Centralised Wage Bargaining - Denmark and Sweden in Comparative Perspective, *Comparative Politics,* 28, 4, July, pp. 399-436.
[72] Pontusson, J. & Swenson, P. (1996) Labour Markets, Production Strategies, and Wage Bargaining Institutions - The Swedish Employer Offensive in Comparative Perspective, *Comparative Political Studies,* 29, 2, April, pp. 223-250.
[73] Op. cit., Visser (1994) p. 76.
[74] Op. cit., Pontusson & Swenson (1996) p. 224.
[75] Op. cit., Visser (1994) p. 36.
[76] Indeed, from 1993, the SAF advocated 'coordinated decentralisation' whereby they questioned centralised industry-level (multi-employer) bargaining, having eliminated peak-level (multi-industry bargaining) by this time.
[77] National Institute For Economic Research (1993) *Sweden -The Autumn Report,* National Institute For Economic Research, Stockholm, p. 1.
[78] The 15 percent figure for unemployment includes estimates of those on training and education schemes. The real figure for 1993 was 8.2 percent; well above the previous ten-year average (1984-1993) of 2.9 percent.
[79] 'Suedosclerosis' became established in the 1980s and the diagnosis was developed by Assar Lindbeck in a series of newspaper articles and more recently advanced in Ståhl, I. & Wickman, K. (1993) *Suedosclerosis - en särskilt elakartad form av eurosclerosis,*

Timbro, Stockholm and Ståhl, I. & Wickman, K. (1995) *Suedosclerosis - The Problems of the Swedish Economy*, Timbro, Stockholm.

[80] Social Democratic (since spring 1991) as well as non-socialist governments have officially acknowledged that the primary policy goal is low inflation rather than full employment and all governments in the 1990s have maintained this stance.

[81] The jury remains out as to whether the impact has been overwhelmingly negative. Dowrik, for example, has argued recently that at least up until 1990, 'there is nothing in the Swedish growth performance which indicates substantial underperformance' or that any potential underperformance is due to the presence of a large public sector. This however, remains the minority view - Dowrik, S. (1996) Swedish Economic performance and Swedish Economic Debate: A View for Outside, *The Economic Journal*, 106, November, pp. 1772-79.

[82] Svenska Arbetsgivareföreningen (1995) *Facts About The Swedish Economy 1995*, SAF, Stockholm, p. 29.

[83] Ibid., SAF (1995) p. 30.

[84] Ministry of Economic Affairs (1981) *The 1980 Medium Term Survey of the Swedish Economy*, Ministry of Economic Affairs, Stockholm, p. 31.

[85] Hallvarsson, M. (1981) *Swedish Industry Faces the 80s*, Federation of Swedish Industries/Swedish Institute, p. 58.

[86] Op. cit., Ministry of Economic Affairs (1981) pp. 81-109.

[87] See ETLA, (1990) *Growth and Integration in a Nordic Perspective*, Frenckell, Helsinki.

[88] Ministry of Economic Affairs (1982) *Growth or Stagnation? The Swedish Economy 1981-85*, Ministry of Economic Affairs, Stockholm, p. 20.

[89] The decision was taken by the government to peg the Krona to ECU in May 1991 in part as a means of displaying its commitment to further European integration.

[90] The substantial devaluation of the Krona by 20 percent between 1992-1993 provided a powerful boost to the Swedish export sector. In the 1990s the trade surplus climbed from SEK 16 billion to SEK 106 billion in 1995, as exports continued to expand faster than imports. Export volumes rose by 17 percent in 1994 and 11 percent in 1995. By 1995, exports accounted for around 40 percent of GDP compared to under 30 percent in 1990. The European average was around 32 percent. Figures taken from Barclays Economics Department (1996) *Barclays Country Report - Sweden*, April, Barclays, London.

[91] Stålvant, C.-E. & Hamilton, C. (1989) *A Swedish View of 1992*, RIIA Discussion Paper, No. 13, Royal Institute of International Affairs, London, p. 3.

[92] Organisation For Economic Cooperation and Development, (1996) *OECD Economic Survey - Sweden*, OECD, Paris, p. 72.

[93] This pressure was especially concentrated and emanated from certain sectors of the Swedish economy which include a higher preponderance of foreign-owned companies and multinationals. Foreign investment from multinationals has tended to cluster in the specific industrial sectors, such as food and beverages, chemicals and machinery in Sweden. - Knudsen, O. (1980) Foreign Investment and Multinational Corporations in the Nordic Countries, *Cooperation and Conflict*, XV, pp. 209-15.

[94] This view is prevalent in most of the key government reports in the 1990s and most recently, by Magnus Henrekson - see Henrekson, M. (1996) Sweden's Relative Economic Performance: Lagging Behind or Staying on Top? *The Economic Journal,* 106, November, pp. 1747-59. However, Jonas Agell in particular, has rejected that the poor aggregate growth record is the result of a large welfare state - see Agell, J. (1996) Why Sweden's Welfare State Needed Reform, *The Economic Journal,* 106, November, pp. 1760-71.

[95] Miles, L. (1995) Transforming Competition Policy: The Case of Sweden in Davison, L., Fitzpatrick, E. & Johnson, D. (eds.) *The European Competitive Environment,* Butterworth-Heinemann, London, pp. 176-92.

[96] Ibid., Miles (1995) p. 181.

[97] The diverse nature of Swedish companies is illustrated by the fact that 97 percent of all Swedish firms employed between 1-19 workers in 1993.

[98] As Kjell-Olof Feldt (Minister of Finance 1982-90) noted the basic concern of the 1980s governments was that Sweden's 'fundamental problem was the low growth and the lack of efficiency in the utilisation of economic resources' - Feldt, K.-O. (1991) *Alla dessa dagar....i regeringen 1982-90,* Norstedts, Stockholm.

[99] See Lane, J.-E. (1994) Sweden: Privatization and Deregulation in Wright, V. (ed.) *Privatization in Western Europe,* Pinter, London, pp. 180-97.

[100] The crisis which engulfed the Swedish banking sector was large affecting all the major banks. In fact, government support measures to the banking sector amounted to 2 percent of GDP in 1992 and 2.4 percent in 1993 and represented 26 percent and 24.1 percent of the government's budgetary deficits in 1992 and 1993 respectively. For a more detailed assessment see Pyggott, J. & Kilmister, A. (1996) *The Financial Crisis in Scandinavia 1990-92,* Occasional Papers in Nordic Studies, No. 2, University of Humberside, Hull.

[101] A sound appraisal of Swedish neutrality doctrine is provided by Brodin, K., Goldmann, K. & Lange, C. (1968) The Policy of Neutrality: Official Doctrines of Finland and Sweden, *Cooperation and Conflict,* III, pp. 19-51 or Andrén, N. (1972) Sweden's Security Policy, *Cooperation and Conflict,* VII, pp. 127-53.

[102] There are a number of detailed discussions on the nature of Swedish neutrality, such as Sundelius, B. (ed.) (1989) *The Committed Neutral Sweden's Foreign Policy,* Westview, Boulder or Miles, L. (1997) Sweden and Security in Redmond, J. (ed.) *The 1995 Enlargement of the European Union,* Dartmouth, Aldershot.

[103] Goldmann, K. (1991) The Swedish Model of Security Policy in Lane, J.-E. (ed.) *Understanding the Swedish Model,* Frank Cass, London, pp. 122-43.

[104] Hakovirta, H. (1988) *East-West Conflict and European Neutrality,* Clarendon, Oxford, p. 7.

[105] The term 'the committed neutral' was most notably coined in the excellent works of Sundelius - op. cit., Sundelius (1989).

[106] Op. cit., Goldmann (1991) p. 124.

[107] Miljan, T. (1977) *The Reluctant Europeans,* Hurst & Co, London.

[108] For a fuller assessment see op. cit., Miles (1997).

[109] See for example, Dörfer, I. (1982) Nordic Security Today: Sweden, *Cooperation and Conflict*, XVII, pp. 273-85.

[110] Kruzel, J. (1989) 'Sweden's Security Dilemma: Balancing Domestic Realities with the Obligations of Neutrality' in op. cit. Sundelius, pp. 67-93.

[111] Mosey, C. *Cruel Awakening*, Hurst & Co., London, pp. 109-17.

[112] Good summaries of Sweden's commitment to the UN in the past are provided by Haekkerup, H. (1964) Scandinavia's Peace-Keeping Forces for UN, *Foreign Affairs*, 42, 4, July, pp. 675 and Pedersen, O. K. (1967) Scandinavia and the UN 'Stand-by Forces', *Cooperation and Conflict*, II, pp. 37-46 and more recently, in Fredriksson, G., Lindskog, L., Pellnäs, B., Persson, S. & Wallensteen, P. (1997) *Sweden at the UN*, Swedish Institute, Stockholm.

[113] Archer, C. (1995) Conflict Prevention in Europe: The Case of the Nordic States and Macedonia *Cooperation and Conflict* XXIX, 4, pp. 367-86.

3   The Early Years 1950-70

It is generally recognised that due to Sweden's status as the largest of the Nordic countries,[1] its trade patterns have substantial repercussions for the entirety of Scandinavia. By the 1970s, the country represented almost half of the combined GNP of the region. Half of all Scandinavian exports (including intra-Nordic exports) originated from Sweden, whilst one-third of all imports, including intra-Nordic trade were similarly destined for the Swedish domestic market. Overall, the dominance of Swedish international trade in the region is undisputed. The figures speak for themselves. Swedish exports and imports, for instance, were three times the size of Finnish equivalents and roughly twice the size of Danish exports and imports during the period 1950-70.[2] In short, Swedish trade policy has exerted a considerable influence on the import markets of the other Scandinavian countries, whilst at the same time, remaining relatively immune from the threat of overwhelming imports originating from the other Nordic states.

Rather the most important trend in Swedish trade since the end of the Second World War is that it has become concentrated on West European markets. In practice, the country's market share of exports with the rest of the world declined from 24 percent share of the market in 1950 to 16 percent in 1970. Yet, Swedish trade patterns were also multi-faceted during 1950-70, with three interacting component trends affecting the country's trade. First, the central importance of intra-Nordic trade. Although close to saturation point, it still accounted for around 27 percent of Swedish trade in 1970. Second, the country displayed a rising dependence on, and interdependence with, West European markets. After 1958, trade levels rose considerably with other members of the European Free Trade Association (EFTA) and also with the European Economic Community (EEC) countries. Swedish exports, for example, to the EFTA and EEC countries amounted to 63 percent of total exports in 1950, rising to 72 percent in 1955 and 74 percent in 1965, before leveling off at around 72 percent in 1970. Third, Sweden continued to rely heavily on trade with one overseas market - namely the UK. Britain's share of Swedish exports amounted to 20 percent in 1960 and although progressively falling (to around 12 percent by 1970) was influential on governmental thinking as regards trade policy.[3] To some extent, the decline in the UK's share of the country's exports reflected the general expansion of Swedish trade, especially with other West European countries, and consequently, the UK's individual share was always likely to fall.[4]

Given the combined impact of these three trends, it is easy to understand why successive Swedish governments pursued greater international trade liberalisation. They favoured this approach as the major barriers to trade would theoretically be removed. Freer trade would also facilitate greater allocation of resources and economies of scale - something Sweden needed to improve upon to maintain her international competitiveness. However, the Social Democratic governments of Tage Erlander were less certain about the strategy to achieve freer trade and especially trade liberalisation through the establishment of common markets. For neutral Sweden, common markets posed a greater threat to national sovereignty and independence of action that was deemed so essential to a credible neutrality policy.[5] In particular, the requirement of ceding authority from national governments to common and supranational institutions in order to first, police any common market arrangement and second, to govern the external economic relations of the common market's members was simply unpalatable to most Swedes. The country's status as a small European state provided a further deterrent to membership of customs unions and common markets. The prospect of a sizable European customs union raised added doubts that if Sweden ever became a member, this peripheral, neutral country could be easily outvoted by other larger West European states, such as Germany and the UK and at the same time would have to accept common decisions which would undermine the level of national autonomy required by neutrality policy.

Successive governments developed a specific perception of free trade. In short, general trade liberalisation was acceptable, yet for the most part, customs unions and common markets were not. The only permissible form of a customs union/common market which the Erlander governments felt comfortable with was a Nordic customs union, under which Sweden would be the largest nation-state and thus, not easily dominated by other members. Hence, there has been a constant friction in Swedish policy-making surrounding aspects of free trade. Between on the one hand, support for the principle of general free trade (deemed so essential to the country's long-term economic prosperity) and on the other, resistance to the formation of European supranational decision-making arrangements which would be most efficient in transforming the principle into practice.

The Swedish strategy for furthering free trade operated at three levels. Governments during the period favoured the creation of free trade areas in Europe as these arrangements required neither supranational institutions nor a common commercial policy with non-member states and even though negotiations on free trade areas produced mixed results before the establishment of EFTA in 1959-60. In addition, Sweden was an active participant in global trading arrangements, such as the General Agreement on Tariffs and Trade (GATT) and the International Monetary Fund (IMF). Furthermore, the Erlander governments supported specialised trade liberalisation measures for the Third World, through, for example, the United Nations Conferences on Trade and Development (UNCTAD) and by high levels of foreign aid to the developing world.

Early Free Trade Initiatives

Broadly, post-war efforts at European integration developed into two general and alternative streams. On the one hand, there were the intergovernmental Pan-European attempts at trade liberalisation and closer European cooperation, such as through the Organisation for European Economic Cooperation (OEEC), Council of Europe and later the EFTA. On the other, were the more ambitious initiatives involving supranational institutions and commitments, such as the European Coal and Steel Community (1951), which ultimately led to the creation of the EC and latter day European Union. In general, successive Swedish governments showed a strong preference for the first (intergovernmental) option. This was more easy to reconcile with national sovereignty requirements and compatibility with the country's neutral status. Yet, early post-war attempts at achieving freer trade involving the Swedes were not strikingly successful, although the blame for such mediocre results does not lie with the Swedes alone. The intention of the chapter is not to chart the actual development of these initiatives and negotiations, but rather to comment upon Swedish governments' perspectives on, and participation within them.

Swedish preferences for European intergovernmental cooperation were displayed early in the post-war period. The first major political initiative at some kind of European political cooperation was the process that eventually led to the establishment of the Council of Europe. This process in fact tried to combine the two approaches to European cooperation and integration into one general objective of a grand European institution and into one main institutional setting. The Swedish government (along with 16 others) agreed to send delegates to the Hague Congress held between 8-10 May 1948, which led to the Council of Europe's creation in May 1949. Nevertheless, throughout the debates of the Council of Europe over the following two years, the Swedish delegation showed 'a general lack of interest and opposition to the establishment of supranational institutions'.[6] Sweden's Social Democratic government was rooted within the 'functionalist' camp, sharing the views of their British, Danish, Norwegian, Swiss and Austrian counterparts in refusing any proposals that would facilitate federal or supranational institutions and/or result in the ceding of national sovereignty.[7]

The Swedish government's position rejected federalism (in particular) on several economic and political grounds. The economic arguments against federalism centred around fears that the country's high standards of living would attract large amounts of foreign labour which would undermine the success of Swedish economic policy if a federal union was based, as it surely must be, around the free movement of people and labour. Further concerns were raised about the implications for Swedish social and welfare policies given that any future European union would most probably apply continental rather than Swedish standards. As long as the British shared Swedish reservations over a federal Europe and remained one of the country's leading trading partners, then successive governments could afford to remain outside any federal or supranational organisation without drastically hurting trade and future prosperity.

In practice, for the Erlander governments, trade liberalisation (especially if it included the other Nordic countries and the UK) was the overriding priority at this time, rather than any grandiose schemes for pan-European supranational integration. Erlander was, for example, more enthusiastic about the establishment of the loose and informal Uniscan - which reinforced economic ties between the Nordic countries and the UK and provided a mechanism for multilateral coordination of economic policies - rather than the ideals of the federal elements of the Council of Europe.[8] Uniscan became the main forum for consultation between Britain and Scandinavia regarding the progress of European economic integration and to coordinate governmental opposition to the development of a federal and/or supranational Europe.[9]

The Swedish elite also spurned a federal Europe on political grounds. The Erlander government saw little attraction in replacing the country's successful and mature national institutions with untried and rather nebulous European ones. The main argument in favour of a federal Europe seemed in Swedish eyes, after all, to be championed by states whose political institutions had been discredited, disintegrated or were unstable as a result of the Second World War. This scenario simply did not apply to Sweden. Social Democracy was perceived as having been effective in tackling widespread depression in the 1930-40s, whilst the success of the wartime governments in maintaining the country's neutrality throughout 1939-45 had enabled the country's political arrangements to remain intact. This essentially chauvinistic pride in the superiority of 'Swedish democracy' was a substantial buffer to the economic attractions of European integration.

When the Swedish government was interested in European cooperation at all, it favoured an incremental and limited approach in keeping with Nordic cooperation. Overall, little time was spent in the Riksdag debating European integration questions, especially if they derived from the Council of Europe's debates. If anything, more attention was placed on the possibilities of either Nordic cooperation or more broadly applied European functional solutions, such as the OEEC. This was especially apparent during the process leading up to the creation of the European Coal and Steel Community (ECSC).

In line with existing thinking on European supranational organisations, the Swedish government paid little attention to the 1951 Schuman Plan (designed to establish a supranational organisation to direct the integration of Europe's coal and steel industries). It stressed that future European trade liberalisation should take place through the existing OEEC. The Erlander government did not take part in any of the major preliminary negotiations and was viewed by the more federalist inclined Six as an ardent 'functionalist' and ally of the British. Indeed, Erlander took comfort from the equally complaisant attitude of the British government. He believed that the plan was unlikely to reach fruition and was in any case undesirable given its supranational nature. The ECSC could not be regarded by Swedish policy-makers as a purely economic organisation. Its supranational structure and wider political aims deemed it to be too controversial for Sweden and its neutrality. For the most part the government stuck to existing policy of 'shadowing' British trade policy. It emphasised the importance of the UK market for Swedish trade and the need to 'wait and see' as to the outcome of the Paris negotiations.

There was hardly any parliamentary or public debate on the ECSC either, except for a limited discussion over the future impact of the Six's integrated coal and steel market on the Swedish manufacturing (and in particular the iron and specialist steels) sector. Traditional intergovernmental objections, neutrality considerations and the British trade policy connection dominated governmental thinking. Ultimately the ECSC was a specific kind of customs union. Thus, it was rejected as incompatible with neutrality (the Diamond's fourth point). If anything, Swedish attention (on the customs union front) was directed at the possibilities for a smaller but more comprehensive Scandinavian variant, which had been introduced on to the political agenda before the Schuman Plan.

a) Nordic Economic Cooperation[10]

After the successful launching of a combined Scandinavian airline - SAS (Scandinavian Airline System, including Denmark, Norway and Sweden) on 1 August 1946, deeper economic cooperation between the Nordic countries seemed an obvious and popular option. Indeed, at a conference of Scandinavian foreign ministers (9 July 1946), a special committee was established to examine the possibilities for expanding economic cooperation between the Scandinavian countries. The ensuing committee, formally known as the 'Joint Nordic Committee For Economic Cooperation' (JNCEC), and led by the Danish banker, C.V. Bramsnaes examined several potential areas (from 1948) and reached its interim conclusions in January 1950.[11] It suggested that a customs union would facilitate specialisation and economies of scale benefits for the Nordic economies.

However, despite limited Swedish governmental support, the early attempts at comprehensive Nordic cooperation were doomed to failure. Successive Norwegian governments were not enthusiastic about the development of a Nordic customs union as they were uneasy about the ability of Norway's industry to compete openly with Danish and Swedish counterparts. This limited progress and led the Erlander government to eventually lose interest in the concept. Further proposals by the Danish government in 1950 to establish a Danish-Swedish customs union (which Norway could join later) were rejected by the Social Democratic government. There would be only marginal benefits without Norway's participation and this would create further divisions within Scandinavia.

For the most part, Norway remained aloof, regardless of further attempts by the Bramsnaes committee at reconciling her fears by limiting the customs union to specific kinds of industrial goods. By the time the JNCEC finally presented its report to the Nordic Council,[12] little concrete progress had been made. Even when a new ministerial level 'Committee of Ministers of Economic Cooperation' and a specialist 'Nordic Economic Cooperation Committee' (NECC) were created at an intergovernmental conference in Harpsund in 1954 to consider the establishment of a Scandinavian customs union, the chances of success were still poor. In effect, the initiative had passed to wider talks on a pan-European free trade area by 1954. Yet, in typical Nordic fashion, the NECC produced several detailed studies on the merits of a Scandinavian customs union between 1955-59 and there were extensive debates in the Nordic Council in 1956 and 1958 [13] before the concept finally ran out of steam.

The option of a purely Scandinavian customs union was never sufficiently persuasive to Erlander unless it included all three Scandinavian countries. Indeed, it is interesting to note that the Swedish government viewed a Scandinavian customs union as less of a threat to neutrality than a wider European variant on the grounds that it viewed the Nordic area as one of low tension and within the emerging concept of the 'Nordic Balance'.[14] Yet, since such a customs union was never likely given the degree of Norwegian opposition, Swedish governmental thinking moved in favour of less ambitious, but more wide-ranging European measures which would include all of Scandinavia and beyond. Swedish policy makers perceived a Scandinavian customs union as only being worth the ceding of national sovereignty if it included all of Scandinavia. The implied loss in sovereignty would then be translated into Swedish economic dominance of the customs union and large opportunities for the country's export industries. This reasoning was reflected in for example, the Erlander government's proposals on harmonising Nordic tariffs presented at the 1966 Copenhagen Nordic Council meeting. Otherwise, European solutions were equally (if not more attractive). They included trade liberalisation affecting the growing continental markets and incorporated the existing trading relationship with the UK.

For a considerable time, Swedish thinking remained unaltered. From a comparative perspective, the response to Danish proposals in April 1968 about a revived Nordic economic community (NORDEK)[15] was similar to that of ten years earlier in that they also failed to invoke any substantial domestic debate either.[16] NORDEK was to some extent, a reaction to the failure of the applications by the UK, Denmark and Ireland to join the EEC in 1967 and reflected Danish aspirations that NORDEK might actually prepare the Nordic countries 'for the day when the door to broad European integration will be opened'.[17] In practice, NORDEK was not supposed to be an alternative to European integration, but a partial and regional catalyst to promote further Nordic participation within it. In common with the previous and less ambitious Scandinavian customs union initiative, the Nordic Council set up a Nordic Committee of High Officials on Nordic Economic Cooperation in April 1968 to compile an investigative report by 15 July 1969. This time, the four Nordic governments were able to reach a preliminary agreement, but the plan was eventually scotched. The Finnish government declared (24 March 1970) that it would refuse to sign a NORDEK Treaty on the grounds of Finnish neutrality and that NORDEK was not an effective organ to further European integration.

In the Swedish case, the whole NORDEK question 'raised little enthusiasm'.[18] The Palme government shared Finnish reservations about the compatibility of NORDEK with neutrality policy especially since the Danish government proposed that any NORDEK arrangement should have common institutions, similar to that of the EEC (see next section). Overall, the Social Democratic government's perspective reflected Palme's unofficial belief that the NORDEK initiative had run out of steam by early 1970. In the Riksdag's debate on NORDEK (29 April 1970),[19] governmental spokesmen limited their statements to merely an understanding of Finland's position and that the NORDEK question would be unresolved until a new Finnish government could be formed. Palme had for the most part lost interest in NORDEK by December 1969, when the EEC Heads of Government agreed to begin negotiations with future membership applicants and thus, governmental attention on the EEC began to resurface. In fact, the entire Riksdag debate was low-key, even if there was some disagreement between the main political parties. The former leader of the Liberal Party, Sven Wedén and the leading conservative, Leif Cassel both called for an immediate acceptance of NORDEK (to be called SCANDEK if it did not include Finland) in the hope that Finland would join later. The Social Democratic government and the leader of the Centre Party, Gunnar Hedlund argued that SCANDEK would have only minimal advantages for Sweden without Finnish participation. Hedlund in particular stipulated that 'freer trade with the EEC ought to be sought, but Swedish neutrality must be respected'.[20] In practice, the NORDEK question stalled by March 1970 (see Chapter Six) and attempts to continue with the project in a more limited SCANDEK form foundered due to the lack of Swedish enthusiasm.

Two of the four points of the 'Swedish Diamond' were predominant - namely, concerns over Sweden's economic interdependence and neutrality. In the Scandinavian customs union and later NORDEK cases, successive governments were cautious about supranational Nordic economic cooperation. For Social Democratic Sweden, a supranational Nordic Community did not offer significant economic advantages to offset its need for preferential trading arrangements with continental Europe and the UK. At the same time, any such supranational Nordic arrangement would imply the dilution of the country's neutral status through the ceding of elements of control of trade policy. This was in Swedish eyes too large a price to pay. In short, the Diamond's third point (economic interdependence) favoured a European, rather than purely Nordic solution to the country's reliance upon international trade.

b) The WFTA and the EEC Negotiations[21]

It was developments in Western Europe that curtailed attempts at closer Nordic cooperation and any kind of Swedish enthusiasm for them. From the mid-1950s onwards, the attention of Swedish policy-makers as regards further trade liberalisation was fixed on Western rather than Northern Europe. In particular, the high point for the Nordic countries concerning trade liberalisation was reached during the 1956-58 Wide Free Trade Area Negotiations. With their failure in 1958, the objectives of Swedish trade policy altered from that of achieving Pan-European free trade to the growing challenge of dealing with the emerging EEC.

According to Miljan, the WFTA concept had two important effects on Swedish (and Nordic) perspectives on free trade. The negotiations illustrated 'the salutary effect of exposing the pragmatic basis of their adherence to the principle of free trade' and its consequent failure led to the development of a realistic Nordic approach with the objective of achieving freer, rather than free trade.[22] In practice, after 1958, the one driving Swedish governmental objective was the need to find an accommodation with the emerging EEC. Nordic attempts at strengthening regional economic arrangements stalled from the 1950s onwards and Swedish policy makers paid much greater attention to wider developments in Western Europe.

Nonetheless, Erlander continued to follow the slow progress of the European Communities 'with a great deal of disbelief and distrust'.[23] He especially treated the 1950 Pleven Plan and the negotiations on a European Defence Community (EDC) with a large pinch of scepticism and perceived its rejection by the French Senate in 1954 as a vindication of his policy that European integration should not infringe into areas of 'high politics' and in particular, security matters. The EDC episode, according to Erlander, reinforced Swedish neutrality and the wisdom of prioritising it above the economic potential of European integration.

Yet, Erlander underestimated the strength of the political forces working for European integration in the continental states and their importance for the emergence of a new Europe. In effect, the notion that centuries-old rivalries must give way to a relationship that made another European war unthinkable was a prevailing force on the continent. Although this was welcomed and accepted by the Swedes as legitimate, most politicians doubted the speed with which it could be realised. It had after all, taken several centuries for the same thing to be achieved in the Nordic region.

It was the Messina Conference in June 1955 that compelled the Erlander government (like its British counterpart) to consider in concrete terms what the cooperation of the Six now implied. The ECSC had by this time been in operation for several years and was widely regarded (at this time) as a qualified success. Nevertheless, Erlander concurred with the strongly negative reaction of the British and again placed the priorities of sustaining exports to Britain above those of trading with the continent. On 1 July 1955, the Swedish Chargé d'Affaires in London, Sverker Åström (along with the Danish and Norwegian Ambassadors) met Lord Reading of the Foreign Office to discuss the implications of the Messina plan for a European customs union. At the meeting, Lord Reading outlined the stern dangers of the plan and that the British government had 'the most serious objections against practically all proposals discussed at Messina'.[24] In fact, the Social Democratic government agreed with many of the objections (although for essentially neutrality based considerations) and was satisfied that the Swedish line would be protected indirectly by British representatives at the Spaak Committee's meeting in Brussels on the details of the customs union.

Overall, the Swedish position on the EEC was filled with 'objections, hindrances and doubts'.[25] Consequently, Erlander argued that liberalisation should take place through the existing OEEC rather than a smaller Six arrangement and supported British proposals in July 1956 that the OEEC examine the creation of a European free-trade area including the Six, the UK and 'other interested countries'.[26] Indeed, the British and the Six's initiatives were the main subjects of discussion at the Nordic Council's Helsinki session (February 1956). The Swedish government (along with Denmark and Norway) realised that if the UK and the Six formed a joint free trade area, then the Nordic countries must join as well. The issue for the Council was if Nordic regional arrangements, such as a customs union, would bolster their own negotiating hand in any wider negotiations on European trade liberalisation.

Therefore, the OEEC Council's decision in February 1957 to establish a Pan-European free trade area must be placed into the context of the process leading to creation of the EEC and EURATOM.[27] In effect, the WFTA concept was also a direct reaction to the decision at Messina in June 1955 by the Six to create a common market and joint action on the development of nuclear power. The proposal of a study on the future establishment of the WFTA originated from the British with substantial Swedish support. The Erlander government, for instance, also jointly proposed that the OEEC Steering Board of Trade would devise a plan for a Europe-wide reduction of tariffs. At the OEEC Council meeting, which took place after the signing of the EEC's Treaty of Rome, the goal of establishing a European Free Trade Area was formally adopted. An intergovernmental ministerial committee headed by Reginald Maudling (the Maudling Committee) was appointed to carry out the detailed negotiations for a free trade area treaty. The Maudling Committee met nine times between November 1957 and November 1958, when negotiations abruptly ended, signalling the failure of the WFTA.

Although for the most part a peripheral player in the WFTA, the Swedish government developed its preliminary position in time for the July 1956 OEEC Council meeting. The government stressed its long-standing desire for tariff reductions. By 1957, Erlander's position was concrete. In a statement by the Prime Minister to the Riksdag's First Chamber (20 March 1957 - also given by the Foreign Minister to the Second Chamber), Erlander argued that:

> 'In view of the fact that a very considerable part of Sweden's external trade is with the United Kingdom and countries of the European continent, it is clear that for Sweden too it is important not to stand outside a free trade area comprising most of the member states of the OEEC. ... The creation of a free trade area is in line with the efforts which traditionally have been one of the main aims of Swedish commercial policy'.[28]

Nevertheless. Erlander was criticised in Parliament by the non-socialist parties for the slow evolution of government policy on the WFTA/EEC and that the issue was being effectively down-played. In general though, parliamentary interest in the WFTA and EEC was also limited and the level of domestic debate was minimal.[29] The government restricted itself to merely informing the Riksdag's Foreign Affairs Standing Committee, issued only a handful of statements on WFTA/EEC policy and was subject to equally few questions in plenary sessions. The lack of debate on the whole WFTA/EEC issues was illustrated by the action of Mr. Antonson, a Centre Party MP who tabled a parliamentary question to the Ministry of Commerce asking why the Riksdag had not been given sufficient information on the progress of the negotiations. Yet, it took until the last day of final parliamentary session of 1958 and only a few days before the suspension of the WFTA negotiations (11 December 1958) for Minister Gunnar Lange to reply.

During the short debate in the Riksdag's (then) Second Chamber in December 1958, there was general approval amongst the main political parties for the government's policy of creating 'a basis for continued negotiation and above all avoid discrimination in West Europe's common trade' - although there was also general disappointment with the slow progress of the WFTA talks.[30] Yet, given that the WFTA negotiations were taking place at the same time as the ill-fated attempts at establishing a Scandinavian customs union, this only helped to confuse the whole debate in the eyes of the parliamentarians. In effect, the government was left to itself to develop policy in this key area.

There was, however, virtually unanimous agreement among the political parties and economic interest groups on two counts - which were to impact on government policy. First, that EEC membership was not attractive to Sweden because of its overt aims of supranational political integration and economic union; second, that the high EEC tariff walls were equally unacceptable to Sweden as a non-member state because of its long tradition of free trade. Although no major parliamentary debates were arranged to discuss either the WFTA or EEC, the Erlander government was careful to consider the interests of Swedish business. A series of high-level meetings were held at the Prime Minister's official country residence - *Harpsund* - in autumn 1958 between the Cabinet and leading members of the country's interest groups in order to accommodate economic interests within government policy - much to the annoyance of the main opposition parties, which were excluded. Erlander himself later admitted that the meeting at Harpsund was 'certainly the most thorough discussion that we have had with the business community about free trade'.[31] There was 'total unity' between the government, the business community and the trade union movement that Erlander should make the WFTA's establishment a priority in order to avoid the discriminatory effects that emerged after the EEC became operational in January 1958.

The Swedish delegation did have at least, some positive influences on the WFTA negotiations. Earlier during the March 1957 preliminary negotiations, the delegation tried to ensure that the positions of the UK and the Six on agriculture questions converged and did, albeit to a limited extent, help to move the process 'at least partially on the way towards reconciliation'.[32] Indeed, the Social Democratic government, despite obvious concerns, refrained from criticising the Danes for their 'open door' policy on EEC membership and sought instead to develop mutually supportive positions in the WFTA negotiations.

Yet the Erlander government was trying to develop concrete trade policy positions in an international setting of shifting sands. The government attempted throughout to support both the Scandinavian customs union and the WFTA. Once the WFTA negotiations faltered Erlander attempted to reinvigorate the Nordic initiative as a second alternative. In summer 1958, during a lull in the WFTA negotiations and with the EEC now in operation, Erlander seized the initiative and pressed for action on the Scandinavian customs union at the forthcoming Nordic Council session in order to counteract any negative effects on Nordic trade. The initiative was, at least in part, based on the political need to strengthen Sweden's negotiating hand with the rest of Europe. In particular, the Swedes argued that if the WFTA negotiations failed, then the Nordic countries as a customs union would be in a stronger position in negotiating tariff agreements with the evolving EEC rather than acting as individual actors. At a series of Nordic Council meetings at Saltsjöbaden (22-23 September 1958), the Minister of Commerce, Gunnar Lange proposed that first, the Scandinavian customs union should be instituted immediately for a limited range of commodities and second, this would be followed by a political decision to expand this to a full common market within two years. On 9 November, Tage Erlander at the Nordic Council's sixth session in Oslo, again warned that,

> 'there is a danger that our countries up here in the North will be subject to discrimination by the Six Powers which is irreconcilable with a close Western European association and that is something which we could not accept'.[33]

Indeed, Erlander made one last effort to call for a united Nordic position during the stagnated WFTA negotiations as 'we are by no means insignificant as negotiating partners' and that 'this new situation (*of the emerging and discriminatory EEC*) would perhaps make it even more essential for the Nordic Market to be a living reality'[34] - both of which proved to be empty gestures. When these initiatives for a limited customs union were also rejected, Erlander quickly moved ahead to bring about an interim solution in the form of the 'Outer Seven' EFTA arrangement. Hence, Swedish position operated 'on the basis of pragmatism, but a pragmatism based on necessity, not preference'.[35]

EFTA - The Next Best Thing?

After the collapse of the WFTA and Scandinavian customs union negotiations in the late 1950s, the Erlander government quickly mobilised a unanimity of views among the 'Other Six'.[36] During the OEEC negotiations, the Swedish delegation proposed the formation of a more limited free trade area to offset the economic power of the EEC. According to Miljan, this was viable due to several reasons. First, that formal economic consultations already existed between the UK and Denmark, Norway and Sweden through Uniscan. Second, that the Erlander government could rely on the support of the British, which shared similar concerns over the supranational EEC. Third, there was also a convergence of views between Austria and Switzerland and the Uniscan members during the 'Maudling negotiations'. Finally, the previous conditions allowed for a consensus among the 'Other Six' (for differing reasons) on the formation of a European free trade area rather than a customs union arrangement.[37]

Yet, in practice, these countries formed a diverse grouping. They were united primarily because a limited EFTA arrangement was the only viable alternative (other than economic isolation) to the Community and by their general dislike of the political integration required by EEC membership. For neutral Sweden, a free trade area was compatible with the requirements of her neutrality precisely because it did not require a common external tariff or commercial policy arrangement. At the same time, the Erlander government could achieve its dual objectives. It could maintain the low tariffs which her industrial structure needed[38] and also allowed the country to be part of a trade bloc which could negotiate market access for Swedish exports with the EEC. The attraction of the EFTA framework for the Social Democratic government was compounded by the fact that Sweden would benefit from a reduction in (the relatively high) British tariffs, which given the UK's status as a major trading partner was attractive to the Swedes. The negotiations that led to the signing of the Stockholm Convention roughly fell into two phases. The first semi-official stage lasted from December 1958 to March 1959 and was characterised by a series of discussions between leading diplomats in both private and official capacities. The second stage was relatively brief lasting only between May-November 1959 and saw continual negotiations between what had now become the 'Outer Seven'.[39]

The rapidity of the government's initiatives (in dealing with the thorny problem of future discriminatory frameworks as a consequence of the EEC's operation) was highlighted by the fact that only two days after Maudling suspended the WFTA negotiations, Erlander (18 November 1958) invited representatives from the 'Outer Six' to meet in Stockholm to discuss the coordination of trade policies. Ironically, Erlander had second thoughts - suspecting this was premature and withdrew the invitations the following day. None the less, this action was significant. The SAF actively supported the initiative arguing that it was in part a governmental reaction to their lobbying activities. Earlier that year the SAF had signed (14 April 1958) a joint statement (Free Trade in Western Europe) of the industrial federations and employers' organisations of the 'Outer Six' in Paris calling for a new OEEC-wide trading arrangement. Later in a joint declaration of the SAF and the Federation of British Industries (17 December 1958), both organisations called for the immediate establishment of an 'Outer Six' trading association. This resulted in an extensive series of discussions between the industrial federations of the 'Outer Six' on the details of such a plan in 1958-59.[40]

The Erlander government's leading role was seen throughout the EFTA negotiations and during both the informal first and formal second stages. At a meeting of senior officials in Stockholm in March 1959 the decision was taken to actively pursue the formation of a free trade area apart from the Community, but (at this time), still within the OEEC framework and with the longer term aim of including all OEEC members. It was also agreed that the 'Outer Seven' should refrain from making separate agreement with the EEC without prior consultation with the other members of the group. At the Stockholm meeting, the leader of the Swedish delegation and Assistant Under-Secretary in the Ministry of Foreign Affairs, Hubert de Besche, was appointed coordinator of the negotiations and was assigned the task of drawing up the free trade area. In typical Swedish fashion, De Besche spent the next month informally touring the capitals of the seven prospective members seeking consensus on, and mobilising support for, the project. General disagreement revolved around two points. First, the transitional period for the implementation of the free trade area and whether there should be the immediate removal or gradual phased reduction of import barriers. Second if EFTA's trade liberalisation rules should apply to agriculture and fisheries, which the British especially opposed.[41] Apart from these two areas, agreement had been reached by all members.

Hence, by the time the second more formal phase of the EFTA negotiations began, the Swedes were central to the process. The Erlander government called for and held the inaugural meeting at Saltsjöbaden (7-13 June 1959) and based the ensuing negotiations around de Besche's report. Indeed, even as the negotiations on a Nordic customs union were being revitalised in 1958-59, the government consistently displayed its preference for the wider EFTA solution

- although at the same time, it did favour the existence of a Nordic customs union as an integral part of a wider free trade area. During a foreign affairs debate in the Riksdag's Second Chamber in March 1959, the government clearly outlined its general preference for an EFTA that should however, include a Nordic customs union.[42] When the Nordic option was buried by the Nordic Council at Kungalv (July 1959), the government continued to champion the EFTA concept regardless. At the July 1959 'Outer Seven' meeting at Saltjöbaden, for instance, Erlander asserted that an EFTA between the countries should still be established.

The EFTA draft convention was subsequently prepared over a series of four meeting in Stockholm between 8 September-18 November 1959, before being finally initialled on 20 November 1959. For the Swedes, the Stockholm Convention included some useful attractions. Unlike the EEC, the Convention permitted a member of EFTA to withdraw provided 12 months notice was given. This removed any longer term concerns that EFTA membership could undermine sovereignty or neutrality and at the same time allowed for the Swedish government to (at times) ponder some kind of future EEC membership. In addition, given that the Stockholm Convention only created a free trade area, the issue of the compatibility of common commercial policy (CCP) with Swedish neutrality never arose as a CCP was not included within the EFTA concept. The EFTA's institutional arrangements were also designed to be intergovernmental and remained minimal, with scarcely 100 people working for its secretariat (even in its heyday) and included no court. Consequently, this reduced any Swedish fears surrounding the prospect of EFTA developing into an overarching European, but undemocratic bureaucracy, which would ultimately threaten Swedish premises of a transparent and accountable democracy. In short, the Diamond's first 'point' - that of protecting the country's integrative and consensual democracy - remained intact and outside the EFTA framework.

Moreover, the Convention was 'built on the twin pillars of free and fair trade'.[43] As well as creating an industrial free trade area and being concerned with the elimination of barriers to industrial goods, it also promoted conditions of fair competition. In practice though, EFTA created a free trade area of a specific kind and industrialised nature. Given that the Convention was almost exclusively concerned with industrial goods, the balance of advantages within EFTA favoured the industrialised members - namely Sweden, Switzerland and the UK. Governmental concerns about maintaining access to the markets of the UK and the Nordic countries were at least partially addressed by the EFTA Convention. Indeed, during both the OEEC and Saltsjöbaden negotiations leading to the creation of EFTA, Sweden showed a remarkable degree of unity with the UK on many issues and especially those related to creating an industrial free trade area.

EFTA was, for the most part, viewed as successful by successive Swedish governments throughout the 1960s. As Archer argues, however:

'any assessment of EFTA's achievements must take into account the dual purpose for which the Association was established - to create an industrial free trade area and to procure a wider settlement of trade differences between all the West European countries'.[44]

It is generally recognised though that EFTA was more successful in achieving the former rather than the latter objective. Industrial free trade within EFTA was achieved some three years earlier than scheduled - in December 1966 - though this was again a reaction to developments within the EEC. The EFTA Council in 1960-61 agreed to accelerate tariffs cuts in order to keep pace with the Community's timetable for tariff reduction and thereby allow any future overall EEC-EFTA trade settlement to be negotiated more easily. Once it was apparent to the EFTA states that such an agreement was not likely, the Lisbon EFTA Council meeting (May 1963) decided to accelerate the tariff cuts timetable in order to enable EFTA's industries to strategically plan their future. For Sweden, as one of the most industrialised EFTA members, this meant that the full benefits of an industrial free trade area were felt more quickly and to the country's overall benefit. The rewards were through increased exports as the country's low tariff levels meant that the domestic market was competitive and Swedish industries were acclimatised to competitive pressures.

Despite considerable variations between the EFTA countries, Sweden enjoyed an average annual increase of around 5-6 percent, which in part can be attributed to EFTA membership. Robertson, for instance, estimated that the total increase in intra-EFTA trade as a result of the reduction in trade barriers and tariffs amounted to $830 million in 1965 and as far as exports were concerned this represented 'a genuine increase in total trade'.[45] Around 25 percent of the total increase in intra-EFTA trade between 1959-65 was directly attributable to the creation of EFTA. In addition, Lundgren argued that the main benefits for Sweden were mainly in those products for which natural resources were not important (machinery, clothes, shoes and finished goods in general) and intra-European trade was viewed as 'mainly a way of reaping the benefits of large scale economies'.[46] Consequently, the Erlander government was also keen to avoid tariff discrimination in key commodities with a high raw material content, such as paper, steel, aluminum products and ferro-alloys. This latter concern was based not on their overall share of total Swedish exports - for in practice this was naturally falling - but rather around their prominence in the public debate due to the roles of key interest lobbies. Both elite and public opinion were opposed to any concept of economic integration involving agriculture in particular.

Despite Robertson's assertions that the EFTA effects on intra-Nordic trade were not as high as that for EFTA as a whole and that 'the creation of EFTA had promoted trade between distant member countries to a greater extent than trade between neighbouring countries',[47] EFTA nevertheless, helped to ensure that the Nordic market took a considerably larger share than the Community of the most rapidly expanding groups of manufacturing exports. It was only in paper and metals that the Community's markets dominated as a recipient of Swedish exports. The EFTA market as a whole represented 41 percent of such exports in 1966 (subjected to duties affected by EEC/EFTA trade liberalisation), whilst the Community accounted for 25 percent and the Nordic market alone for a further 26 percent. For Sweden, the Nordic market was the most important for chemicals, motor-cars and other finished manufactures. Exports of machinery were more evenly distributed between the Nordic area, the EEC and the rest of the world.

The achievements of EFTA were important for the growth of machinery exports, which were perceived to be a growth sector for Sweden. EFTA was an important stimulus and helped ensure total exports of manufactures rose faster to the Nordic area and EFTA than to the Community. By the late 1960s, EFTA (and especially other Nordic markets) represented around 13 percent of total Swedish exports in machinery. EEC discrimination did not prove to be such a large threat as first appeared. In practice, machinery suppliers were able to absorb the Community's discriminatory tariffs so that machinery exports to the EEC were around 8 percent of total exports in the late 1960s.[48] In part, Swedish industry was already internationalised and more easily able to overcome tariff barriers. Yet, this did cut into the profit margins of Swedish industry and made it more vulnerable. In particular, there was growing concern throughout the 1960s regarding the sluggish performance of the paper and pulp industries. EFTA also helped to maintain Swedish trade with the UK. Whilst total exports increased by only 64 percent between 1959-66, exports of Swedish manufactures to the UK (excluding ships) increased by 167 percent, which was roughly equivalent to the increase in the EEC market. Thus as Lundgren argued 'the commodity-country structure of Swedish exports of manufactures is such that Swedish industry has on the whole done very well in EFTA'.[49]

None the less, the Ministry of Commerce expressed concern in the late 1960s that the economic benefits of EFTA would only be short-term. Doubts arose surrounding the difficulty of gaining access to new, rather than existing markets and that this would be the future challenge for Swedish trade policy. The SAF, in particular, highlighted that the country's manufacturing exports to the

Nordic market would soon reach saturation point and that then the natural expansion into continental markets would be seriously hindered by the EEC's external tariff. There was also a sharp upswing in Swedish direct investment in the Community, especially in the Netherlands (1966 onwards), which, in part, indicated the growing pessimism of Swedish industry towards the chances of reaching a general EEC-EFTA agreement.

The Erlander government's other major objective of using EFTA as a tool to deliver parity in future discussions with the Community was not fully realised. EFTA's attempts to accelerate tariff liberalisation to encourage future discussions with the EEC only served to force the Community to speed up its own liberalisation programme in May 1960 - ironically causing the EFTA states to again respond by revising its own timetable for tariff cuts in February 1961.

Sweden did however, enjoy a rather high profile position within EFTA during the 1960s and, albeit to a limited extent, acted as a mediator between the large and industrialised UK and the smaller and more agriculturally based Norway and Denmark. Sweden benefited from 'two cross cutting trends - her Scandinavian connection and her agreement with Britain on industrial free trade questions'.[50] Consequently, the problems associated with neutrality only really became important during the later set of EEC applications in 1961 and not really within EFTA. Indeed, the country's useful role as mediator was illustrated during the 1964 'surcharge crisis', when Britain imposed a 15 percent surcharge on most EFTA industrialised imports as a means of dealing with the problems confronting the UK regarding sterling. All the Scandinavian countries argued that this was in fact a breach of the Stockholm Convention and demanded that the UK recognise that this was the case. Gunnar Lange, the (then) Minister of Commerce, for example, replied to a question in the Riksdag, by stating that the government 'considered such an admission was of importance from the point of disciplinary action under the Convention. The reoccurrence of such a step will be more difficult'.[51]

Ironically, although Swedish trade was more affected by the surcharge that that of either Denmark or Norway (given that that 45 percent of Swedish exports to the UK were of the industrial type compared to an EFTA average figure of 36 percent), the Erlander government was moderate in its criticism of the UK. In part this was due to the fact that Sweden, unlike its Scandinavian neighbours, was a member of the 'Group of Ten' within the International Monetary Fund that had agreed to support sterling during the November 1964 British financial crisis. Erlander felt compelled to be more sympathetic towards the UK's imposition of a surcharge. Hence, the Social Democratic government's approach towards EFTA was two-fold in the 1960s. On the one hand, it recognised the central importance of the UK to Swedish trade and EFTA. As Gunnar Lange succinctly noted in 1965 at a Nordic Council meeting,

> 'What happens in the United Kingdom is of decisive importance to us but what happens with us is not so important to our British trading partner. ... It bears witness to the weakness intrinsic in the method of foundation of the free trade association and its whole structure. ... .we should see that we do not make future cooperation too difficult for the member which provides us with 30 percent to 40 percent of our market and only takes 15 percent of our trade'.[52]

On the other hand, the government acknowledged the growing importance of intra-Nordic trade within EFTA. Erlander endeavoured to warn against extreme Nordic options and stressed the significance of the Scandinavian countries within EFTA. Mr. Lange's speech highlights four elements of governmental attitudes towards the Association which were well developed by 1965 and continued to dominate Swedish thinking on EFTA until the UK left the Association (31 December 1972).

First, the prime aim of Swedish policy within EFTA was to maximise national interests. This could be done best by using the Association to align Swedish interests with those of other members. On this point, Erlander enjoyed the dual support of domestic industrial and trade union groups but also the support of the other EFTA governments. The Swedish government's focus was on moderation and consistency. Mr. Lange in the same speech admitted that it was essential to make reasonable requests rather than use brinkmanship. Second, it was the government's task (in order to achieve the first aim) to dilute the more extreme demands of the other EFTA governments and to obtain the greatest possible unity over specific proposals as possible.

Third, Swedish ministers, whilst recognising its limitations, stressed the importance of EFTA as a vehicle for six small states to influence one large one, (the UK) and to encourage the Nordic brethren to introduce moderate proposals. In practice, this produced some positive results - for example, the establishment of an EFTA Economic Committee to discuss economic cooperation.[53] Finally, the government constantly evaluated the alternatives to EFTA. However, Mr. Lange at the 1965 Nordic Council Meeting also recognised that during the 1960s, there was little likelihood of either a single market for the entirety of western Europe or Swedish EEC membership in any form, 'the EFTA we have now - an EFTA which is by no means in an ideal way today - is at any rate better than any alternative that can be available in the immediate future'.[54] In reality, future Nordic cooperation, such as NORDEK, 'was in addition, not an alternative to EFTA'.[55]

However, for the Swedes, perhaps the greatest achievement in EFTA coordination was the London Declaration (June 1961). This Declaration represented an agreed position by the seven EFTA countries over the question of future negotiations with the Community. Whilst it was accepted that individual EFTA countries would desire different forms of arrangements with the EEC, it was agreed that the Association should be maintained until all the members had satisfied their 'various legitimate interests'.[56] In practice, it meant that the EFTA countries would consider each other's position when making overtures and conducting negotiations with the emerging EEC. Indeed, Swedish perspectives on European integration were to be discussed in depth approximately four times before the eventual application for membership was submitted in July 1991.[57] Two of these major debates were to take place during the 1960s and it is to these discussions that this chapter will now turn.

Laying the Foundations: Swedish Debates on European Integration in the 1960s

a) 1961-1963: Domestic Debate in Favour of Association

The major domestic debates on Swedish relations with the emerging EEC during the 1960s occurred in 1961-63 and 1967. Ironically they took place after the Community had been established. The decision by the Erlander government to stay outside had long since been taken and therefore the debates revolved around if Sweden should join the Community in existence rather than whether she should participate in shaping its evolution.

The first debate arose as a direct result of the British application for full membership (July 1961) and ended just as abruptly when the British application was rejected by France's President Charles De Gaulle in 1963. In part, the debate reflected the quandary then surrounding the basic tenet of Swedish trade policy which had traditionally been to follow the line pursued by the British government. After all, as long as Sweden and the UK shared the same intergovernmental functional approach to European integration, there were great commonalties between the two countries' trade policies. During the late 1950s for example, there had been very little domestic discussion on the governmental position vis-à-vis the emerging EEC. It was almost taken for granted in all quarters that Sweden would not contemplate joining the Community without Britain and as long as the UK remained sceptical the EEC was not a major domestic issue. However, once the Macmillan government shifted its policy on the full membership then this created the need for a new Swedish response to it.

Yet, the 1961-63 debate was comprehensive and healthy. Within the lengthy discussions, a number of differing schools of thought on Sweden's relationship with the Community developed and the whole spectrum of options were debated - 'from membership, through association agreement - which was the line adopted by the Social Democratic government under Tage Erlander - to total rejection of any relationship whatsoever with the new "European" power'.[58] Bergquist in his classic study of the 1960s argued that the 18 month long debate on the EEC membership issue between 1961-63 was in practice, 'the liveliest, and in many respects the most thorough, on Swedish foreign policy since the discussion in the late 1940s about the plans for a Nordic Defence Community'.[59] The problem of Sweden's relations with the Community was politicised to the extent that it became the dominant theme of political discussion between the 31 July 1961, (the day that the British Prime Minister Macmillan issued his statement to the House of Commons) and General De Gaulle's press conference (14 January 1963). Indeed, it was also a major issue in one Swedish election - namely the 1962 local elections.

In reality, the problems for the Erlander government in 1961 were threefold. First, and as always, Sweden remained concerned about securing her access to foreign markets, especially as some 25 percent of the country's GNP derived from foreign trade and by 1961 some 67 percent of exports went to the Six. A Community which would also incorporate the UK (and its additional trade implications for Sweden) created 'a compelling argument for forming some kind of relationship with the EEC'.[60] In effect, the 'Swedish Diamond's' third point (economic interdependence) was compounded by the fact that if Britain joined the Community in the future, most of the country's key export markets would be within this emerging trading bloc. Second, there was the political problem of Swedish neutrality and more specifically, whether EEC membership could be reconciled with a credible neutrality policy. In short, the Diamond's fourth point became more prominent within governmental perspectives. Finally, there were the ideological problems associated with full membership. The long years of Social Democratic government, the success of its economic policies and its concerns about the continuation of the welfare state all reinforced the first and second points of the Diamond. They tended to suggest that there was a domestic 'predisposition on the part of many to look at continental Europe with some reluctance'.[61]

The debate initiated within a few days of the British and Danish announcements of their intentions of requesting EEC membership (31 July) when Foreign Minister, Östen Undén expressed his scepticism over the possibility of combining full membership with Sweden's neutrality policy in a press interview (5 August 1961). He argued that the EEC's development was proceeding in a direction intended to eventually produce a political federation. Sweden, he argued, was only interested in purely economic arrangements because such political objectives were contrary to its interests. Consequently, if EEC membership had to be excluded either because of the position taken by the Six or due to the fact that Sweden could not accept it then other options would need to be found. As the Minister suggested 'an economic association agreement would constitute a completely different question'.[62]

As Bergquist highlights even if the government had not formally taken a position at this time, Undén's interview was significant in that it set the parameters for the ensuing debate.[63] The interview was quickly followed (17 August 1961) by a meeting of the Riksdag's Standing Committee on Foreign Affairs which discussed the question of negotiations with the Community in general terms. On the same day, the Prime Minister issued a statement in which he stressed the willingness of the Social Democratic government 'to negotiate on closer economic cooperation in Western Europe', although he was also careful to stipulate that 'the outcome of the negotiations must not be allowed to change the conditions that made it possible for Sweden to pursue its policy of neutrality. The economic coordination with the EEC that we sought thus presupposes special provisions to make this coordination compatible with our policy of neutrality and to satisfy other vital Swedish interests'.[64] Shortly afterwards, the initial policy lines of the various parties began to form. On 19 August, for instance, Gunnar Hedlund, the leader of the Centre Party publicly announced his support for association with the Community and that he was against Swedish full membership.[65]

Hence, the Swedish domestic debate revolved around three options. The first two were derived from the articles of the existing Treaty of Rome, which allowed for twin possibilities for European countries wishing to participate with the existing EEC members in working for economic integration - accession (article 237) or association (article 238).[66] The third option was for the Swedish government to do nothing at all - which was widely regarded by most domestic parties as unwise and unacceptable given that British overtures to the Community were likely to continue in the future. The solution chosen by the government in 1961 was to seek association.[67] The main reason for this lay in the country's wish to maintain her neutral status.

The classic official statement on the government's position regarding full membership was outlined in an address given by the (then) Prime Minister, Tage Erlander to the annual congress of the Metal Workers' Union (22 August 1961).[68] This speech and the rationales contained within it, formed the backbone of governmental policy towards the Community until 1991 - long after the demise of Erlander himself. In his 'Metal' speech, the Prime Minster stipulated why

Swedish full membership of the Community was not a realistic option. His speech incorporated all four aspects of the 'Swedish Diamond' to varying degrees. During its early parts, the Prime Minister stressed the country's economic interdependence with Europe and in effect, the Diamond's third point. Erlander recognised that Sweden is 'a low-tariff country and which has pursued a policy favourable to free trade for a long time' and that EFTA had been successful in realising the goal of tariff reduction (as internal tariffs had been reduced by 30 percent by 1961).[69] Indeed, the government was, for the most part, happy with the country's trading relationship with the EEC mainly because the main exports to the Community were raw materials (iron ore and pulp) which already entered the EEC duty-free.[70] Yet, Erlander also specifically acknowledged that a new situation had arisen for the country now that the UK and Denmark have applied to join the Community.[71]

Sweden's economic interdependence with the Community would rise (and the Diamond's third point was increasingly important) - although the Prime Minister also clarified that his government would not follow suit as the reasons for the British and Danish applications 'do not have the same force in the case for Sweden'.[72] In particular, Erlander argued that Sweden's healthy economic situation did not require or 'provide a reason for re-planning our trade policy'.[73] Employment was 'at an extraordinary high level' and unemployment was on the decrease. Industrial production rose during 1960 by 7 percent; total investment to industry increased by 11 percent in 1960, whilst foreign trade expanded with imports up 10 percent and exports rising by 16 percent respectively.[74]

However, the political aim of strengthening the Atlantic alliance was perceived, according to Erlander, to be no inducement tó Swedish participation in supranational European integration. To Erlander, the most convincing arguments against full membership centred around three main areas - the two traditional concerns over compatibility with Swedish neutrality and sovereignty and the third broadly related to maintaining Sweden's identity and distinct features - most of which were an integral part of the 'Swedish Diamond'. In sum, Erlander was referring to the fourth, first and second points of the Diamond which (at the time) influenced attitudes against full membership. In his 'Metal' speech, Erlander categorically stated that the government had come to 'the conclusion that membership of the European Economic Community set up in accordance with the Treaty of Rome, in its present form, would not be compatible with the Swedish policy of neutrality'.[75] Erlander argued that neutrality was 'the key issue' and thus, the Diamond's fourth point was the most influential. His most significant objections relating to this point focused on several grounds:

- that the EEC Treaty provided for a common commercial policy and presupposed that all commercial agreements with third countries, after the transitional period, would be negotiated and concluded by the Community. This Erlander argued, would mean 'that in this sphere it would be no longer possible for Sweden to pursue an independent trade policy' and that 'supranational institutions would be authorised to direct Swedish trade policy in a way that was a complete departure from our commercial policy hitherto'.[76]

- that Community rules applied in wartime as in peacetime. Under this interpretation, Sweden would not be entitled in wartime to renounce EEC obligations with a view to applying measures in line with its neutral status.

- that the Community would in the future foster the political unification of Europe and strengthen the Atlantic Alliance, which Sweden must remain detached from in accordance with her neutrality policy.

- that the Six were 'taking it for granted that the Treaty of Rome is a step on the way to a real federation'. If Sweden was to join, the government would require major changes effecting 'the very lifeblood of their (the Six) cooperation'.[77]

For these reasons, the Prime Minister believed that neutrality could not be reconciled with full membership, especially as any future application may actually be interpreted 'as a political move signifying that we are prepared to depart from our policy of neutrality and to seek membership of the Atlantic Pact'.[78]

In addition, the government also disliked the obligations of full membership because of the implications it would have for Swedish sovereignty. The Prime Minister stipulated on the record that some of the Treaty of Rome's provisions implied that full members 'must yield their sovereignty to supranational institutions governed by majority vote'.[79] Erlander especially deemed this to be unacceptable. Apart from the neutrality concerns (the Diamond's fourth point), the Prime Minister stressed the continuation of complete control over economic policy and thereby also implied the importance of the second aspect of the Diamond - that of maintaining the country's organisational model. In general, the governing Social Democratic Party and the labour movement were unenthusiastic about any policy initiatives that would remove governmental action, such as the regulation of capital movements, whilst the free mobility of labour was also seen as controversial.[80] The SAP and trade union leaderships highlighted that the country's governments had implemented economic policies since the 1930s which were, to some extent, different from those followed on the continent. As the Prime Minister indicated the government's right to follow an active labour market policy was 'right at the centre of our attention'.[81] To a degree, Erlander's arguments against EEC membership 'reflected the solid confidence at the time in the success of the Swedish model, Swedish industry and the emerging welfare state'.[82] Most importantly, there was a widespread belief within public opinion that there were differences between the Swedish and continental welfare states, that the Swedish example was superior and that full membership would compromise its future development.[83]

The speech provoked a reaction from the other mainstream parties and helped to crystallize party policy on the EEC question in time for the Riksdag's 'market debate' in October. On 25 August, the Liberal Party argued that Erlander's actions were premature in writing off full EEC membership. The government it argued should first, initiate a domestic consultation process with various economic and labour organisations before taking further action and second, make an attempt to discover whether it would be possible to become a full member with certain 'escape' clauses to satisfy Sweden's neutrality policy. If this was not viable then the government should seek an association agreement. On 28 August, the leader of the Conservatives, Gunnar Hecksher took the same position as the Liberals. Three days later (31 August 1961) the Centre Party (whose agricultural wing wished to protect farm subsidies) issued a statement agreeing with the governmental position. The Party recommended association whilst contact with the other EFTA neutrals should also be consolidated. Last of all, the central committee of the Communist Party declared (10 September 1961) that it was totally against either full EEC membership or association in any form.

Erlander accommodated some of the demands of the non-socialist parties for a twin approach to the EEC - even if the outcome was still the same in preferring association with the Community. Erlander held a meeting at Harpsund (4 October) with representatives of the key industrial and agricultural organisations. In general, the industrial and forestry representatives highlighted the dangers of isolation from the Community's markets and for the most part advocated membership, whilst the agricultural delegation stressed the dangers of the CAP for Swedish farmers and the need for a self-sufficient agricultural sector to support neutrality policy. In addition, the government sought closer contact with Austria and Switzerland as fellow EFTA neutrals resulting in a ministerial meeting in Vienna (19 October). A consensus between the governments was found and the ensuing press release highlighted that all three saw the problems relating to their future relationship with the EEC 'in the same light'. Although the press release stressed the problems raised by the EEC for neutral countries, the three governments did agree that 'neutrality does not constitute an obstacle to their participation, through association in an appropriate form, in the economic integration of Europe'.[84]

Yet to all intents and purposes, EEC membership was not an option for Sweden in 1961 and had only been considered for essentially reactive reasons. Although there was broad cross party support for a closer relationship with the Community, there were substantial differences between the parties on the form of the strengthened relationship. There were two main areas of contention for the domestic political parties. First, whilst most of the mainstream political parties were keen not to see Sweden subject to raised tariff barriers between itself and an expanded EEC (including most of her major trading partners), reservations were expressed about the position of agriculture. Second, the Community's institutional characteristics once again led to internal and vocal concern over its impact on Sweden's traditional foreign policy.

The Social Democratic government with the support of the Centre Party declared its intention to submit an application for association to the Community in the Riksdag's 'market debate' on the EEC (25 October 1961). Despite a lengthy debate, the positions of the parties remained unchanged. The Conservatives and the Liberals, backed by the industrial and business lobbies canvassed for full membership, albeit with specific preconditions. In the debate, both parties stressed the importance of access to protect the country's export interests, whilst at the same time highlighting the need to secure specific escape clauses in order to satisfy Swedish neutrality. In reality, these variations were little more than differences of emphasis, based on varying desires to achieve partnership in European economic integration and most of all, on tactical considerations.

The Communists remained opposed to an arrangement in any form.[85] The Social Democrats and Communists, for example, maintained that the Community was based on conservative political ideas and therefore full membership (and for the Communists even associate status) should be resisted. This seemed especially persuasive given that there were conservative governments in Britain, Germany, Italy and France and social legislation was generally thought to be backward compared to Swedish standards. The Social Democrats were also officially concerned about the implications for neutrality especially as regards participation in the Community's CCP and that full membership explicitly required adherence to future political integration as outlined in the EEC's July 1961 Bonn Declaration. Hence, the governing Social Democrats stressed the twin dimensions of the character of the Treaty of Rome and its incompatibility with the main traits of neutrality.[86] The Centre Party was equally sceptical and the party's agrarian interests and nationalism also reinforced its opposition.

Ultimately, the government's decision to apply for associate membership was approved by a large parliamentary majority. In effect, a consensus had been formed around the notion that Sweden should seek some form of adherence to the Treaty of Rome, but without jeopardising its policy of neutrality. The application for associate membership delivered together with the those of the Austrians and Swiss (15 December 1961) reflected this delicate consensus. Erlander, with some conviction was able to claim in a statement made on the day of the application:

> 'Our country's interest in participating in the economic cooperation now developing in Europe, and our will to do so, has the support of practically unanimous Swedish public opinion. ... At the same time Sweden has steadfastly resolved to abide by her neutrality. ... Thus what we want to achieve for Sweden is an economic association with the European Economic Community which is compatible with our neutrality'.[87]

Yet, as Miljan notes, the emerging consensus 'did not indicate unity: the differences in orientation of the pro-membership and anti-membership partisan blocs remained'.[88] Indeed, the type of association envisaged by Erlander at this time remained far from clear especially as at this time only one prior association agreement (excluding former member state dependencies) existed (with Greece).

The EEC issue allowed for a slight re-alignment of the Swedish political spectrum. The Centre Party once again shared sympathies with the governing Social Democrats (as it had done so between 1951-57, but had moved in favour of the opposition parties since then). Equally, the rapprochement between the Centre Party and the Liberals was slowed. Indeed, the Liberals and Conservatives enjoyed a convergence of views throughout 1961-62 on the membership issue.The Liberals and Conservatives were accused of a willingness to dilute Swedish neutrality in the 1962 local election campaigns.

As regards the key sectoral interest groups in Sweden, the main organisations split on similar lines with the social democratic sympathetic trade union movement favouring associate status. In contrast, the Federation of Swedish Industries (*Sveriges Industrifordund*) forcibly entered the debate (at the end of 1961) and called for full membership. It argued that there would be few differing practical effects for industry and/or the Swedish economy between membership and association, save for the country's absence from decision-making bodies.[89] The Erlander government did however, move some way in early 1962 to accommodate the economic concerns of the industrial and commercial interest groups and tried to convince them of the benefits of EEC association.Yet, in most cases, full membership was deemed to be not worth the price of losing the country's neutral status.

However, the Swedish decision (alongside those of other EFTAns) to seek association was greeted with some reluctance on the part of the Community institutions and received some hostile reactions from within the EEC itself. In general, the Community was keen to ensure that any kind of association would not result in the same rights as full membership. Paul Henri Spaak, the Belgian Prime Minister, for instance, in his speech during the EEC's Consultative Assembly on the neutrals' problems in May 1962 highlighted some of the problems for the Community. After recalling the efforts made by the Six to create the EEC and recognising that the Community had developed its own traditions over its five-year existence, he suggested,

> 'suddenly nine or ten countries come to us simultaneously and say: now you must rethink it all, for we want to join or be associated; each of us wants to join or be associated and bring you his particular problems. You must realize that you put us (the Community) in a very difficult position'.[90]

The Swedish position in this debate was conciliatory and reflected that by early 1962, the government had become slightly more positive towards the prospect of deeper European integration. Gunnar Lange was keen to illustrate the government's flexibility in its interpretation of associate status:

> 'As a neutral country, we would wish to keep a certain liberty of action and to reserve the competence to negotiate and sign agreements with third countries in our own name. On the other hand, we are prepared, within the institutional arrangements for consultation, to coordinate our tariff and trade policy closely with that of the Community. Experience leads us to expect that there should in practice be no significant divergence between Sweden's policy and that of the Community. ... But we are nevertheless willing to discuss how the functioning of the integrated market and the interest of the Community could be safeguarded if divergence were in fact to occur on some point'.[91]

Again on 28 July 1962, when Gunnar Lange addressed the Council of Ministers, he was careful to accommodate the EEC's tough line on the prospects for association, emphasising Sweden's acceptance of the provisions of the Treaty of Rome and its economic implications, such as the immediate and full tariff cuts. Lange also claimed that 'we share the view of the Community that integration... entails a number of economic and social measures designed to ensure a good result. ... We are ready to negotiate with the Community in an instructive and positive spirit'. However, the Minister was also vocal in his demands for a right to suspend or even withdraw from the association in event of war in order to maintain Swedish neutrality policy. Lange argued that his government was 'meticulous in not letting economic interests as such influence our position. We take our policy of neutrality much too seriously'.[92] In the speech, the Minister drew attention to three reservations on neutrality: the independence of Swedish trade policies with third countries, the safeguarding of certain supplies vital to wartime and the ability of Sweden to take or abstain from measures essential to the maintenance of neutrality.

There were sighs of relief from both the Swedes and the Community when all these efforts came to nothing and the membership issue virtually disappeared from the Swedish political agenda once the British application for full membership was vetoed by the French in January 1963. Nevertheless, the 1961-63 EEC episode was politically significant. The government had come to a detailed, well-articulated view on full membership which was to be the mainstay of Swedish policy towards the EEC for the next two decades. With the issue now resolved, Swedish EEC policy between 1963-67 was 'more or less dormant'.[93] Governmental attention focused on the development of EFTA and plans for a EEC-EFTA rapprochement. In addition, three other factors meant that the EEC issue was no longer a major priority for the Swedish government - the onset of the GATT's Kennedy rounds, De Gaulle intransigence inside the Community and finally that in October 1964, the UK elected a new Labour government under Harold Wilson that was more cautious on the idea of full membership for Britain. Overall, these events reinforced Erlander's view that Sweden should stay outside the EEC.

b) 1967: A Temporary Interjection

The second Swedish debate on full membership arose out of another British (and subsequent Danish) membership application and was as a result of the reversal in the Wilson government's perspectives on full membership. The 1967 debate this time proved much shorter. The respective governmental and party positions on the EEC were already developed and, in any case, the British and Danish applications met the same ill-fated ends. In fact, the Swedish debate lasted only a few months - from the time of the submission of the British application in summer 1967 to De Gaulle's second veto in November 1967.

Interestingly, this time the Swedish governmental attitude was more positive than in 1961 and the government chose not to declare what status it desired with the Community and referred to a letter to the Commission in Brussels to Swedish interest in 'participating in a widening of the EEC'. In reality, the government had changed its mind about the form of participation and left that open to the envisaged negotiations. In part, this more flexible and open Swedish attitude was a reflection of the fact that the Community itself seemed to be moving away from its more ambitious political aims and supranationalism and more towards evolving into an intergovernmental framework. It was not so much that the Swedish position had dramatically altered, but rather than the EEC was moving to be more in line with what was acceptable to the Swedes. This view was articulated in Sweden by the business community and the political Right and was based, for example, on the constant rebuffs by President Charles De Gaulle towards extending Qualified Majority Voting (QMV) in the EEC.[94] From the Swedish perspective, the January 1966 Luxembourg Compromise in which the other EEC members had agreed with France that major decisions would require unanimous consent in the Council of Ministers, 'reduced the significance of the European Community as a political organisation'.[95]

Moreover, in Swedish eyes, the Community's long-term goals 'seemed extremely diffuse' with more division than unity between the Six over the precise content of the EEC's common political objectives.[96] This uncertainty over what the EEC actually stood for allowed the Erlander government to contemplate an 'open' application for full membership in 1967. It seemed that by this time the government no longer regarded it as impossible to negotiate membership status with a few exceptions to safeguard its neutrality - namely the three reservations on the Community's treaty-making power, self-sufficiency for certain strategic products and the right of withdrawal.

There had also been some interesting developments in domestic attitudes since 1962. The government, of course, was careful to reaffirm its position and its general reservations surrounding EEC membership. It stated in its March 1966 declaration that 'the government would like to repeat its wish to see an all-European economic market realised. Within the limits set by Swedish foreign policy we want to do all we can to contribute to this aim'.[97] Of course, both the Liberals and the Conservatives argued that the governing Social Democrats had changed their minds on the EEC issue and accepted their perspectives but this was strenuously denied by the SAP. Ironically by 1966, the Liberals and the Conservatives seemed to be moving away from full membership as a result of growing pessimism over the chances of agreement on accession between the EEC and the UK.

Yet, Swedish farmers also seemed to be taking a more favourable attitude towards the EEC based mainly on the fact that proposed Swedish agricultural reforms in the late 1960s would result in lower subsidies to farmers than that provided by the EEC's CAP membership. In reality, Swedish farmers would receive more favourable treatment under the CAP than the government's reformed regime. Yet, the nature of agricultural support would also require changes, so making the effect on agriculture far from clear - and never resulted in change of policy by the Centre Party. Not surprisingly, the trade union movement in line with its close ties with the governing Social Democrats supported closer economic links with the EEC and thus concurred with the open negotiating stance of the government. It was however also keen to show its reluctance to sanction any major concessions of Swedish sovereignty. The position of private industry was equally as predictable with the Confederation of Swedish Employers, the General Export Association of Sweden and the Federation of Swedish Industries all urging that the country must join the EEC in order to secure market access - otherwise the country's standard of living would eventually suffer.[98] Party and/or even elite consensus on future strategy remained as confused as ever; other than general agreement that neutrality must remain intact.

Consequently, the Erlander government decided to seek 'open' negotiations with the EEC 'with a view to enabling Sweden to participate in the extension of the European Economic Community in a form that is compatible with a continued pursuit of the Swedish policy of neutrality'.[99] It sent an application for negotiations on 26 July 1967. It accompanied the application with an oral declaration in which the government once again declared that its goal was to attain 'extensive, close and durable economic relations with the EEC' and noted that 'as far back as in 1961-62 the Swedish government considered membership an advantageous form in certain respects'.[100] In short, the form of Sweden's application was left explicitly open and could include a new special kind of EEC membership. It thus went significantly further than that of any other neutral country.

These overtures were treated with scepticism by the Community. EEC officials may have intimated that the possibility might exist for negotiating a preferential tariff agreement or an unusual and ambiguous form of association with Sweden, but the EEC was genuinely 'disinclined to grant special concessions to the neutrals on the grounds that neutrality should not serve as an excuse for a nation's avoiding the costs of membership while seeking its economic advantages'.[101] After all, neutral Sweden was not, in the EEC's eyes, being forced into full membership; the country was sufficiently free of international constraints to be able to exercise a free choice on whether to join the Community or not. For the majority of the Community's existing members, the real choice for non-member states was either full membership or an association agreement.

The gestures were, in any case, to prove futile. De Gaulle again vetoed the respective British application in November 1967. Indeed, the application was never properly dealt with by the Community, especially once talks between the Six and the UK stalled in autumn 1967. The Commission was asked to evaluate the full membership applications made by the UK, Ireland, Denmark and Norway. Yet, the Swedish application, which officially remained on the Council of Minister's agenda was not examined, except in passing in the Commission's report to the Council of Ministers in autumn 1967. In its report to the Council of Ministers, the references to Sweden intimated that full membership was only a realistic option, if the ensuing negotiations revealed her government's ability to accept the Community's 'finalité politique'. Thus, as Stålvant argued, the burden of initiative had already shifted to the Swedish Cabinet. The prospect of any eventual agreement allowing for a special status for Sweden was dependent on the willingness of at least one of the founder six members advocating acceptance of Swedish reservations on membership.[102] Indeed, De Gaulle offered some small glimmers of hope to the Erlander government. At the 27 November 1967 press conference (which brought the entire episode to an abrupt end), De Gaulle indicated that alternatives to full membership did not exclude the comprehensive type of solution proposed by Sweden.[103]

Conclusion

The debates in 1961-63 and 1967 were crucial. They acted as a catalyst for the formulation of party opinion on the EEC issue inside Sweden and facilitated an extensive EEC policy on the part of successive Swedish governments. Yet, for many, the challenge of an emerging EEC remained as problematic as ever for Sweden. In spite of two applications - one associate, the other 'open' - Swedish trade policy had still to secure either a comprehensive formal free trade arrangement with the Community or some kind of membership of the EEC that was compatible with the constraints of neutrality. By the late 1960s, the only major trade liberalisation in Europe involving Sweden, was through proposed GATT, EFTA or NORDEK structures.

In short, the governments of Tage Erlander, despite formalising the government's position through reference to the 1961 'Metal' speech were still trying to balance the two main points of the 'Swedish Diamond' - on the one hand, growing economic interdependence with the Community and on the other, the country's neutral status. The problem for Sweden as regards the Community remained the same in 1961-63 and 1967. How could Sweden gain the benefits of full membership without incurring the obligations of that membership and in particular, its negative implications for neutrality policy? Throughout the 1960s, the Diamond's two main points (third and fourth) seemed irreconcilable. It was only in the early 1970s that the Palme government was able to, at least partially, square this 'Diamond'. It is to this era in the Swedish-EEC history that the next chapter will now turn.

Notes

[1] Sweden's Gross Domestic Product (GDP) in 1970 was twice that of Denmark and roughly three times the size of Norway and Finland.

[2] Figures taken from Miljan, T. (1977) *The Reluctant Europeans,* Hurst & Co, London, p. 64.

[3] Ibid., Miljan (1977) p. 65.

[4] It has been argued by authors such as Wijkman, that throughout the post-war period two countries - Germany and the UK - acted as the core markets or poles for the entirety of international trade in Europe. However, to a large degree, the UK (as the EFTA core) declined as one of the main poles and was effectively replaced by the expanding German market (as part of a dynamic EEC core) after 1960.

[5] This point was confirmed by Tage Erlander himself during the critical period of 1958-60 and directly affected thinking on the EEC/WFTA/EFTA. In a speech made by the Prime Minister to the Riksdag's Second Chamber (24 November 1959), the interrelationship between neutrality and independence of action was addressed by Erlander: 'If, without binding ourselves by undertakings made under an alliance, we nevertheless fervently and constantly take the part of one side in the political groups existing in our divided world, we should lose every chance we have of working for peaceful coexistence and the reconciliation of the peoples of the world. We should thus forfeit the chance to undertake an important and positive task which is otherwise a natural one for a country like ours' - Ministry of Foreign Affairs, (1960) *Documents on Swedish Foreign Policy 1959,* UD, Stockholm, pp. 46-7.

[6] Ibid., Miljan (1977) p. 82.

[7] Little distinction was made at either the Swedish elite or public level between supranationalism and federalism as concepts. Any continental attempts at European integration were presumed by the Swedes to have overt political objectives. Any resulting bodies were regarded as political as well as economic organisations. Therefore, the arguments applied against supranationalism and federalism were similar and intertwined in the Swedish domestic debate.

[8] Ibid., Miljan (1977) p. 85.

[9] Twenty meetings of Uniscan took place during the 1950s - see Barclay, G. S. J. (1965) Background to EFTA: an Episode in Anglo-Scandinavian Relations, *Australian Journal of Politics and History,* XI, 2, August, pp. 185-97.

[10] A detailed discussion of Swedish perspectives on Nordic cooperation can be found in Chapter Six.

[11] See for example, Wendt, F. (1979) *Cooperation in the Nordic Countries,* The Nordic Council, Stockholm.

[12] The Nordic Council had been established with Swedish governmental and parliamentary support in 1952 - see Chapter Six.

[13] Anderson, S. V. (1967) *The Nordic Council,* Praeger, New York, p. 131

[14] Useful summaries of perceptions of the 'Nordic Balance' in the 1960s are Brundtland, A. O. (1966) The Nordic Balance: Past and Present, *Cooperation and*

Conflict, II, 1, pp. 31-63 or Moberg, E. (1968) The 'Nordic Balance' Concept: A Critical Commentary, *Cooperation and Conflict*, III, 1, pp. 2-4.

[15] For a more detailed discussion of NORDEK - see Chapter Six.

[16] NORDEK was to comprise of Denmark, Finland, Norway and Sweden. Iceland was excluded.

[17] Haekkerup, P. (1970) The Role of the Nordic Countries in European Economic Cooperation, *Annaire Europeéne*, 16, p. 81.

[18] Op. cit., Miljan (1977) p. 107.

[19] The debate had already been delayed for nearly two months due to the government's taxation proposals being discussed in March 1970 - illustrating the general lack of importance attached by the government to the NORDEK project.

[20] *Nordisk Kontakt*, (1970), 7, p. 420.

[21] The term Wide Free Trade Area (WFTA) was only coined after the later European Free Trade Association (EFTA) was formed in 1960 to distinguish the two. Originally, the later EFTA proposal was referred to as either the Free Trade Area or the European Free Trade Area. However, for simplicity the term WFTA will be used to describe the developments of the Maudling proposals in question.

[22] Op. cit., Miljan (1977) p. 116.

[23] Åström, S. (1988) The Nordic Angle I: Sweden's EC Dilemmas, *World Today*, 11, p. 191.

[24] Taken from a presentation given by Sverker Åström at the Nordic History Association, University College London, London, December 1994.

[25] Taken from a presentation given by Sverker Åström at the Nordic History Association, University College London, London, December 1994.

[26] Op. cit., Wendt (1979) p. 106.

[27] The representatives of the Six met in Rome on 25 March 1957 to sign the treaty establishing the EEC and EURATOM (which was to come into force on 1 January 1958) only a month after the OEEC decision and the Nordic Council's Helsinki discussions.

[28] Ministry of Foreign Affairs, (1957) *Documents on Swedish Foreign Policy 1957*, UD, Stockholm, pp. 23-4.

[29] The issue of EEC membership did attract the attention of certain business quarters. In particular, the anti-EEC forces were swollen by the support of the Swedish farmers' organisations. The farmers were afraid that as the EEC included the Common Agricultural Policy (CAP) and that the Swedish farming sector had been protected from lower-cost competition from continental agriculture, the impact on the sector would be negative. This was a rational fear since Swedish agricultural policy had incorporated a high price system since 1947 to attain income parity between farmers and industrial workers and to promote self sufficiency in food production in the interest of a credible neutrality policy. In contrast, the pro-EEC forces were essentially the economic and commercial lobbies led by the Federation of Swedish Industries and the Federation of Swedish Wholesale Merchants. They argued that as the export sector was critical to national income it was imperative that Sweden associate with the EEC in some way.

The fact that the industrial and commercial lobbies were the only supporters of full membership and that their arguments were strictly economic prevented the EEC issue from prompting an extensive domestic debate on foreign policy.

[30] *Nordisk Kontakt,* (1958) 15, p. 816.

[31] *Nordisk Kontakt,* (1958) 14, pp. 772-3.

[32] Ministry of Foreign Affairs (1959a) *Negotiations For a European Free Trade Area, 1956-58,* UD, Stockholm, p. 41.

[33] Ministry of Foreign Affairs (1959), *Documents on Swedish Foreign Policy 1958,* UD, Stockholm, p. 37.

[34] Ibid., Ministry of Foreign Affairs (1959) p. 37.

[35] Op. cit., Miljan (1977) p. 127.

[36] The 'Other Six' were Austria, Switzerland, Denmark, Norway, Sweden and the UK.

[37] Op. cit., Miljan (1977) p. 143.

[38] Swedish industries could continue to import most raw materials and semi-manufactures either tariff-free or at low tariff rates.

[39] Portugal had by this time joined the 'Outer Six' on the basis of a firm draft convention drawn up by the Swedish government.

[40] Camps, M. (1964) *Britain and the European Community 1955-63,* Oxford University Press, Oxford, p. 213.

[41] Archer, C. (1990) *Organizing Europe,* Edward Arnold, London, pp. 122-3.

[42] *Nordisk Kontakt* (1959) 5, pp. 245-9.

[43] Op. cit., Archer (1990) p. 123.

[44] Op. cit., Archer (1990) p. 126.

[45] Robertson, D. (1970) Effects of EFTA on Member Countries in Corbet, H. & Robertson, D. (eds.) *Europe's Free Trade Area Experiment - EFTA and Economic Integration,* Pergamon Press, Oxford, p. 90.

[46] Lundgren, N. (1968) The Nordic Countries in Study Group, Graduate Institute of International Studies, Geneva, *The European Free Trade Association and the Crisis of European Integration,* Michael Joseph, London, p. 72.

[47] Op. cit., Robertson (1970) p. 96.

[48] Op. cit., Lundgren (1968) p. 73.

[49] Op. cit., Lundgren (1968) p. 113.

[50] Archer, C. (1976) Britain and Scandinavia: Their Relations within EFTA 1960-68 *Cooperation and Conflict,* XI, 1, p. 5.

[51] Ministry of Foreign Affairs (1965) *Documents on Swedish Foreign Policy 1964,* UD, Stockholm, p. 127.

[52] Ibid., Ministry of Foreign Affairs (1965), pp. 137-8.

[53] Op. cit., Archer (1976) p. 9.

[54] Op. cit., Ministry of Foreign Affairs (1965) p. 138.

[55] Op. cit., Archer (1976) p. 10.

[56] Ministry of Foreign Affairs (1962) *Documents in Swedish Foreign Policy 1961,* UD, Stockholm, pp. 108-9.

[57] See for example, Huldt, B. (1994) Sweden and European Community-building 1945-92 in Harden, S. (ed.) *Neutral States and the European Community*, Brassey's, London, pp. 104-43.

[58] Ibid., Huldt (1994) p. 110.

[59] Bergquist, M. (1969) Sweden and the European Economic Community, *Cooperation and Conflict*, IV, 1, p. 1.

[60] Ibid., Bergquist (1969) p. 3.

[61] Ibid., Bergquist (1969) p. 4.

[62] The details of the press interview are reported in and taken from Bergquist, M. (1970) *Sverige och EEC*, Nordstedt & Söner, Stockholm, p. 46.

[63] Ibid., Bergquist (1970) p. 46.

[64] Op. cit., Ministry of Foreign Affairs (1962) p. 111.

[65] Op. cit., Bergquist (1970) p. 47.

[66] Lambert, J. R. (1962) The Neutrals and the Common Market, *The World Today*, 18, 10, October, p. 444.

[67] Nevertheless, the government made no reference to association as a preferred form of adherence to the Treaty of Rome until the 'market debate' in the Riksdag (25 October 1961).

[68] Bergquist points that however that the President of the LO had made a speech similar in tone to the Prime Minister's in which he had specifically supported association with the EEC two days earlier. This is not surprising given the close relationship between the SAF and LO and Erlander's preference for close consultation with key interest groups in the 'spirit of Harpsund' - op. cit., Bergquist (1970) p. 47.

[69] Op. cit., Ministry of Foreign Affairs (1962) p. 113.

[70] Lundgren, N. (1970) Nordic View of Temporary Arrangements in Corbet, H. & Robertson, D. (eds.) *Europe's Free Trade Area Experiment - EFTA and Economic Integration*, Pergamon Press, Oxford, p. 170.

[71] Op. cit., Ministry of Foreign Affairs (1962) p. 114.

[72] Op. cit., Ministry of Foreign Affairs (1962) p. 115.

[73] Op. cit., Ministry of Foreign Affairs (1962) p. 115.

[74] Op. cit., Ministry of Foreign Affairs (1962) p. 116.

[75] Op. cit., Ministry of Foreign Affairs (1962) p. 119.

[76] Op. cit., Ministry of Foreign Affairs (1962) p. 120.

[77] Op. cit., Ministry of Foreign Affairs (1962) p. 121.

[78] Op. cit., Ministry of Foreign Affairs (1962) p. 122.

[79] Op. cit., Ministry of Foreign Affairs (1962) p. 122.

[80] Op. cit., Lundgren (1968) p. 77.

[81] Op. cit., Ministry of Foreign Affairs (1962) p. 123.

[82] Op. cit., Huldt (1994) p. 111.

[83] Op. cit., Lundgren (1968) p. 68.

[84] Op. cit., Ministry of Foreign Affairs (1962) p. 127.

[85] Their impact on the debate was minimal as Communist representation in the Upper House was a mere two representatives and there were five in the Lower House.

Consequently, the Communists were not critical to any parliamentary consensus on EEC policy - Arter, D. (1993) *The Politics of European Integration in the Twentieth Century*, Dartmouth, Aldershot, p. 222.

[86] Op. cit., Bergquist (1969) p. 5.

[87] Op. cit., Ministry of Foreign Affairs (1962) p. 139-40.

[88] Op. cit., Miljan (1977) p. 247.

[89] Op. cit., Lambert (1962) p. 451

[90] Taken from Lambert, op. cit. (1962) p. 447.

[91] Taken from Lambert, op. cit. (1962) p. 450

[92] Ministry of Foreign Affairs (1963) *Documents on Swedish Foreign Policy 1962*, UD, Stockholm, p. 151.

[93] Op. cit., Bergquist (1969) p. 8.

[94] The Conservatives and Liberals in particular argued that the political thrust of the EEC had been dissipated even further since the 1961-63 debate due to General De Gaulle's policies.

[95] Hancock, M. D. (1972) Sweden, Scandinavia and the EEC, *International Affairs*, 48, 4, July, p. 429.

[96] Stålvant, C.-E. (1974) Neutrality and European Integration: A Comparison of Finland's and Sweden's EEC Policies, *Scandinavian Studies*, 46, 4, p. 415.

[97] Taken from Lundgren, op. cit. (1968), p. 119.

[98] Op. cit., Bergquist (1970).

[99] Ministry of Foreign Affairs (1968) *Documents on Swedish Foreign Policy 1967*, UD, Stockholm, p. 152.

[100] Ibid., Ministry of Foreign Affairs (1968) pp. 153.

[101] Op. cit., Stålvant (1974) p. 416.

[102] Op. cit., Stålvant (1974) p. 417.

[103] Op. cit., Stålvant (1974) p. 417.

4 Keeping a Friendly Distance 1970-84

As part of British attempts to become an EEC member in the 1960s, the UK government was careful to assure its fellow EFTA members that it would not join the Community before agreeing satisfactory arrangements able to 'meet the various legitimate interests' of all the EFTA countries, and in effect allow them also to participate in an integrated European market from the same date. This commitment, agreed by the EFTA states in the London Declaration (27-28 June 1961), was quoted by Swedish administrations as the basic governmental position, ensuring that full membership was merely an option rather than a necessity. Nevertheless, the Swedish experiences of 1961-63 and 1967 illustrated that the British pledge would be difficult to keep, especially as the Community 'appeared to be ready to open the door to let the United Kingdom in, but showed every sign of wishing to shut it quickly so as to bar the way to those in the rest of the queue'.[1] Yet, the problem never emerged in the 1960s as the EEC closed the door to Britain as well, thereby allowing the Swedes to remove the membership issue from the political limelight.

None the less, 'when the EEC thaw set in, in December 1969, it was total and complete'.[2] The Community agreed at the 1969 Hague Summit to re-open the question of British accession and EEC enlargement. This decision eventually provoked a Swedish response. The country's 1967 'open' application remained in quiescence with only limited action having been taken by either side and therefore could easily be re-activated.[3] Swedish-EEC relations between 1970-73 entered a new phase of heightened activity, and ultimately led to the signing of a Free Trade Agreement (FTA) on 22 July 1972. The FTA entered into force at the same time as the UK, Denmark and Ireland became full members (1 January 1973) and through it, the Palme government achieved its (then) aim of continued access to EEC markets. The agreement was to become the platform for Swedish-EEC relations for next two decades. It was regarded by both sides as a success story. An assessment of this period, as well as the FTA's details and overall performance, is therefore essential to any comprehensive appreciation of the relationship between Sweden and European integration.

1970-72: Elaborating on the Swedish Position

Dominating Influences

By the early 1970s, four developments led to further reappraisal of governmental policy vis-à-vis the EEC. First, Sweden's economy and in particular, her sensitive engineering, steels and electronics industries had become firmly integrated into the Common Market and by this time the need for a formal economic and trading arrangement had become an overriding priority. Second, the chances of the EEC enlarging to include the UK and Denmark were now real since the election of the more sympathetic Georges Pompidou to the Elysée Palace. Sweden was now confronted with the possibility that two of its major trading partners would soon be full EEC members, leading to a subsequent reduction in exports to her most important markets due to trade diversion.[4] This seemed likely as after the failure of the 1967 applications, the Six had never completely ruled out potential future enlargement of the Community. In a statement publicised in autumn 1969, for instance, the European Commission outlined the preconditions for accession. Third, the chances of the Palme government negotiating EEC membership in a form compatible with neutrality seemed better, if never particularly good. The Commission stated that accession negotiations could start if the Palme government demonstrated its willingness to accept, without restrictions, the 'finalité politiques' outlined in the Preamble of the Treaty of Rome.[5] In addition, Pompidou's insistence at the December 1969 Hague Summit that Britain could not join the Community until agreement was reached with the EFTA 'non-candidates' seemed to offer a glimmer of hope over more varied forms of negotiations with the EEC.

Finally, by early 1970, it was apparent that Palme's European policy of operating on two levels - one Nordic (i.e. NORDEK) and one European (i.e. EFTA cooperation and seeking negotiations with the EEC) was in danger of collapse. The government's 'Nordic' strategy of using the creation of NORDEK as a 'second best solution' and as a catalyst for Community accession was doomed to failure. When the proposed NORDEK treaty was scotched by the Finnish President Kekkonen (6 April 1970),[6] it was inevitable that the Nordic elements would amount to little more than political cooperation. At the same time, the other main element - EFTA membership - was reaching saturation point. Nearly all of the association's trade liberalisation plans were now complete. An accommodation with the EEC looked to be the most attractive future avenue for Swedish trade policy. The issue in early 1970s (as in 1967) was whether this accommodation should take the form of EEC membership (either full or associate, and provided it was compatible with neutrality policy) or whether a free trade agreement would be sufficient.

Reactions of the EEC Member States and the other Applicants

The flexible nature of the Swedish 'open' application caused problems for the Community. For the EEC institutions, the key choice regarding the application was that of membership or non-membership and by resolving this issue, the actual contents of any future negotiations and treaty with Sweden would be, for the most part, determined.[7] The Community made a crucial distinction between those states applying for full membership under article 237 (the candidates) and the other EFTA members (known as the 'non-candidates') namely - Austria, Finland, Iceland, Portugal, Sweden and Switzerland.

In contrast, the Palme government sought to downgrade any problems with the EEC by expressing its willingness to negotiate special terms with the Community on the basis of the 1957 Treaty of Rome. In reality then, the Swedish application 'went significantly further than that of any other neutral country'.[8] Indeed, the Swedish government through EFTA communiqués had already stipulated that it was also prepared to explore the prospect of full membership anyway (provided it met the usual condition of compatibility with neutrality). Hence, the initial problem for both the Palme government and the Community was agreeing similar terms of reference on which to base future negotiations in 1970.

The Community tried to shift the onus of initiative to the Swedish government, with the prospect of any special agreement between the EEC and Sweden reliant upon Stockholm's ability to persuade at least one of the existing six member states to advocate in the Council of Ministers acceptance of any special Swedish conditions. Moreover, the Prime Minister, Olof Palme, used several channels to argue the Swedish case and, for instance, visited the major European capitals in spring 1970 in order to lobby the existing member states. Palme in an address in London (7 April 1970), justified this strategy by stressing,

> 'the fact that the political objectives of the Rome Treaty were interpreted in different ways by the member countries. It was not easy in advance to assess how far Sweden's neutrality was compatible with these aims. This could hardly be clarified without discussions with the EEC countries themselves'.[9]

Throughout 1970 and early 1971, the Palme government made a concerted effort to persuade leading officials in the member states that Sweden should be considered as a front-runner and as a candidate, rather than as 'non-candidate' content with negotiating new free trade arrangements.

The Community's general response was also unsympathetic. Ultimately, the Palme government was unable to convince the Six that it was pondering full membership seriously, especially if it created further complex problems with the rest of the Nordic region. The most that was gained was little more than an acknowledgement of the preconditions arising from the country's neutral status, rather than any larger commitment to championing the Swedish cause in any EEC Council of Ministers' meetings. Even in the Commission's report to the Council of Ministers on the Swedish case, the Commission noted that membership would not be a realistic option unless the ensuing negotiations revealed that Sweden displayed an unreserved measure of acceptance of the Community's 'finalités politiques'.[10]

The rather ambiguous positions of the Six in 1970 illustrated their general scepticism in the feasibility of the Swedish proposal. Germany for instance, whilst recognising that Sweden posed key problems regarding the Community's political objectives discussed at the 1969 Hague Summit, also agitated for the removal of the economic divide between the EEC and EFTA. The Benelux countries and Italy were the most negative towards the Swedish application. These countries were, after all, enthusiastic about the prospect of a supranational Community and foreign policy coordination and were therefore wary that the inclusion of neutral Sweden would undermine such future developments by strengthening internal EEC support for intergovernmental forms of cooperation. In spite of continual Swedish overtures that the Community should consider seriously the enlargement of the EEC to include Sweden (as well as the four other applicants), the Community for its part did not perceive the country to be a realistic prospect for full membership. In other words, 'the balance sheet embraced only a Community of Ten',[11] and not the prospect of eleven. For the Palme government, this meant that the country would be grouped by the Community as a 'non-candidate' (rather than as a candidate) and with states with much lesser ambitions than those of Sweden.

The Palme government could also not rely on the wholesale support of the UK, despite its status as the largest and leading applicant for full membership. The British government tried to distance itself from the EFTA neutrals. To the (then) Labour government, full membership seemed the only option if the UK was to be granted full equal rights to influence the Community's future development from within and to counter French political dominance. The British government was apprehensive of the Swedish initiative. It raised first, the prospect (at least at the beginning of 1970) of partial or new types of comprehensive solutions, which the Community may have then have offered to the UK in lieu of full membership and second, it was feared that if the British and Swedish talks were 'in tandem' then Britain's accession could be held up if negotiations on special Swedish arrangements were problematic. Harold Wilson provided a precise statement of the British position when Olof Palme visited London (April 1970):

'We shall be negotiating Britain's entry into the Communities ourselves, and not as a member of a general team. ... It will be their (the Swedes') job to establish with the Commission or the Common Market ministers how closely the economic arrangements can be fully consistent with their position of political neutrality'.[12]

The suspicions on the parts of the Commission, the member states' governments and even the British were reinforced by the Palme government's proposals in early 1970 for a negotiating procedure that was favourable to Swedish perspectives. Interestingly, the suggestions were not restricted to which procedure should be adopted for her own discussion. It was generalised to include the whole of the deliberations and was aimed at reconciling the division of the EFTA group into candidates and 'non-candidates' with two differing sets of negotiations and procedures. Palme tried to synchronise the timing of the two sets of discussion in order to change the context of the talks, influence the bargaining process and thereby turn the other parties' attention to different problems.

The Swedish Minister of Trade, Gunnar Lange, for example, at a meeting in Brussels with Commission representatives in March 1970 stressed the common problems faced especially by the Nordic EFTAns and argued for simultaneous talks. Yet, these 'parallel negotiations' were not possible because of the form and timing of the talks that the EEC chose, which sought to avoid negotiating on subjects not yet defined and whose legal implications were uncertain'.[13] For the Community, negotiating a unique deal for the Swedes and, at the same time, conducting negotiations with both the candidates and 'non-candidates' was neither exciting nor attractive. Rather it was perceived as being time-consuming and fraught with political difficulties, especially as the Community had agreed that any EEC accessions and agreements with the 'non-candidates' would have the same date of entry into force.

The Community's internal developments created further unpalatable problems for the Swedes and their search for some kind of flexible relationship with the Community. By 1970, the Community was in the final stages of agreeing on future monetary integration. The Werner Report on Economic and Monetary Union (EMU) was being devised, which struck at the heart of Swedish concerns over the country's neutrality. In addition, the Davignon Committee's report to the Community's Foreign Ministers in May 1970 also recommended the establishment of a system of consultation on foreign policy, which was treated with disdain by the Palme government. The Davignon Report, which was adopted at the EEC's Foreign Ministers' meeting (27 October 1970), emphasised the connection between full membership and participation in foreign policy measures aimed at furthering political unification. Unluckily for the Swedes, Davignon even proposed that any future applicant country must adhere to the report as a part of full membership, which would thereby act as an important vehicle for realising the political aims of the Treaty of Rome. These developments, which were now seen as part and parcel of the emerging Community, took place at the very time when the Palme government was considering negotiations with the EEC. The Social Democratic government would, if it wanted the country to be an EEC member, have to participate in aspects which it had great reservations about.

Thus, the EEC's internal developments were not conducive to ensuring successful negotiations between Sweden and the Community. As part of its strategy, the Palme government even went as far as proposing a Swedish-EEC customs union in 1970, allowing for fuller economic integration, whilst maintaining the premise of avoiding political integration.[14] However, the Community's unfavourable reaction to these various Swedish approaches, combined with its later adoption of the Davignon (political integration) and Werner (EMU) plans effectively killed these initiatives as they were perceived by the ruling Social Democrats as threatening the country's neutral status. Hence, it was primarily due to internal EEC developments during winter 1970-71 that culminated in Sweden's rejection of membership or any form of association that would lead to membership.[15]

Negotiating With the Community

Negotiations between the Community and Sweden took place in three approximate stages - exploratory talks during winter 1970-71; internal EEC consultations from April 1971 and formal negotiations from December 1971- July 1972. Sweden accepted the invitation of the Community to 'enter into discussions at ministerial level in the autumn on Sweden's relationship to the Common Market' (5 August 1970). The formal opening of talks was marked by the declaration of the new Swedish Minister of Trade, Kjell-Olof Feldt, to the Council of Ministers (10 November 1970). The Minister's speech was also attached to the application (already delivered in 1967, but in quiescence). Once the Swedish proposals for simultaneous negotiations between the candidate and 'non-candidate' groupings had fallen on the deaf ears of the Commission and that it seemed that the forthcoming British talks would set the pace of any negotiations, the Palme government had by November 1970 shifted its position. In his nine-page statement, Feldt specified that Sweden wished 'to conduct, as far as possible our discussions parallel with Norway and Denmark'.[16] In addition, he emphasised that the coordination between the EFTA countries would not be too complex or push each others' claims too hard for fear that this would delay the opening of formal negotiations even further.

In the policy statement (10 November 1970), Feldt formally elaborated on its position regarding the EEC and made direct reference to his government's concerns over the Community's future plans in the monetary and foreign policy spheres. The Minister emphasised the 1967 position and outlined Sweden's reservations over the compatibility of its neutrality with full membership with great precision - stating that:

> 'international ties cannot be accepted which make the possibility to choose neutrality in the time of war illusory. The policy must be supported by a strong military defence and the economic life so organised that the nation can endure a large scale blockade during a fairly long period. We cannot participate in such forms of cooperation on foreign policy, economic, monetary and other matters which, in our judgement would jeopardise our possibilities to pursue a firm policy of neutrality. This means that we cannot participate within a certain group of states in a cooperation of foreign policy which is binding and which aims at working out of common policies. Limits are also set to our responsibilities to accept a transfer of the right of decision-making from national to international institutions within the framework of an economic and monetary union'.

Swedish governmental objectives in November 1970 were to achieve dual outcomes, namely participation in a customs union with the Community and the CAP. In order to achieve these aims, Sweden was willing to harmonise domestic legislation with the Community's trade rules and practices in both areas, although a 'neutrality clause' would be insisted upon by the Swedes to allow them to disassociate themselves from any of the Community's future trade policies with a 'political intent'.[17] However, the Council's initial reaction was lukewarm. The German Foreign Minister and chairman of the meeting, Walter Scheel, stated that the general opinion in Brussels towards possible Swedish EEC membership was negative.[18] In particular, the Council stipulated that only full membership would enable access to the CAP. In response to this, the Social Democratic government's ambitions regarding agricultural policy were speedily abandoned.

In Stockholm the opposition party leaders reacted to Feldt's statement in Brussels by reiterating their now familiar positions. The Left Party leader, Hermansson, repudiated both the membership and customs union concepts. He viewed the statement as surprisingly friendly towards the Community and argued that Sweden ought to be (at the most) satisfied with a trade agreement with the EEC. The Centre Party (Gunnar Hedlund) and Liberal Party (Gunnar Helén) leaders by and large approved the statement but underscored that much would depend on the ensuing negotiations. The pro-membership leader of the Conservatives, Yngve Holmberg, expressed disappointment with the governmental position and that it had not sought to ascertain whether it would be possible to combine full membership with neutrality. This view was echoed by most of the leading business organisations.

Exploratory talks were held on the level of administrative experts in order to exchange information, define goals and resolve technical problems. These fact finding talks began on 17 December 1970 and for roughly ten weeks, Swedish experts led by the chief negotiator, Ambassador Sverker Åström, met with officials of the Commission. The resulting data served as the basis for the Commission's report (on the relationship between the enlarged EEC and the remaining EFTA members and associate members) to the Council of Ministers, which was published on 16 June 1971, although it then took several months for the EEC ministers to agree the precise mandate for negotiations with Sweden.[19]

During winter 1970-71, the Social Democratic government was unable to establish an effective platform to influence the form of the future negotiations with the Community. It could therefore not ensure that they were to be flexible enough to accommodate neutrality and/or make full membership viable. During these exploratory talks it became manifestly apparent to the Palme government that the Community was not willing politically to treat Sweden either as a special case for full membership or as one of the candidates rather than 'non-candidates'.

Swedish concerns at events were apparent as early as the general parliamentary debate (19 January 1971) on the application's progress. As Miljan comments,

> 'It was not so much a debate as an attempt to show moderation and increase the consensus, as all party leaders - except for the Communist Party leader, who stood fast in his anti-EEC attitude - attempted to come to grips with the conflicting political demand of neutrality and the economic demand of close participation with the EEC'.[20]

Palme, for example, argued that it was also in other countries' interests that Swedish neutrality be firmly followed and that foreign policy cooperation remained out of the question. The Prime Minister highlighted that the government would continue to 'gather a broad opinion around the base lines of Swedish foreign and trade policies and attempt to reach a constructive agreement with the EEC'. However, the opposition parties remained far from convinced of the likelihood of achieving the latter. Hedlund (Centre Party) for instance, declared that whilst he did not exclude Swedish EEC membership, he was now more pessimistic as a result of the Davignon Report. The Liberals criticised the 'national self-sufficiency' of EEC opponents in Sweden and that the country 'will have to pay dearly if even a customs union at the very least does not materialise'. The new Conservative party leader, Gösta Bohman, stressed the inflexibility of the party positions and 'political superstitions which marked large parts of the Swedish EEC debate'. According to him, the government 'must create as good conditions as possible within Swedish opinion and at Brussels which will best safeguard Swedish and European interests'.[21]

Rejection of Full Membership

By early 1971, the Social Democratic government had tried most avenues for future cooperation and had still to find a way of reconciling any form of EEC membership with Swedish neutrality. Yet, the impetus for a final political decision on the part of government came quickly in early 1971. At its session (8-9 February), the EEC Council of Ministers endorsed the Werner Committee's recommendations that EMU should be created by the early 1980s. On 8-12 March, Swedish and Commission delegates reviewed the views on economic co-operation that had been compiled by experts on both sides since December and after evaluation and preliminary consultations with the Community, the Palme government abandoned the equivocation of its 'open' application. Consequently, the government unilaterally issued a memorandum (18 March 1971) announcing that participation in the Community's EMU and within the Davignon Report's proposed foreign policy coordination would, after all, be inappropriate. In effect, the Swedish government had ruled out full membership or an association agreement leading to future membership - much to the relief of the Commission.

The memorandum argued that any future EMU would imply 'economic cooperation which is far more binding and which limits the freedom of action of the participating countries to a larger extent than the kind of cooperation we have hitherto been prepared to participate in'. In particular, the ruling Social Democrats disliked the supranational and institutional implications of the Werner Report which they claimed would reduce any chances of using a Swedish veto.[22] Once again, the memorandum argued that it was the neutrality question that predominated and that the economic ramifications of any EMU would require 'a curtailment of a freedom of action in the field of economic policy on the scale which .... reduces the possibilities to pursue the policy of neutrality'.[23] In addition, the memorandum also referred explicitly to the problems arising from the Community's envisaged foreign-policy cooperation. The government acknowledged that full membership 'would result in cooperation in the field of foreign policy along the lines of the Davignon Report'.[24] The crux of the question depended on whether 'cooperation in the field of foreign policy in accordance with the Davignon plan is compatible with the policy of neutrality'.[25] Not surprisingly this was rejected by the government on several grounds:

- Foreign policy cooperation and the promotion of joint actions between mainly NATO and WEU members would be a direct violation of neutrality.

- Any joint action would reduce governmental ability to take up position freely and that it 'did not want to give ... the impression that our conduct is dependent upon consultations with a certain group of states'.

- that future co-operation did not exclude defence cooperation, which according to neutrality doctrine was clearly out of the question.

Hence, it was these new developments by the Community that scotched any chances of full membership and not the contents of the Rome Treaty *per se*. At the same time, these developments also made it easy for the Community to reject Swedish overtures for a customs union in industrial and agricultural goods. In effect, the agenda had moved on for the Community. Nevertheless, the memorandum did incorporate the seeds of continued governmental policy towards the Community. Despite having 'come to the conclusion that membership is not a realistic possibility so far as Sweden is concerned', the government did claim that it would 'seek to attain close, comprehensive and durable economic relationships with the Communities having regard to our policy of neutrality'.[26] It was willing to agree to concrete obligations and would continue to look for a special agreement which could guarantee Swedish access to EEC markets.

In response, the Riksdag passed a virtually unanimous parliamentary resolution removing the issue of membership from the domestic political agenda on the grounds of its incompatibility with neutrality. It remained out of the political limelight for some considerable time. As Waite argued Sweden developed a 'Paradox' in which it officially divorced political and economic relations with the Community from one another. In practice, it sought closer economic ties with the EEC whilst remaining politically aloof on the grounds of its neutrality.[27] The government continued to press for a far-reaching free trade agreement. This provided a forum for workable alternatives, based around satisfying Swedish objectives concerning industrial products:

- any agreement must 'rest on a stable and durable foundation creating favourable conditions for planning by government and enterprises'.

- any accord would 'cover important fields besides customs duties and trade regulations'.

- future agreement must 'permit further development so that cooperation could be widened and deepened'.[28]

The government also argued that any agreement based on industrial goods would be most effective if the signatory countries applied the same customs duties in trade with third countries. This implied Sweden was first, willing to adopt the Community's common customs tariff (CCT) and quota regime on industrial goods on a similar timetable to those adopted by the joining new members; second, that it would adjust its tariff over a five-year period in order to correspond with the CCT; third, it would harmonise its trade policies. The Swedes in particular, still argued that an innovative treaty would be needed with a consultative institutional framework based on mutual rights and obligations and even suggested some form of cooperation at the parliamentary level between the Riksdag and the European Parliament. In general, Swedish perspectives were positive, relatively ambitious and included a willingness to make unilateral concessions in order to achieve its wider free trade aims.

In part, this strategy was a political manoeuvre to limit the Community's ability to demand extensive exceptions to the agreement, such as Swedish paper and pulp products, which the government mentioned explicitly in the memorandum. The ruling Social Democrats were keen to ensure that any agreement would be evolutionary and allow for cooperation in other fields such as, in medium-term economic planning, monetary questions and research and development. In many ways, the government was still calling for special status so that in effect, the country would 'become an annex of the Communities, but an annex in which its formal independence would have been retained'. Such an agreement would allow Sweden to apply the same rules and policies as the Community but by her own decision'.[29]

For the Community, the statement was received with some relief and at least helped to clarify matters for the future formal negotiations, even if parts were still deemed to be unacceptable. The Commission's opinion (published 16 June 1971) argued that Sweden presented three specific problems for the Community. The first concerned agriculture and the fact that a non-member could not be part of the CAP; the second was the problem of defining special institutional arrangements for Swedish membership of Community policies; the third was that the application of a general safeguard clause based on neutrality would never be fully operable without a firm institutional framework (which again reinforced the second problem).[30] In the eyes of the Community, Sweden had formally stipulated that she was now a 'non-candidate'. The Commission could now choose between two alternatives when dealing with the problems of the 'non-candidates' arising from enlargement. Either that existing trade barriers remained the *status quo* between the Community and the 'non-candidates' for a tentative two-year period (which the Commission itself favoured) or that the problems could be solved immediately by special agreements with the 'non-candidates'. Both the Palme government and the Council of Ministers chose the second option. On the 18 June 1971, the Swedish government declared that the free trade proposal for industrial goods implied by the second proposal constituted a good basis for forthcoming negotiations, whilst the Council of Ministers (26-27 July) decided to base any future negotiations on the free trade proposal. On 6 September 1971, Sweden delivered a memorandum outlining its preferences for an agreement.

In the following November, the Commission was formally authorised to begin negotiating with Sweden, Austria, Switzerland, Finland, Portugal and Iceland, but this was to be based on procedures established on 10 November 1971, which dictated that the Community would be negotiating not only on behalf of the Six but also the four applicant countries as well. The interests of the existing member states were also openly protected with the Commission generally favouring a limited agreement only in industrial goods and with a series of sectional exceptions. The first meeting at representative level between the Commission's Mr. Wallenstein and Sweden's chief negotiator Mr. Åström took place on 4 December 1971.

Once the Swedes had abandoned any pretence over access to the Community's CAP, the negotiations focused exclusively on the possibilities of reaching a special agreement in the form of a customs union with the Community. Although the Swedish delegation reserved the right to return to the ideas it had previously presented about a flexible framework, its negotiators found it difficult to find satisfactory solutions within the free trade remit. The Commission's position limited Swedish ambitions in two ways. First, the narrow negotiating mandate of the Commission made it impossible for the Swedes to expand the scope of the talks. Second, the Community had already adopted three principles to govern any negotiations with those countries that had not applied for full membership - namely that there would be no new barriers to intra-European trade; that there would be the complete maintenance of EEC autonomy and that the treaty would be consistent with GATT rules. In practice, this made the achievement of a customs union virtually impossible. The Swedes officially abandoned the idea of a customs union in early June. The government's policy of 'general harmonisation and specific sector integration' was deemed incompatible with the Community's existing structure.

Most of the problematic issues in the negotiations concerned sensitive products. The Swedish delegation were particularly opposed to a three-year tariff freeze on steel, pulp and paper products and any special arrangements discriminating against special steels. In fact, the Commission eventually abandoned its proposed freeze on tariffs and instead negotiated more tolerable (at least for the Swedes) small reductions over the first four years. There were also disagreements over foodstuffs and especially which products were to be included in an accord on processed foodstuffs. The Swedish negotiators insisted on prior consultations on competition issues (especially on the procedures concerning a breakdown in competition rules), on the imposition of safeguard clauses (which were partly met) and for an arbitration clause (which they failed to achieve).

Towards the end of the negotiations, the discussions were complex, with bilateral talks being held by the government with Denmark and Norway alongside its own dialogue with the Community. In addition, Sweden (with Finland) opened discussions with the UK on the levels of tariffs that were to be temporarily re-imposed and on the size of duty-free import quota on Swedish pulp and paper exports to Britain. There was generally a feeling of compromise and urgency to the negotiations, with the Free Trade Agreements being drafted in July 1972. On the one hand, the Palme government made some final concessions on agricultural products. It agreed to suspend duties on for example, fish fillets provided that Denmark maintained the existing landing rights for Swedish fishermen and that the Community did not introduce any tariffs on Swedish herring exports.[31] Yet, it also generally remained disappointed about the Community's treatment of Swedish special steels and the government negotiated to extend the transitional period for the abolition of tariffs on the imports of special steels from 5-6 years. In exceptional circumstances, the Social Democratic government also reserved the right to apply indicative ceilings on alloy steel, high carbon steel and steel tubes and pipes. In part these actions 'revealed a certain irritation with the bureaucratic features hidden in the form of the rules of origin and toward EEC's protective measures'.[32]

Final agreement was reached between Sweden and the Community with the final treaty draft being initialled on 21 July 1972 and the formal agreement being signed the following day. Ultimately *de facto* economic integration was intensified by the creation of a free trade agreement with the Community, while *de jure* political integration was studiously avoided. For Sweden, the Free Trade Agreement (FTA) with the EEC (22 July 1972) secured access to the Community's markets. However, this argument is not as convincing or as simple as first appears. Although the FTA appeared to 'represent a way out of the insoluble problem of obtaining the benefits of economic integration without subscribing to the political commitments', the very fact that Sweden was formally linked to 'a bloc with distinctly political ambitions' meant that, albeit to a limited degree, Sweden had already sacrificed the appearance of 'complete neutrality'.[33] Indeed, for the Palme government the negotiations had been informally one of almost continual retreat with the Swedes in turn abandoning its aspirations for a qualified and flexible membership of the Community, a common Nordic front, or even any special status with the EEC based on a customs union. In the final stages of the negotiations with the Community, the government further diluted its position to one similar to those of the other EFTA 'non-candidates' and sought a more limited free industrial trade agreement - a far cry from the original aspirations of the 1967 'open' application for full membership.

Domestic Reactions

As regards domestic politics, the controversies over the EEC issue altered between 1967-72. During this time, and as a result of the 'open' application, the domestic debate had initially focused on tactics within the political parameters of a universal acceptance of neutrality policy. Indeed, the decision by the EEC at the Hague (1-2 December 1969) to proceed with the opening of negotiations with Britain on enlarging the Community 'created little enthusiam in Sweden'.[34] As late as 29 April 1970, the overwhelming consensus amongst parliamentarians during the Riksdag's foreign and trade policy debate was that the EEC question would not be solved for some years. Later when confronted by increasing political opposition to full membership and that the government sought to negotiate a free trade agreement with the Community (once the March 1971 memorandum ruled out full membership), domestic party cohesion faltered. In general and as Bergquist argues, party divisions continued to revolve around the publicised arguments formulated previously during the 1961-63 and 1967 debates.[35] At no point did any of the leading Swedish politicians suggest that Sweden should relinquish its policy of neutrality.

However, two facts helped alter governmental and domestic perspectives in favour of the FTA and promoted the need for an FTA with the Community. First, the country's declining economic growth during 1970-71 re-emphasised the country's dependence on international trade. Second, the 'young Europeans' in the Social Democratic government, such as Olof Palme, Trade Minister Kjell-Olof Feldt and the Foreign Minister, Krister Wickman lost influence within the domestic debate as the party suffered electoral losses in September 1970. What was clear from the 1970 electoral campaigns was that most voters were unenthusiastic about the formation of a comprehensive link with the EEC and were suspicious of its implications for the credibility of neutrality policy. In particular, grass roots SAP members and supporters doubted the viability of full membership.

Once the government announced its decision to favour a more limited free trade arrangement, its position was supported by most notably the Centre Party, but also by some Liberals and Conservatives. In practice and as Hancock has argued, Sweden's decision in March 1971 that full membership and neutrality were incompatible, restricted governmental policy choice to an industrial free trade agreement and 'effectively insulated the domestic political system from a major ideological confrontation'.[36] Yet, it was also evident that the main discussion and final decision on the membership issue was taken almost exclusively at the political elite level within Sweden.[37]

Nevertheless, the domestic debate over the FTA became most pronounced during autumn-winter 1970 and spring 1971. It was during this time that the main political parties re-affirmed their positions on the issue of full membership before its ruling out in March 1971. Yet, for all the main actors participating in the domestic debate, the Community issue was seen from an economic perspective and in particular, whether the EEC would deliver Swedish economic objectives. Bonham, for example, in his survey of Scandinavian parliamentary attitudes towards the EEC suggested that in Sweden, most parliamentarians viewed the Community almost exclusively in economic terms.[38] With striking accuracy, he argued that until the majority of the domestic elite changed their attitudes with respect to accepting deeper political integration, the chances for any form of regional political union involving Sweden remained small. In general terms, the domestic elite were of three schools - those favouring closer, but conditional relations with the Community, those proposing full accession (as long as it is compatible with neutrality) and those advocating non-accession.

Ironically, the ruling Social Democrats' policy 'was officially ambiguous on the issue',[39] and in spite of being (along with the Centre Party), the main advocates of closer, but conditional relations. The SAP's main policy premise was that it would not support any type of arrangement with the Community which would be against the essential pre-requisites of maintaining independence in foreign policy and a credible neutral stance. The party was deeply split on the issue. Its youth wing, for example, actively campaigned against Swedish full membership.[40] It was not surprising that in order to maintain at least the premise of party unity and given the relative size of the Social Democratic parliamentary majority, the SAP leadership 'monopolised the inner circle of the foreign policy elite'.[41] It was responsible for the party's position on the membership question. The most influential SAP figures, of course, remained the Prime Minister, Olof Palme, Minister of Trade, Kjell-Olof Feldt and Minister of Foreign Affairs, Krister Wickman. These elite figures also enjoyed the support of key legislative leaders in the LO, who were more than usually active in paying close attention to the EEC issue. For the most part, the ruling Social Democrats stressed that closer cooperation with the Community would reinforce the economic interdependence between Sweden and its main overseas markets and lead to substantial efficiency gains within the domestic economy.

Supporting the Social Democratic governmental view were the leaders of the LO, the Centre Party and, at least tacitly the Liberals.[42] The Centre Party strongly advocated a favourable agreement with the Community, although for the most part, their main reasoning for such an agreement derived from a Nordic perspective and that a divided region - with some countries as full members and others not - would be to Sweden's disadvantage. In general and with equal ambiguity, the Centre Party supported the government's policy. This action, like that of the SAP, attracted criticism from the Centre Party's youth wing and also from Johannes Antonsson (vice-chairman of the party during the 1970 election campaign) who favoured the creation of a Nordic free trade area as the basis of future negotiations for a regional arrangement between the region and the Community.

In addition, the Liberals, whilst formally favouring full membership, continued to support government policy throughout the domestic debate. Like the Centre Party, the Liberals supported the need for a united Nordic front, but were also deeply concerned that Swedish interests must be guaranteed through participation in EEC decision-making in at least some form. As usual and in line with their previous policy, it was the Conservatives that were the most fervent in promoting full membership; although mainly on the same grounds as the Liberals - that Sweden needed to participate in Community decisions. As late as 4 September 1971 the Conservatives on the Riksdag's Foreign Affairs Standing Committee at a meeting called to consider the letter delivered to the Council (on Swedish preferences on the form of the FTA) still protested that the government should ask for association as the bare minimum. Yet, this was not 'an all-out fight' between the main political parties. Once the March 1971 declaration was issued, the need for foreign policy consensus (in line with the neutrality requirements of the 'Swedish Diamond') prevailed and the Liberal and Conservative parties' criticisms were not as widely made as could have been.[43] As Hancock argues a comparison of the government policy and the views of the political Right revealed a consensus on the economic importance of joining an expanding Community. It was the degree of institutionalisation between Sweden and the Community that created differences.[44] The government suggested the primacy of maintaining political independence, whilst the Conservatives prioritised closer economic contact.

The Left Party was also consistent. They were the main grouping advocating non-accession and maintained outright opposition to the Community and Swedish affiliation in any form. For this party, the EEC issue 'was one of the most vital issues facing the Swedish political system'.[45] The Left Party opposed the EEC on ideological grounds, fearing that it would reinforce international capitalism, undermine the government's ability to control the excessive power of multinationals and that trade union influence on policy-making would also be reduced because of the Community's supranational decision-making structures.

The main interest groups also followed the EEC issue with vigour. The SAF favoured full membership; the LO shadowed government policy stressing a cautious 'wait and see' approach. However, both groups were active in trying to influence any governmental negotiations with the Community on labour market and industrial investment issues. In contrast, the white-collar, trade union - the TCO - were much less active, but still established a 'Market Committee' to evaluate the effects of the Community on the trade union movement. Not surprisingly the Federation of Swedish Industries (SI) was the most vociferous and openly favoured full membership, (provided it was compatible with neutrality policy). In January 1972, for instance, the Federation (in conjunction with the Export Association) organised a two-day meeting of 175 business leaders who sharply criticised the government's handling of the EEC question. For the SI, the fact that more than 60 percent of Sweden's trade was with the Six and the four applicants was decisive. However, it played a flexible hand suggesting that it would accept an arrangement short of full accession, provided it guaranteed access to the Community's decision-making.

Following the conclusion of the negotiations, the Riksdag quietly ratified the FTA treaty (12 December 1972) by an overwhelming majority of 298-15. Only the Left Party directly opposed the agreement, although both the Liberals and the Conservatives were not completely satisfied. The Liberals called for new negotiations to improve Sweden's terms, whilst the Conservatives predictably called for eventual full membership. Ultimately, the Swedish FTA treaty 'was endorsed with near parliamentary unanimity and with no special conditions attached'.[46]

Once the treaty entered force in January 1973, it opened the way for achieving the basic objectives of those favouring closer but conditional arrangements with the Community - the Social Democrats, the LO, the Centre Party and the Liberals - by allowing for the expansion of Swedish-EEC trade 'at minimum political cost'.[47] Yet, the agreement did not receive universal approval. The limitations of the FTA were raised by the Swedish business community. Erik Braunerhielm, Director of the SI in July 1972, for example, argued that there were four main problems with the FTA:

- The FTA's rules of origin and restrictions on Swedish exports were much stricter than those prevailing in EFTA. In most cases, Swedish firms would find it difficult to procure raw materials and components from outside Western Europe, affecting the country's development policy with the Third World.

- There were still restrictions on free trade. There were long transitional periods for paper, special steels and ferro-alloys and some processed foods were not covered in the FTA.

- There was still a high degree of uncertainty for Swedish exporters as the FTA incorporated a large number of safeguard clauses.

- Swedish interests were still excluded from large areas of economic and industrial cooperation with the Community. They faced major handicaps due to the country's status as an outsider and would have to work hard to maintain its position in EEC markets.[48]

The FTA: A Brief Evaluation

The FTA, which came into force on 1 January 1973 alongside the accessions of Denmark, Ireland and the UK had three major advantages for Sweden. First, it provided a political framework for governing Swedish relations with the Community; second, it allowed for the setting up of a free trade area in industrial products between Sweden and the EEC; third, the FTA was governed by the same rules and principles as other FTAs between the Community and the EFTA 'non-candidates'. This reinforced a feeling of equality and cooperation between the EFTA countries and made the creation of a large industrial free trade area between the Community and the EFTA states a reality. The Swedish government had gone some way to achieving one of its primary objectives - namely an industrial free trade area spanning most of Western Europe.

In particular, the FTA provided for the successive elimination of tariffs on approximately 80 percent of Swedish-EEC industrial trade over a 5-year period, beginning with the first of five scheduled 20 percent reductions on 1 April 1971 and ending with the final instalment on 1 July 1977 (see Table 4.1). The FTA was discriminatory against two of Sweden's major exports, imposing an 11-year transition (until 1 January 1984) for the abolition of residual tariffs on paper products and on certain types of finished steel. In particular, the discrimination against Swedish paper and steel was prompted by the desire of the EEC countries (and most notably the new member state, the UK) to protect their own industries.

The FTA also excluded most agricultural products. The contracting parties did however, express their readiness in the agreement 'to encourage the harmonious development of agricultural trade while respecting each other's agricultural policies'.[49] When signing the FTA, Sweden did autonomously grant certain reciprocal concessions in the agricultural field, such as exports of beef to the EEC, imports of wines, certain fruit and vegetables and fishery products from the Community. At that time they contributed less than 8 percent of Sweden's total trade with the EEC.[50]

Table 4.1   General Rule Tariff Reductions Between Sweden and the EEC

Time Period	Percent Reduction
1 April 1973	20
1 January 1974	20
1 January 1975	20
1 January 1976	20
1 January 1977	20

Source: Taken from Skandinaviska Enskilda Banken, (1972) Sveriges Avtal med EEC, *Utlandsnytt,* 10 October 1972, p. 5.

As a result of the FTA, Sweden enjoyed duty-free access to the markets of the Six for the first time. The country also gained open trade with Ireland (which was neither a previous EEC or EFTA member) and at the same time, retained free trade with the other new EEC members (UK and Denmark). In addition, Sweden continued to benefit from mutual free trade with its other EFTA partners, which had not become members of the Community in 1973. Furthermore, the Palme government retained the individual right to impose external tariffs and as a consequence within the Swedish-EEC free trade area, both sides had differing external tariffs on non-member state goods. None the less, essential 'rules of origin' were introduced by the FTA to ensure that only goods originating inside the free trade area were exempted from duty. Under these new rules of origin, a product was regarded as originating from within the Swedish-EEC free trade area if it was either wholly produced there or had undergone sufficient processing or working there. In short, the FTA provided Sweden's political and business elite with significant economic advantages and had, for the time being, psychologically addressed the requirements of coping with the evolving and expanded Community. Ulf Bernitz, for instance, argued that the FTA was among Sweden's 'most important international agreements of an economic nature, *perhaps* the most important'.[51]

On the down side, the FTA was restricted to essentially manufactured goods and even then, there were specific rules for key 'sensitive' products. In particular, the FTA's rules extended the five-year transitional period to 1 January 1980 for special steels, certain metals and rayon wool and to 1 January 1984, for paper board (except fibre building board) and paper products.[52] Moreover, tariff reductions only applied to Swedish imports which fell below predetermined annual ceilings and new paper tariffs were temporarily imposed by the EFTA countries joining the EEC in 1973. The agreement was not as generous or as comprehensive as first appeared. Unfortunately for the Swedes, the FTA did also not permit direct influence on Community decisions as the Conservatives and Swedish industrial lobbies had so clearly wished.

On the positive side, the agreement did not impose formal constraints on Swedish sovereignty and therefore did not compromise the country's neutrality policy. At the same time though, the FTA incorporated an all-important 'development' or 'evolutionary' clause, which the Swedish delegation had strenuously insisted upon in the negotiations. The clause required the parties 'to examine the possibility to develop and broaden their ties, when it appears advantageous for their economies to extend [such ties] to areas that are not covered by the present treaty'.[53]

The FTA also included institutional provisions and created limited mechanisms to ensure its proper functioning. A Swedish-EEC Joint Committee represented the core of the institutional arrangement; supposedly to meet at least once a year to supervise the proper implementation of the agreement, especially as regards customs questions, rules of origin and the application of safeguard clauses.[54] However, the FTA was from a legal and institutional perspective underdeveloped. In short, the economic significance of the FTA was not adequately reflected in its legal structure.[55] As Bernitz points out, the text of the FTA was concise and matter of fact orientated, containing few detailed rules. This of course can be partly explained by the Community's wish to sign almost exactly the same agreements with all the EFTA 'non-candidates' and led to the Community trying to find the lowest common denominator between the positions of the various EFTA countries.[56] In the Swedish case, this was illustrated by the fact that the Palme government pushed for a fully-fledged customs union with the EEC, but had to settle for an industrial free trade area, which was all the Finns, Austrians and Swiss were ever going to accept.

In particular, the FTA only incorporated a primitive system for dispute resolution. The Joint Committee established by the FTA to supervise future relations and developments was a diplomatic body and not a judicial organ. In essence, the Agreement only provided for consultations between the parties as the primary source of remedying disputes. As a last resort, each of the parties could under the FTA's terms unilaterally decide to introduce safeguard measures, such as customs duties or quantitative restrictions. Sweden along with Switzerland, was especially disappointed that no system of judicial control or review formed part of the agreements.[57] Ironically, despite facilitating international trade, the country's legal status as a duallist state meant that the FTA provisions did not form part of domestic law.[58] Overall, the FTA raised the degree of contact and cooperation between Sweden and the Community to a higher more formal, if at times still limited, level.

Swedish-EEC Relations: Assessing the FTA 1973-84

For the most part, the FTA was implemented on schedule. By mid-1977, free trade in industrial products had been achieved on the whole as nearly all customs duties had by then been abolished. The longer transitional period for Community imports of aluminium and some other metals ended again on schedule (31 December 1979), whilst the remaining Community import duties on pulp and paper products from Sweden continued to be dismantled gradually and disappeared entirely on 31 December 1983. To all intents and purposes the FTA signed by the Community and the respective EFTA countries allowing for a free trade area in industrial goods of some 300 million consumers was completed by the early 1980s.

The degree of economic interdependence between Sweden and the Community continued to grow and indeed the Agreement functioned exceedingly well. The rise in international trade between Sweden and the Community was striking during the 1970s and must, albeit to a limited extent, be as a result of the FTA. The Community's imports from Sweden in 1979 (ECU 10.3 billion) were just over two and half times the total of 1972 (ECU 4.1 billion), the year before the FTA came into force.[59] In similar vein, the Community's exports to Sweden in 1979 (ECU 10.4 billion) were also slightly more than two and half times the 1972 amount (ECU 4.0 billion). Interestingly, Swedish-EEC trade was nearly always in equilibrium throughout the 1970s, with the balance of trade between the two sides not exceeding ECU one billion surplus in either direction since the beginning of the 1970s. In most years, it was well below ECU 400 million.[60] From an economic perspective, the FTA was clearly a success. By 1980, roughly one-half of Swedish exports went to the Community compared to little over 5 percent to the United States and in the same year, 49 percent of imports derived from the Community.[61]

For the most part, there were very few trade disputes between Sweden and the Community. There are no known Swedish court cases concerning the application or interpretation of the FTA, even if this is because of the ambiguous status of the FTA in terms of Swedish law. Nor has there been any major cases in which anti-dumping measures have been instituted against enterprises exporting to Sweden from the Community or other EFTA countries. There were of course some controversial areas, such as the so-called Swedish shoe case concerning Swedish restriction on shoe imports between 1975-77, but these remained relatively minimal. In the shoe case, the government officially imposed quantitative restrictions (quotas) on all shoe imports on the grounds that the decline in the Swedish shoe industry necessitated a general import limitation if national supply readiness for this sector was to be maintained in the event of a war. In other words, the restriction was linked to neutrality policy and thus in line with article 21(c) of the FTA. The Community and the other EFTA countries rejected this - claiming (quite correctly) that the Swedes were actually trying to deal with the acute economic problems of the shoe industry (and therefore should have cited article 26 which allowed for safeguard and anti-dumping duties). This required consultations with the Community. As a response, the Community refused to grant successive tariff reductions on Swedish paper for a time.

Furthermore, the FTA facilitated institutionalised relations between Sweden and the Community which progressively increased throughout the 1970s. Although the FTA for example, only required that the Joint Committee meet once a year, the Committee met regularly twice a year from 1973. In addition and as a reflection of the growing degree of political co-operation between the two sides, the Community and the Swedish government decided in 1980 that one of the two annual sessions normally attended by officials would be raised in status to full ministerial level. High-ranking representatives conducted the discussions and allowed for major policy issues to be more extensively debated. The first such meeting took place on 29 June 1981, when the Commission Vice-President, Wilhelm Haferkanp, responsible for external relations visited Stockholm.

The FTA also provided the backdrop for further agreements on co-operation between Sweden and the Community. Following the imposition of measures by the Community as part of the Davignon Plan's attempts to deal with the 'manifest crisis' in the steel industry, for example, arrangements were made between the two sides in February 1978 to ensure that traditional trade flows were maintained. There were no new protectionist measures and the Community's price regulating measures were observed by Sweden. The first framework agreement between the Community and Sweden was also signed in 1977 on the management of fish stocks in the Baltic and Kattegat and the granting of reciprocal fishing rights.

As the Agreement's tariff timetable was 'ultimately completed without any significant hitch' and that it provided 'the infrastructure through which to extend the relationship with the Community into new fields',[62] the Swedish government was keen to push for greater cooperation in other areas. Sweden had after all been an associate member of the Community's monetary 'snake', but decided to withdraw in August 1977. At the summit meeting of the EFTA Heads of State and Governments in Vienna (May 1977), the government expressed its readiness not only to maintain the achievements of the FTA, but also to complete and expand them by supplementary cooperation with the Community. In turn the

Community's Council of Ministers in 1978 deemed it desirable 'to improve and round out those agreements in all sectors where this might be useful'.[63] Consequently, Swedish participation in the Community's thermonuclear fusion (JET) and scientific and technological (COST) research programmes were extended (Sweden first joined in JET in 1976). There were also regular consultations between the two sides on, for instance, environmental protection, the paper and pulp industries and state aids.

Overall, the status of diplomatic contacts between Stockholm and Brussels was progressively raised. Ola Ullsten's visit to the European Commission (June 1981) represented the first time that a Swedish Minister for Foreign Affairs had visited this body. By the early 1980s, the level of diplomatic contact reached such a high degree that it would have been perceived as inconceivable during the early years of the FTA. In practice, the rising levels of economic interdependence and political dialogue between both sides made it inevitable that the relationship would be further deepened. The next phase extending cooperation between Sweden and the Community was to begin in 1984 and it to this era that the next chapter will now turn.

Notes

[1] Curzon, V. (1974) *The Essentials of Economic Integration - Lessons of EFTA Experience,* Macmillan, London, p. 227.

[2] Ibid., Curzon (1974) p. 227.

[3] Hancock, M. D. (1974) Scandinavia and the Expanded European Community, *Scandinavian Studies,* 46, 4, p. 319.

[4] Indeed, in 1970, it seemed that the expansion of the EEC would include three of Sweden's major trading partners. Norway had applied with the UK, Denmark and Ireland for full membership, but did not eventually go to accede to the Community due to the rejection of Norwegian full membership in the 1972 referendum.

[5] Commission of the ECs (1969), Le nouvel avis del la Commission Europeanne sue les candidatures a l'adhesion, *Europe,* 545, Brussels, Commission of the ECs, 6 October, p. 1.

[6] Although ironically on the same day as Kekkonen announced the decision not to participate in NORDEK, the Finnish government established a clear EEC policy line. It was announced that it would not be seeking either associate or full membership, but rather that it wanted to open negotiations on a special bilateral trade arrangement with the EEC, in a form that would be compatible with Finland's neutrality policy - Nielsson, G. P. (1971) The Nordic and the Continental European Dimensions in Scandinavian Integration: NORDEK as a Case Study, *Cooperation and Conflict,* VI, 2, p. 179.

[7] Op. cit., Hancock (1974) p. 416.

[8] Op. cit., Hancock (1974) p. 417.

[9] Ministry of Foreign Affairs (1971) *Documents on Swedish Foreign Policy 1970,* UD, Stockholm.

[10] Commission of the ECs (1967) *Avis de la Commission au Consiel concernant les demandes d'adhesion,* Commission of the ECs, Brussels, 9 September 1967, p. 19.

[11] Stålvant, C.-E. (1973) Sweden: The Swedish Negotiations with the EEC, *Scandinavian Political Studies,* 8, 2, pp. 236-45.

[12] Hansard (1970) *Commons,* 9 April, pp. 747-9.

[13] Op. cit., Stålvant (1973), p. 240.

[14] Sweden was willing to adopt the EC's common external tariff (CET) autonomously provided future changes were made the object of consultation. This offer was rejected by the EEC on the grounds that it would allow the Swedish government negotiating rights similar to those of member states without incurring the full obligations of EEC membership - op. cit., Curzon (1974) p. 230.

[15] Stålvant, C.-E. (1974) Neutrality and European Integration: A Comparison of Finland's and Sweden's EEC Policies, *Scandinavian Studies,* 46, 4, p. 418.

[16] Statement by Minister of Trade, Kjell-Olof Feldt, in Brussels between Sweden and the EC on 10 November 1970 - op. cit., Ministry of Foreign Affairs (1971).

[17] Op. cit., Stålvant (1974) p. 420.

[18] Nordisk Kontakt (1970) 14, p. 869.

[19] Taken from a speech by Sverker Åström given to the Nordic History Association, University College, London, 16 December 1994.

[20] Miljan, T. (1977) *The Reluctant Europeans,* Hurst & Co., London, p. 253.

[21] Op. cit. Nordisk Kontakt (1970) p. 174.

[22] Ministry of Foreign Affairs (1972) *Documents on Swedish Foreign Policy 1971,* UD, Stockholm, p. 212.

[23] Ibid., Ministry of Foreign Affairs (1972) p. 213.

[24] Ibid., Ministry of Foreign Affairs (1972) p. 213.

[25] Ibid., Ministry of Foreign Affairs (1972) p. 213.

[26] Ibid., Ministry of Foreign Affairs (1972) p. 214.

[27] Waite, J. (1973) The Swedish Paradox: EEC and Neutrality, *Journal of Common Market Studies,* 12,1, pp. 319-36.

[28] Ministry of Foreign Affairs (1972) *Regeringens Memorandum den 6 september 1971, Utrikes frågor 1971,* UD, Stockholm.

[29] Op. cit., Stålvant (1973) p. 241.

[30] Commission of the ECs (1971) *Europe,* Document 886, Commission of the ECs, Brussels, 21 September, p. 4.

[31] Op. cit., Stålvant (1973) p. 243.

[32] Op. cit., Stålvant (1973) p. 241.

[33] Moxon Browne, E. (1973) The Special Relations Agreements, *The World Today,* August, pp. 337-41.

[34] Op. cit., Miljan, T. (1977) p. 253.

[35] Bergquist, M. (1970) *Sverige och EEC,* Nordstedt, Stockholm.

[36] Op. cit., Hancock (1974) p. 324.

[37] For an extensive evaluation of elite level interaction see Hancock, M. D. (1974b) Swedish Elites and the EEC: Models of the Future, *Cooperation and Conflict*, 4, 2.

[38] Bonham, G. M. (1969) Scandinavian Parliamentarians: Attitudes Toward Political Integration, *Cooperation and Conflict*, 3, 3.

[39] Op. cit., Waite (1973) p. 327.

[40] Op. cit., Waite (1973) p. 327.

[41] Op. cit., Hancock (1974b) p. 229.

[42] Hancock, M. D. (1972) Sweden, Scandinavia and the EEC, *International Affairs*, 48, 4, July, p. 432.

[43] Svensson, S. (1971) Ingen strid om EEC men M och Fp kritiska, *Dagens Nyheter*, Stockholm, 18 March, p. 12.

[44] Op. cit., Hancock (1972) p. 433.

[45] Op. cit., Waite (1973) p. 329.

[46] Op. cit., Stålvant (1974) p. 425.

[47] Op. cit., Hancock (1974b) p. 231.

[48] Braunerhielm, E. (1972) *Swedish Industry in a Free Trade Europe*, UD, Stockholm, December, p. 1.

[49] Commission of the ECs (1981), *Europe Information - External Relations*, 48/81, Commission of the ECs, Brussels, June, p. 1.

[50] Ibid., Commission of the ECs (1981) p. 1.

[51] Bernitz, U. (1986) The EEC-EFTA Free Trade Agreements with Special Reference to the Position of Sweden and the Other Scandinavian EFTA Countries, *Common Market Law Review*, 23, p. 567.

[52] Skandinaviska Enskilda Banken (1973) *The Agreement Between the EEC and Sweden*, Skandinaviska Enskilda Banken, Stockholm, p. 2.

[53] Taken from a speech by Sverker Åström given to the Nordic History Association, University College, London, 16 December 1994.

[54] Op. cit., Commission of the ECs (1981) p. 3.

[55] Op. cit., Bernitz (1986) p. 568.

[56] Despite the fact that the FTAs were negotiated separately between the Community and each 'non-candidate', the texts are in every case almost identical - op. cit., Moxone-Browne (1973) p. 337.

[57] This point is discussed in Danelius (1973) Sveriges avtal med de europeiska gemeskaperna, *Svensk Juristtidning*, UD, Stockholm, p. 110.

[58] Op. cit., Bernitz (1986) p. 579.

[59] Op. cit., Commission of the ECs (1981) p. 2.

[60] Op. cit., Commission of the ECs (1981) p. 2.

[61] Op. cit., Commission of the ECs (1981) p. 2.

[62] Op. cit., Commission of the ECs (1981) p. 4.

[63] Op. cit., Commission of the ECs (1981) p. 4.

5   Declining EFTA Alternatives 1984-90

The new impetus in EC-EFTA cooperation dated back to April 1984, when the 18 Community/Association countries held their first meeting at ministerial level. This occasion was of dual importance. First, it celebrated the successful implementation of the Free Trade Agreements (FTAs) between the Community and the respective EFTA countries - by 1984, an industrial free trade area covering the entirety of EC-EFTA had been completed. Second, it provided an opportunity to build on this firm foundation and to identify new areas and common tasks for future EC-EFTA cooperation. Sweden, as an EFTA member supported these measures. The Palme government highlighted that since most quantitative restrictions on EC-EFTA trade had been removed, the Association fulfilled one of its primary functions and 'was on the lookout for a new role'.[1]

The formal initiative proposing closer multilateral dialogue came from the EFTA, and more specifically Swedish side. Somewhat ironically, it was a Social Democratic government which moved Swedish (and subsequently EFTA) relations with the Community 'to a higher plane'.[2] During Olof Palme's official visit to the European Commission in February 1983 (the first by any Swedish Prime Minister), he emphasised his government's 'desire to participate actively in the final realisation of ... a free Western European market, characterised by social and international solidarity'.[3] Later during a routine meeting in 1984, the (then) Minister of Trade, Mats Hellström, suggested the starting of an EC-EFTA multilateral dialogue to his French counterpart, Claude Cheysson and was somewhat surprised to hear Cheysson's positive response. The Swedish idea suited the pro-integration line of the French socialists and with the European Parliament's 1984 direct elections approaching, the French government thought it appropriate timing to launch such an initiative.[4]

Yet, the Swedish government abandoned any pretext of seeking an EFTA substitute to full membership by the end of 1990 and was by this time, in the process of seeking parliamentary consent to submit an application. Indeed, with the lodging of a full membership application (1 July 1991), the Carlsson government formally recognised that the attempts to negotiate an advanced EC-EFTA free trade area in the shape of the European Economic Area (EEA) were now merely a transitional arrangement paving the way for Swedish EC membership. The chapter will argue that the successive Social Democratic governments gradually became discontented with, and pessimistic about, partial arrangements with the Community and finally accepted that there were no comprehensive alternatives to full membership. It will focus on Swedish and Community's attitudes to the Luxembourg Process and the European Economic Space (EES - to be later renamed the EEA) in order to evaluate why Sweden eventually discarded its preferences for an EC-EFTA arrangement and took up the option of full membership.

A Positive Start: The Luxembourg Process

The process leading to closer EC-EFTA collaboration was strengthened by a culmination of positive trends on both the EC and EFTA sides. The Community was by 1983, deliberating ways of revitalising the stagnant EC. The Single European Market (SEM) was deemed to be an appropriate issue for reinvigorating the Community and formal proposals for its establishment were presented in the Commission's *White Paper on Completing the Internal Market* in 1985. The EFTA Secretariat had also been revived during the early 1980s by a new dynamic secretary-general, the Norwegian Per Kleppe. In addition, EC-EFTA cooperation had been seen to work. A free trade area in industrial goods, with the exception of a few sensitive products, had been established through the various FTAs by 1 July 1977. As early as May 1977, the EFTA governments stipulated that 'it would be desirable to develop the existing cooperation ... in varying degrees of intensity - between the EFTA countries and the European Community'.[5] Indeed, it was Per Kleppe, who floated ideas within EFTA of a common multilateral approach instead of each country focusing on its bilateral relations with the Community. Representatives of multinational companies from the EFTA countries had also been involved in the preparation of the SEM project through the European Round Table of Industrialists established in 1983.[6] They pressured for closer EC-EFTA cooperation as a means of ensuring access to the SEM programme.

At the first joint EC-EFTA ministerial meeting in Luxembourg (9 April 1984), which had been convened in order to celebrate the successful implementation of the FTAs and the abolition of the last remaining tariff/quantitative restrictions affecting trade in industrial products, Claude Cheysson in his opening statement outlined four areas for future EC-EFTA activity - research and development; industrial cooperation through the SEM; common action on the international level (especially regarding monetary policy), and collaboration with regard to the Third World.[7] At Luxembourg, the ministers stressed the importance of further EC-EFTA cooperation aiming to create 'a dynamic European Economic Space (EES)'. This new multinational dialogue came to be known, not surprisingly, as the 'Luxembourg Process'. In 1984, a joint EC-EFTA High Level Contact Group (HLCG) was established including the EFTA ministers and members of the European Commission.

The Palme government welcomed the Luxembourg Declaration as it included the attractive concept of a European Economic Space and in spite of the fact that it was not given a clear definition, (apart from that it should be dynamic and homogeneous). The government recognised that any dynamism would 'accrue from the expected benefits of removing trade barriers and partly from the intention of both EFTA and EC to continue to enlarge the scope of their cooperation'. The homogeneity of the EES was interpreted by the Swedes as referring to the parallel changes in the EC-EFTA relationship which would correspond to SEM developments.[8] It was not surprising that the Palme government was quick to support the Luxembourg process, especially as at face value, neutrality would not be undermined by such a limited concept. Indeed, the process was a piecemeal affair with cooperation only being advanced in certain areas, such as a Common Transit agreement. It remained too limited to accommodate the dynamism of the Community and its evolving SEM programme.

However, the re-launch of the European integration process in the mid-1980s around the twin concepts of the SEM programme (for EC member states) and the Luxembourg Process (for non-member states) demonstrated the need for a reevaluation of existing policy towards the Community. According to Jerneck, the government continued its groping, 'wait and see' attitude towards European integration and followed a cautious policy in which the maintenance of neutrality policy was of paramount importance. In general, Sweden's renewed interest in European integration entered three phases: 1984-85, 1987-88 and 1990-92.[9]

During the earliest phase (1984-85) which dealt with the evolving Luxembourg Process, Swedish policy incorporated two assumptions. First, that the FTA's industrial free trade area with the Community would alone be insufficient to accommodate Swedish economic requirements of closer trading relations with the Community. Second, that the Social Democratic government needed to keep contact with the rapid integration process. The dynamism emanating from within the Community needed to be accessed through the existing, albeit somewhat improved, channels of communication of the Luxembourg Process. Hence, the Palme government participated in the ever enlarging institutional framework (that had been initially set up for supervising the 1972 FTA) but which by 1985 amounted to 30 working groups of EC-EFTA officials.

The existing Swedish policy was therefore pragmatic, evolutionary and at least, in the government's eyes, did not require (at this point) any major revisions in the long-standing posture established towards the Community in March 1971.

Despite various motions by the Liberal and Conservative parties in 1984, the Riksdag's influential Foreign Affairs Standing Committee rejected demands for a reformulation of EC policy.[10] In terms of emphasis, the government's EC policy was beginning to alter though. In the 1970s, it had stressed the need for bilateral links with the Community (of which there were over 70 by 1990). This gradually changed. Ministers increasingly highlighted the need for EFTA common action in order to avoid Swedish isolation from EC markets.[11]

The EC-EFTA rapprochement took place quietly and without great public attention in any of the EFTA countries or in the Community. From 1985, the EFTA ministers were meeting with representatives of the Commission annually to review progress, covering some 30 policy areas. In particular, the HLCG prioritised the issues of technical barriers to trade, rules of origin, simplification of border formalities and cooperation in research and development. In May 1987, the first two multilateral agreements between the Community and EFTA were signed in Interlaken without notice by the Swedish public - one convention agreed a common transit procedure and the other introduced a single administrative document (SAD) for all trade between the EC and EFTA countries.

Progress was slowed due to the need for EFTA to agree a common position before approaching the Community - something that could have been problematic for the Swedes given their emphasis on national independence in order to maintain their neutrality policy. In addition, the EC Commissioner for external relations, Willy De Clerq, declared in 1988 that three basic principles would govern the Community's perspectives when negotiating with EFTA - that the EC's internal integration (and especially the SEM programme) would be the overriding priority and could not be compromised; that the Community would preserve its decision-making autonomy and that there would need to be a balance between benefits and obligations for both sides.[12] In many ways though, the Swedish government[13] had no objections to these three pre-conditions - the SEM's priority, the Community's autonomy and the need for reciprocity - as the ruling Social Democrats would in any case assert the principle of autonomy for decision-making and required reciprocal measures if any agreement was to be politically acceptable back home.

Overall then, the Luxembourg Process was important for Sweden. It required the EFTA countries to further institutionalise their own cooperation within the Association and thereby provided a new rationale for the future development of EFTA. At the same time, the process furthered the Social Democratic government's declared aims of closer and durable economic relations with the Community. Yet, the Luxembourg Process did not require any major concessions of sovereignty and could be defended by the Swedish government on an economic basis and not as a major threat to the credibility of neutrality policy.

Nevertheless, the long list of problems still to be tackled by the end of 1988 'showed that the Luxembourg Process was slow, costly and inadequate'.[14] It was in any case supplanted by the Community's SEM programme. As Church argues, the Luxembourg Process did not bring the EFTA countries 'much closer to their goal of a "special relationship" with the Community which would give them a share in the decision-making process'.[15] The agreement was insufficiently extensive to cope with the requirements of an integrating Europe and especially lacked a complex institutional framework capable of governing it.

Ultimately, it was the rapidity with which the concept of the SEM was developing within the Community that helped to speed up EC-EFTA relations. As Schwok has succinctly argued the rationale for Swedish and EFTA cooperation was simple. If the Community's SEM was 'not extended to the EFTA states, exporters from those countries will continue to pay at EC borders for administrative charges and bureaucratic delays. ... If they were left out of the internal market, EFTA firms would not obtain the benefits of economies of scale or the effects of competition'.[16]

The 1987 Government Policy Paper

The impact of the Community's 1992 project was noticeable within governmental thinking and led to rising levels of domestic debate on the implications of the SEM for Sweden. According to Åström, the Swedes began to actively discuss again their country's relationship with the EC once the 1992 programme became a reality.[17] Barely four months after the Single European Act came into operation (July 1987), Anita Gradin (Minister of Foreign Trade) in her speech to the Council of Europe (19 November 1987) hinted that the Swedish government was willing to consider participation in initiatives aimed at maintaining the cohesion of the EES in the light of the emerging SEM.[18] Increasing emphasis was placed within governmental documentation of the time on the country's precarious economic position. In 1987, for instance, 52.2 percent of Swedish exports went to the Community. Over half of this number consisted of intermediate-export technology, (such as motor vehicles, chemicals, non-electrical machinery, plastic and non-ferrous metals). The share of machinery and transport equipment alone of overall exports was 43 percent.[19] Equally Swedish industry was now a large foreign investor. The share of employment in Swedish producing subsidiaries in the EC amounted to 33 percent of total industrial employment in 1987. Swedish investment in Community had already risen sixfold between 1985-88 in anticipation of the Single Market. In short, the SEM programme sent shock waves through Swedish industry and was something that the government could not ignore or be isolated from.

Indeed, the government submitted its policy paper (in the form of a government initiated bill) to the Riksdag outlining its preferences for shaping future policy with the Community (entitled 'Sweden and West European Integration') in December 1987. It summarised national policies and regulations within all the fields covered by the Community's SEM programme. It was eventually endorsed by the Swedish Parliament by 288 votes to 17.

The policy paper 'conveyed a statement of Sweden's European identity'.[20] The government argued that it was adhering to the traditional philosophical and cultural path that the country had always followed. It stressed that the country's future was, as always, intertwined with that of the rest of continental Europe - 'Sweden is part of Europe. ... Developments in Europe are of great importance when we draw up today's and tomorrow's policies'.[21] Interestingly, for a governmental paper, it denied that the country's interest in the EC was solely based on economic concerns; 'these commitments also reflect a feeling of affinity that has several dimensions other than purely economic ones. There is a community of values that includes concepts, such as democracy and defence of human rights'.[22]

Yet, the paper (incorporated into the government bill) to the Parliament did establish certain guidelines for Sweden's participation in 'broad West European cooperation'.[23] As Hamilton notes, the proposals were far reaching. In effect, the government was suggesting that 'Sweden should be prepared to become a member of the Community in all respects, except for requirements regarding common discussions of foreign policy and security issues'.[24] The possibility of becoming an associated member of the Community was especially mentioned and not excluded.[25] The policy paper also touched on the issues of environmental and research and development collaboration. These themes were outlined further by Ingvar Carlsson during his tour of Madrid, Brussels, Bonn and London in spring 1988.

Overall, the Social Democratic government began to canvass for a more comprehensive policy dealing with the evolving dynamism of the Community from late 1987. In practice, the 1971 position, whilst still universally accepted as the foundation of the government's position, was being modernised to take account of the development of the SEM programme. After all, the SEM presented more of a concrete challenge to Swedish policy-makers than the Community's past overtures about foreign policy and monetary cooperation (which in reality had still only been superficially developed by 1987).

In many ways, the Swedish government was reacting to political pressure that had been mounting as the SEM programme gained momentum. The Carlsson government rationalised the timing of the policy paper on two grounds - that EC-EFTA cooperation was by this time regular and institutionalised and that the domestic debate needed to be informed and led accordingly. As Carlsson himself noted, 'the Riksdag and the general public have shown an increased interest in related questions'.[26] This was an accurate picture. The issue of European integration figured more frequently in Riksdag debates during the next two years than it had during the twelve years that the Free Trade Agreement was in force.[27] This was neither surprising nor amounted to a great deal as for most of the 1970s-80s, the EC issue was perceived to have been dealt with by the March 1971 policy declaration. In effect, the issue was settled and hardly featured in the domestic political debates at all. Indeed, the Riksdag's Foreign Affairs Committee (in reaction to motions from leading Conservatives and Liberals) declared that the majority of parliamentarians supported the government's view that full membership was still not a viable option during the 1986-87 session.[28]

The governmental policy paper evoked a response from parliamentarians and did, albeit to a limited extent, lead to a more informed domestic debate on Swedish policy towards the Community in the late 1980s. The policy paper led to extensive deliberations in the Riksdag. It resulted in four motions being tabled by parties and nine private member's bills. The main plenary debate took place almost six months later (5 May 1988). The relatively wide-ranging scale of the debate was also illustrated by the fact that all specialised parliamentary committees (other than defence) were involved, with overall coordination and responsibility residing with the Foreign Affairs Standing Committee. This enabled the Committee to determine the issues to be discussed and in practice, left the government with some freedom of manoeuvre.

In May 1988, the Riksdag accepted that the SEM would require a comprehensive response if the government was to ensure that the Community would not invoke protectionist measures against Swedish consumers and firms. In practice, the government's argument of avoiding a 'Fortress Europe' were telling on the Parliament. In its parliamentary decision, it was stated that,

> 'with regard to the proposals in the Community's White Paper on the Internal Market, Swedish consumers and Swedish firms should have the same rights and the same obligations as consumers and firms of the Community's member states, and that Swedes and Swedish firms in no way whatsoever shall be discriminated against'.

Next the government 'should try to abolish all types of border controls between Sweden and the Community in a way parallel to the abolition of border controls between member states of the Community'. The country 'has a clear interest in coordinating the free Nordic labour market and passport union with the (equivalent future) system of rules of the Community'.[29]

The parliamentary decision was, as always, the result of compromise between the (then) four leading parties in the Riksdag, with the Left Party (with equal consistency), maintaining its outright opposition to any kind of closer link with the Community. Ultimately, it was party politics rather than the government's prerogative, supported by a reserved and acquiescent opposition, that was decisive in defining the eventual policy outcome.[30] This was partly due to the more cautious attitude of Carl Bildt's Moderate Party, which was careful to stress that any future cooperation must be compatible with neutrality and that foreign policy cooperation would be excluded.[31] It was also equally acceptable to the Social Democrats and the Centre Party, who were wary of letting splits within their respective parties on the EC issue resurface. The basis of party accord surrounding the March 1971 declaration remained relatively intact. There were no motions in the Riksdag suggesting that the Swedish government should apply for EC membership and equally, the absence of party proposals outlining any alternatives to the government's flexible approach on institutional solutions for future EC-EFTA cooperation. There were of course still areas of disagreement between the parties on the EC issue. First, the Conservatives' motions - proposing a customs union as the most desirable goal for any future negotiations with the Community (as in 1971) was rejected by the other parties. Second, other proposals for joining the Community's European Monetary System (EMS) also fell on deaf ears.[32]

Nevertheless, given the relatively high degree of consensus maintained between the main parties, the Foreign Affairs Standing Committee reached the conclusion 'that membership of the Community is not the objective for the negotiations which are now starting'. To some extent, the Luxembourg Process (and until 1990, the later EEA initiative) were viewed as alternatives to full membership.[33] The bill was finally approved by 288-17 highlighting the degree of consensus, with only the Greens and the Left Party opposed. This 'historic compromise' between the main political parties at least allowed the government to claim that its broad policy approach to future cooperation with the Community had general support - as long as the government observed the constraints of neutrality. In practice, this was important and the government's freedom of manoeuvre was slightly curtailed.

As Stålvant and Hamilton note the original policy paper stressed two aspects - that Sweden was prepared to become an EC member 'in all respects, except for such foreign policy requirements as could diminish the credibility of the policy of neutrality' and that the country must participate in EC-EFTA cooperation that aimed to create a freer movement of goods, services, persons and capital in Western Europe. Yet, in the Riksdag's decision, this was transformed into the government 'working for the establishment of a common market encompassing all 18 EC and EFTA countries'. The Commission's White Paper became the terms of reference for Swedish policy towards EC-EFTA cooperation. The domestic consensus had at its heart the desire to develop policies in parallel with the SEM programme. Governmental policy would critically revolve around efforts aimed at abolishing existing frontier barriers as far possible and to ensure non-discriminatory treatment in the entire West European market'.

For domestic reasons, the government stressed that the developments in Swedish EC policy (including its primary aim) were to take account of the SEM, rather than any specific desire to apply for full membership. At first sight, it seemed that Swedish policy towards the Community had been modernised rather than fundamentally altered and the revised policy stance could remain relatively intact for the foreseeable future. Yet, the change in policy was more significant than first appeared, especially in the context of the 'Swedish Diamond'. First, the fact that the government raised the possibility that the country should consider becoming an EC member (in the 1987 policy paper) was an acknowledgment that the Diamond's third point (economic interdependence) was now the central feature of EC policy. The only question was once again whether this aspect of the Diamond could override another - namely the considerations of a credible neutrality policy.

Second, that the Diamond's third point was also interfering with wider deeply-held concepts of national sovereignty and in particular, another variable of the Diamond - namely the country's integrative and consensual democracy.[34] In January 1988, the Under-Secretary of State for Foreign Affairs, Pierre Shori highlighted the movement in governmental thinking when he officially stated that the fear of loss of economic sovereignty was now groundless and that majority voting and the acceptance of EC legislation was now acceptable. It was now only the concerns over neutrality that made full membership inappropriate.[35] From June 1988, the government, with parliamentary consent, decided that all new national legislation relevant to the SEM programme would be considered with a view to voluntary harmonisation with Community law. The government was *de facto* shadowing Community legislation and imposing voluntary constraints on its freedom and scope to legislate in certain SEM-related areas. In typical thorough fashion and in line with Sweden's integrative and consensual democracy, the government created 'a panoply of centrally coordinated organisations' in order to facilitate consensus on EC issues - directly recognising the rising importance of the EC for domestic policy-making.[36]

Next, the third point also had ramifications for the Diamond's second aspect - Sweden's corporate model. Swedish firms, multinationals and consequently the SAF and SI were increasingly concerned about the country's position outside the emerging SEM and the potential negative impact of a 'Fortress Europe' on Swedish trade with the Community. At the same time, the trade union movement was also beginning to consider the implications of the SEM programme for the country's future international competitiveness, its welfare model and its influence on the future labour relations within the Social

Democratic government. In short, the role of key interest groups in championing the need for closer integration with the Community was also a central aspect in changing the Carlsson government's policy towards the Community (see Chapter Seven). The seeds of policy change were planted, consciously or unconsciously, by the 1987 policy paper and albeit to a limited extent, allowed for the sacred March 1971 policy position on the EC issue to be modernised. It would now be easier for the government to open the debate again. After all, the issue had been discussed recently. There had been information dissemination to the Parliament and the Swedish political elite. From now on, the Carlsson government could, with some credibility, use the EC's dynamism to initiate a future policy discussion.[37]

Yet, the Community remained a peripheral and almost non-existent issue in the autumn 1988 general election campaigns. The Moderate Party was the only party to canvass membership under the party slogan 'Sweden Needs Europe More than Europe Needs Sweden', but even then (compared to taxation reform and privatisation), it was not a major campaign theme for the Conservatives. In any event, they were to remain in opposition. Ingvar Carlsson declared on polling night that his re-elected minority Social Democratic government would not consider EC membership before the completion of the SEM in 1992 at the earliest.[38] In addition, the Left Party leader, Lars Werner, also stated that further drifts towards closer EC cooperation or full membership would be opposed by a coalition of his party, the Greens and (at this time anyway) the Centre Party.[39] Probably the most notable outcome of the 1988 election was the strengthening of the anti-EC camp - with the introduction of the Greens to the Riksdag - even if the EC issue was not at the forefront of the election campaigns.[40] The Greens illustrated their opposition to the EC by introducing some 36 motions urging the government to halt harmonisation with the Community in their first parliamentary term alone.[41]

Nevertheless, what Ross labels as the 'Politics of Economic Realism', were beginning to tell on Swedish policy-making. Overall, the Diamond's third (economic interdependence) point was strengthened by the parallel and ongoing efforts within EFTA to adopt a common negotiating stance towards the Community. The economic considerations arising from the SEM programme also impinged upon the integrative democracy and corporate model points of the 'Swedish Diamond'. It was only, as always, the need to maintain the Diamond's fourth point - a credible neutrality policy - that restricted the government's freedom of manoeuvre on the EC issue. In contrast to 1971, the supplementary arguments of maintaining national sovereignty and domestic policies in order to reinforce neutrality policy, had been undermined by the onset of the SEM programme. To a large extent, this had been recognised indirectly in the government's 1987 policy paper. The issue was, not as to whether sovereignty was affected (as the decision in June 1988 to shadow SEM legislation acknowledged that this was already the case), but rather how much sovereignty was now affected and to what degree, sovereignty could, after all, be protected. In effect, the four points of the 'Swedish Diamond' were shifting in emphasis.

The 1989 Delors Initiative

Although the Luxembourg Process officially continued, it was clear to all sides that the 1984 Agreement was too limited to cope with the new dynamics of the post Single European Act (SEA) Community. Nearly all the EFTA countries accepted that EC-EFTA cooperation would need to be further strengthened and expanded. In particular, the Austrian government seemed to be moving further. It shifted rapidly from a position of autonomous adaptation to favouring a full membership application during winter 1987-88. This was symbolically and psychologically important. A fellow EFTA neutral seemed to be willing to set a precedent within the Association.

It was with some surprise and even relief, on the part of the EFTA countries, that Jacques Delors, the President of the Commission, initiated the next logical step in EC-EFTA relations. On 17 January 1989 in a speech to the European Parliament, he suggested that the Community and the EFTA countries look for,

> 'a new, more structured partnership with common decision-making and administrative institutions to make our activities more effective and to highlight the political dimension of our cooperation in the economic, social, financial and cultural spheres'.[42]

The 'Delors initiative' as it became known, envisaged a bloc association based on the 'two pillars' of the Community and EFTA and was radical in several ways. First, Delors was in practice not just calling for the further institutionalising of EC-EFTA cooperation 'by switching from a sectoral to a global approach', but the offer also implied the creation of a common regime between the two organisations with cooperation on a broad rather than piecemeal level.[43] Internal EFTA cooperation would need substantial strengthening for, as Delors recognised, the only other alternative would be 'a system based on Community rules, which could be extended - in specific areas - to interested EFTA countries'.[44]

The initiative by Delors was welcomed in the EFTA capitals, including Stockholm. At EFTA's Oslo Summit (14-15 March 1989), the member countries agreed to take up the challenge, strengthen their internal decision-making structures and called for negotiations that would facilitate:

'the fullest possible realisation of free movement of goods, services, capitals and persons with the aim of creating a dynamic and homogeneous European Economic Space'.[45]

There were of course, divisions within EFTA especially over whether such cooperation would lead to the formation of an EC-EFTA customs union.[46] The Carlsson government in line with the previous 1988 Riksdag decision, was willing to go further than most in adapting to the Community. Indeed, the governmental view was reinforced by the downturn in the Swedish economy during 1989 which highlighted the need for a European-wide restructuring of market access to ensure the future competitiveness of the country's firms. As a result of an informal EC-EFTA ministerial meeting in Brussels (20 March 1989), a joint High-Level Steering Group (HLSG) was created (April 1989) to examine the scope, content and institutional potential of future cooperation. In particular, this action was warmly received in Stockholm. It convinced the ruling Social Democrats that there was a strong political commitment to the EES on the Community's part.

The Commission's motives for embarking on further EC-EFTA cooperation were relatively transparent.[47] Apart from the obvious fact that each side was the other's largest trading partner and the Community had an implicit economic interest in consolidating economic ties with the Association, the EEA (as it later became known) was also attractive for political reasons. Not only were there key member states with a direct stake in securing closer relations with EFTA, such as the UK or Denmark, but the Commission also viewed the EEA process as a means of avoiding any future applications for full membership until the Community had completed its present stage of deepening and the SEM at the very least. The Commission also feared that in the longer term, the absorption of the neutral EFTA countries could jeopardise its future evolution into a genuine political entity with a common foreign policy and place considerable strains on its existing decision-making machinery. Hence as Schwok argues,

'to keep the EFTA countries outside the organisation by granting them the 1992 internal market was a way to preserve the very identity and existence of the Community'.[48]

For the Community at least, the EEA was a delaying tactic and a way of deterring the EFTA countries (at least in the short-term) from applying for full membership in a reaction to the SEM programme. The details of the EEA was to be extensively negotiated with the EFTA partners. Broadly, the development of the EEA fell into three phases:

- *Fact-finding talks* (March-October 1989). Five working groups were established by the HLSG to examine the free movement of goods, the free movement of services and capital, the free movement of persons, the flanking and horizontal policies and institutional and legal questions respectively. The main outcome was identification of the Community's relevant 'acquis'.

- *Exploratory talks* (December 1989-March 1990). During this period the objectives of the EEA were agreed. The Community outlined its three governing principles, namely a coordinated approach requiring EFTA to act as one pillar, a reasonable balance of benefits and advantages and that the EEA's institutional arrangements must not jeopardise the EC's decision-making autonomy.[49] In January 1990, Delors further qualified the limitations of the Community's position by claiming that that although there would need to be an 'osmosis' between the Community and the Association to enable EFTA's interests to be accommodated within EC decision-making, this would stop short of joint decision-making which would imply full Community membership.[50]

- *Formal EC-EFTA Negotiations* (June 1990-March 1993). These talks were continually delayed. A number of areas of dispute appeared - most notably, derogations from the Community's 'acquis' (at least initially); arrangements on Fish, Transit and the creation of an EEA Cohesion Fund; the nature of the EEA's institutional arrangements (especially the level of EFTA influence on EC decisions i.e. 'decision-shaping' or 'decision-making') and the EEA's legal apparatus. The European Court of Justice formally objected to the role of any EEA Court between December 1991-April 1992. Even when the EEA agreement was finalised, the fiasco did not end. On 6 December 1992, the ratification procedure (by all 19 relevant parliaments) was de-railed by the Swiss people's rejection of the EEA in a referendum, leading to parts of the agreement having to be renegotiated to take account of Switzerland's exclusion. The agreement was eventually signed in Oporto (2 May 1992) and came into force a year later than the SEM (1 January 1994).

Swedish Frustration with the EEA: Moving out of the Slow Lane

At face value, the advantages of the EEA for all the EFTA countries was clear to see. The EEA would 'create a single market in Western Europe: a market of some 380 million'[51] and in practice, would extend the majority of the SEM programme to cover the EFTA countries. It established 'a dynamic and homogeneous integrated structure based on common rules and equal conditions for competition' and even more significantly, was 'intended to give fresh impetus to the privileged relationship' between the Community and the EFTA countries.[52] Indeed, the signed copy of the EEA agreement contained 13 different languages, some 15,000 pages and weighed around 100 kgs.[53] However, this did not mean the complete adoption of the four freedoms by the EFTA countries, but merely the fullest possible realisation of them and crucially the establishment of an advanced free trade area, rather than a full customs union. The EEA agreement also had several major exceptions to free trade and did not, for the most part, include agriculture. None the less, the EEA was a comprehensive agreement. It went 'beyond purely economic cooperation and also covers areas of more direct interest to the public'.[54] It included 'flanking and horizontal policies' incorporating the environment, research and development, education, social and consumer policies and a sophisticated institutional structure to administer the EEA.

The Swedish position regarding the development of the EEA was two-fold. On the one hand, the Carlsson government had 'first and foremost chosen to manage relations with the European Community in an EFTA-context ... Sweden has opted for a broad approach to West European integration'.[55] The Social Democratic government therefore welcomed Delors' ideas of a structured partnership and accepted the concept of a common EFTA multilateral approach to the following negotiations. The government's Advisory Council, for example, concluded that the strengthening of EFTA would be the first priority. It stressed that a common EFTA (and especially Nordic approach) to the SEM was essential to avoid the emergence of discrimination between the EFTA countries. This would officially take account of 'the two compounds' of Swedish EC policy - the protection of neutrality and the accommodation of the country's corporate model.

On the other hand, the government's priorities were to gain access to the SEM and the Community's ensuing decisions shaping it. As both Anita Gradin, the Minister for Foreign Trade and Kjell-Olof Feldt, the Minister of Finance, recognised in December 1989, the government's overriding priority was gaining 'the fullest possible participation in the four freedoms'.[56] Swedish policy was solidly within the framework established by the 1988 parliamentary decision. The government stressed simultaneously the need to take part in the SEM 'as far as possible' and that 'neutrality is incompatible with membership' of the Community. This led to a dual-pronged strategy (from 1988) which combined multilateral coordination at the EFTA level and unilateral adaptation to Community rules. Sweden was, along with Austria, the EFTA country with the fewest specific demands regarding the EEA and had minimal objections to the Community's 'four freedoms'. The only major and common concern on the part of the Carlsson government revolved around the loss of sovereignty in a number of policy areas, such as competition policy and public procurement, under any

EEA regime.[57] In short, the undercurrents emanating from the 'Swedish Diamond' remained an important influence on policy-makers.

The Carlsson government therefore took the decision that its strategy would be exploratory and use a variety of multilateral, bilateral and unilateral approaches. Where there were common EFTA or even Nordic interests, such as on issues relating to social policy or the free movement of people, which affected the Nordic Labour Market and/or Passport Union, a multilateral approach was adopted. In other cases, Sweden simply unilaterally adopted EC legislation to mirror the SEM.[58] Stålvant & Hamilton estimated in 1991 that the majority of the Commission's White Paper could be unilaterally adopted.

Carlsson also put in place political and administrative structures to facilitate this dual-strategy. At a governmental level, he streamlined its cross-departmental organisational network and established an ambitious set-up which was unique in Swedish constitutional history.[59] A new sub-committee was formed within the government, chaired by the Prime Minister and responsible for framing 'integration policy'; its high-profile indicating the rising status of EC relations. Besides the Prime Minister, the sub-committee included the Foreign Minister and the Ministers of Foreign Trade, Finance and Industry. It was assisted by a select group of high-level Under-Secretaries of State representing the core ministries. In addition, another 25 issue-specific working groups were established to examine the consequences for Sweden of the SEM's development. These were coordinated by the chief Swedish EEA negotiator, Ulf Dinkelspiel, who chaired the policy-preparatory group composing of all the chairmen of the 25 working groups and took charge of the EC/EFTA negotiations. A Secretariat for Integration Questions was also created - responsible for internal adjustments and the implementation of domestic integration policy - which complemented the function of Division 1 of the Department of Foreign Trade (which dealt with external contacts).

In addition to these comprehensive inter-ministerial arrangements, the government also established an Advisory Council, whose members came from key industrial and corporate bodies. The size and extent of these administrative changes illustrated the seriousness with which the government considered the challenge that the SEM presented for Swedish policy-making. In effect, the Carlsson government's decision to shadow EC legislation in order to achieve all the benefits of the SEM meant that it was necessary to take the Community's 'acquis' into account constantly. This was unprecedented in the Swedish case, especially given the need for policy-makers to (officially) maximise national independence in order to maintain a credible neutrality policy and that there was a lack of contractual recognition between Sweden and the Community. In short, a comprehensive review of decision-making procedures was undertaken.

The extent of the operation was officially outlined in an unusual decree adopted by the government as early as June 1988. It stressed the need for a

'Community consciousness' and advised that every expert inquiry or Royal Commission working in fields relating to the SEM would 'account for the proposal's relevance to corresponding EC regulations and Commission proposals'. If its decision diverged from that of an EC regulation then the body would have to stipulate its reasons and motives.[60]

The importance of these new structures should not be under-estimated. In his study of the participation of Swedish national officials in meetings with EC representatives in Brussels between 1985-91, Ekengren argues that a so-called 'contact-zone' was created between them and their EC counterparts which facilitated a more systematic approach to diplomatic relations between the two sides.[61] The Foreign Ministry assumed overall responsibility for conducting negotiations with the Community on the EEA. For the most part, it used the opportunity to centralise Swedish decision-making as regards EC-related matters. According to Ekengren, these structural changes in Swedish-EC relations can be interpreted at the macro-level 'as the beginning of a new era for the Swedish state. In relation to the Community, the state was given a new role - the role of the outward-looking centralised European negotiator'.[62] In addition, these structures were useful in acclimatising national officials to the demands of EC cooperation throughout the Swedish national administration.

The Carlsson government soon began to air the first elements of disillusionment with the EEA. The preliminary phase during which fact-finding and exploratory talks took place were protracted - diminishing initial Swedish enthusiasm for the EEA project. The EEA after all, was only ever going to be an advanced free trade area, and not even as ambitious as the customs union that Swedish government had called for some 20 years earlier. Moreover, by late 1989 events were unfolding which allowed the Social Democratic government to consider alternatives other than the EEA, which had previously been perceived as impractical. In reaction to the SEM, the Austrian government had been intensively deliberating (from December 1988) the possibilities of the country becoming an EC member. This was always the primary policy objective, which the coordination of the EFTA countries was supposed to prise from the Community. In particular, the Austrians extensively debated the relationship between EC membership and neutrality and still went on to lodge a full membership application (17 July 1989).

This was important for Sweden for political reasons. The Austrian government had chosen to apply when 'the changes in the old European political contours were not yet evident'.[63] Austria's submission was chiefly explained as a reorientation of EC policy, an expression of the concern over the speed of European integration and in part and related to the other two, an implicit recognition that the EEA concept did not provide a sufficiently credible alternative to full membership. The EEA was thus deemed a transitional vehicle rather than a substitute for EC membership. The Austrian application did however, still include a specific reference to neutrality. This had important implications for governmental thinking. First, Austria represented the first EFTA state to break ranks and was especially significant given the expanded EEA concept was reaching fruition. Austria had chosen not to wait for the EEA and had set a precedent - formally recognising that full membership was the superior option. Second, the Austrian application provoked a major debate in Sweden and left several senior politicians and experts, such as Sverker Åström, 'marvelling at the temerity of the Austrians in applying' especially as their neutrality was thought to offer far less freedom of action than that of Sweden.[64] The sacrosanct nature of Swedish neutrality was now itself in question. The incompatibility of neutrality policy with EC membership (which after all was the dominant element of the 'Swedish Diamond') was now seriously challenged from an economic perspective. In December 1989, with the EEA negotiations imminent, the Moderates and Liberals in the Riksdag requested a study of the conditions for Swedish EC membership, with particular reference to the consequences of membership on the country's neutrality.[65]

It was during spring 1990, that events and the possibilities of considering a full membership application moved rapidly. Officially, the Carlsson government remained committed to the completion of an EEA agreement and that neutrality and full EC membership were still incompatible. In May 1990, Ulf Dinkelspiel, for instance, continued to stress that there was strong support in Sweden for pursuing the 'third way' of the EEA between full membership and isolation.[66]

According to Ulf Dinkelspiel, the government was still in favour of an EEA agreement with 'as broad a coverage as possible'. He also stated the government's support for concentrating on exceptions from the agreed starting point as the basis for future EEA negotiations as this 'would be quicker than testing the acceptability of each piece of legislation one by one'.[67] However, a number of problematic areas were identified by him. Any attempts by the EEA to include 'a political dialogue' would need thorough examination by the Swedes. Dinkelspiel was suspicious of any moves relating to foreign policy cooperation. Equally, it would not be 'politically acceptable' for the EEA to include any 'flanking policies' which would 'lower environmental protection and health and safety to Community norms'. In addition, he outlined Sweden's emphasis on 'genuine participation in the EEA decisions in substance and in form. Sweden would seek involvement at all stages of the legislative process'.[68]

However, the government was frustrated with the EEA's slow progress and several elements of the government started to question the overall benefits of the EEA concept.[69] During the exploratory EEA negotiations in 1989-early 1990, it was increasingly clear to the government that there could be an imbalance between the benefits of the EEA and the obligations imposed by it upon Sweden.

The EEA would and did include substantial concessions on the part of the Swedes as regards their national sovereignty and their general reservations surrounding supranationalism. In short, Sweden would have to adopt large parts of the Community's 'acquis communautaire', amounting to some 12,000 pages of existing EC legislation. The country would have to also accept many of the principles pertaining from EC law as they would be implicit within the effective functioning of many of the EEA's SEM related policy areas.[70] The EEA would also require the establishment of an EFTA supranational pillar to govern the Association's remit within common EEA policy and the creation of, for example, an EFTA competition surveillance authority to administer the EU-based EEA competition policy. Ironically, the Carlsson government was, albeit to a limited degree, confronted with many of the same dilemmas as those arising from full membership. The EEA required that Sweden accept supranationalism and constraints on national independence in many areas of policy.

In one sense, the EEA seemed to be even worse for Sweden. The government was frustrated with initially, the slowness of the negotiations on, and then with the nature of, the EEA's future institutional arrangements. At the start of the negotiations, Ulf Dinkelspiel stated that the degree of adequate parallelism and access to EC decision-making would be the '$64,000 question'. In practice, it soon became clear to the Swedish delegation - as a result of Delors' comments on limitations of an EC-EFTA osmosis and various statements on the three principles governing the Community's perspectives on the EEA - that the Commission sought to maintain its decision-making autonomy almost completely. In May 1990, for example and after some delay in order to take account of the European Parliament's demands that the EFTA countries would only obtain limited participation rights, the Commission submitted a preliminary negotiating position to the EC Council of Ministers, (which as one of its four principles) stipulated that there could be no compromise as regards EC decision-making. This was accepted by the Council of Ministers (18 June 1990) and formed a major element of the Commission's negotiating mandate. In effect, the Commission was only willing to allow the EFTA countries a consultative 'decision-shaping', rather than a full 'decision-making' role when the Community was devising SEM-related legislation.

The frustration on the part of the Swedish government was further reinforced by the fact that it held the EFTA Presidency during the first half of 1990 and was responsible for spearheading the EC-EFTA progress on the EEA. Anita Gradin, speaking at the EC-EFTA Brussels summit (19 December 1989) as the incumbent EFTA President, mentioned the significance of 'some kind of conceptual breakthrough' by June 1990. Whilst stressing existing progress, she paid attention to the lack of it in key areas and that 'genuine participation in a joint EEA decision process is of crucial importance for the political acceptability of a wide-reaching EC-EFTA integration treaty'.[71] She highlighted that any successful EEA blueprint must cover three broad areas - the scope and structure of the EEC agreement, lists of derogations and transitions due to fundamental national interests and legal and principles for future cooperation.

Yet, little progress was made during the last stages of the exploratory talks (March 1990). More attention was directed by the EFTA governments towards the changes in Eastern Europe. It took until the EFTA Heads of Government summit in Göteborg (13-14 June 1990), celebrating 30 years of the Association and to which the EC Commission Vice-President, Frans Andreissen, was invited, to get the formal negotiations launched and the talks back on track. By now it was obvious to Swedish policy-makers that the asymmetry between the EEA obligations and benefits meant that the arrangement would fail to safeguard future long-term interests. It 'infringed Swedish economic sovereignty, without allowing proportionate influence on EU decisions. In practice, rather than pacifying political concerns, the EEA threatened Swedish concepts of independence'.[72]

Domestic developments also helped change governmental perceptions of the EEA. Swedish business and leading industrialists from 1989 were openly countenancing that the EEA was only the bare minimum and that full membership was now preferable. In the same year, the SAF launched a comprehensive campaign to influence public opinion, including later (on 8 May 1991), a campaign concert to commemorate the 40th anniversary of the Schuman Plan - attended by 40,000 Swedes.[73] Both the employers' federation and the major trade unions raised the issue of attracting inward investment to counter the country's emerging economic problems and to stem outwards investment to the Community, which had dramatically increased since 1989 (see Chapter Seven).

As a result of these pressures and in response to increasing frustration with the prospects of the EEA, Carl Bildt and Bengt Westerberg, leaders of the Moderate and Liberal parties respectively, raised the domestic stakes. They announced in May 1990 (in connection with a pro-Community speech given by the Danish Foreign Minister Ulf Ellemann-Jensen in Stockholm), that their parties would now raise the issue of full membership at the next general election in September 1991 and would demand the submission of a full membership application by any successive government. This in turn put the spotlight on the Social Democratic government and required a response to take account of the changing domestic political realities.[74]

The response was rapid. On 27 May 1990, the Prime Minister had published an article in *Dagens Nyheter*. Despite its title - 'EC membership will become impossible - Sweden cannot be a member of the Community if political union becomes a reality' - and that the Prime Minister specifically stated that 'first we want the EEA. Then watching what happens in Europe and the EC, we will decide whether we want to seek membership', the article was interpreted somewhat differently. Certainly, it implied that the debate on the EC was formally re-opened and that a change in the policy of the Social Democratic Party was now being contemplated. However, in the article, Carlsson also stipulated two main conditions for Swedish EC membership:

- that prior to any application there would have to be a new security order, with alliances dissolved and lasting peace guaranteed.

- there would be no Swedish participation whatsoever in a political union.

Yet, ironically despite support from the Centre Party, these comments were either not taken seriously or openly criticised as lacking ambition. It was with little surprise then that the domestic debate on the EC warmed up during summer 1990 (by Swedish standards). It slipped further into the political limelight with the announcement (as a footnote in an austerity package - 26 October 1990), that the Carlsson government now intended to apply for full membership (see Chapter Seven). Sweden's drive from the slow lane of European integration and being content with EEA participation was now over - the country was now accelerating towards full membership.

As this chapter has argued the EEA's slow development was an integral part of the change in the pace and direction of governmental policy towards the EC. By mid-1990, Sweden's commitment to the EEA was on the wane and was made worse, and reinforced by, the problems with the EEA negotiations in September 1990. As part of the opening statement by EFTA at the start of the formal negotiations (20 June 1990), the EFTA countries stressed two specific issues - the number of permanent derogations from the Community's 'acquis' and the reluctance of the Community to enter into substantive talks on the institutional arrangements for the EEA. Negotiations made little headway during the next two months and the HNLG (17-18 October) proved to be in Pedersen's words 'a downright disaster' with no progress on either issue at all.[75] In the light of Sweden's movement towards full membership, the Carlsson government informally signalled to its EFTA partners throughout September-October 1990, that unless rapid progress was made, the whole EEA process would be overtaken, reduced in significance by a series of membership applications and would become a prelude to membership.[76] Although at an informal meeting of the EFTA ministers (23 October) in an attempt to break the impasse with the Community, it was decided to withdraw the demands for permanent derogations and replace them with transition periods, safeguard arrangements and non-discriminatory measures, this concession was conditional on the Community accepting the need for a genuine common decision-making mechanism. This of course, looked equally unlikely and reinforced Swedish views that the EEA would be unsatisfactory. Three days later, the government announced that it would be seeking full membership.[77]

Conclusion

The EEA proposal was eventually submitted for parliamentary approval. Due to its size and complexity, the proposal was 3,000 pages in length, making it the largest single government bill ever to be placed before the Riksdag. A special committee was appointed to examine the EEA treaty. However, the almost universal attitude of the main parliamentary parties in favour of the EEA ensured that all of its members - except for Gudrun Schyman of the Left Party - voted to approve the treaty. The Riksdag, given the recommendation of the Committee, likewise consented to Swedish participation in the EEA with an equally large majority. Of course, to most members of the Parliament, approval was now perceived as 'a decisive step towards full EC membership'.[78]

The EEA agreement came into operation on 1 January 1994, some 12 months later than originally planned. In many ways, the EEA was another move forward in Swedish-EU relations. The country remained an EEA participant (on the EFTA side) until it joined the EU as a full member on 1 January 1995. Most of all, Swedish business gained access to most aspects of the SEM as a result of EEA membership before full accession.[79] The country benefited from being part of the most advanced free trade area arrangement that could be realistically negotiated with the Community by non-member states. The EEA was, despite its weaknesses, a clear improvement on the industrial free trade area provided for by the 1972 FTA and the later Luxembourg Process and reinforced the importance of the economic interdependence point of the 'Swedish Diamond'. Yet, the Carlsson government regarded the EEA with mixed views. Overall, it was deemed to be a disappointment and as a 'lame duck' by late 1990. Rather than being a substitute for membership and as a deterrent to future EC applications, the slowness of the negotiations designing it, combined with its obvious conceptual weaknesses, meant that the EEA process acted as a catalyst for full membership in the Swedish case.

For both the Carlsson government and the European Commission, the advantages of the EEA gradually disappeared. The agreement was attractive to the ruling Social Democrats because it facilitated access to the SEM programme whilst being compatible with neutrality policy and to a lesser extent, with concerns over supranationalism and the protection of national sovereignty.[80] However, by late 1990, it was clear to the Carlsson government that the EEA imposed such large obligations and at the same time, provided for proportionately less influence on the EC decision-making. Even though the Swedish government had from the time of the December 1987 policy paper accepted that national sovereignty would be constrained by EEA participation, this was conditional on gaining limited derogations and sufficient influence on EC decisions. During the ensuing EEA negotiations, the Commission made it equally clear that it would not be entirely forthcoming on either count. At the same time, as the Carlsson government was losing interest in the EEA so was the Commission. By 1990, Delors' original rationale of deterring membership applications had failed, whilst the difficult negotiations raised problematic questions for the Commission about differences between full and EEA membership.

The EEA imposed limitations on national independence. It required participating governments to accept supranational decision-making - such as a multilateral surveillance authority to govern the EFTA pillar of the EEA's competition policy. Two of the Social Democratic government's original arguments for opposing full membership as stipulated in the March 1971 Declaration (which remained the foundation of policy even in 1990) were now compromised. The Carlsson government had accepted, albeit to a limited extent, supranationalism and limitations on its sovereignty as part of the EEA agreement; then (on these two issues) there seemed little variation between EEA and full membership.

For the Carlsson government, the main difference between EEA and full membership now revolved entirely around the neutrality arguments. However, to some degree, even the compatibility of Swedish EEA participation and the maintenance of a credible neutrality policy was far from obvious. According to official neutrality doctrine, a credible neutral stance could only be maintained if the government reserved as much freedom of manoeuvre in domestic and foreign policy-making as possible in order to reinforce its predictability and reduce potential aggressors. The fact that the EEA was a free trade area and did not include a common EEA Common Customs Tariff (CCT) and policy (CCP) was a case in point. Yet, if EEA membership necessitated governmental acceptance of a degree of institutional supranationalism, the 'acquis' and subsequent limitations on its sovereignty, then the EEA itself had some negative implications for the practical implementation of neutrality policy. In one sense, the EEA itself reinforced the growing influence of the Diamond's third (economic interdependence) point and partially downgraded its fourth point (neutrality) which stipulated that full membership was inappropriate. The EEA meant that, in reality, Sweden was halfway on the road to ensuring that full membership and neutrality were compatible.

However, these arguments were in many ways academic. The revolutions engulfing Eastern Europe in 1989-90 and the virtual disintegration of the Soviet Union and the Warsaw Pact by 1991 meant that the traditional constraints imposed by neutrality also disappeared. As Chapter Seven illustrates, security policy itself was revised in response to alterations in the external strategic environment. In short, from late 1990-early 1991, neutrality was considered in a more flexible light and with it, governmental preferences for the EEA over full membership were removed. From this time, there was little difference between EEA and full membership in terms of obligations, apart from the fact that as a full member Sweden would enjoy the economic benefits of membership and, at the same time, maximise its political influence on the EC decision-making (the latter the EEA could not provide).

Notes

[1] Pedersen, T. (1994) *European Union and the EFTA Countries,* Pinter, London, p. 27.

[2] Ross, J. F. L. (1991) Sweden, the European Community, and the Politics of Economic Realism, *Cooperation and Conflict,* XXXVI, 3, p. 119.

[3] Viklund, D. (1989) *Sweden and the European Community: Trade Cooperation and Policy Issues,* Swedish Institute, Stockholm, p. 32.

[4] For further details see Pedersen, T. (1988) *The Wider Western Europe: EC Policy Towards the EFTA Countries,* Royal Institute of International Affairs (RIIA) Discussion Paper, No. 10, RIIA, London.

[5] EFTA, (1977) Declaration of the Meeting of the EFTA Heads of Government and Ministers, Vienna, 13 May 1977, *Seventeenth Annual Report of the European Free Trade Association 1976-77,* EFTA Secretariat, Geneva, p. 53.

[6] For an extensive discussion of the Luxembourg Process see Gstöhl, S. (1996) The Nordic Countries and the EEA in Miles, L. (ed.) *The European Union and the Nordic Countries,* Routledge, London, pp. 47-54.

[7] *Agence Europe,* 9-10 April 1984, p. 1.

[8] Op. cit., Gstöhl (1996) p. 50.

[9] For a discussion of the three phases as understood by Hermann's foreign policy model see Jerneck, M. (1993) Sweden - the reluctant European? in Tiilikainen, T. & Petersen, I. Damgaard, (eds.) *The Nordic Countries and the EC,* Copenhagen Political Studies Press, Copenhagen, pp. 23-42.

[10] See Foreign Affairs Committee Report, (1984-1985), 2405, SOU, Stockholm.

[11] Church, C. (1990) The Politics of Change: EFTA and the Nordic Countries' Responses to the EC in the early 1990s, *Journal of Common Market Studies,* XXVIII, 4, June, p. 418.

[12] De Clerq, W. (1987) *Speech at the EC-EFTA Ministerial Meeting, 20 March 1987, Interlaken,* Commission of the EC, Brussels, pp. 5-6.

[13] The Social Democratic governments were by this time led by Ingvar Carlsson, after the assassination of Olof Palme in 1986.

[14] Op. cit., Gstöhl (1996) p. 52.

[15] Church, C. (1989) 1992 and the EFTA Countries, *European Access,* 4, August, p. 14.

[16] Schwok, R. (1991) EC-EFTA Relations in Hurwitz, L. & Lequesne, C. (eds.) *The State of the European Community, Volume I: Policies, Institutions and Debates in the Transition Years*, Longman, London, pp. 330-1.

[17] Åström, S. (1988) Sweden's EC Dilemma, *World Today*, 43, 11, pp. 191-3.

[18] Council of Europe, (1987) DOC CM (87) 216, Council of Europe, Strasbourg.

[19] For an appraisal of EFTA's economic interdependence with the Community see Nell, P. G. (1990) EFTA in the 1990s: The Search for a New Identity, *Journal of Common Market Studies*, XXVIII, 4, June, pp. 321-59.

[20] Stålvant, C.-E., & Hamilton, C. B. (1991) Sweden in Wallace, H. (ed.) *The Wider Western Europe - Reshaping the EC/EFTA Relationship*, Pinter/RIIA, London, pp. 194-5.

[21] Riksdagen (1987) *Sverige och den västeuropeiska integrationen*, Proposition 1987-1988, 17/12/1987, Riksdagen, Stockholm, p. 1and Riksdagen, (1988) *Utrikesutskottets betänkande 1987-88*, 21/4/1988, Riksdagen, Stockholm.

[22] Ibid., Riksdagen (1987) p. 1.

[23] Op. cit., Stålvant & Hamilton (1991) p. 201.

[24] Hamilton, C. B. (1991) *The Nordic EFTA Countries' Option: Seeking Community Membership or a Permanent EEA-Accord*, Discussion Paper No. 524, Centre For Economic Policy Research, London, p. 4.

[25] Op. cit., Riksdagen, (1987) p. 24.

[26] Op. cit., Riksdagen, (1987) p. 3.

[27] Op. cit., Stålvant & Hamilton (1991) p. 201.

[28] Riksdagen (1987) *Foreign Affairs Committee 1986-87*, 18, Riksdagen, Stockholm.

[29] Taken from the Riksdag's decision of May 1988.

[30] Stålvant, C.-E. (1990) Rather a Market than a Home, but preferably a Home Market: Swedish Policies Facing Changes In Europe, in Laursen, F. (ed.) *EFTA and the EC: Implications of 1992*, European Institute of Public Administration, Maastricht, p. 150.

[31] Taken from a speech given by C. Bildt at the Swedish Institute of Foreign Affairs, 13 May 1987 see op. cit., Stålvant & Hamilton (1991) p. 202.

[32] Sweden did none the less go on to peg the Krona to the ECU in 1991.

[33] Riksdagen, (1988) *Foreign Affairs Committee 1987-88*, 26, Riksdagen, Stockholm, p. 19.

[34] Op. cit., Stålvant & Hamilton (1991) p. 206.

[35] Taken from Schori, P. (1988) *Sverige och den Västeuropeiska Integrationen*, AIC Seminar Report 29-30 January, UD, Stockholm.

[36] Jacobsson, R. (1990) *Sweden and West European Integration*, UD, Stockholm, p. 16.

[37] Indeed, an opinion poll published on 19 November 1987 indicated that Swedish attitudes towards full membership were softening with 36 percent in favour and 36 percent against EC accession.

[38] Arter, D. (1988) A Tale of Two Carlssons: The Swedish General Election of 1988, *Parliamentary Affairs*, 42, 1, pp. 84-101.

[39] Arter, D. (1990) The Swedish Leftist Party: Eco-Communism or Communist Echo?, *Parliamentary Affairs*, 44, 1, pp. 60-79.

[40] Hamilton, C. B. & Stålvant, C.-E. (1989) *A Swedish View of 1992*, RIIA Discussion Papers No. 13, Royal Institute of International Affairs, London, p. 19.
[41] Op. cit., Stålvant & Hamilton (1991) p. 204.
[42] Taken from *EFTA Bulletin*, (1990), 3, EFTA, Geneva, p. 1.
[43] For a more detailed analysis of the EEA see Gstöhl, S. (1994) EFTA and the European Economic Area, *Cooperation and Conflict*, 29, 4, December, pp. 333-66.
[44] Delors, J. (1989) Statement on the Broad Lines of Commission Policy, *Bulletin of the European Communities*, Supplement, 1/89, Commission of the ECs, Brussels, p. 17.
[45] European Free Trade Association, (1989) Final Declaration of the Meeting of the EFTA Heads of Government, Oslo, 14-15 March, *EFTA Information*, 6/89/SP, EFTA, Geneva, pp. 1-2.
[46] In Iceland, for instance, there was domestic political criticism that the Oslo Declaration was too adventurous, see op. cit., Church (1989) p. 15.
[47] For a summary of the Community's Policy towards EFTA see Laursen, F. (1990) The Community's Policy Towards EFTA: Regime Formation in the European Economic Space (EES), *Journal of Common Market Studies*, XXVIII, 4, June, pp. 303-25.
[48] Schwok, R. (1992) The European Free Trade Association: Revival or Collapse? in J. Redmond, (ed.) *The External Relations of the European Community*, Macmillan, London, p. 62.
[49] Andreissen, F. (1990) *Intervention of Frans Andreissen, Vice-President of the Commission, Ministerial Meeting with EFTA, Brussels, 19 December*, Commission of the ECs, Brussels, p. 1.
[50] Delors, J. (1990) Introduction of the Commission's Programme for 1990 by the President of the Commission of the European Communities, *Bulletin of the European Communities*, Supplement 1/90, Commission of the ECs, Brussels, p. 9.
[51] European Free Trade Association, (1992) *The EEA Agreement*, EEA 2/92, EFTA, Geneva, February, p. 1.
[52] European Free Trade Association, (1992) *European Economic Area*, Press Release 5944/92, Oporto, 2 May, EFTA, Geneva, p. 6.
[53] Norberg, S. (1992) The Agreement on a European Economic Area, *Common Market Law Review*, 29, p. 1171.
[54] Op. cit., EFTA (1992) p. 1.
[55] Gradin, A. (1989) West European Integration: The Swedish View, *European Affairs*, 4/89, Winter, p. 22.
[56] Feldt, K.-O. (1989) Nordic Cooperation, *European Affairs*, 4/89, Winter, p. 94.
[57] Op. cit., Pedersen (1994) p. 47.
[58] By May 1990, for instance, Sweden had already adopted 20 pieces of SEM legislation into national law.
[59] Op. cit., Hamilton & Stålvant (1989) p. 17.
[60] Riksdagen, (1988) *Kommittedirektiv*, 43, 20-6-1988, Riksdagen, Stockholm, p. 43.
[61] Ekengren, M. (1996) *Statsförvaltningens europeisering i tid och rum - En studie av den politiska tidens förändring till följd av EU-samarbetet*, Research Report 25, Swedish Institute of International Affairs, Stockholm.

[62] Ekengren, M. (1997) The Europeanization of State Administration - Adding the Time Dimension, *Cooperation and Conflict*, XXXI, 4, March, p. 393.

[63] For a more detailed discussion see Koch, K. (1994) Austria: The Economic Logic of Accession in Redmond, J. (ed.) *Prospective Europeans*, Harvester-Wheatsheaf, London, pp. 40-58.

[64] Huldt, B. (1994) Sweden and European Community-building 1945-92, in Harden, S. (ed.) *Neutral States and the European Community*, Brassey's, London, p. 116.

[65] The response was a study undertaken at the Swedish Institute of International Affairs - see Stålvant, C.-E. (1991) Sweden and the European Community in 1990, *CEPS Yearbook 1991*, CEPS, Brussels.

[66] Op. cit., House of Lords (1990) p. 21.

[67] Evidence given by Dinkelspiel to the British House of Lords Select Committee on the European Communities (22 May 1990) - House of Lords, (1990) *Relations Between the Community and EFTA*, 14th Report, HMSO, London, p. 11.

[68] There were differences in the EFTA camp on this issue. Dinkespiel implied that the normal machinery would be for the Commission and the EC Presidency to hold discussions with the EFTA Presidency. In contrast, the EFTA Secretariat, Switzerland and Austria were determined to see all the EFTA countries' delegations involved and that this constitued a real 'osmosis' - ibid., House of Lords (1990), p. 16.

[69] Ulf Dinkelspiel, the chief negotiator was especially concerned about the issue of reciprocity. Dinkelspiel flagged that there were problems in agreeing Swedish financial contributions to the proposed EEA Cohesion Fund and in gaining Spanish acceptance of levels of regional financial support. He especially mentioned that it would be difficult for the government to explain the need for Swedish financial contributions to the EEA if the Community was unwilling to give up its decision-making autonomy. They would in effect, be paying out money without having a say in its usage. For a fuller discussion of these asymmetry issues - see Wallace, H. (1991) *The Wider Western Europe*, Pinter, London.

[70] This started a process which led to the overhaul of Swedish competition policy - see Miles, L . (1995) Transforming Competition Policy: The Case of Sweden, in Davison, L., Fitzpatrick, E., & Johnson, D. (eds.) *The European Competitive Environment*, Butterworth-Heinemann, London, pp. 176-92

[71] European Free Trade Association, (1990) *EFTA Bulletin*, 4/99-1/90, XXX-XXXI, March 1990, p. 11.

[72] Miles, L. (1994) Sweden and Finland: From EFTA Neutrals To EU Members in Redmond, J. (ed.) *Prospective Europeans*, Harvester-Wheatsheaf, London, p. 70.

[73] For further details see Milner, H. (1994) *Rational Choice and Swedish Social Democracy*, Routledge, London, p. 208.

[74] The initiative by the non-socialist opposition provoked an immediate internal review of policy by the SAP leadership - taken from an interview with Conny Fredriksson, International Secretary of the SAP, in Stockholm on 16th September 1994.

[75] Op. cit., Pedersen (1994) p. 49.

[76] Taken from an interview with Jón Águstsson Valfells at the EFTA Secretariat building, Brussels in April 1994.

[77] Frustration with the EEA continued throughout 1991. Carl Bildt, for instance, urged the government to reach a bilateral interim agreement to pave the way for Swedish full membership of the EC on 31 July 1991. He argued that the slowness of the EEA negotiations meant that it would be operational too late to bring any benefits to Sweden before it eventually joined the Community - Buchan, D. (1991) EC and EFTA worry time is not on side of Economic Talks, *The Financial Times*, 31 July 1991, p. 2.

[78] Hadenius, S. (1997) *Swedish Politics During the 20th Century - Conflict and Consensus*, 4th edition, Swedish Institute, Stockholm, p. 163.

[79] There were several major studies of the benefits of the EEA to the Nordic Countries. All of which identified that the EEA would 'result in a substantial increase in trade in manufactured goods' - Lundberg, L. (1992) European Economic Integration and Nordic Countries Trade, *Journal of Common Market Studies*, XXX, 2, June, pp. 157-73. See also Lundberg, L. & Fagerberg, J. (eds.) (1993) *European Economic Integration: A Nordic Perspective*, Avebury, Aldershot; Norman, V. (1989) EFTA and Internal European Market, *Economic Policy*, 9; Norman, V. (1990) 1992 and EFTA in Winters, A. & Venables, A. (eds.) *European Integration: Trade and Industry*, Cambridge University Press, Cambridge; Weiser, T. (1992) European Economic Integration: Concepts, Measurements and Degree of Nordic Integration in Lyck, L. (ed.) *The Nordic Countries and the Internal Market of the EEC*, Handelshojskolens Forlag, Copenhagen.

[80] Taken from an interview with Conny Fredriksson, International Secretary of the SAP, in Stockholm on 16th September 1994.

6 The Nordic Dimension

Politicians and political scientists have often highlighted the potential of Nordic cooperation in offering the Scandinavian countries either a step towards, or an alternative to European integration. Swedish governments have intermittently stressed the benefits of such cooperation and, at various times, introduced initiatives aimed at expanding its scope. However, Nordic cooperation has also been criticised with equal regularity for failing to realise its potential and that in practice, it has proved to be something of a sideshow. Sundelius and Wiklund, for instance, have labelled it as 'the ugly duckling of regional cooperation',[1] whilst Andrén argued that it was best analysed through a 'cobweb theory' - whereby the cooperation represents a complex 'web' of social, political and economic contacts, rather than a vehicle for strong political initiative.[2]

The chapter will discuss the importance of intra-Nordic relations in influencing Swedish governmental perspectives on European integration. It is not the intention to provide a chronological study of Nordic cooperation, but rather to concentrate on its influence on Swedish thinking. The chapter will initially examine the dynamics underpinning Nordic cooperation and assess the legacy of post-war attempts at strengthening such collaboration on governmental attitudes. Despite its elaborate nature, it will be argued that such cooperation was progressively abandoned by Swedish governments as a substitute to European integration. Rather governments perceived Nordic cooperation as a catalyst to further Swedish interests on the continent. Its most important role has, and will be, in coordinating Nordic strategies towards the Community, which could continue throughout the 1990s and beyond.

The Dynamics of Nordic Cooperation

At first glance, cooperation between the Nordic countries seems a logical and natural progression. The five countries of Denmark, Finland, Iceland, Norway and Sweden share many common characteristics. They are relatively homogeneous, affluent, secularised, industrially advanced and with the exception of Denmark sparsely populated and also have similar political and social institutions, ideology and party systems.[3] As Solem noted as long ago as 1977, the

Nordic countries 'appear to be more integrated even economically, than any other group of independent states in the world'.[4]

In terms of converting these factors into practical measures and political initiatives, then this homogeneity should not be over-emphasised. The slow pace of Nordic integration can in part, be attributed to the variables operating between the countries and the political history of the Nordic region. First, there is the inherent rivalry between the two major and largest (in terms of population) countries - Denmark and Sweden - for leadership of the region. This 'major-major' rivalry has dominated the development of the region since the 16th century. Second, there has been the problem of friction between the two 'majors' and the three 'minors' (Finland, Iceland and Norway) within the Nordic grouping. Finnish, Icelandic and Norwegian governments have often stressed the protection of their national sovereignty, primarily because they are comparatively newly independent states, gaining full independence in 1917, 1944 and 1905 respectively. In particular, Norway has been wary of Swedish domination. It was joined in a union with Sweden as recently as 1814-1905 and twice during the last two decades of the union nearly went to war with its larger neighbour.[5] The outcome of this 'major-major' and 'major-minor' tension 'has been a problem of over-familiarity, which certainly breeds suspicion, if not contempt'.[6]

Given this tempestuous background, Nordic integration has taken a specific, if not necessarily unique, form. Supranationalism was traditionally rejected by all of the Nordic countries and therefore, their approach to integration was based upon the premise that political amalgamation between the countries would be resisted and that 'simple and easily-performed tasks and objectives serve as stepping stones for future strengthening of their organisation'.[7] This 'microintegration'[8] implies a cautious attitude towards integration in which 'the degree of multilateral implementation of regionalism is limited to that desired by the least regionally minded member'.[9]

Probably the most famous way of describing Nordic cooperation is Nils Andrén's 'cobweb theory'.[10] Although it should not be forgotten that Nordic cooperation represents only one aspect of international integration in which these countries participate, Andrén recognised that integration takes place at various levels and in differing forms. He argued (in 1967) that the Nordic variant was most active at 'rather low levels in the system' - in areas which have little significance towards integrating the countries in the vital areas of defence and security and of common institutions'.[11] It was, amongst other things, based upon a 'cooperation ideology' - a broad attachment to 'Nordism' and to a 'utilitarian-pragmatism' perspective that regional cooperation would bring material benefits.

Nordic cooperation was based on the universal rejection of supranationalism. It assumed that continuous consultation and coordination existed precisely because it did not impose any formal limitations on the sovereignty of participating states.[12] Nordic cooperation was developed by contact between existing national institutions and not through specially established supranational organs.[13] It is, for the most part, conceptualised as a process 'that reaches across the various national entities rather than links these with a higher, regional level of activity'.[14] At face value, Nordic cooperation provided the seeds of a practical alternative to European integration based on loose 'cobweb integration' - 'in which the significance and strength of a single thread or mesh is very small but the total result in many fields may be recognised as considerable'.[15] In a study by Thomas (1995), it was recognised that Andrén's 'cobweb theory' and Solem's 'microintegration' are still valuable as a framework for analysing the development of Nordic integration.[16]

Alternatively, Sundelius argued that Nordic cooperation can be gauged according to three dimensions - social, attitudinal and political integration. It also represents a useful paradigm for conceptualising the extent of Nordic links.[17] Social integration is broadly defined as the process whereby the societies become increasingly interconnected through growing transnational ties and networks. Attitudinal integration is characterised as the process whereby the Nordic peoples develop favourable attitudes towards their neighbours and to the joint management of regional problems. Finally, political integration is defined as the process whereby the public authorities increasingly manage national problems in conjunction. Overall, there has been broad improvement in all three aspects, which ensured that Nordic cooperation could act as a compliment to European integration and possibly even as a rival to it.

Yet, such cooperation was always deemed to be a limited affair, primarily due to the constraints voluntarily imposed upon it by its membership and sceptical governmental attitudes towards supranational regionalism covering any major policy areas. These variables ensured that Nordic cooperation, despite various political initiatives by its members and at differing periods of history to the contrary, was never able to realise its potential. Consequently, it was secondary to more ambitious integration on the European continent.[18]

Failures in Nordic Cooperation

Sweden, as Anderson notes, 'has been consistently permissive in her attitude toward Scandinavian regionalism'.[19] With an eye on her mainland European and British trading partners and with 150 years of successful neutrality, Swedish governments were conscious to keep any Nordic initiatives in perspective and not divorce the country from the wider European environment. Moreover, as the largest of the Nordic countries - whether measured economically, militarily, by population or geographic area, the governing elite did not fear domination by its Nordic neighbours. Hence:

'Perhaps to avoid accusation of regional imperialism, ... the Swedes have, for the most part, let other countries initiate proposals for new forms of Scandinavian cooperation. Sweden has then lent ready support to the others' proposals, even those which envisaged supranationality, while insisting that they not jeopardise Swedish non-alignment in the Cold War'.[20]

It can be argued then that Swedish governments are not without blame for restricting the development of Nordic cooperation. From a historical perspective, intra-Nordic relations were characterised 'as much by disintegration as by cooperation'.[21] The limitations of Nordic cooperation, for instance, was no better illustrated than by the events of the Second World War, when a common response was conspicuous by its absence. During the Winter War (1939-40), Finland put considerable pressure on Sweden to enter the war as an ally - something that the Hansson government refused to countenance. In spite of the fact that the Soviet Union's attack on Finland (30 November 1939), 'created overnight a militant spirit in Sweden' and culminated in a demand for active intervention on the Finnish side by some groups such as *Centrala Finlandshjalpen* or *Samfundet Nordens Frihet*,[22] Prime Minister Per Albin Hansson preferred to lend support to Finland as a 'non-belligerent' - much to the disappointment of the Finns. Although this fell short of a declaration of neutrality and that the domestic mood swung towards benevolent neutrality in favour of Finland, the government rejected a request from the British and French governments to allow their troops passage across Swedish territory (2 March 1940).[23] Hansson also refused to militarily intervene (apart from approving 8,500 volunteers as part of an international brigade), but did provide Finland with economic and military aid, estimated to amount to as much as $125,000,000.[24]

Foreign policy was governed by the principle of not provoking either the Soviet Union or Nazi Germany (thereby avoiding Sweden's entry into the war). When Denmark and Norway were occupied by German troops (April 1940), Sweden as the only country reasonably able to defend itself, insisted on strict neutrality rather than 'non-belligerence' as in the case of Finland in 1939.[25] Swedish-Norwegian relations worsened further during the 'Engelbrecht Division' episode (June 1941).[26] Hansson, in clear breach of his 'strict' neutrality policy, permitted 15,000 German troops transit across Sweden to Finland.[27] Later, when it was obvious that Nazi Germany would be unable to defeat the Soviet Union, the Prime Minister conducted a *volte-face* and allowed the training of Norwegian 'police troops' on Swedish soil from 1943.[28] During the early post-war years (1945-50), intra-Nordic relations were damaged by the legacy of Sweden's rather flexible approach to neutrality. Recent events illustrated to many Norwegians and Danes that they could not completely trust Sweden on foreign policy matters.

It was partly due to this that the Swedish government was one of the first to embrace the ideas of reviving Nordic cooperation in the post-war era. Yet to a large extent, Swedish initiatives were prompted by international events. The period 1947-60 marked the first phase in post-war attempts at deepening Nordic integration and illustrated to all concerned that ambitious supranational initiatives were doomed to failure. Early examples were the initiatives (by the three Scandinavian countries) to establish a Defence Alliance and a Customs Union.

a) Scandinavian Defence Alliance 1948-49

Ironically, one of the first initiatives at Nordic integration was in one of the areas, which seemed least attractive to Sweden, namely security cooperation. After all, foreign policy coordination was deeply embedded in the realms of 'high politics' - something that was always going to be problematic for neutral Sweden.[29] The Foreign Minister implied this was the case in a statement before a joint session of the (then) bi-cameral Riksdag. He refused to consider the possibilities of signing the Brussels Treaty in March 1948 and stipulated that 'Sweden will not join any Western or Eastern political bloc. Sweden will remain neutral'. Even at this time, the government indicated its preference for furthering Nordic cooperation and that a Scandinavian defence pact was preferable in Swedish eyes to a Western European one.[30]

As Abrahamsen comments, 'in 1948, Sweden was placed in the precarious position of having to withstand a possible Russian attack; her solution was to attempt the establishment of a Scandinavian regional defence'.[31] Yet, throughout 1948, the government also made it clear that it would 'consent to such an alliance only if Norway abandoned her westward orientation and joined Sweden's more than a century-old policy of strict neutrality'.[32] To a large degree, the governmental proposals were in response to wider European dynamics and in particular, the Czechoslovakian communist coup (February 1948) and the process leading to the creation of NATO. On 1 May 1948, Foreign Minister Östen Undén tentatively raised the issue of a defence pact with Denmark and Norway, but included the condition that any arrangement would have to include both countries. During September 1948, the Foreign Ministers of the three countries met in Stockholm to discuss a joint defence. As a result, a Scandinavian Defence Committee (*Skandinavisk Forsvarskomite*, (SFK)) was created to explore the possibilities of a joint defence of Denmark, Norway and Sweden in October 1948.

Ironically and given her previous statements about neutrality, it was Sweden which played a major part in proposing such a joint defence arrangement. At a meeting of the three Scandinavian Prime Ministers, Foreign Ministers and Defence Ministers in Karlstad (5-6 January 1949 - and after a series of consultations between the three government during summer-autumn 1948), Prime

Minister Erlander offered Norway and Denmark a 10-year military alliance which appeared to be 'the first step toward a joint Scandinavian Parliament', but only on the condition that they refrained from joining the emerging Atlantic Alliance. In Karlstad, the Prime Minister stipulated that he was willing to accept an alliance based on the principles set down by the Scandinavian Defence Committee, which meant that an attack on any one of the signatories would be regarded as an attack on all of them.

At first glance, Sweden's offer of a military alliance could be regarded as a radical departure from the country's traditional neutrality. However, at Karlstad and at the two later conferences convened in Copenhagen (22-24 January 1949) and in Oslo (29-30 January 1949) to negotiate a Scandinavian Defence Alliance, it was clear that what Erlander intended was actually a flexible interpretation of neutrality. In other words, the extension of the principle of collective neutrality to the entirety of Scandinavia - the staying out of any involvement in a war with any of the major powers in Europe.[33] As early as 18 January 1949, the Foreign Minister reported the events at Karlstad to the Riksdag and reiterated the governmental position that a Scandinavian defence alliance would be conditional on remaining outside any wider western defence organisation. This was something that Norway in particular was never likely to accept as from the start of the consultation its government insisted that a Scandinavian arrangement must be linked to a North Atlantic Pact. As Barbara Haskel succinctly notes,

> 'Sweden of course did not want to participate in anything which might cast doubt on the permanence of its foreign policy stance. Norway, on the other hand, did not want to create the impression that its possible future commitments to a Western pact might be half-hearted'.[34]

Erlander's thinking was relatively transparent. He was conscious of the growing ideological divide sweeping Europe and the growing militarisation of the continent. The question of a defence union for the Nordic region was revived shortly after the Communist takeover of Czechoslovakia (February 1948) and as a direct consequence of Swedish fears over the rapid deterioration in relations between the Western Powers and the USSR. The country's Defence Staff for instance, in direct response, to the Czechoslovakian coup pleaded for increased military forces and a special appropriation of $56 million was added later that year. At the same time, the country was eager to maintain her policy of neutrality. Consequently, Sweden did not want to join the newly emerging North Atlantic Treaty Organisation (NATO) in 1949. In addition, if Denmark and Norway chose (as was likely) to participate in NATO, then this constellation inside the Nordic area would place Sweden between rival blocs. This was seen as highly undesirable from the Swedish perspective. Although the country's participation in

NATO was out of the question because of neutrality, the fear of greater marginalisation would place severe strain on its credibility and additional pressure on Sweden if the neighbouring Nordic countries to the west and south became firmly committed to NATO.

It was as an alternative to, or at least as a means of softening the damage inflicted, by these two challenges that the Erlander government suggested a Scandinavian pact based on mutual defence and neutrality. To the Swedes, any Scandinavian defence alliance must be independent of the two power blocs emerging in Europe and therefore also of NATO. Each of the three countries involved presented draft proposals in the 1948-49 negotiations. The Swedish version is well-known due to Foreign Minister Östen Undén's statement to the Riksdag (9 February 1949). Undén envisaged a Scandinavian defence alliance for 10 years that would adopt a Swedish-type policy of neutrality and thus the region would be turned into a neutral zone. As Undén summarised,

> 'An attack on one of the countries was to be considered an attack on all of them and the two others would be obliged immediately to render military aid. Plans for joint defence should be worked out immediately in the coming into force of the pact. In the pact the contracting parties should declare their intention to try in the case of war to keep out of the conflict provided that they were not drawn into it through an armed attack on one of them. ... During a war, in which the parties do not take part, they should consult on the application of their neutrality rules and on the maintenance of their neutrality. From time to time, joint discussions should take place on the character and scope of the defensive measures of the parties. ... A joint defence council should be set up. A close collaboration in the field of foreign policy should be established. None of the contracting parties should have the right to enter into a military alliance with a third power. The pact should be valid for a period of 10 years'.[35]

Overall, the Swedish proposals included three main principles:

- there would be a joint pledge from all three states that an attack on one of them would be regarded as an attack on all - in other words a collective security guarantee.

- that a declaration of neutrality would be made and none of the states would be able to sign military treaties with third parties (article V of the Swedish proposed treaty) - thereby removing the prospect of Danish or Norwegian NATO membership.

- the joint Scandinavian neutrality would be supported by common plans for defence, control of armaments, a joint military defence council and close cooperation in the field of foreign policy.[36] From a Swedish perspective, this was quite a radical departure from her strict policy of neutrality. She was the only country in the proposed alliance with a high degree of modern armament. Erlander was in reality taking a calculated risk in offering to come to the rescue of Sweden's neighbours if they were attacked.

At the two January conferences, it became evident that the negotiations on a future Scandinavian defence pact would most likely be unsuccessful due to the differing defence priorities of the respective countries. Erlander quickly became disillusioned with the prospect of defence alliance once it was clear that the Norwegians and Danes would not commit themselves to a guaranteed rearmament in order to achieve a credible strong defence for the alliance. Swedish experts on the Scandinavian defence committee established to examine the details of such an alliance stressed that without guarantees from Denmark and Norway to such a rearmament, they could only recommend 'looser' forms of cooperation which the committee was also appointed to investigate.[37] Indeed, with the announcement by the United States that no military aid would be given to such an alliance (14 January 1949) and that the Norwegians proposed extending any plan to include a unilateral US military guarantee, the Erlander government had by 30 January 1949 recognised that its plans were likely to fail. Undén privately interpreted the US position on supplying arms as a device to prevent the negotiations succeeding.

After the relatively nasty experience of occupation and the lack of Swedish assistance, Denmark and Norway chose to join NATO in order to secure American defence guarantees. In effect, there was a degree of mistrust on the part of Danes and Norwegians that Sweden would ever come to their aid in any arrangement (as the experiences of 1939-45 war illustrated). They also disliked for 'national psychological' reasons the prospect that any Scandinavian defence alliance would be dominated by Sweden and its forces. Finland was also wary of antagonising the Soviet Union once again, and had only just signed a Treaty of Friendship in 1948, imposing limitations on Finnish foreign policy. Thus her future membership was also impossible. In essence, Sweden's neighbours no longer believed that neutrality, armed or otherwise, would be successful in keeping them out of any future war between the emerging superpowers. The Norwegians refused the Swedish proposals. The Danes at least in passing considered the possibilities of a bilateral arrangement between the remaining two countries, which Sweden in any case, rejected as an inadequate substitute.

The Oslo conference marked 'the final attempt by Sweden to neutralise the Scandinavian region' and the final communiqué admitted that there were no possibilities of reconciling the opposing views of the Scandinavian countries. Undén in his later speech to the Riksdag (18 January 1950) re-stated the government's continued support for neutrality and that a defence union would have meant 'in a way a departure from neutrality'. He also reiterated that any future Northern defence union would continue to be conditional on standing outside the superpowers and with a commitment to keep out of any future war. The Swedes accepted that their 'generous offer' had been coolly received and domestic support for neutrality remained strong. Indeed, just as the original governmental offer received the almost universal approval of all the major political parties in the Riksdag, its eventual failure met with equal disappointment.[38]

Nevertheless, the negotiations on the proposed defence alliance were important for several reasons. First, they reinforced Swedish perspectives that if neutrality was to be maintained it would need to be complimented by a strong defence, although the government refrained from applying the country's technological capability to the development of nuclear weapons. In effect, the fourth point of the 'Swedish Diamond' - neutrality - was reinforced by these events. The maintenance of a credible neutrality policy by Swedish actions alone and without being compromised by international obligations was highlighted. Second, the government became concerned about the gulf developing between the Scandinavian national interests, especially given the need to establish some kind of Nordic arrangement to ensure that Swedish influence on its neighbours was maintained. Swedish support for the future Nordic Council was therefore assured. There was no animosity between the Scandinavian partners over the breakdown and the disagreement over a joint defence alliance caused no lasting damage to intra-Nordic relations.

Interestingly, the spectre of a Scandinavian Defence Alliance briefly re-emerged within the Swedish domestic debate in 1965, but sank without trace just as quickly. On 16 September 1965 under the headline 'Swedish-Norwegian defence pact being considered', Eric Silver, (*Guardian* correspondent) asserted that specialist study groups (at each countries' Institutes of International Affairs) had been established in Norway and Sweden to explore the implications of a defence pact to come into force in 1969. This was repeatedly denied by the (then) Minister of Defence, Sven Andersson,[39] and the Director of the Swedish Institute for International Affairs, but did not prevent a lively debate appearing in the Swedish press in October 1965. Tage Erlander was forced to make a categorical denial in a speech at Karlstad (17 October 1965) in which he expressed little desire to attempt to influence Sweden's Nordic partners and that 'For Sweden, Nordic military cooperation is today not a current issue'.

b) Scandinavian Customs Union 1947-59

The other major plan aimed at promoting Nordic cooperation was also stimulated by international events shortly after the end of the war. Marshall Aid convinced most of the Nordic countries that discussions on a Scandinavian customs union could be worthwhile. At this time such cooperation was doomed to failure due to the countries' reservations surrounding the issue of supranational institutions and in particular, the implications for Swedish neutrality.[40] What is striking about the early attempt at creating a Scandinavian customs union was that the ensuing negotiations illustrated how different the views of the countries actually were.

The concept of a Scandinavian customs union received a rather low priority status and yet, simultaneously enjoyed high political 'visibility'. At the end of summer 1947 and with Swedish support, the Scandinavian Foreign Ministers announced that they intended to establish a cooperation committee of experts to discuss Nordic economic cooperation. This was created in February 1948. The committee's mandate was wide-ranging. Under the general proviso of making a contribution to the economic recovery of the region after the war, the committee was ordered to examine a variety of issues ranging from the need to introduce a common tariff as a prerequisite to a Nordic customs union to the broader issues of the division of specialisation and labour. It took until the Committee's preliminary report in January 1950 for it to provisionally conclude that:

- a customs union would benefit Scandinavia as a whole.
- there would be transitional difficulties for some industries in all three countries.
- there would be a reduction of trade restrictions phased over 10 years.
- there were problems of such magnitude in agreeing these that there was at present no basis for agreement.

Thus, the first attempt at creating a customs union more or less ended in early 1950, with the Committee's recommendations that the three countries should not establish a customs union because of the anticipated difficulties between them and especially for Norway. In order to save the initiative, the Committee (at the request of the Norwegians), was given a more limited mandate (November 1950) to investigate those industrial areas for which the elimination of restrictions could be agreed. It took until 1953 for Committee to again report.

In general, the speed of progress on the Scandinavian customs union was hardly inspirational. The initiative was only allowed to continue as a consequence of the launch of the Nordic Council (see later) in 1953. In March 1954, the

Committee submitted its final report. The degree of division between the three delegations was indicated by the fact that it had split conclusions with the Swedes and Danes writing a joint and generally optimistic summary and the Norwegians a sole and mostly negative one. The report contained extensive surveys of 21 different branches of industry associated with the proposed customs union and covered 50 various industries. The report showed overwhelmingly positive support from Swedish industry for the concept.

The upshot of this activity was that at the October 1954 Cabinet level conference at Harpsund, the three Prime Ministers agreed to upgrade the Scandinavian negotiations with the Ministers of Trade now responsible for the investigations and contact with economic organisations. In essence a second attempt at a customs union was made to revive the process by raising the status of the participants and negotiators. However, even this higher profile, with the most important ministers being involved, did not change the fact that the mandate of the new Nordic Economic Cooperation Committee (NECC - devised to survey Scandinavian trade to see where tariffs may be eliminated) was no stronger than in 1948. Thus, the problems in gaining agreement between the three governments remained the same.[41] From January 1955, the Nordic Council received a number of studies from the Committee examining Scandinavian trade and an NECC report was debated for the first time (January-February 1956). By the time of the July 1957 NECC report and its supplement (autumn 1958), several areas including an immediate common customs tariff covering 80 percent of the Nordic countries were agreed,[42] but negotiations continued until as late as May 1959.

As with nearly every attempt at Nordic cooperation, the link with European integration was influential and led to the undermining of the customs union process. Two months after the failure of the OEEC negotiations, representatives from Denmark, Norway, Portugal, Switzerland, the UK, Sweden and Austria met in Oslo to explore the possibilities of forming a free trade area. In effect, the whole concept had been eclipsed by the process leading to the formation of EFTA (see Chapter Three). Despite the work of the NECC being completed in July 1959, no action was ever taken. The Scandinavian customs union was stillborn. At a Nordic ministerial meeting in Kungälv, the ascendancy of larger European projects over purely Nordic ones was no more clearly illustrated. The plans for the customs union were shelved in the light of the possibilities of a broader market solution (and which ultimately led to the establishment of EFTA on 3 May 1960).

Swedish governmental perspectives on the development of the customs union are especially of interest. Haskel, for instance, has argued that in fact, the whole reason why the Erlander government was interested in a Scandinavian customs union related to external developments and was in reality a reaction to outside events.[43] The decision to set up a committee of experts in 1948 was supported by Sweden because of the lack of unified Nordic position regarding the US Marshall Plan. By supporting regional initiatives, the Swedes could avoid being pressured into involvement in larger European customs union. To some extent, the Swedish government viewed the project as a defensive strategy and as a counterweight to diplomatic developments on mainland Europe. Indeed, it is doubtful whether the Erlander government ever viewed the chances of its completion seriously. This is why the Scandinavians insisted (at least at first) on low-level investigations and not high-level diplomatic initiatives.

In general, the advantages of the customs union from an economic perspective were related to Sweden's position as the economic leader in the region. Her government's aim was relatively simple - 'to expand market opportunities for its thriving industries. Its main argument was the comparative thesis of classical economics: all parties would gain by the increased division of labour in a larger market'.[44] Sweden as the largest economy would be the greatest beneficiary. Moreover, because the country was the most industrialised and was by the 1950s developing a more differentiated economy with strong iron and steel, ball-bearing and machine tools industries, the Erlander government perceived that the country would be able to strengthen its already positive balance of payments surplus with its Nordic neighbours. In essence, governmental attitudes towards the Nordic initiative were similar to those associated with broader European endeavours. They were essentially liberal. The governmental view of Nordic economic cooperation tended to be based on a maximalist perspective. If Sweden was to benefit and be compensated for its losses of economic sovereignty, its role as a regional leader must be maximised. The government insisted on a customs union as the very minimum. Otherwise a wider European free trade area offered better economic advantages for Sweden (see Chapter Three).

Prime Minister Erlander argued in June 1954 that Sweden would benefit. Owing to its present situation of having no balance of payments problems, the country would be a natural exporter of capital and was 'on the threshold of a period of increased investments both private and public'.[45] Ironically, Swedish industry whilst consistently favouring the country's participation in a customs union was cautious especially over plans for joint investment or capital transfers. At a meeting of the Swedish Chamber of Commerce (February 1956) convened in part to discuss the potential for capital arising from Nordic cooperation, doubts were expressed about the attractiveness of investing in Norway for instance. The Erlander government was, consequently, careful to argue in the negotiations that since joint gains could be expected, (including for Norway), Sweden should not have to pay 'side-payments' or compensation for the liberalising of the other countries' economies. The Swedish delegation subsequently stressed the technical benefits associated with trade liberalisation.

When the Norwegian government opposed a fully-fledged customs union, Erlander offered some, if rather late, concessions. The lateness of these concessions was due to two reasons. First, Erlander's belief (at this time) that there would be a Nordic pillar in any future European free trade area. Closer coordination at the Nordic level would strengthen European cooperation rather than provide an alternative to it. Second, that the government doubted the will or ability of the Norwegian parliament to ratify any Scandinavian plan. Thus, from a pessimistic viewpoint, the concessions could be perceived as empty gestures.

In 1957, some 10 years after the start of the project, the Swedish government improved its offer concerning the embryonic Nordic Investment Bank and volunteered to contribute almost all the Bank's capital by counting as the contribution of the others their payments on post-war loans. In addition, longer and unilateral transitional arrangements were offered in 1959 - removing Swedish insistences on reciprocity - and allowing for transitional arrangements of up to 12 years duration for certain Finnish and Norwegian industries. This allowed for a gradual opening of their markets to foreign exports whilst at the same time gaining immediate access to Swedish (and Danish) markets. Although the concessions were recognised by all sides as relatively significant, the depth of division had been too wide for too long. The project had foundered. It was overtaken by the speedy development of EFTA.

The Nordic Council - Concrete, if Piecemeal Progress

The Scandinavian Defence Alliance episode confirmed Erlander's assertion that successful areas of Nordic cooperation must be carefully chosen, applicable to sectoral areas and mainly in the domain of 'low politics'. It was not surprising then that his government was at least partly responsible for the initiatives on uniform citizen laws in 1950 and on improving communications in 1951, which eventually formed the basis of a passport union between the Nordic countries. In August 1949, after three years of deliberations, a committee of experts submitted a report for a new law on citizenship, which was essentially the work of the committee's Swedish secretariat. Again on 19 January 1951, it was the Swedish Social Democrat, Rolf Edberg, who introduced a motion to the Riksdag urging the creation of an inter-parliamentary committee for the facilitation of travel among the Scandinavian peoples. Edberg argued that the elimination of restrictions on movement and transit would be 'a quiet beginning to something which in substance can be characterised as a Nordic citizenship'.[46]

After gaining the support of the floor leaders of the various parliamentary parties, the Standing Committee on Foreign Affairs presented a unanimously favourable report, which was accepted without dissent (11 April 1951). Swedish support for a passport union was consequently more or less gained. It allowed for the later establishment, with Swedish participation, of a Nordic parliamentary committee for Traffic Freedom. Between 1952-56, the committee (created in July 1951) produced 12 reports dealing with issues such as passports, customs allowances and traffic rules. From July 1952, passports for Scandinavian travel were abolished, and as a consequence intra-Scandinavian travel increased by around 9.5 million in that year.

It was the creation of the Nordic Council, that represented the main forum for such cooperation and was the breakthrough. This body was sporadically raised as being (if dramatically improved) a possible alternative to European integration. Without providing a long chronology of the Nordic Council's evolution, which is not the main objective of this study, it came into being in 1952. The Nordic Council in effect coordinated existing cooperation through ministerial conferences, government departments and permanent bodies.[47] Above all, the Nordic legislative assemblies were drawn into the work on a much greater scale than ever before. As Frantz Wendt suggests, probably the greatest impact of the Council was that it ensured that Scandinavian cooperation came 'to occupy a central position at government level'.[48]

The practical benefits of the Council were felt almost immediately in Sweden and by Swedes living abroad in the other Nordic countries. The creation of a Nordic Passport Union was reinforced by two further major agreements under the auspices of the (later) Nordic Council. First, the Common Nordic Labour Market Treaty (signed in 1954) abolished the existing system of work permits and established the general principle of free labour mobility in the region (excluding Iceland). Second, the 1955 Convention on Social Security (which consolidated 16 reciprocal agreements into one Convention) provided for all social security benefits of one country to be extended in principle to the citizens of the other Nordic states living in that country. It became effective on 1 November 1956. As a result of this convention, one of the major items on the Council's agenda - namely the realisation of a Nordic Passport Union - was completed (1 April 1958). Passports were now only controlled at the external ports of entry into the region. The Passport Union also accelerated Nordic cooperation in other practical areas, such as common systems for issuing visas. From 1958 for instance, the Swedish and Norwegian governments coordinated their customs authorities at all crossings on their long common frontier, with each countries' officials carrying identification from both services.

Since the establishment of the Nordic Council, its administrative arrangements have been strengthened and its institutions widened. Later it was joined by the high-profile Nordic Council of Ministers and cooperation became more institutionalised as a result of the signing of the Helsinki Treaty (March 1962). At more or less the same time and after agreement (21 November 1961), the Nordic countries under the auspices of a Swedish negotiator acted as a body in the GATT Kennedy Round. This collective action has been regarded as an almost unique incident in the history of Nordic cooperation. In this instance the governments 'chose to make a political decision first and then negotiate on concrete details - i.e. the exact opposite to their manner of proceeding during the three attempts to form a customs union'.[49]

In many ways, the inter-relationship between Nordic cooperation and European integration was no better illustrated than by the Helsinki Treaty itself. The 1962 Treaty was drawn up mainly to provide an international basis for Nordic cooperation and so that it could be safeguarded during Norway and Denmark's negotiations for EEC membership during the 1960s.[50] The differing positions of the countries as regards their relationship with the Community - with some seeking full membership (Denmark and Norway) and others association (Sweden) - demonstrated the weaknesses of such cooperation and that a split on the EEC issue was impending. As Erlander himself commented, the Helsinki Treaty was needed to further codify Nordic integration and lessen the gulf between the countries on the EEC issue:

> 'It was vital that we attempted to formulate the draft so that it did not hinder those entering into European negotiations, and we sought to make it an aid to each of us in the forthcoming negotiations on economic cooperation, no matter in what way we choose to pursue those negotiations'.[51]

The Treaty allowed for cooperation to be secured, itemised future areas and identified the means as being ministerial meetings (article 35). When the membership overtures of Denmark and Norway came to nothing after General De Gaulle's veto of the British application (January 1963), the Helsinki Treaty provided a partial fall-back position for the countries - highlighting Nordic cooperation's twilight position as both a limited replacement for, and at the same time a complement to, European integration.

The Treaty was revised as a result of European integration in 1971, when Norway and Denmark were again in the midst of membership negotiations with the Community. The revision was also brought about by the failure of the other major attempt at pushing forward Nordic economic integration - namely a Nordic Economic Union (NORDEK). Indeed, its failure was at least in part because of its implications for certain states' relations with the Community. The countries disagreed over the relationship of NORDEK with the EEC, which two of them, after all, intended to join. The revised Helsinki Treaty therefore provided for the Nordic Council of Ministers which could by unanimity and subject to parliamentary approval make binding decisions.

The significance of the Nordic Council and its achievements should not be underestimated. Certainly Swedish policy-makers have constantly stressed that the country is in a far better position within it, than without it. As Tage Erlander succinctly summarised as early as 1964,

> 'I believe that every cabinet Member ought to be able to provide examples of how the Nordic Council in reality has served as an effective *pressure group*, sometimes irritating and troublesome - that I will not deny - but often extraordinarily useful'.[52]

The Failure of Nordic Economic Cooperation - NORDEK

Compared to the two previous attempts at forming a Nordic customs union in the 1950s, the remarkable feature of the NORDEK case was the speed with which the planning phase progressed, even if like its forebear it also ended in failure. The proposal to establish a Nordic customs union was made by the Danish Prime Minister, Hilmar Baunsgaard at the Nordic Council session in February 1968 and met with a favourable response from the Swedish government. Once again this new attempt at Nordic cooperation seemed to ride on the back of wider European events and the failure of European integration. Baunsgaard's initiative came only six weeks after De Gaulle's third veto of enlarging the Community in December 1967. There seemed to be a consensus amongst the Scandinavian political elites that entry into the Community was effectively blocked until at least 1972. According to this interpretation, Nordic cooperation would seem to be a second best and more feasible alternative. As Baunsgaard himself noted during the general debate of the Nordic Council (17 February 1968), De Gaulle's veto 'gives us every reason to consider the place of the Nordic countries in the debate on the European market'. More importantly, NORDEK could also be used as a negotiating tool to further the participating countries' European aspirations. NORDEK by formulating a common Nordic negotiating stance would provide the foundation for special trade arrangements with the Community since membership negotiations were frozen.

In usual fashion, when the Prime Ministers met later (April 1968) they agreed to establish an Inter-Nordic Committee to examine the potential for closer economic cooperation. The Nordic Committee of Government Officials was appointed in June 1968. It produced its first preliminary report in January 1969 - having already succeeded in reaching agreement in substantial areas, such as 85 percent of the items covered by customs union duties and corresponding to 75 percent of Nordic imports from third countries. The planning stage was further accelerated in March 1969, when the Nordic Council agreed that the Committee of Government Officials should formulate firm proposals for a Nordic Economic Union, including a Draft Treaty. By 17 July 1969, the final report, 'Expanded Nordic Economic Cooperation', was completed. In November 1969, the Nordic

Prime Ministers met in Oslo to negotiate the few outstanding issues, such as agricultural policy, raw materials duty and its financial and institutional arrangements. NORDEK had been confirmed at the highest political level and the likelihood of completion looked good.[53]

The actual details of the arrangement were quite ambitious. As Nielsson comments, 'the classification of NORDEK as an economic union is accurate and appropriate because the treaty proposal provided for integrative features far beyond the establishment of a customs union'.[54] The plans provided for NORDEK to, amongst other things, advance the region from an EFTA-based free trade area to a customs union in two stages. First, the common external tariff for industrial goods would be established in January 1972 for 90 percent of the headings of goods. The last 10 percent would have been the subject of further negotiations and there was to be a transitional period lasting until 1 January 1974. In negotiations concerning the common customs tariffs, the countries would act jointly in relation to third states and in international organisations.[55] Second, the development of a common market in agriculture would also have begun in 1974. The ambitious economic features of the NORDEK treaty also included the gradual development of designated time deadlines for other policy areas. Before 1 January 1974, for instance, the governing Council of Ministers was to lay down the basic principles for cooperation in taxation, budgetary policy, credit policy and regional policy. NORDEK would have provided the basis for a very significant extension of socio-economic and political integration in Scandinavia.

Yet, the limitations of Nordic cooperation were still apparent - highlighting its attraction as an intergovernmental alternative to supranational European integration. NORDEK did not include any provisions for supranational authority in policy-making.[56] Policy decisions were still to be made by intergovernmental means and on the basis of unanimity, with the chief institutional body governing NORDEK being a Council of Ministers and its permanent delegate equivalent - the Permanent Committee of Government Officials. In the tradition of Nordic consensual policy-making, nine Cooperation Committees were to be an integral part of decision-making, having responsibility for planning and deliberating on policy proposals. Ultimately the link between NORDEK and the intergovernmental Nordic Council was formalised.

Nevertheless, NORDEK was seen as a supplement and not as an alternative to European integration by the majority of the Nordic countries. The NORDEK treaty's preamble was careful to stipulate that the Nordic Economic Union would not affect the foreign and security policies of the four countries and at least to the Swedes could be reconciled with the country's neutrality. In addition, NORDEK was seen as a complement to their existing membership of EFTA, especially as the preamble also stipulated that 'the cooperation must be organised in a manner that will facilitate the four countries' participation in or cooperation with an enlarged European market'.

There seemed to be a notable difference of perspective on the part of the Swedish government during the NORDEK negotiations when compared to their previous attitudes to the customs union plans of the 1950s. In part, this was due to the fact that by 1961, the government and public had more or less fully debated their country's relationship to European integration and had stipulated that full membership was incompatible with the country's neutrality. Moreover, the economic results of EFTA membership for Sweden has been beneficial. The Erlander government had a greater self-confidence in the sturdiness of the Swedish economy and was content by the fact that the country was already enjoying the benefits of a European free trade area. During the first decade of EFTA membership, there was a significant increase in intra-Nordic trade. The Scandinavian markets, for example, made up 16.3 percent of Sweden's entire imports and 24.6 percent of total exports in 1968, compared with figures of 8.3 percent and 19.7 percent in 1958 respectively. For Sweden, EFTA had served the dual function of safeguarding her substantial trade with the UK and at the same time, providing for a regional intra-Nordic trade to improve in the 1960s.

The Social Democratic government therefore viewed NORDEK as a way of consolidating the gains of the last decade. Tage Erlander pointed out during a Nordic TV program (23 April 1968) to discuss NORDEK between the four Nordic Prime Ministers, that although this was the first time that a Nordic customs union and finance fund had been sketched out in detail, he believed that the cooperation did not signify a new departure for Sweden. It should be viewed as a further evolution of the intensive cooperation already taking place in the Nordic area.[57] Erlander took a more benevolent attitude towards NORDEK than the previous 1950s proposals. During the NORDEK negotiations, he offered that Sweden would contribute more than ever to such an arrangement, including contributions to joint funds for transitional measures for industry and for structural reform in agriculture. The Social Democratic government proposed in 1969 that Sweden would pay 25 percent of joint bank reserves of $50 million, plus 46 percent of the three funds for agriculture, fishing and industry. In reality, Sweden was offering to pay $340 million in 1969 compared with $300 million in 1958. As a result of Sweden's economic confidence, Erlander's insistence on purely technical assessments of the benefits of such a customs union was also dropped. In practice however, NORDEK would only allow for joint tariffs against non-EFTA countries, (compared with a joint tariff wall against all non-Scandinavian states in the 1950s). Thus the economic benefits of NORDEK in terms of tariff protection would at face value seem less.[58]

As early as 18-19 January 1969, at a series of meetings at Stockholm, the Swedish government's 'non-technical' approach to NORDEK was illustrated. At one of the meetings, Erlander stressed that if an examination of each detail of NORDEK was undertaken, probably a negative balance would be the result. Swedish small and medium sized industry, for example, would benefit, whilst heavy industry in the country had less to gain from cooperation. Yet, NORDEK would produce overall political benefits for Sweden. Erlander throughout 1969 also regarded the timetable for reaching an agreement as optimistic. The process, he argued, should not be weighed down by a specific time-frame, not least out of consideration for the national parliaments. Erlander's only continual proviso was the importance of the full completion of NORDEK's customs union. To him at least, the customs union was the practical symbol of an integrated economy. It was the real asset which would strengthen future negotiations within EFTA and/or with the Community. Despite the generous offers of financial aid, Erlander still demanded a complete customs union as a precondition for contributing SEK 1,000 million to NORDEK's joint funds.[59]

A major statement on this very point was made by the Minister of Finance, Gunnar Strang, during a general policy debate in the Riksdag (29 October 1969). The Minister highlighted in his first detailed comment on NORDEK, the link between the costs to Swedish agriculture and the benefits to the country arising from the completed customs union. Strang stipulated that 'the customs union is an absolute prerequisite for a settlement, which must not leave essential parts to be decided in the future. Sweden must have a customs union in actuality and not merely in name'.[60] He stressed that the question of increasing agricultural imports from Denmark had to be coupled with the lowering of Swedish levels of self-sufficiency in agriculture. The exports of capital (amounting to SEK 200 million annually) which NORDEK required of Sweden would put substantial strains on the country's currency reserves. If the government was to make these sacrifices, Swedish gains from the customs union must be substantial and not be frittered away. This view was also shared by the new Prime Minister, Olof Palme, who was present at Nordic Council and NORDEK meetings from November 1969.

To some extent, it also seems that Swedish governmental perspectives on NORDEK can be correlated to its hope that a Nordic Economic Union would mitigate some of the economic burden of maintaining a neutral foreign policy. Once again, the tension between two points of the 'Swedish Diamond' - growing trade and economic interdependence on one side and the continuation of credible neutrality policy on the other - is of relevance. During the negotiations, the main employers' organisations and *Svenska Dagbladet* and *Dagens Nyheter* (the largest Conservative and Liberal newspapers in Sweden respectively) all urged the government to be generous in the financial aspects of the package in order to maintain Swedish economic influence in the region.[61]

Yet, most of all, NORDEK was seen as an integral part of future governmental strategy towards Europe.[62] The arrangement would bolster Swedish influences in EFTA and push the possibilities of securing either a wider free trade arrangement with the Community or at this time even the possibility of some kind of flexible Swedish membership of the Community. As Tage Erlander commented in his statement on television (15 January 1969), his interest in the provisions of NORDEK depended 'upon the weight one attaches to a common Nordic stance in the European context'. In essence, NORDEK supported the two strategic goals of Erlander. First, that Swedish interest in a Nordic customs union would decrease the risk of isolation from an enlarged EEC, whilst still maintaining the country's neutrality policy. Second, it would increase Swedish diplomatic leverage in any future EEC negotiations by consolidating ties which would make it impossible to leave the country out. As Sweden (along with the other EFTA states) had agreed to act in unison when dealing with the EEC, the formation of NORDEK was, according to the Social Democratic government, a reinforcement of that strategy. If anything it would actually improve the chances of a common Nordic approach towards the Community. It was for political rather than economic reasons that Sweden remained committed to the project.

Unlike in the 1950s the Swedish government was more than ever convinced of the benefits of further trade liberalisation. It perceived any Nordic arrangement as being healthy and as a catalyst for, and not an alternative to, wider European trade liberalisation. Although in 1969, Erlander discounted any reformulating of the 1967 'open' application to the Community and that no immediate enlargement in his view could be expected, his government was always keen to stress the relationship between European integration and Nordic cooperation. During a major debate in the Riksdag (5-7 February 1969), for example, the NORDEK plans were discussed. The Minister of Foreign Trade, Gunnar Lange, replied to a leading representative of the Centre Party (who asserted that an expanded European market rather than a Nordic one could solve the marketing difficulties of Swedish agriculture), by stating that the Community itself was grappling with surpluses and that price levels in Sweden were 5 percent higher than in the Community. In practice, even cooperation at the Nordic level would pose some transitional difficulties but these would be balanced by advantages in other sectors.[63]

Furthermore, the domestic debate on NORDEK was striking for two things. First the relative and nearly unanimous party and to a lesser extent, interest group support in favour of NORDEK. Second, the subsequent lack of major debate on the issue in terms of domestic politics. As regards the main political parties, the governing Social Democrats strongly supported NORDEK. The SAP issued positive statements at the various joint meetings with other Nordic Social Democrats. The party's newly elected leader, Olof Palme, claimed at the SAP's congress (4 October 1969) that important decisions on Nordic cooperation were imminent and welcome. Support from the Centre Party was also evident. Its leader Gunnar Hedlund, emphasised during the Riksdag's debate on general policy (29 October 1969) that the current NORDEK negotiations were a step in the right direction - although because of its reliance on the agrarian vote, the party did also highlight concerns over the impact of NORDEK on Swedish agriculture. In similar vein, the Liberal's new leader Gunnar Helén, at the party's extraordinary conference in early November 1969, also stressed the need for the party to concentrate on two international questions - the country's relationship within NORDEK and/or with the Community. The Liberals supported NORDEK because of the perceived overall benefits for Sweden. In addition, the Conservatives in line with their party's position favouring closer ties with Europe, showed a similar attitude to that of the Liberals. In terms of emphasis, it was the Social Democrats, Liberals, Conservatives and Centre Party that were most in favour of NORDEK.

Owing to this high degree of domestic consensus between the main political parties, the issue was not controversial. At the parliamentary level, for example, the issue was dealt with intermittently, and even then only as part of general economic and foreign policy discussions, with no special debate on NORDEK taking place in the Riksdag. None the less, when it did appear, talks focused around five main aspects - NORDEK's relationship to the Community; its impact on Swedish agriculture; a future fisheries policy; its institutional arrangements and finally, the creation of common funds, its investment bank and the corresponding size of Swedish financial contributions.

A large degree of interest from key interest groups was discernible. In part, this was due to the fact that the Erlander and later Palme governments encouraged the main interest groups to submit official comments. The groups perceived it necessary to be involved in any economic plan, such as NORDEK, that could have substantial implications for their members. Representatives of the interest organisations also played a prominent role in the actual negotiations. The contact between the government, interest organisations and even various influential firms, meant that the interest groups had a direct input into the government's proposals on NORDEK. During the negotiations, for example, it was agreed that the condition for eliminating Norwegian fiscal duties on automobiles was that the Swedish automobile industry (namely Volvo) pledged to buy more parts from Norway. It was therefore essential for the main interest groups to publicise their attitudes towards NORDEK.

The interest groups most strongly in favour were not surprisingly the export orientated Federation of Swedish Industries (SI) and the Swedish elements of the Nordic labour movement. NORDEK was greeted with cautious optimism by the trade union movement. In particular, the main trade unions, along with the

SI, supported the concept of a Nordic Investment Bank, claiming that it would support new infrastructure and create jobs in Sweden. The four main Nordic trade union confederations expressed their positive opinion in NORDEK at a joint meeting in Gothenburg (7-8 November 1968). This was reaffirmed after another joint meeting (this time including the Social Democratic parties of the four countries) at Harpsund on 8-9 February and again on 29 September 1969.

Greater criticism arose from the main farmers' organisations. They feared that the creation of a NORDEK agricultural policy would lead to fewer measures aimed at protecting Swedish agriculture, greater competition and most of all, a reduction in price support to farmers. Sweden's agricultural organisations especially disliked the idea of a customs union. They argued it would lead to greater costs for consumers and industry through higher import duties on raw materials, semi-manufactures and machinery. Equally, the Swedish Federation of Fisheries' Unions expressed strong fears that the proposed cooperation in fisheries would have serious and mostly negative implications for the country's small fishing industry. The Swedish Bankers' Association whilst generally in favour of NORDEK's customs union, also raised the issue of increased costs for the Swedish economy, suggesting a figure of SEK 500 million as a conceivable estimate of the increased burden on the economy.

The reasons for NORDEK's collapse have been examined in detail elsewhere. In the context of this study only a few points need to be made from the Swedish perspective.[64] In effect, its completion was thwarted by the reaction of the Finnish government to the EEC's ministerial meeting at the Hague (1 December 1969). Once again, it was the external European environment that provided the rationale for, shaped the configuration of, and eventually sounded the death knell of Nordic integration plans. At the Hague Summit, the six member states agreed to re-open the enlargement question and future negotiations with the outstanding applicants by 1 July 1970. From then on there was a complete change of prospects for NORDEK as the original reasons why Baunsgaard proposed the arrangement disappeared, Yet again, the enlargement of the Community was on the agenda. NORDEK was soon to be eclipsed by wider European developments.

The Finns declared that they disliked the possible attachment of NORDEK to the Community. They reserved the right to cease the NORDEK talks if any of the Nordic countries started formal negotiations with the Community on membership (which after all was likely). Once the arrangement came into force, the Finnish government would also protect their right to take any necessary precautions in order to maintain the country's neutrality if another Nordic state eventually joined the Community. The Finns suspected (as the rest of the Scandinavians intended) that NORDEK would be a stepping stone towards EEC membership or at least provide a framework for close relations with the Community - which they believed would compromise their neutrality towards the

Soviet Union.[65] Hence, despite the Nordic Governments' Officials Committee reaching agreement and the negotiations on the NORDEK treaty being more or less completed by the time of the Nordic Council session in Reykjavik (20 February 1970), there were further delays in signing the treaty. The Finnish government insisted on waiting until after its March elections. Finally, on 31 March 1970, the Finnish government announced that it could not sign the treaty on the grounds of its incompatibility with its neutrality and which effectively brought an end to the NORDEK concept.

Sweden, Nordic Cooperation and European Integration

Despite the mixed success of attempts at Nordic integration and indeed, various degrees of enthusiasm on the part of successive Swedish governments, it seems fair to say that a 'Nordic orientation' represented 'an ever-present force in the formulation of policy'.[66] Stålvant, for instance, argued that the foreign policies of Northern Europe (thereby including Sweden) has been largely shaped by four international orientations - namely the Nordic, European, Atlantic and global levels and these could be seen as 'concentric circles'.[67] In the Swedish context, it would appear that the first two levels (i.e. the Nordic and the European) were especially important and thus worthy of special attention.

To some extent, the relationship between the Nordic and wider European influences on Swedish policy has been defined by the fact that the Nordic dimension has become subservient to the wider European influences. In particular those arising from ambitious supranational integration plans centred on the continent and thus 'from the open-ended nature of the European idea itself'.[68] The ideals of Nordic cooperation were overtaken by those of European integration. This led to a greater stress within Swedish policy that any Nordic plans needed to be complimentary and supportive of integration taking place on the continent. Swedish optimism for further Nordic cooperation, for example, was based on the point that General De Gaulle would remain in power at least until 1972. He would therefore keep the door to any kind of Swedish membership of the EEC firmly shut. Later when this door was opened at the 1969 Hague Summit, Swedish policy again reflected the linkage between the Nordic and European 'concentric circles' by trying to accommodate the three interconnected objectives of NORDEK, the Community and its traditional neutrality policy.

The subordination of Nordic cooperation to wider 'European' needs continued throughout the 1970s. Yet, Swedish perceptions of the importance of maintaining at least partially the premise of close contact between the Nordic countries remained strong. The significance of Nordic ties was reinforced by two trends during the 1970s-80s. First, that the economic ambitions of Community had direct implications for practical aspects of Nordic cooperation, such as the

Nordic Passport Union and the Nordic Labour Market. Second, the possibility that the region could be split between full members and non-members of the Community impinged on the operation of these arrangements. Danish and Norwegian EEC membership would, for instance, imply that the Community's external barrier would run down the middle of the Nordic region.

During the time of the enlargement negotiations of Denmark and Norway with the Community in the 1970s, the Nordic Prime Ministers agreed at several meetings on the need to prevent a re-erection of tariff barriers between the countries as a result of some becoming full EEC members. Moreover, the diverse forms of applications to the Community, with Sweden for instance, insisting on a flexible form of membership, but one compatible with its neutrality, meant that a common position between the Nordic governments would be virtually impossible to achieve. Even this issue was not a genuine Nordic undertaking. It was subsumable under the wider interest of EFTA. The ministers also agreed to safeguard and maintain other common Nordic institutional achievements - the labour market, social security legislation, the harmonisation of civil law and the agreements on educational matters. What is clear is that the ministers consistently differed on the emphasis that they attributed to the Nordic cause. Certainly, Swedish enthusiasm for Nordic cooperation was converted during the 1970s negotiations on full membership into a continued insistence on parallel negotiations between the Community on the one side and Denmark, Norway and Sweden on the other.

When this failed, and it was apparent that Sweden would not become a full member of the Community and Denmark (and at this stage, Norway) would, the linkage between Nordic cooperation and European integration appeared in other forms. In 1971, the possibilities of a wider European agreement resulted in the reactivating of Nordic institutionalised cooperation through a revision of the 1962 Helsinki Treaty. From the Swedish governmental perspective this improvement was welcomed simply because the Swedes had already closed the door on full membership by March 1971. Strengthening Nordic cooperation was seen as an integral part of reinforcing Swedish influence during negotiations with the Community.

From 1973, the Community influenced Swedish perspectives on Nordic cooperation in two ways. First, the development of the Community's internal policies strengthened Danish ties with the other member states. Second, through the evolution of EEC relations with the European non-member states. The Palme government continued to express its interest in developing closer economic ties with the Community. Thus, the relationship between the two main rivals in the Nordic region - Denmark and Sweden - was once again central. On the one hand, Sweden represented the *de facto* leader of the Nordic non-member states due to its traditional influence and the size of its trade contact with the Community. On the other hand, Denmark perceived its role as the 'bridge-builder' between the Community and the Nordic non-member states, thereby challenging Sweden's leadership role.

At least initially, it was expected that Danish-Swedish cooperation would intensify. Both countries shared an intergovernmental view of European integration, or at least a resistance to federalism. However, rather than Danish-Swedish trade contacts deepening, Danish trade moved towards the (then) Community of Nine and in particular, Germany. None the less, the continued importance of economic and political interdependence between the Nordic countries and the Community was highlighted at the 1977 summit meeting of EFTA, even though little actual concrete progress resulted from it. The Community also proposed that a regular annual meeting should be held at ministerial level with Sweden and Norway respectively in the future.

However, the majority of Nordic Council's work - the arm of Nordic cooperation - remained introvert. Cooperation continued throughout the 1970s-80s, with, for example, the extension of the Helsinki Treaty in 1975 to cover transport and communications, the 1975 decision on a Nordic Investment Bank and the signing of a 1976 Convention on environmental cooperation.

At the Nordic level, there was no immediate reaction to the Commission White Paper on completing the Single European Market (SEM) or the later Single European Act (SEA). It was only when the realisation of the SEM drew nearer that the Nordic Council of Ministers discussed its role in the European integration process at its Oslo meeting (7 December 1987). Once again, the European level was to take priority. Negotiations with the Community took place under the auspices of EFTA rather than through the Nordic Council of Ministers.

In practice the negotiations between the Nordic Council and the Community could never be an option due to dual membership of Denmark in both organisations. Ironically from 1973, although the Community's influence on such cooperation was increasingly apparent and thus the need for negotiations between the Nordic and European level was ever present, the feasibility of the Council playing an institutionalised and potentially supranational role became less and less due to the shifting nature of membership. As Goldschmidt aptly notes,

> 'Direct negotiations between the Nordic Council of Ministers and the EC, would however, be out of the question as Denmark, an EC Member State, could not sit on both sides of the table, while the four other countries had their loyalties to the other EFTA countries'.[69]

Given the limitations of Nordic cooperation in terms of its scope and that it has little potential as a supranational platform either as an alternative to, or as negotiator with, the Community, such cooperation has been essentially reactive since the early 1970s. As Sundelius and Wiklund have elaborated upon elsewhere, this is due to conceptual differences between the dynamics governing Nordic cooperation and that of European integration. These authors argue that there are two important differences between Nordic cooperation and European integration. First, there has been 'the delayed development of joint institutions in the Nordic area', compared to its Community rival. Second, that the expansion of the institutional features of Nordic governmental cooperation has 'been coupled with a recent strengthening of nongovernmental structures in the area'.[70] In effect, there has only been a limited movement towards supranationalism at the governmental level in the Nordic context, with larger degrees of societal, rather than political integration. For the most part, the authors' claim that these differences are due to the varying goals of Nordic cooperation and European integration. Unlike the latter, the Nordic example has no general vision of what cooperation is supposed to end up achieving. The main goal of such cooperation, they alleged,

> 'is not to merge the Nordic countries into one political unit, but to facilitate constructive and mutually beneficial management of various regional problems. In contrast, the continental European cooperation effort was aimed more directly at the unification of the separate European countries. ... One could characterise the EC experience as a case of integration that reaches down to the societal level from the original political level of decision and interaction. In contrast, the Nordic case has its roots in the societal linkages and gradually builds up political relations as they are needed to manage problems associated with societal interdependence'.[71]

In short, the Community has been seen by Swedish policy-makers as the major challenge and that Nordic cooperation would always be a subsidiary to it. After all, the main initiatives for regional integration were spawned by the Community with EFTA and the Nordic Council responding to them. At the beginning of 1988 for example, the Nordic Council of Ministers initiated a comparative analysis of the development of the SEM programme on the one side and proposed Nordic cooperation on the other. This 'Norden in Europe' evaluation (finished in May 1988) identified areas where the countries were lagging behind the EC in terms of cooperation. In the second half of 1988, the findings were examined in order to identify future action. The outcome of this work was the 'Norden in Europe II' report, published at the end of 1988, which was discussed by the Nordic Council in Stockholm (February 1989). This report identified two priorities for Nordic cooperation in the wider European context, which have remained underlying themes ever since:

- the need for the internal strengthening of Norden in order to provide companies and citizens with the best possible basis for participation in the European integration process. In other words the consolidation of Norden as a domestic market, the creation of Nordic transport market, a 'cultural and educational community' and greater rights especially in terms of labour market policy.

- the strengthening of Nordic influence in Europe, especially in terms of citizens' safety and health and environmental, social and consumer policy.

The objectives fulfilled two important rationales. First, an economic rationale aimed at ensuring coordination with Community policies and achieving the eventual removal of discrimination for Nordic firms and citizens as part of the SEM process. Second, the political rationale of maximising the Nordic countries' influence on the EC's future development. The immediate practical evidence of this was the adoption of the 'Working Programme - Norden in Europe 1989-92' (19 June 1989) which consisted of 7 chapters and 82 respective actions. The Nordic Council committed itself to a number of actions up until the end of 1992 'in order to bring Nordic cooperation on par with and, in some fields, ahead of the process of European integration'.[72] There has been closer cooperation between the countries on for instance, technical standards and progress aimed at, albeit to a limited extent, mirroring the liberalisation of the EC's transport markets.

In particular, the Council has been concerned that its lead in terms of labour market policy coordination and the Nordic Passport Union is maintained so that when future countries join the Community (as Sweden and Finland did in 1995) then Nordic cooperation can act as an example for future EC integration in those areas. In a sense, this is a reactive strategy aimed at ensuring that future full membership for any of the countries could not be converted into the dilution of the successful areas of existing Nordic cooperation. The Nordic Committee for Social Policy has for example since 1989 set up a senior officials' committee to examine possible forms of connection and adjustment between the Nordic Social Convention and corresponding EC rules.

The 1990s: From Nordic to Baltic Cooperation

Ole Wæver has argued that 'Nordic identity is in crisis. With the revolution of 1989-91, the meaning of 'Norden' has become unclear'.[73] He suggests that the Nordic identity has been compromised by the fact that it was characterised as a 'low security arrangement' - directly related to the 'Nordic Balance' - and as a model society - about being better than Europe. It seems relatively indisputable that, to a large extent, the challenges facing Nordic cooperation (and Swedish participation within it) have been transformed by two factors during the early 1990s. First, the post-1989 revolutions in Eastern Europe and the disintegration of the Soviet Union in 1991 led to a greater instability on the borders of the Nordic region. In particular, the re-establishment of the three Baltic Republics - Estonia, Latvia and Lithuania - as independent sovereign states opened up the prospect of wider Baltic cooperation in which the Nordic countries would play a central role. Swedish governments since 1991 have continually reiterated their support for Baltic cooperation and that the country will play a prominent role in supporting it.

Second, the recent development of the European Union has raised fresh challenges for Nordic cooperation and especially Sweden's role within it. In practice, Nordic cooperation is now dealing with the fact that the countries participate in the EEA and since 1995, the majority of its members are now in the EU rather than outside it, It can no longer be regarded in any sense (no matter how superficially it was in reality) as a potential alternative to the Community. Rather its main future role may be to act as a Nordic pressure group within the Community directed at influencing EU decision-making and as a more concrete bridge between those countries who are full members and those who are content (at least at this time) with EEA participation.[74]

As Strom suggests 'European Union enlargement will bring Nordic cooperation beyond low politics'.[75] Existing areas of collaboration, such as the Passport Union and police cooperation will continue but perhaps with renewed enthusiasm. Nordic cooperation will be extended to include aspects covered by the existing EU's policy portfolio and the ambitious and far more problematic, areas deemed to be appropriate for future integration as part of the Treaty on European Union (TEU). Issues such as the coordination of economic and monetary policies will have to be extensively deliberated within Scandinavia. In effect, the scope of Nordic cooperation will be modified. At the March 1995 Reykjavik Nordic Council summit, it was agreed that Nordic cooperation could be used as a platform for pursuing 'Nordic advantage (*nytte*)' and to exert an influence on the EU's agenda in order to maintain the harmonisation of legislation.[76] Cooperation will focus on three main areas:

- *intra-Nordic cooperation will be given a sharper focus.* It will continue 'in the pursuit of a shared perception of democracy, a healthy environment and fundamental social rights'. For the most part then, Nordic cooperation will not focus as much on wider issues, but rather deal with more problematic ones, such as the relationship between the Nordic Passport Union and the Schengen Agreement.[77]

- *Cooperation with Europe:* Nordic cooperation will also aim to influence the European agenda and 'the coordinated implementation of EU and EEA directives'.[78] To some extent, this is simply a modification of the traditional aim of acting as a bridge-builder between the Community and the Nordic countries who remain involved in European cooperation through the EEA agreement (Iceland and Norway).

- *Coordination with the areas adjacent to the Nordic region* - the Baltic Sea and the Arctic, including the Barents Sea: the areas which are increasingly important since the post-1989 changes in Europe.

This new 'three-pillar structure therefore provides a framework for future cooperation in the 1990s and beyond. It was heavily influenced by impact of the Union. It also has implications for Swedish policy in several ways. Sweden has become an EU member and now must balance the obligations of full membership with Nordic cooperation. Its relationship within Nordic cooperation has essentially changed since 1995. The country moved from being the leading Nordic non-member state to arguably, the leading Nordic EU member. Certainly, Denmark's influence as the Nordic bridge-builder will be curtailed. Fenno-Swedish affinity and their coinciding interests in many policy areas, together with the country's economic power, is likely to place Sweden at the centre of Nordic collaboration within the European Union.

In the short-term at least, Swedish policy-makers see the advantages of reconciling Nordic cooperation with the future EU objectives. The government for example, supported the construction of the Øresund bridge on the basis that it would link Sweden not just with Denmark but with the rest of the EU as well.[79] Moreover, the government view Nordic cooperation as a way of gathering support in order to influence EU-based outcomes. It wants to see the EU establish procedures incorporating Nordic decision-making principles such as greater openness and transparency, active parliamentary and public participation, and policy initiation on labour market and environmental questions.[80] As Carl Bildt summarised as early as 1994, one of the most important tasks for Sweden will be 'to give the European Union a clear Northern European dimension'. The existing Swedish position is not one of the abandonment of Nordic cooperation *per se* - although clearly the Swedes have reinforced their view that Nordic cooperation could never be a complete alternative to European integration.

Rather the government stresses that the main emphasis of it will be on EU matters and based within the boundaries of EU policy endeavours. In Swedish eyes at least, the link between Nordic cooperation and European integration has been strengthened. As Pedersen comments, Swedish and Danish efforts 'to turn

Nordic cooperation into a platform for European Union cooperation ... as well as an increased Norwegian participation in forums outside its immediate sphere of interest promises a continuation of Nordic cooperation on the basis of shared social practices'.[81] After all, the EU's decision-making procedures actually encourage collaboration between the Nordic EU members. The Council's qualified majority voting (QMV) rules 'provide extra impetus to Nordic cooperation'.[82] The practical necessity for EU members to cooperate in order to form majorities or 'blocking minorities' that will enable them to influence decisions on proposed EU legislation means that informal Nordic cooperation will be the norm. Given their commonality of interests, Sweden, Denmark and Finland will naturally align on certain issues.

In addition Swedish policy making has also impacted on EU external policies. Since the lodging of membership applications by the three Baltic states in late 1995, the Social Democratic government has expressed its wish to see them pushed into the fast lane for membership. Sweden, along with the other Nordic member states, acts as an internal EU sponsor of their respective applications. Yet, the effect of EU membership on the attitudes of Swedish policy-makers has also resulted in governmental pressure for the Nordic Council's operation to be slimmed down and tailored to the EU (and Baltic questions). Sweden has already cut payments to the Council by about SEK 150 million and from late 1995, the Council's operations have been targeted at specific issues.

For the most part, the Swedes perceive the future of Nordic cooperation as also lying within a wider Baltic context. As Bildt commented (again in 1994), 'Few things are as important ... as facilitating the building of ever closer networks of contacts, commerce and cooperation in the entire Baltic area'. He underlined that Sweden could not afford to take a detached attitude to what happens in the three Baltic countries. Indeed, his political advisor on foreign affairs, Krister Wahlbäck wrote an article in the same year which elaborated on this point. He claimed that it was not possible for Sweden to remain neutral on Baltic questions and that,

> 'Probably, Sweden's attitude concerning the question of the Baltic countries carries more weight in Moscow and in the Western capitals than it does on almost any other question'.[83]

The impact of the changes in the Eastern Baltic had already affected the workings of the Nordic Council in some ways. At the beginning of the 1990s, the Council began to discuss security questions which had previously been outside the organisation's traditional remit. The Nordic Foreign Ministers in May 1992, for instance, discussed the questions of disarmament, economic cooperation and environmental security. This act was significant. As Neumann argues, the fact that the Council discussed security questions meant that it had 'jumped some of the hurdles of formal cooperation ... in the form that one knows from the days of the Cold War'.[84] Future Nordic cooperation is now more flexible and incorporates questions of security in the Baltic region. However, it remains to be seen how useful this potential role may be.

To a limited extent, the Carlsson and Persson governments have seen the future of Nordic cooperation lying within three spheres. On the one hand, as an internal foundation for the Nordic and European environments and on the other as a bridge-builder and initiator of cooperation in the wider Baltic region. If this is put in the context of Stålvant's 'concentric circles' then there is now an additional dimension - the Nordic, *Baltic*, European, Atlantic and the global. Nevertheless, from the Swedish perspective, the immediate future of Nordic cooperation lies as an intermediary with the three Baltic Republics and beyond. Although relations with the Baltic region will in part take place within the context of the European Union (as all three countries have applied for full EU membership) a wider policy towards the region is perceived as valuable by the Swedish government.

After all, the area has significant economic potential for Sweden. Some 50 million people live in what can be described as the Baltic region. It is estimated that the area has strategic value as a possible bridge between the 350 million inhabitants of the industrialised EU and the 250 million people in the rapidly progressing Eastern Europe.[85] As Wæver nicely puts it 'the Nordic project belongs to the old Europe, the Baltic to the new'.[86] Indeed, when the three Baltic states eventually join the EU in the next century, the politicians will most probably replace the term Nordic cooperation with a more broader Baltic one.

The Swedish government and the European Commission were quick to recognise the potential of the Baltic region. Sweden, along with all the other Nordic countries joined the Council of the Baltic Sea States (CBSS).[87] The backbone of official Swedish involvement in the Baltic Sea is to found in the programme for cooperation with Central and Eastern Europe adopted by the Riksdag in late 1995 and which terminates in 1998. The government is committed to spending SEK 4 billion during these three years, with the Baltic states taking the lion's share. About one third of the support is channelled through the EU and additional comprehensive export credits should facilitate Swedish corporate efforts at strengthening trade relations in the Baltic region. In 1995, Ingvar Carlsson also took the initiative. He proposed the holding of a conference 'to give new political force to cooperation in the Baltic region as a dynamic, democratic and stable region in the new Europe'.[88] At the same time, the European Commission established the 'Baltic Sea Region Initiative'.

The culmination of Swedish governmental activity was the hosting of the Baltic Sea Business Summit in Stockholm (24-25 April 1996) and the Baltic Sea

States Summit (3-4 May 1996) at Visby.[89] This latter Summit was especially important not just because it included all the members of the Council, but also included the President of the European Commission and the Prime Minister of Italy, who at that time held the EU's Council Presidency. At the Visby conference, the governments discussed levels of democracy, international cooperation, trade, economy, environmental protection and cultural matters.[90] In the Visby Presidency Declaration, they 'affirmed their support for the process of cooperation in the Baltic Sea Region' and 'confirmed the instrumental role of the Council of the Baltic Sea States (CBSS) in furthering their aims'.[91] They also agreed a number of key topics, such as support for Estonia, Latvia, Lithuania and Poland in their preparation for EU membership, the realisation of the free trade area between the three Baltic Republics and the strengthening of the Baltic Sea Joint Comprehensive Environment Action Programme. Sweden's leading role in the process was confirmed by the fact that the country's new Prime Minister, Göran Persson, was given the task to 'assure, for the time being, the coordination of the Baltic Sea Cooperation'[92] - a role which he has publicly stated he intends to fulfil with vigour.

There is evidence that Persson's government treats this new role seriously. As Foreign Minister Lena Hjelm-Wallén commented in 1996, 'Regardless of whether or not they become EU members, the Baltic states will increase their own cooperation. This cooperation has a value of its own and is not to be found in some EU waiting room'.[93] The Swedes supported the 'five plus three' formula for Nordic ministerial meetings (in which the three 'Balts' are represented). They have unilaterally assisted with financial and technical help to especially reduce the environmental degradation in the area. The Persson government, for instance, contributed funding for the construction of 25 municipal sewage-treatment plants in the region.

Conclusion: Nordic Cooperation and the 'Swedish Diamond'

It can be argued that Nordic cooperation bolstered aspects of the 'Swedish Diamond' and there has been a close interrelationship between the two. Nordic cooperation for example, strengthened Swedish commitments to the principles of consensual democracy by proving that aspects of it, such as the rules adopted in the operation of the Nordic Council's Cooperation Committees and the Nordic Parliamentary Assembly can be translated to regional level. Of course, this it not an entirely Swedish phenomenon. Many of the principles of consensual democracy are apparent in the other countries and there is a high degree of similarity between some of their domestic political procedures and systems.

Ironically, it can be argued that rather than acting as an alternative to European integration, the tangible results of Nordic cooperation have actually reinforced and even increased the interdependence between the countries and the rest of Europe. During the 1960s, for example, there was a noticeable rise in intra-Nordic trade, increasing by 200 percent between 1959-67 and leading to corresponding climb in levels of economic interdependence between the Nordic economies. In part, this was due to the wider benefits of EFTA membership and cemented together the fortunes of Nordic cooperation and European integration.

This of course, has implications for the 'Swedish Diamond'. One point of the Diamond - that of economic interdependence - was bolstered by the three aspects of rising Nordic, EFTA and EU trade. In practice, this meant that the performance of the Swedish economy was physically intertwined with that of its Nordic neighbours and to an increasingly high degree. This was fine when all the Nordic countries, for the most part, belonged to the same economic organisations, such as EFTA. But once Denmark (and Norway) considered joining the Community from the 1960s, the importance of intra-Nordic trade, placed additional pressure on Swedish policy-makers to deal with the issue of EC membership. In effect, Nordic cooperation was modified into a vehicle for gaining closer Swedish ties with the Community. Indeed, since Danish EC accession (1973), Nordic cooperation has been more or less subservient to the dynamics of European integration.

The secondary position of Nordic cooperation has been further reinforced by the inclusion of Sweden and Finland as full EU members since 1995. Yet, in some ways, their accessions have brought a new lease of life to the Nordic Council by, once and for all, confirming that the most of its future role (if any) will be as a platform for common Nordic approaches to EU policies. To some extent the Nordic Council has a better future as a special kind of interest group within the Community. However, Nordic cooperation will not be solely tied to the fortunes of the EU as the Baltic initiatives mean that in this context it can also act as junior partner to the EU. Whatever the scenarios for Nordic cooperation, Sweden's leadership position within it is relatively secure. Sweden is in the rather unusual position (and has in some ways replaced Denmark in these roles) of being central to all of the future scenario for Nordic cooperation. Its new status as a full EU member means that its profile has risen within the Nordic Council and will be instrumental to the Council's EU platform role. At the same time, its position as an initiator of Baltic cooperation within the CBSS was consolidated by Sweden's recent mandate to coordinate its work in the region. The Persson government enjoys the strong position of being critical to both aspects and has clearly reinforced the long-standing view that Nordic cooperation and European integration are mutually reinforcing.

Notes

[1] Sundelius, B. & Wiklund, C. (1979) The Nordic Community: The Ugly Duckling of Regional Cooperation, *Journal of Common Market Studies*, XVIII, 1, September, pp. 59-73.

[2] Andrén, N. (1967) Nordic Integration, *Cooperation and Conflict*, II, 1, pp. 1-25.

[3] For a more detailed discussion of Nordic cooperation see for example, Stålvant, C.-E. (1990) Nordic Cooperation in Wallace, W. (ed.) *The Dynamics of European Integration*, Pinter, London, pp. 125-40.

[4] Solem, E. (1977) *The Nordic Council and Scandinavian Integration*, Praeger, New York, p. 170.

[5] For an extensive study of the Swedish-Norwegian political union see Lindgren, R. E. (1959) *Norway-Sweden Union, Disunion, and Scandinavian Integration*, Princeton University Press, Princeton.

[6] Op. cit., Solem (1977) p. 150.

[7] Op. cit., Lindgren (1959) p. 277.

[8] Op. cit., Solem (1977).

[9] Anderson, S. V. (1967) *The Nordic Council A Study of Scandinavian Regionalism*, University of Washington Press, Washington, p. 9.

[10] Andrén's 'cobweb' theory with its emphasis on 'a fine-meshed net of small interdependencies' has attracted criticism 'because it focuses on the strength of the whole web rather than on that of the individual threads' - see Haskel, B. (1967) Is there an Unseen Spider - A Note on 'Nordic Integration', *Cooperation and Conflict*, II, 3-4, pp. 229-34.

[11] Op. cit., Andrén (1967) p. 3.

[12] Op. cit., Andrén (1967) p. 11.

[13] Op. cit., Andrén (1967) p. 13.

[14] Sundelius, B. (1982) The Nordic Model of Neighborly Cooperation in Sundelius, B. (ed.) *Foreign Policies of Northern Europe*, Westview, Boulder, p. 182.

[15] Op. cit., Andrén (1967) p. 17.

[16] Thomas, A. (1995) The Concept of the Nordic Region and the Parameters of Nordic Cooperation in Miles, L. (ed.) *The European Union and the Nordic Countries*, Routledge, London, pp. 15-31.

[17] Op. cit., Sundelius (1982) pp. 177-95.

[18] Gunnar P. Neilsson however, has argued that Nordic cooperation should not concentrate on the political structural transformation leading to the replacement of separate states by a larger regional state, but rather focus on the process of changes in behavioural codes of conduct among existing states. Thus, the Nordic example is rather more than a pale shadow of European integration - Neilsson, G. (1978) The Parallel National Action Process: Scandinavian Experiences in Taylor, P. & Groom, A. J. R. (eds.) *International Organisation: A Conceptual Approach*, Pinter, London, pp. 270-316.

[19] Op. cit., Anderson (1967) p. 12.

[20] Op. cit., Anderson (1967) p. 12.

[21] Op. cit., Sundelius & Wiklund (1979) p. 60.

[22] For an evaluation of Foreign Policy in the Second World War see Abrahamsen, S. (1957) *Sweden's Foreign Policy*, Public Affairs Press, Washington, D.C.

[23] Ibid., Abrahamsen (1957) pp. 31-4.

[24] According to information disclosed by the Ministry of Defence on 25 March 1940, Swedish military aid to Finland included heavy field artillery, Bofors anti-aircraft and anti-tank guns, rifles, machine guns, 25 airplanes, and large quantities of light ammunition and other supplies.

[25] The proclamation of strict neutrality was erroneous anyway. It did not, for instance, prevent the government approving German requests for the transit of soldiers on leave to Germany, the transit of war materials from Germany to Norway or from one part of Norway over Swedish territory to another part of Norway. Sweden showed during the early parts of the war a 'benevolent neutrality' towards Nazi Germany.

[26] Hadenius, S. (1985) *Swedish Politics During the 20th Century*, Swedish Institute, Stockholm, pp. 53-5.

[27] This was after Finland had re-entered the war on the side of Germany in order to regain territory lost to the Soviets during the previous 1939-40 Winter War.

[28] Op. cit., Abrahamsen (1957) p. 48.

[29] For a survey of the relationship between Nordic cooperation and levels of political sensitivities see for example, Ørvik, N. (1974) Nordic Cooperation and High Politics, *International Organization*, 28, 1, Winter, pp. 61-88; Bonsdorff, G. V. (1965) Regional Cooperation in the Nordic Countries, *Cooperation and Conflict*, I, 1, pp. 32-8 or Wendt, E. (1968) The Power of the Weak, *Cooperation and Conflict*, III, 1, 157-68.

[30] Taken from Ahman, B. S. (1950) Scandinavian Foreign Policy in Ahman, B. S. (ed.) *Scandinavia Between East and West*, Cornell University Press, Ithaca.

[31] Op. cit., Abrahamsen (1957) p. 69.

[32] Op. cit., Abrahamsen (1957) p. 74.

[33] For extensive discussions of the Scandinavian Defence Alliance see Brundtland, A. O. (1964) Hvorkor ikke skandinavisk forsvarsforbund? *Internasjonal Politikk*, 3. or Dörfer, I. (1965) Stalins nordiska balans, *Internasjonal Politikk*, 2 or Haskel, B. G. (1965) Forsoket pa a skape et Skandinavisk forsvarsforbund, *Internasjonal Politikk*, 2.

[34] Haskel, B. G. (1976) *The Scandinavian Option*, Universitetsforloget, Oslo, p. 44.

[35] Ministry of Foreign Affairs, (1950) Östen Undén, Speech by the Foreign Minister of Sweden, 9 February 1949, *Documents on Swedish Foreign Policy, 1949*, UD, Stockholm.

[36] See Hirschfeldt, L. (1949) Skandinavien och Atlantpakten, *Världpolitikens dagsfrågor*, 4-5, p. 35.

[37] For more details see Lange, C. & Goldmann, K. (1966) A Nordic Alliance 1949-1965-197?, *Cooperation and Conflict*, II, 1, pp. 46-63.

[38] The political parties in general maintained their commitment to neutrality, although the Liberals and Conservatives were more sympathetic to the West. Some of the leading independent Liberal newspapers however, openly advocated Sweden joining NATO, but this did not lead to change in the Liberal Party's policy on Europe - see Tingsten, H. (1963) *Mitt liv. 1946-52*, Bonniers, Stockholm.

[39] The most notable statement by Andersson was to the Riksdag (13 October 1965) - Riksdagen, AK 1965, 22, p. 45f. or *Svenska Dagbladet*, 14 October 1965, p. 1.

[40] Archer, C. (1990) *Organizing Western Europe*, Edward Arnold, London, p. 133.

[41] Op. cit., Haskel (1976) p. 92.

[42] From summer 1956, the NECC included Finland as well.

[43] Op. cit., Haskel (1976) p. 94.

[44] Op. cit., Haskel (1976) p. 98.

[45] Ministry of Foreign Affairs, (1955) Address by the Prime Minister to the Foreign Press Association in Stockholm, 1 June 1954, *Documents on Swedish Foreign Policy, 1954*, UD, Stockholm, p. 35.

[46] Edberg, R. (1954) Osynliga gränser i Norden, *Nordisk tidskrift*, KF's forlag, Stockholm, p. 198 or Edberg, R (1952) *Öppna grindarna*, KF's forlag, Stockholm.

[47] For a survey of the levels of the Council's activity see Sundelius, B. (1977) Trans-governmental Interactions in the Nordic Region, *Cooperation and Conflict*, XII, pp. 63-85.

[48] Wendt, F. (1959) *The Nordic Council and Cooperation in Scandinavia*, Munksgaard, Copenhagen, p. 101.

[49] Wiklund, C. (1970) The Zig-Zag Course of the NORDEK negotiations, *Scandinavian Political Studies*, 5, pp. 307-36.

[50] Op. cit., Archer (1990) p. 136.

[51] Taken from Wendt, F. (1979) *Cooperation in the Nordic Countries*, The Nordic Council, Stockholm, p. 41.

[52] Taken from op. cit., Anderson (1967) p. 118.

[53] For a good appraisal of the NORDEK process see op. cit., Wendt, E. (1979).

[54] Nielsson, G. P. (1971) The Nordic and the Continental Dimensions in Scandinavian Integration: NORDEK as a Case Study, *Cooperation and Conflict*, VI, 2, pp. 173-81.

[55] Nordisk Udredningsserie, (1969) *Expanded Nordic Economic Cooperation*, Nordisk Udredningsserie, Stockholm, 17.

[56] Op. cit., Nielsson (1971) p. 175.

[57] Op. cit., Wiklund (1970) p. 312.

[58] However, this point made by Haskel ignores the fact that the NORDEK arrangement was more ambitious than the 1950s proposals. It included areas, such as agriculture and a common market - op. cit., Haskel (1976) p. 127. If NORDEK had been completed then the economic implications were more substantial than those of the 1950s proposals.

[59] Erlander wanted a full customs union (without exceptions) introduced as quickly as possible. If this demand was not met, Erlander declared that Sweden was not prepared to pay its share (46 percent) of the contributions to a number of financial institutions.

[60] Riksdagen, (1969) *Riksdagens protokoll*, Forsta kammeren, Risdagen, Stockholm, 29 October, p. 32 ff.

[61] See for example, *Svenska Dagbladet*, 31 December 1968 or 16 January 1969; *Dagens Nyheter*, 19 January 1969.

[62] Haskel identified this as the so-called 'EEC factor'. It was the major determinant of governmental interest in the NORDEK project - Haskel, B. (1969) External Events and

Internal Appraisals: A Note on the Proposed Nordic Common Market, *International Organization*, 23, 4, Autumn, pp. 960-68.

[63] Riksdagen, (1969) *Riksdagens protokoll,* Andra kammaren, Riksdagen, Stockholm, 4, p. 101 ff.

[64] Gunnar P. Nielsson for example, develops a number of economic, ideological and domestic political and international political factors and places NORDEK within the context of the 'Nordic Balance' to explain its failure - op. cit., Nielsson (1970).

[65] NORDEK could be viewed as a stepping stone towards EEC membership, which the Soviet Union at this time viewed as an economic extension of NATO.

[66] Stålvant, C.-E. (1982) Nordic Policies Toward International Economic Cooperation in Sundelius, B. (ed.) *Foreign Policies of Northern Europe,* Westview Press, Boulder, p. 107.

[67] Ibid., Stålvant (1982) p. 109.

[68] Ibid., Stålvant (1982) p. 113.

[69] The problem became even worse once Sweden and Finland joined the EU and Iceland and Norway form part of the EEA. The Nordic Council and the EU now have three of the Nordic countries as full members of both organisations - Goldschmidt, E. (1990) The European Community and the Nordic Countries: A View From the Nordic Council of Ministers in Laursen, F. (ed.) *EFTA and the EC: Implications of 1992,* European Institute of Public Administration, Maastricht, p. 86.

[70] Op. cit., Sundelius & Wiklund (1979) pp. 69-70.

[71] Op. cit., Sundelius & Wiklund (1979) p. 71.

[72] Ibid., Goldschmidt (1990) p. 88.

[73] Wæver, O. (1992) Nordic Nostalgia: Northern Europe After the Cold War, *International Affairs,* 68, 1, p. 77.

[74] For a preliminary analysis of the potential Nordic influences on the Community see Miles, L. (1995) The European Union and the Nordic Countries: Impacts on the Integration Process in Rhodes, C. & Mazey, S. (eds.) *The State of the European Union, Volume III - The Building of a Euro-Polity?* Longman, London, pp. 317-34.

[75] Strom, K. (1992) Norway, Sweden and the New Europe, *Scandinavian Studies,* 64, 4, p. 513.

[76] Op. cit., Thomas (1996) p. 28.

[77] Nordic Council, (1995) Nordisk och europeisk passunion via ESS, *Nordisk Kontakt,* 20, pp. 8-9.

[78] Op. cit., Thomas (1996) p. 28.

[79] Pedersen, F. S. (1995) Nordic Cooperation and the European Union in Lovenduski, J. & Stanyer, J. (eds.) *Contemporary Political Studies 1995, Volume 3,* PSA/Short Run Press, Exeter, p. 1199.

[80] Hellström, M. (1994) The Swedish View of Europe, *The European,* 2-8 December, p. 2.

[81] Op. cit., Pedersen (1995) p. 1202.

[82] Miles, L. (1995) Enlargement of the European Union and the Nordic Model, *Journal of European Integration,* XIX, 1, Fall, p. 65.

[83] Wahlbäck, K. (1994) Sveriges hållning vid hot mot Balticum, *Briefing från Utrikesdepartmentet,* 2, UD, Stockholm, pp. 26-39.

[84] Neumann, I. (1996) Nordic Security Cooperation in a Homogenized Political Setting, *Cooperation and Conflict,* XXXI, 4, December, pp. 417-32.

[85] Ministry of Foreign Affairs, (1996) *Baltic Sea States Summit 1996 - Facts and Background, No.1,* UD, Stockholm, 25.3.1996, p. 1.

[86] Op. cit., Wæver (1992) p. 96.

[87] The first meeting of the CBSS took place in Copenhagen in March 1992. A Baltic Assembly and a Baltic Council were also established for the Baltic states. They were modelled on the Nordic Council and the Nordic Council of Ministers.

[88] The full membership of the CBSS are Sweden, Finland, Russia, Estonia, Latvia, Lithuania, Poland, Germany and Denmark. Although Norway and Iceland are not usually perceived as part of the Baltic area, they also participate on the grounds that they have a natural interest in the region.

[89] In the eyes of many, the Visby Summit can be seen as 'Carlsson's political testament', especially as Baltic Sea Cooperation has a strong popular foundation in Sweden - Crona, E. (1996) The New Baltic Sea, *Current Sweden,* no. 413, Swedish Institute, Stockholm, p. 2.

[90] Op. cit., Ministry of Foreign Affairs (1996) p. 2.

[91] Ministry of Foreign Affairs, (1996) *Presidency Declaration Visby 3-4 May 1996,* UD, Stockholm, p. 2.

[92] Ibid., Ministry of Foreign Affairs (1996) p. 5.

[93] Taken from op. cit., Crona (1996) p. 2.

7   Contemplating Membership 1990-93

The period 1990-93 is crucial to any comprehensive understanding of why Sweden eventually went on to become a full EC member on 1 January 1995. Numerous domestic and external influences had emerged by 1990 that made full membership both attractive and tenable. The speed with which the Carlsson government moved from ruling out the prospect of membership (1989), to considering the merits of accession (1990), to finally submitting a full membership application (1 July 1991) was exceedingly quick (at least by Swedish standards). As Ole Wæver denotes, the year, 1991 marked the country's 'almost complete acquiescence' to the perceived necessity of joining the Community'.[1]

This chapter will evaluate the domestic process leading to the application and the political considerations that persuaded the government of Social Democrat, Ingvar Carlsson to announce that it would seek full membership. The author will argue that there were substantial domestic and external pressures that influenced Carlsson's policy towards the Community. It was alterations to these pressures that in turn enabled the government to propose in 1990 that EC membership was now compatible with the country's consensual democracy, declining corporate model and neutrality. In other words, it was changes in and between the four points of the 'Swedish Diamond' that accelerated the movement in governmental, party and public thinking on the EC between 1990-93.[2]

Moving Towards Membership

The change in Swedish perspectives towards the European Community took barely two years and to some extent, was treated with a mixture of trepidation and surprise from practitioners and academics alike. Compared to the previous domestic debates on full membership (1961-63, 1967 and 1971 respectively), the Social Democratic government moved speedily towards seeking accession during 1990.To a limited degree, this was due to the impact of the Single European Market (SEM) programme which was being dealt with as part of the European Economic Area (EEA) initiative (see Chapter Five). However, what was noticeable was the rapid change in elite perspectives towards the membership question arising from Swedish frustration with the EEA process. Full EC membership was increasingly attractive due to the limitations of any of the proposed alternatives - be it EFTA or Nordic based.

As early as December 1989, with the changes affecting Eastern Europe now in full swing, the Moderate and Liberal parties re-activated their stances in favour of EC membership. They argued that there were major external changes in Europe which would remove some of the constraints on governmental EC policy. In that month, their parliamentary parties requested a study of the conditions for Sweden becoming an EU member, with specific reference to the consequences of membership for neutrality.[3]

A number of critical events occured during spring 1990, which widened the discussion of full membership. In general, there was growing criticism of the emerging EEA concept across the political spectrum, despite all the major political parties and interest groups supporting its development. Increasingly, the main political parties viewed full membership as the most attractive option and there was a minor race between the parties to establish their positions as pro-EC parties. The governing Social Democrats were placed in the unenviable situation of reacting to initiatives and a pace set by their political opponents. The EC issue, after all, had always been sensitive for the SAP especially at the grass roots level. As Huldt notes,

> 'For almost 30 years it had rejected the European Community, in its various forms, and the party's leader, Ingvar Carlsson, on visits to the Community's capitals in 1988, had reasserted that neutrality remained an insurmountable obstacle to Sweden's membership. The party and the Cabinet needed time - which was never granted to them'.[4]

The EC debate was pushed very much into the limelight, when the key opposition leaders - Carl Bildt of the Moderates and Bengt Westerberg of the Liberals - declared that a change of policy was now a realistic possibility. They announced in May 1990 that their parties would demand a full membership application in their manifestoes at the forthcoming 1991 general election.[5] Westerberg in particular, had been the first major Swedish politician to publicly recognise the significance of the fall of the Berlin Wall, when only five days after (14 November 1989) he had stated that this historic event opened up new possibilities for Sweden with regard to Europe.[6]

In short, the governing Social Democrats suspected that the political initiative on the EC issue was moving away from them. Consequently, the Prime Minister himself responded in an article in *Dagens Nyheter* (27 May 1990) with the audacious title 'EC membership will become impossible - Sweden cannot be a member of the Community if the political union becomes a reality'. The article outlined the main conditions for Swedish full membership. It included two main pre-conditions. Prior to an application there would have to be the creation of a new stable security order in Europe (including the dissolution of the (then) two existing blocs) and that Sweden would not participate whatsoever in any political union orchestrated by the Community.

Unfortunately for the Prime Minister, rather than clarifying the government's position on the EC issue, the article attracted widespread criticism for its total lack of ambition. Carlsson's newspaper piece was quickly followed by a succession of similar articles from the other main political leaders and certain key figures. Carl Bildt's critical response, for example, was published in the same newspaper several days later (3 June 1990). After a series of similar attacks from such notable experts as Carl B. Hamilton, Kjell Goldmann and Bo Huldt, members of the Cabinet were called upon to support Carlsson's position (for instance, Rune Molin, 3 June 1990). In particular, criticism from the unexpected quarter of Ambassador Sverker Åström, former Permanent Under-Secretary of State for Foreign Affairs under the Palme administrations and closely identified with Social Democratic and neutrality policy[7] caused greater concern within the Carlsson camp. Åström continued throughout 1990 to point to the inconsistencies appearing in Swedish security policy.[8] The criticisms of Carlsson's article obliged the Prime Minister to issue another statement in which he declared that he had been misunderstood and was not after all, opposed to membership.

The Prime Minister's position gained the support of the traditional elements of the Centre Party. Its leader, Olof Johansson, intermittently attacked the pro-EC positions of the Moderates and Liberals and especially, their pushing of full membership whilst the EEA process continued.[9] During early summer, the debate became quite heated by Swedish standards.[10] The main interest groups became openly involved in the EC discussion. The SAF, which had supported full membership for a long time, began an orchestrated publicity campaign in favour of membership. It publicly reiterated its position that its support for the EEA was conditional on it leading to an eventual full membership application.[11]

In addition, the LO's EC Committee began the process of converting the main blue-collar trade unions to full membership with a series of reports for the LO's governing management board.[12] In May 1990, the EC Committee produced its report. It discussed eight main scenarios governing future Swedish relations with the Community and stated that the membership option was now viable. Attention was drawn to the fact that the Community was developing a social dimension which reduced some of the concerns of the labour movement as regards European integration.[13] After extensive negotiations within the trade union's leadership during summer 1990, its management board finally approved a cautious acceptance of full membership (August 1990) on the basis that only by maintaining continual export growth could employment be protected and welfare provisions maintained.[14] The EC Committee's 1990 report epitomised their thinking stating that the country 'must participate in integration for economic reasons. A sound economy is necessary to uphold full employment, reduce the social divide and improve social standards'.[15] In short, the LO leadership was convinced that the Swedish welfare model would be endangered unless the country's export industries possessed adequate foreign outlets for their products and ultimately full access to the EC's integration process. However, to some extent, the change in the LO's position on full membership was a tactical manoeuvre. Its leadership wished to have its policy on the issue in place before the opening of the September 1990 congress of the Social Democrats and thus, allow the LO to exert maximum influence at the forthcoming event.[16] By autumn 1990 both the main employers and employee organisation came out in favour of EC membership.

At the September 1990 SAP congress, 'a more positive view towards EC cooperation and possible Swedish participation was informally conveyed'.[17] Whilst official statements by the Prime Minister remained cautious and in spite of the fact that the EC issue was virtually neglected in the debates, a general movement in the position of the Social Democratic leadership was being considered.[18] However, a clear indication by the SAP leadership to the grass roots membership that a policy change was in the offing was not officially given. The motions on the Community that were carried were preceded by little debate. They were ironically almost a carbon-copy of the previous declarations approved by the LO's management board - a point missed by both the SAP mass membership and the Swedish press.[19] Even at this point, the seeds of change were being planted. Certainly, the 1988 informal agreement between the main political parties that membership was not an option and that the EEA should be steadfastly pursued was now quietly forgotten.

As Huldt notes, 'Sweden had now left the door ajar for the Community'.[20] At the Riksdag's opening session (2 October 1990), Ingvar Carlsson introduced a vision of a developing Europe without dividing blocs and that significantly in such a situation, membership of the Community would be compatible with the country's neutrality. The Prime Minister hinted that 'the Community's cooperation on foreign and security policy might not be of such a nature that it entails a binding defence policy'. Nevertheless, it was economic factors that supposedly provided the next step and allowed the government to announce that it would seek full membership.

The Social Democratic government had already fallen into chaos in spring 1990 after a Cabinet crisis over an emergency economic programme to deal with the deep economic recession. In fact, the cabinet had resigned, been reformed and returned to power. This economic sub-text provided the ideal rationale for moving forward with the full membership issue. By October, the

Swedish currency market was highly unstable and estimates of capital moving out of the country were exceedingly high. The Carlsson government was faced with another confidence crisis. The business lobbies pressured for action to deal with the large capital flight in the short term and the implications for full employment in the longer term.

The government suddenly announced (26 October 1990) as part of an economic austerity package that 'Swedish membership of the EC while retaining Swedish neutrality is in our national interest'. It would 'work for a new decision by Parliament about the policy towards Europe, which more clearly and in more positive wording clarifies Sweden's ambitions to become a member of the European Community'.[21] This shock announcement was also disguised as a 'footnote' to a short-term austerity package, which gave the impression that this was either a hasty decision or a political manoeuvre to facilitate full membership by the back-door. The Riksdag's Foreign Affairs Standing Committee was not fully consulted on the 'footnote' decision (even if individual members were) prior to its announcement. Given the committee has a coordination role in the Parliament and is the source of considerable expertise on foreign policy questions, the apparent lack of consultation on the part of government was deemed to procedurally incorrect and/or politically unwise by most parliamentarians.[22] Whatever the scenario the reality was that this decision was the culmination of a much longer process'.[23]

The problem for the Social Democratic party elite was that the SAP had traditionally been identified with strong opposition to full membership on the grounds of neutrality, as the 1961 Declarations by Erlander and 1971 by Palme were cases in point.[24] Carlsson was careful to argue that the policy change had been facilitated by the post-1989 strategic changes in Europe and more importantly as being forced on the government by the economic crisis engulfing Sweden by late 1990. This view was neither accepted nor liked by the majority of the party's mass membership. Just as in the previous Danish and British examples and even the later Finnish one, full membership had been rationalised on essentially economic grounds and as a reactive, rather than pro-active policy.

The decision to apply for membership was also a populist reaction by the government to the mood of the country in order to increase public support for (at this time) a relatively unpopular administration. Carlsson's personal rating had fallen to under 30 percent in the polls by April 1990 and consequently, the Social Democrats could not afford either the Moderates or the Liberals to lead the election campaigns in 1991 on the EC issue. Polls taken during May 1990 also indicated that a large majority of Swedes favoured full membership, with only 21 percent opposed to EC membership and 20 percent undecided. The Social Democrats saw considerable political advantage (in 1990) in being labelled as the party (and government) that had transformed Swedish EC membership into a real possibility.[25] In effect, the government dropped the previous conditions for full membership outlined in Carlsson's newspaper article (27 May 1990). In less than six months, the Social Democrats changed tack and policy, partly in response to domestic pressures from the opposition parties and also in the light of external influences.

On 12 December 1990, the Riksdag voted by 289-28 in favour of applying for full membership, although it still insisted on the reservation that it must be in a form compatible 'with the retention of neutrality'. Some 90 percent of the Riksdag's members voted in favour providing a resounding endorsement of the government's change of heart and for a democratic mandate to seek EC membership. With equal consistency, those parliamentarians that opposed such a move came from the Greens and Left Party. Once again, the parliamentary statement (December 1990) sparked a minor debate on the consequences of combining full membership with the country's neutrality. Key figures, such as Sverker Åström, repeated their demands for a thorough review of Swedish policy on this point. This resulted in some minor concessions on the part of the government. Carlsson promised in February 1991 that any possible Swedish EC membership would have to be approved by a preceding national referendum.[26]

During spring 1991, the government embarked on a domestic exercise aimed at replacing the traditional consensus on neutrality policy with one that would accept that full membership and neutrality could be reconciled, (especially as there would soon be a summer break and then a general election in September 1991). In short, the Carlsson government needed to act relatively fast if it was to move from declaration to actually seeking full membership. This consensus-building process extended to the formulation of a rather unusual parliamentary procedure. In May 1991, a hearing was called by the Riksdag's Foreign Affairs Standing Committee (after an initiative of the opposition parties) to deal with the specific question of whether the Community would develop a common defence policy which would act as a barrier to Swedish full membership. For the most part, this was a publicity exercise aimed at airing all the major viewpoints on EC membership. It acted as a means of further 'rubber-stamping' the government's decision, rather than altering the actual policy outcome.[27] The Committee came (not surprisingly) to the same conclusions as the Carlsson government:

> 'The prerequisites for Swedish security policy are also changing. The question of avoiding foreign policy ties which was previously of crucial importance is no longer posed in the same way. Full participation in European cooperation - already in the CSCE, and in membership also of the European Union - is, on the contrary, for any country a prerequisite for being able to influence developments and to actively contribute to the establishment of a new peace and security order in our continent. ... In this new situation, Swedish security

policy is ... characterised by active and full participation in efforts to achieve the objectives which are now shared by all European states'.[28]

In addition, the government decided in May 1991 to become a 'shadow-member' of the EC's Exchange Rate Mechanism (ERM) and to peg the value of the Krona to the European Currency Unit (ECU). The Krona was fixed to a band 1.5 percent either side of the ECU. The decision was rationalised by Carlsson on several grounds. First, linking the Krona to the ERM was part of the government's attempts at bringing down domestic inflation. In other words, it was part of the overall strategy at dealing with the current recessional conditions in Sweden. Second, the ERM appeared (at least at this time) to offer a stable exchange relationship with the country's key trading partners (the UK, Denmark and Germany). In effect, Sweden was once again following the economic lead of the UK which had become a full member of the ERM in 1990. Third, it would strengthen trade possibilities with the rest of Europe and promote greater Swedish export sales abroad. Finally, it was a further attempt on the part of the government to establish the country's EC credentials. It would be seen as a symbolic gesture by Sweden towards the notion of eventually joining the Community.

Whilst receiving a positive reaction generally from the political elite as a means of strengthening Swedish participation in European integration, concerns were raised in certain quarters about the timing of the decision. Certain elements of the business community questioned the wisdom of tying the country's exchange rate policy and reducing its freedom of action at a time of recessional difficulties. Sweden after all, was only a 'shadow member' of the ERM. The country would not be party to ERM-related decision-making inside the EC. It would remain outside the collective support networks of the EC's central banks - restricting the Riksbank's ability to mount an effective defence of the Krona's pegged rate against market speculators. It would also be difficult for the Riksbank to convince the foreign exchange markets that the value of the Krona was sustainable given the present weakness of the Swedish economy.[29] The decision also attracted some criticism from the opposition parties on two points. First, that it was not based solely on economic considerations. They alleged that this was a political manoeuvre to revitalise the popularity of the ruling SAP in time for the forthcoming September election. Second, the Greens, the Left Party and to a lesser extent, the Centre Party, highlighted its implications for neutrality policy. They argued that the country's credibility as a neutral was once again in question given that Sweden's economic policy would be even more firmly tied to the EC.

Fortunately for the Social Democratic government, the only parliamentary groups that were resolutely opposed to full membership were the Greens and the Left Party, which whilst acting as a thorn in the side of the government, were so numerically small (in terms of parliamentary representation) as not to be essential to any parliamentary consensus for the new policy. Their opposition was more than balanced by the pro-EC stances of the Moderates and the Liberals.

The change in the Centre Party's orientation to the European Community was gradual and at times, far from clear or uniform. Shortly after the government's announcement (October 1990) for instance, the party's Riksdag group backed a committee proposal to investigate the possibilities of Swedish membership and the party later supported the Parliament's decision (June 1991) to submit an application.[30] The Centre Party leader, Olof Johansson, emphasised that EC accession would be conditional on the twin aspects of being subjected to public approval by referendum and that neutrality would remain intact. Johansson's caution was understandable and politically astute. With its traditional identification with the agrarian communities and neutrality, it was vital that the Centre Party's internal unity and electoral popularity was maintained by ensuring that any overtures to the Community incorporated a declaration safeguarding Swedish neutrality. The party's strategy was essentially a 'wait and see' attitude.

In May-June 1991, the representatives of the major political parties completed the text of a governmental declaration on full membership. Consequently, with a relatively firm consensus already in place, the Prime Minister spoke on the official motives for full membership (14 June 1991). Carlsson stressed the link between EC accession and neutrality and that Swedish EC membership was now 'compatible with the requirements of our policy of neutrality'.[31] As Karvonen and Sundelius suggest a new multi-party premise for security policy had been attained:

> 'Due to the new European security order, the classic and previously supreme demand for upholding the credibility of neutrality was no longer an obstacle to membership within the dynamic West European economic integration process'.[32]

In reality, the June 1991 governmental declaration was a compromise between the major political parties. Special attention was paid to the traditional positions of the Social Democrats and the Centre Party on neutrality. In typical Swedish policy-making style and with the ground-work done, the Carlsson government lodged its full membership application (1 July 1991). Yet, to some extent, the overwhelming parliamentary majority supporting the government's decision allowed Carlsson considerable flexibility on presenting the application. When the formal application was presented to the Dutch Council Presidency, the request for membership was surprisingly (and unlike 1967) reduced to one sentence. It included no specific reference to the country's neutrality.[33] At the European

Council's meeting (29 July 1991), the member states welcomed the Swedish application and set in motion the procedure applying to the accession of applicant states (under articles 98 ECSC, 237 EEC and 205 EURATOM Treaties).

Ironically, the rapid change in Social Democratic thinking (in less than a year) was unable to save them at the September 1991 general election.[34] The size of the Social Democratic defeat was historic. The SAP's share of the vote fell to 37.7 per cent of the overall vote, with the non-socialist parties gaining mostly. During the campaigns, the major political parties adopted a generally pro-EU platform, although to varying degrees and with differing success. The Moderates in their campaign tried to take credit for pushing the Social Democratic government forward on the issue, whilst the SAP campaigned for a new mandate to work for a more Swedish style 'Social Europe'. The results were mixed if the perspectives of the respective parties on European integration are compared. The two main anti-EC parties - the Greens and the Left Party - lost seats, as did the (then) governing and cautious (but still pro-EC) Social Democrats. In contrast, the Moderates, New Democracy and the Christian Democrats, (which were in favour of full membership) gained seats.[35]

The new government was this time a non-socialist coalition, headed by the charismatic Moderate party leader, Carl Bildt. From the perspective of the membership application, the new government, whilst widely regarded as more pro-EC than the previous Carlsson administration, still endured internal strains undermining its cohesion. The Bildt government did not have an outright parliamentary majority. Differences between the Moderates and the Liberals on the one side and the Centre Party on the other, on issues like the Øresund bridge project and EC membership were obvious. At the same time, the internally weak new government was faced with the daunting task of coping with economic recession and public pressure for a strong governmental approach to deal with it. Upon assuming office, the government issued a declaration. It explicitly stated that EC membership was a prime objective, but at the same time, eventual accession would be conditional on approval by popular referendum and that environmental concerns would be accommodated within any final accession deal. These qualifications could be interpreted as concessions to the Centre Party in the governmental coalition. They highlighted the pivotal role of this relatively small political party on the EC issue.

Within the four party non-socialist Bildt government, the administration was roughly split into what Miles and Widfeldt identify as two groups as regards their views on full membership. On the one hand, a group of 'core enthusiasts' (the Liberals and Moderates) and on the other, a cohort of 'recent converts' (the Centre Party and the Christian Democrats).[36] The leading Liberals and Moderates maintained high profiles and ensured a strong pro-EC orientation within the composition of the Cabinet. Apart from the fact that the new Prime Minister was enthusiastic about Swedish EC membership, the Moderate Ulf Dinkelspiel was appointed as Minister with special responsibility for European issues and the ensuing accession negotiations. Bildt and Dinkelspiel also enjoyed the active support of the two most senior Liberal ministers, party leader Bengt Westerberg (Deputy Prime Minister and Minister for Social Welfare) and Anne Wibble (Finance Minister). In all, the government was overwhelmingly pro-membership and designed to ensure that Sweden would eventually join the Community.[37] None the less, the Liberals and Moderates were conscious of the Centre Party's tentative position on the EC. They were careful to accommodate their demands for approval by referendum in particular.[38] As Miles and Widfeldt comment elsewhere all the parties were in favour of EC membership on the elite level (even if the Centre Party deemed it necessary to handle the issue with care), whilst on the lower levels all the parties were split, albeit to various degrees'.[39]

The rapidity with which the Bildt government sought to establish its pro-EC credentials was apparent even in its first governmental declaration (4 October 1991).[40] Bildt underlined Swedish future commitments as part of EC membership and in which he described neutrality as no longer relevant to post-Cold War Europe. The Prime Minister introduced a revised 'foreign and security policy with a European identity' and with neutrality at best, reduced to merely an explicit reference to 'non-participation in military alliances'.[41] According to Bildt, the policy revision was rationalised on several grounds. First, that there had been important changes in Europe, allowing for greater flexibility. By the end of 1991, not only had the Warsaw Pact been dissolved but the old Soviet Union was on the verge of break-up, emphasising the point that one of the main blocs in Europe had virtually disappeared. Second, the unanimity requirement for decisions would be maintained in any future EC foreign policy endeavour. The non-socialist government was confident that it could avoid any commitments which would compromise its revised security policy.

However, there was some criticism of Bildt's actions because substantial alterations to traditional policies were made without adherence to the long-standing norm of policy consultation. After all, there had been no major public debate on altering the country's security policy. This seemed to fly in the face of the usual requirement that security policy be governed by an 'unflinching' consensus.[42] Party and public support for the policy revisions seemed far from comprehensive. Carlsson's Social Democrats, now free from the shackles of defining governmental policy, accused Bildt of being premature in removing the strict interpretation of neutrality before it was certain the changes in Europe were permanent. Technically, they did seem to have a point. The Riksdag's approval for lodging a full membership application (12 December 1990) stipulated that it must be in a form compatible with neutrality. The Parliament did not sanction major changes to neutrality policy itself, especially if this was motivated by the governmental desire to join the Community. Yet, from a pragmatic perspective, the non-socialist government was merely reacting to wider demands for a more appropriate response to the wider changes engulfing Europe. It is difficult to estimate for how much longer the new government could have credibly continued with the pre-1989 doctrines of neutrality policy in any case.

Ironically, the Centre Party also entered the foray. It accused Bildt of ambiguity on security policy in spite of the fact that they were also part of the governing coalition. However, the main issue for the two anti-EC parties - the Greens and Left Party - and several well-known intellectuals was the cavalier attitude of the Bildt administration and the lack of consultation on the changes. In a series of articles in *Dagens Nyheter* (12 December 1991 - for example, *Är medlemskap redan ett faktum?*), Bildt was criticised for 'arrogance and disregard of democratic values'. As Huldt suggests it looked 'as if Sweden had gone through a revolution in 1990-91, but that a counter-revolution was now underway'.[43]

To some extent, the domestic debate, which had a tendency to be based on a rather static appraisal of EC development, was eclipsed by events taking place within the Community. As early as November 1991, the Bildt government committed itself to accepting the text of the Community's intergovernmental conference to be held at Maastricht (given the mandate to shape the Community's evolution into the late 1990s and beyond). On 10 December 1991, the (then) twelve member states' governments agreed to transform the Community into a European Union (EU) with a three-pillar structure based on the EC, a Common Foreign and Security Policy (CFSP) and Justice and Home Affairs (JHA). The Swedish debate was consequently given a new impetus.[44] It changed from discussing the implications of changes in governmental policy to dealing with the actual nature of future EC membership in early 1992.

The Changing 'Swedish Diamond'

At first glance, the speed of the transformation in the Carlsson and later Bildt governments' perspectives on the European Community (and later European Union) was nothing short of breathtaking. This remarkable policy transition was not only quick in taking approximately twelve months, but also represented 'one of the most fundamental shifts in Swedish post-war foreign policy'.[45] These changes can be more adequately dealt with in the context of the 'Swedish Diamond' and more importantly, that alterations in governmental policy were, in part, a reflection of the changes affecting the Diamond itself. The Diamond's four points - Integrative and Consensual Democracy, the Corporate Model, Economic Interdependence and the External Strategic Environment - will now be examined in the context of the events of 1989-93.

a) Point 1: Integrative and Consensual Democracy

This aspect was defined (Chapter Two) as a mature parliamentary democracy characterised by long traditions of decision-making by consensus, low degrees of opposition to the governing political system and a high level of open democratic government and public access to government documents. In general, Sweden can still be regarded as a 'consensual democracy', but there have been a number of trends which have at least altered the emphasis within this concept of a democracy. To some extent, Swedish democracy has been less consensual and has been in a state of flux since 1988. This trend has been compounded by the changes in policy towards Europe since 1989-90 in particular. A number of internal tensions within the consensual democracy were obvious when European integration was brought on to the centre political stage as the EC issue tended to be divisive and made consensus-building more difficult.

Certainly, the rising and dominant role of Cabinet government was illustrated by the decision by the Carlsson administration to go for full membership. In essence, the decision was discussed within the Social Democratic elite and without the widespread support (or in some cases) knowledge of mass membership of the SAP. Again with the formation of the succeeding Bildt government, the rapid re-formation of security policy was discussed within the elite of the Moderate, Liberal, Centre and Christian Democratic parties - although in the first two cases, the decision posed few problems for their respective grass roots which were generally in favour of Swedish full membership in any case.

The secondary role of the Riksdag was also apparent, even if the Carlsson and later Bildt governments were careful to ensure that a parliamentary majority could be relied upon to support government policy. In part, this was due to the general trends within the consensual democracy - towards greater individualism, a more unstable party system with lower party coherence and the introduction of new or stronger minority parties into the Riksdag since the late 1980s. There has also been evidence of greater volatility amongst party members and voters, making the party leaderships more sensitive to the concerns of their (at least perceived) less reliable members and supporters.[46] Amongst Swedish voters, the number of individuals stating a party preference is declining. Surveys by the SOM (Society, Opinion and Media) Institute at Göteborg University estimated that the percentage of the population that were 'very convinced or partly convinced' party supporters dropped from 63 percent in 1987 to 48 percent in 1990. This did recover to 65 percent in 1991 as this was an election year.[47] Carlsson was especially conscious that the EC issue was a divisive one for the SAP's parliamentary party, at the mass party level and that party cohesion would be difficult to maintain. This was also reinforced by the fact that the Prime

Minister's own popularity rating fell dramatically during 1989-90 within the party membership and among the public.[48]

In addition, gaining a consensus on a change in policy was more difficult because the Riksdag now contained four revived or new political forces - two of which were openly hostile to Swedish full membership of the Community. The Left Party enjoyed a revival, whilst the anti-EC Greens entered the Riksdag at the 1988 general election. These two anti-EC parties, whilst not being critical to any government consensus due to their small parliamentary representation, were a thorn in successive governments' sides by keeping the EC issue in the political limelight.

The small party aspect was also given a disproportionately higher profile simply because both the Carlsson and later Bildt governments were minority administrations reliant to some extent upon political allies which were at best, less than enthusiastic about the prospect of Swedish full membership. In the case of the Social Democrats, Carlsson needed intermittent Left Party or Centre Party support. Later, with the formation of the non-socialist government, Bildt was reliant not only on maintaining the tenuous internal solidarity of the four coalition partners (and especially the EC cautious Centre Party and Christian Democrats), but also that of New Democracy which was a vibrant political force between 1991-94. In essence, one of the main aspects of Sweden's consensual democracy - that of consensus policy-making - was now difficult for both the socialist and non-socialist camps.

Most of the consensus-building seemed to be achieved after the government announced (26 October 1990) that it would seek full membership; although there were notable movements during spring-summer 1990, which allowed certain key elite leaderships to come out in favour of membership - the LO for the Socialists and the SAF, Liberals and Moderates for the non-socialists. The most important period of consensus building - certainly at the parliamentary party level - happened almost after the fact and from October 1990. As Sundelius concurs:

> 'In Swedish politics, building an authoritative consensus behind major policy initiatives is an important ingredient of successful decision-making. In this particular case, the elaborate process of consensus-building spanned the 1990-91 parliamentary session'.[49]

The Centre Party (at this time part of the non-socialist opposition) was the prime target. Its support was central to gaining sufficient parliamentary votes to carry the bill on the EC application in December 1990. It acted as the *de facto* guardian of Swedish neutrality within the government and party machinery - partial evidence that consensus-building still operated.

In the latter parts of the Carlsson government (from 1990-91), there were attempts at maintaining the consensus-building aspects of the 'Diamond'. Its emphasis changed slightly though - from gaining a consensus before a decision is taken (the ante or pre-decisional stage) to achieving a consensus to support a decision after it has been made (the post-decisional stage). The main public and parliamentary discussions (including parliamentary commissions) came after October 1990 and not before the application. However, to some extent, the process reflected the sizable impact of the economic downturn on the country during 1990. It was influenced by public, media and party pressure for an immediate response to these problems. It was by no means coincidental that the decision to apply for full membership came as part of an emergency austerity package and was not seen by the media or the public as a well-deliberated decision on the part of the government.

Another motivating factor behind the search for consensus during winter 1990 and spring 1991 was that the Social Democratic government wished to neutralise the threat made by the non-socialist opposition that they would make EC membership an issue in the September 1991 general election campaigns. The prolonged consensus-building activities of the Carlsson government ensured that a potentially difficult issue for them was diffused. All the main political parties (with the exception of the fringe Left Party and Greens) were officially in favour of EC membership. It did, however, fail to keep the Social Democrats in power.

Ironically, this high level of consensus allowed the non-socialist government to take policy-decisions once in power (from October 1991) without further consultation. Bildt claimed that the virtually unanimous parliamentary resolution of December 1990 and the consensus-building between the political parties during spring 1991 provided the foundation for policy revisions. It was only later during the 1993-94 accession negotiations that the government again sought to build bridges with the opposition parties in order to quell the rising anti-EC mood of the public.[50]

Overall, as regards the democracy point of the 'Diamond', the EC debate made existing internal friction transparent and consensus-building an arduous task for the Carlsson and Bildt governments. According to the SOM Institute, confidence in Sweden's policy-making institutions (and its consensual democracy) was estimated at a mere 28 percent in 1990. To a limited degree, moves towards EC membership were part of a 'crisis of confidence' that was in any case engulfing the country.[51] Levels of party dissension between the executive and parliamentary and between the elite and mass party membership were apparent. The EC issue consolidated those trends, such as party instability and fragmentation, that had been first seen in the late 1980s.

b) Point 2: The Swedish Corporate Model

The linkage between the emergence of a serious domestic debate on full membership and the onset of major economic recession in Sweden is of major significance. Carlsson stressed in the *Economist* (8 November 1990) that the reasons for the October change in government policy had been principally due to economic difficulties[52] reflected in Sweden's high inflation, big budget deficits and low growth.[53] The combination of the EC debate and the widespread desire to see governmental action to deal with economic recession reinforced changes to the country's corporate model that were already underway. It is not surprising then that the benefits of EC membership were portrayed (at this time) mostly in economic terms and related to Sweden's poor economic performance during 1990-91.

Elements of the traditional Swedish corporate model were already in a state of crises before either the onset of recession or the debate on full membership re-emerged.[54] Pressure to cut welfare provision and curb the size of the country's public sector, for example, had been intermittent throughout the 1980s. The dominance of Social Democracy had also been called into question, as the SAP's popularity amongst voters became more volatile.[55] The era of continuous Social Democratic government, which had been rudely interrupted by the non-socialists between 1976 and 1982, looked under serious threat once again.

Of course, (and as Chapter Two identifies) the traditional elements of Swedish economic policy and industrial relations were in the process of being revised from the late 1980s onwards. The blue-collar trade union congress (LO) was like its Social Democratic party counterpart, facing serious competition, notably from other white-collar unions, for the title as the main voice of the country's workers. The general appearance of the trade union movement was that it was becoming on the one hand, fragmented and the other, that its traditional close links with the Social Democrats were tenuous. The main trade unions increasingly criticised Social Democratic economic policy. They stressed that the increasing power of the multinationals and the necessity of maintaining continuous direct investment in Sweden had outmoded traditional, nationally based economic strategies.[56] Although the trade union movement and the Social Democrats continued to highlight that one of the goals of economic policy was full employment, sizable rifts appeared over the attention paid to other indicators such as inflation, public expenditure and budgetary deficits.[57]

Crucially, the norm of annual, centralised, collective bargaining on wage increases - the core of Swedish industrial relations - had slowly disintegrated in the 1980s. As Olsson argues, this element of the Swedish model was changing. It had originally been sustained by a bi-polar system, dominated by two powerful and important agents - the SAF and the LO (1946-65) - and later with centralised private and public negotiations (1966-73). The collective bargaining system was transformed into a multi-polar system by the mid 1980s with multiple arenas and powerful coalition formations including other actors.[58] Even this multi-polar system was unable to control wage developments by 1990. In economic terms, although centralised negotiations started off the wage bargaining process (at least until 1990), the system increasingly allowed for 'wage drift' whereby centrally negotiated wages were subject to local negotiations at industry and plant level. Central bargaining was virtually abandoned after 1990.

Nevertheless, the twin aspects of economic recession and full membership also reinforced and in some cases, accelerated the speed of disintegration of the corporate norms. Although the industrial relations dimension of the Swedish model was in transition, the process was speeded up by the dramatic rise in unemployment, which rose from around 2 percent (which was the average during the 1970s-80s), to 8 percent in 1993, with another 5-6 percent of the labour force in various public employment and training schemes. The impact was especially severe in manufacturing and construction sectors with employment falling by 25 percent alone in manufacturing between 1990-93. According to the SOM Institute, 38 percent of the population felt the country's economic performance was worsening in 1989, reaching an astonishing 81 percent in 1990 and 80 percent in 1991 - increasing pressure on the Carlsson administration to deal with the country's economic problems as its number one priority.[59] To a degree, this was reflected in long-term unemployment figures which rose from 17 percent of the total unemployed in 1989 to 27 percent in 1994.[60]

Thus, the Swedish economy 'was characterised by serious imbalances' by the early 1990s.[61] According to the International Monetary Fund assessments, the 1990-93 recession, which was the country's 'longest and deepest since the 1930s' could only make matters worse.[62] The country slipped from third position in the OECD's GDP per capita league in 1970 to twelfth place in 1991. Yet, the inflexibility of the wage bargaining system resulted in high wage inflation and a slowing down of productivity growth.[63] Even in 1990 hourly earnings increased at an annual rate of 10 percent, whilst economic confidence was further depleted by difficulties in the financial and real estate markets (which entirely collapsed in 1991-92 with several large banks on the verge of bankruptcy).

For most of the 1980s, the SAF had insisted on industry-level negotiations only, but in the early 1990s critics of centralisation became more ambitious. Having more or less eliminated (multi-industry) bargaining, the organisation increasingly questioned centralised industry level (multi-employer) bargaining. After closing its collective bargaining and statistical units in 1990 and withdrawing its representatives from most corporate bodies in 1991, the SAF argued that general terms of employment should be regulated at the industry level, whereas wage bargaining would occur at the firm level. In the same year (1991) major engineering firms such as ABB, began signing partnership contracts at the firm level encompassing white-collar and blue-collar employees and wage and non-wage issues.

However, since 1993, it has been the question of whether industry-level negotiations will determine wage setting (rather than peak-level bargaining) that has emerged at the source of contention between the employers and unions. As Pontusson and Swenson suggest, the SAF whilst rejecting old forms of corporatism now sees its new role 'as public policy advocate' and the champion of 'coordinated decentralisation'.[64] In its program adopted in 1990 (Multiplicity and Markets), the SAF paid no attention to the issue of collective bargaining. It concentrated on broader political and ideological concerns, such as the full membership question and the employment crisis - signalling the perceived link between the decentralisation process and internationalisation of industrial relations questions. Indeed, the SAF was careful to always stress that decentralised wage bargaining was accompanied by macro-economic changes, including public spending cutbacks, a restrictive monetary policy and to a lesser extent, EC membership.

In sum and according to Iversen, the combined impact of internationalisation, controlled growth in public sector wages and rising levels of real and threatened unemployment has several important effects on Sweden.[65] First, it relaxed market-induced wage push emanating from the privileged sectors of the economy. Second, it made a decentralised and flexible bargaining system increasingly attractive to powerful groups of employers and workers. In other words, it consolidated demands for a process of decentralisation, liberalisation and internationalisation.[66] After all, the initiative to break with decades of centralised bargaining came from export-orientated engineering employers and unions dominated by highly skilled and relatively well-paid workers. Iversen argues that the decentalisation process seems to be 'irreversible'. The strongest signal for this conclusion coming from the SAF when it shut down its central bargaining and statistical units and since then has withdrawn from virtually all government bodies, including the Labour Market Board (AMS).[67]

Part of the problem of the Swedish economy was (later) estimated to be the slowdown in growth resulting from too low investment ratios. Gross domestic investment as a share of GDP declined from 25 percent in the late 1960s to 17 percent in 1992.[68] The stagnation of domestic investment was matched by increases in foreign direct investment (FDI) abroad by the country's largest firms. Swedish investment in the EC member states was especially large during the late 1980s, when the FDI outflows amounted to over 3 percent of GDP annually. In 1990, nearly two-thirds of the total labour force of Swedish multinationals were employed in foreign affiliates. The corresponding inflows of FDI into Sweden was much smaller.

The trade unions and the employers federations were put on the defensive. Both sides accepted that greater flexibility within the work force was needed to maintain and boost job numbers. On one main aspect, there was a striking affinity of viewpoints between the traditional arms of the Swedish model - the government, employers and the trade unions. The competitiveness of firms (and the maintenance of low unemployment) was reliant upon continued access to export markets and inward investment into Sweden. This would be reinforced by EC membership.

Following the same line of reasoning, it was also argued by most of the main political parties (although to varying degrees) that the future of Sweden's generous welfare provision was directly tied to export growth.[69] Greater demands were placed upon the welfare state after 1990 as economic recession hit hard - at a time when the government expenditure was already stretched. By 1991, public spending whilst not at an all time high, still amounted to 64 percent of GNP. The main political parties reluctantly accepted that levels of welfare provision would have to be reduced if successive governments were to remove budgetary deficits and limit the size of the country's public debt.[70]

Ultimately, the long-standing principle that the welfare provision would be universal, based on the notion of citizenship and solidarity in purpose was dropped. The welfare state was reformed on the basis of targeted and means-tested provision. Key elite 'think-tanks', such as the Swedish Centre for Business and Policy Studies' (SNS) Economic Policy Group were arguing by the early 1990s that the welfare state 'in its current proportions and design - constitutes a severe threat to future employment and growth in Sweden'[71] and that the real problem for the economy lay in the country's high expenditure ratio.[72] Moreover, there was general public support for the trimming of welfare provision in 1990. The SOM Institute reported that three times as many respondents wanted to see a cut in public spending as resisted reductions.[73] Support for privatisation also peaked in polls conducted in 1990.

Ironically, most of the main political parties also argued that EC membership, whilst not in itself solving the problems of the Swedish economy, would at least reinforce any governmental solutions by providing the most advanced framework for guaranteeing exports and consequently, long-term job security. It was generally accepted that the Social Democratic government by applying for membership, was effectively surrendering its belief in the superiority of the Swedish model. In return, it expected that membership would provide a new external discipline that would make it easier to control, and lighten the burden of, an overgrown public sector.[74]

In short, the Swedish corporate model itself was challenged by the recession of the early 1990s, accelerating underlying trends to the point that many elements of the model had to either be modified, suspended or in some cases, simply removed. Many of the viewpoints linked to the model which had made EC membership unpalatable on sovereignty grounds were now less persuasive. Arguments, such as the overriding need to protect Sweden's superior welfare provision and to maintain complete control over the economic policy, were less convincing. These changes strengthened support for EC membership. The underlying rationale of the protecting Swedish jobs and welfare provision by increasing levels of international competitiveness became associated with the economic benefits that would supposedly accrue from joining the Community. It was doubtful whether these benefits would ever be a reality. None the less, it did not prevent the economic arguments promoting changes to the corporate model from indirectly pushing forward the prospect of Sweden becoming an EC member. The second point of the 'Diamond' rather than being an obstacle to membership, now acted to further it.

It is by no means coincidental that Carlsson's decision to apply for EC membership in October 1990 was preceded by the LO coming out in favour of full membership during the previous summer. It provided a firm foundation for government policy as the decision was now supported by both the main trade union and employers interest group elements. In many ways, the traditional consensual approach of mobilising key interest group support behind a policy initiative held true for the EC case. Equally, once the Social Democrats went into opposition in late 1991, the SAP became more pessimistic about EC membership, partly because of doubts expressed not just within the party but also with the LO's mass membership. In effect, the LO also became more cautious on EC membership. Throughout the early 1990s the debate between key interest groups on the future of the corporate model and the discussion on EC membership were inter-linked. During 1990-93, most of the arguments regarding the reform of the corporate system also, albeit to a limited extent, facilitated support for Sweden becoming an EC member.

Nevertheless, this did not prevent the Bildt government, and in spite of criticism in 1992 to the contrary, from reverting back to traditional consensus-building measures to discuss future changes to economic policy and the merits of full membership. On 10 December 1992, the Bildt government appointed a commission of independent academics (*Ekonomikommissionen*) to analyse the economic crisis and suggest ways to solve it. The Commission, chaired by Assar Lindbeck, presented its final report on 9 March 1993. In the same month as the Commission delivered its final report, the government appointed a parliamentary committee (later to be known as the EU Consequences Committee) to assess the economic merits of full membership (see Chapter Eight). It finished in March 1994. In both cases, each body supported the government's bid to become a full member of the Community, but primarily because of the economic benefits that would accrue from it in the long-term. To some extent, they legitimised existing governmental policy rather than necessarily shaped it.

c) Point 3: Economic Interdependence

The 1989-93 era was also important for strengthening the dominance of economic interdependence arguments influencing governmental, party and public opinion in favour of joining the Community.[75] In effect, this point of the Diamond was strengthened, rather than dramatically revised. It enabled the Diamond's economic interdependence arguments to overwhelm the previously dominant fourth point - neutrality and the importance of the strategic environment.

The Bildt government (and the Lindbeck and EU Consequences Commissions) claimed that EC accession would provide a new external discipline to reinforce ongoing economic reforms, such as the reform of domestic competition policy and a programme of privatisation. Full membership was attributed (at this time) with providing, amongst others, two potential benefits to the Swedish economy:

- A reinforcement of Sweden's continuing internationalisation. It would ensure greater competitiveness of exports and (implied) employment. As the EU Consequences Committee summarised, 'In our view, membership will make it possible to create an environment for growth and real wage development which will facilitate the wage formation process'.[76]

- EC accession would improve business confidence in the Swedish economy. Levels of inward investment would increase and reduce the outflow of capital, which had supposedly been very high during 1990-91. The country's investment ratio (i.e. investments as a share of GDP) was at the lowest level for more than 40 years. The EU Consequences Committee later estimated that the full membership would 'have an immediate effect in the form of a higher level of investment'.[77] The overall investment ratio would rise since direct investment would increase by up to one percentage point of GDP and that these investments would be more specialised.[78]

However, these views were not universally shared. André Sapir for example has argued that there was no *prima facie* evidence of a fall in investment in Sweden corresponding to the Community's 1992 programme. Indeed, according to the OECD, the ratio of investment to GDP in Sweden was 18 percent in 1982, 1983 and 1984, 19 percent in 1985 and 1986, 20-22 percent between 1987-91, and 19 percent in 1992. Sapir was however, willing to concede that 'joining the European

Union should promote investment and increase growth, but it will not solve the country's problems'.[79]

Yet, regardless of these reservations, the two general arguments of strengthening liberalisation and reversing the decline in investment into Sweden were central to the economic debate on full membership. They provided, at least in the public's eyes, a firm link between the merits of becoming a full EC member and dealing with Sweden's economic problems. Full membership, whether rightly or wrongly, was identified by the politicians and the public alike as being part of the antidote to the country's poor economic performance. Thus, the economic interdependence point of the 'Diamond' was strengthened.

d) Point 4: External Strategic Environment - Changes to Neutrality[80]

The Diamond's fourth point also faced fresh challenges. The frosting of relations between the two superpowers during the early 1980s created two new security problems for Swedish neutrality. First, the 'High North' was transformed from a traditionally low-threat area to one with a much greater profile due in part, to the considerable build-up in Soviet naval forces in the Kola peninsula.[81] Consequently, Sweden gained a higher strategic profile within Europe and led to criticism of existing Swedish military thinking which had been based on the long-standing 'marginality thesis'.[82] It was questionable whether the neutrality would be tenable even in the 1980s and whether large military forces would be sufficient to deter a conventional attack, if the region was viewed as an area of high, rather than low tension. This new friction also made the 'Nordic Balance' - with neutral Sweden balancing the NATO members of Denmark, Iceland and Norway to the West and the tentative friendship of Finland with the Soviet Union to the East - less convincing.

Second, the continuing violations of Swedish territorial waters and airspace, allegedly by the Soviet military forces also made it seem that neutrality was, in any case, not viewed seriously by at least one of the superpowers. Åström and Hakovirta's insistences on neutrality being credible, predictable and respected by others had been cast into doubt by these actions.[83] More and more reports of unidentified foreign submarines leading in many cases to publicised Swedish anti-submarine manoeuvres were logged after 1980.

However, it was the 'Whiskey on the Rocks' episode which illustrated the blatant disregard for the country's neutral position and the weakness of Sweden as a small state when dealing with one of the superpowers.[84] On 28 October 1981, a Soviet 'Whiskey' class submarine (U-137), suspected of carrying nuclear weapons was discovered run aground within a restricted Swedish military zone. According to Stern and Sundelius, the 'Whiskey' case can be regarded as a typical example of the problems confronting a small state, when dealing with 'an asymmetrical crisis'.[85] The sensitivity surrounding neutrality was further emphasised during the equally serious 1982 Härsfjärden intruder incident and raised greater doubts over the ability of the country to maintain its territorial integrity in a bi-polar Europe. In spite of forceful protests by the Palme government against the Soviet incursions and exchange visits at ministerial level being discontinued for a long time, there were those who suggested that Sweden should look for alternative security arrangements, such as a mutual assistance agreement with NATO.[86] Overall, these incidents collectively reinforced Vital's conclusions that 'the survival of small, politically isolated states as independent powers is thus precarious, depending on a multitude of factors over which they themselves have little influence'.[87]

Already during the 1980s Sweden's security policy of 'non-alignment in peacetime for neutrality in war' had 'been the subject of unaccustomed foreign scrutiny and intense domestic discussion'.[88] To most Swedes, neutrality remained 'a dogma as embedded in the national character as democracy',[89] but there was growing public apprehension over its future. Concerns over the inability of Swedish forces to prevent submarine excursions combined with a progressive decline in defence spending during the 1980s indicated that there seemed to be a growing gap between external threats and domestic resources.[90] By 1990, for example, Per Gyllenhammar, (then) Director of Volvo, argued that neutrality had outlived its usefulness and that once it was abandoned, the country could take the welcome step of moving towards full membership of the Community.[91]

The doubts of the Swedish political elite over the future viability of neutrality policy were further reinforced by the dramatic changes of the 1990s. The post-1989 revolutions in Eastern Europe allowed for Swedish neutrality itself to be revised and defined more flexibly and with this, accelerated the demise of some of the traditional preconceptions surrounding neutrality policy. Once Eastern Europe moved on the road towards greater democracy, (and later both the Warsaw Pact and the Soviet Union disintegrated), so did the rationale of maintaining strict neutrality to allow Sweden to remain independent of the two competing blocs in Europe. In effect, one of the blocs had disappeared leaving the political elite with the problem of rationalising what neutrality policy was supposed to be neutral against.

Pierre Schori, the influential Permanent Under-Secretary of State for Foreign Affairs in the Carlsson administration indicated that this was very much the case in an interview for *Dagens Nyheter* (8 November 1990). He argued that the changing EC policy had little to do with the present state of the Swedish economy, nor was it a question of trying to change the poor electoral fortunes of the Social Democratic Party. According to him, the crucial factor was the changing security situation which made neutrality less significant.[92] It remains to be seen as to how accurate Schori's statement was. Certainly, he underestimated the fact that the economic problems that were apparent also allowed successive governments to claim that a 'peace dividend' was on offer. Defence spending could be cut as part of general austerity packages aimed at getting fiscal policy back in the black. For political reasons, neutrality remained (at least at this stage) in order to maintain at least a minimal consensus on security policy. But the last major obstacle to full membership had been removed. EC membership was now compatible with neutrality because the country's neutral status was no longer tied to the strict doctrines of complete independence in policy making and the maximisation of national sovereignty.

In the famous statement by Carlsson (14 June 1991), he argued that EC membership was now compatible with neutrality for two reasons. First, there had been significant changes in Europe and that 'the previous division into two rival power blocs is now a thing of the past'. This, he suggested, allowed the Social Democratic government to have flexibility regarding neutrality on the grounds that 'important aspects of Sweden's security policy situation have thus improved markedly ... the final assessment is that the risk of war in Europe involving the great powers is extremely limited'.[93] Second, that the unanimity requirement for taking decisions would 'in all probability be maintained' within the Community as regards future foreign policy cooperation. As Carlsson stated 'Today EC membership involves coordination, but not uniformity in foreign affairs ... in the government's view it will be possible to avoid commitments which could compromise the credibility of Swedish security policy'.[94] The Prime Minister believed that given these conditions, EC membership 'would bring considerable advantages to Sweden, outweighing the drawbacks'.[95]

Later, when the newly formed non-socialist government shifted security policy further away from the traditional maxims of neutrality, Bildt was able to argue that the new doctrine of defence policy retained the hard core of neutrality, but was now only applicable to how national defence was organised and independently conducted.[96] The new security policy was reduced to the rump of 'non-participation in alliances' giving the government considerable flexibility.[97]

Overall, all four points of the 'Swedish Diamond' had been gradually altering since the 1980s, leading to an accelerated change in Swedish perspectives towards the prospect of full membership. For the most part, however, these changes had been agreed upon at the elite level, with the cautious support of key interest and party groupings. These perspectives were however, not discussed or entirely shared by wider public opinion.

Widening the Debate: Swedish Public Opinion 1990-93

By early 1991, the outcome of a popular referendum on EC accession (which had been agreed would be held during the inter-party negotiations) 'looked to be a foregone conclusion'.[98] Public support for the membership had risen steadily between late 1989 and December 1990, when most polls indicated that it reached a plateau at around 60-65 percent. It dipped to just below 60 percent in June 1991.[99] None the less, a gradual decline in support for Swedish accession was detected between October 1991 to March 1992, with pro-EC support dropping to around 45 percent by March 1992.[100] In a study published by the newspaper, *Göteborgs-Posten* (December 1991) for example, twice as many citizens supported membership as opposed it, but now with 48 percent in favour, 24 percent against, with 27 percent undecided.[101] According to Arter, this survey illustrated the contrasting voter stereotypes on the EC question:

> 'The typical 'pro-Marketeer' emerged as a male aged 50-64 years who owned his own business, lived in a larger town and voted Liberal. The typical 'anti-Marketeer' was an older woman, employed in the public sector, resident in a small town and a supporter of the Leftist Party'.[102]

Yet, within a year, there had been a striking turnaround in public attitudes towards full membership. During the first six months of 1992, public opposition rose sharply. Polls in March 1992, for instance, - only three months after the previous survey - indicated that opinion was hardening against Swedish accession. Rising numbers of previously undecided voters came out against EC membership; 44 percent were now in favour, (with anti-EC support up to 36 percent and the undecided segment reducing to 20 percent.[103] Later in May 1992, the growth in public opposition to full membership was indicated by another survey which showed a majority (40 percent) now opposing membership. Pro-EC support reached a plateau with 35 percent in favour, and 26 percent undecided.[104] The most striking movement was amongst undecided voters on the EC issue. Numerically they seemed to be moving from initially boosting the 'Yes' camp towards rejecting membership in 1992.

To some extent, the swing in public opinion was due to a general lack of confidence in the future of the Swedish economy struggling against deep recession, negative economic growth and sharply rising unemployment. Interest tended to shift from the positive effects of full membership to its potential negative implications. Political issues which generally came to the fore during time of economic insecurity became more visible - such as the loss of national sovereignty, the (perceived) risk of a heavy influx of foreign labour and growing bureaucratic meddling from Brussels - and dominated the debate during 1991-92. In a survey by the University of Göteborg the arguments on full membership were classified into 10 main groups: democracy, industry, the state of the economy, the welfare state, women's rights, labour market issues, consumer prices and standards, environmental protection, neutrality and a catch-all, miscellaneous 'other areas'.[105] Whilst the neutrality and democracy arguments were the most frequently mentioned, different emphases were placed on issues by the 'Yes' and 'No' camps (see Chapter Eight).

The resistant attitude of the Swedish public was further affected in late 1992 by 'the strong contagious effect' of the Danish people's rejection of the Treaty on European Union (TEU) in the June 1992 referendum.[106] To the average Swede, the wafer-thin rejection of the TEU by the like-minded Danes raised even greater questions about future obligations arising from joining the (renamed) European Union (EU). In a high profile survey by the University of Göteborg's SIFO Institute and the newspaper *Göteborgs-Posten* published on 14 June 1992 (covering the 4-10 June 1992), the impact of the Danish result on public opinion was revealed.[107] There was a decline to 32 percent in favour of full membership and a striking 47 percent now against it.[108] Ironically, by July 1992 - 12 months after the membership application - there had been a reversal in public opinion on the EC question. It now seemed that the drive towards EC membership would be flying in the face of public wishes. The EC issue seemed to be more divisive that ever before.

The change in perceptions was also reflected within the membership of the mainstream political parties. The EC application had been facilitated by an elite consensus of party leaders and parliamentarians in 1990-91. Indeed, there seemed to be a partial reaction against this 'elite conspiracy' in 1992 amongst the 'grass roots' of the respective parties. In short, there was, albeit to a limited extent, growing discord between the party leaderships and their wider membership on the EC issue in most of the mainstream political parties. In the case of the Social Democrats and the Centre Party, this actually led to a more cautious policy approach to full membership from 1991 as their respective leaders tried to quell unrest amongst their mass membership.

The Social Democrats, which after all and whilst in government were responsible for lodging the application, were now openly critical of the prospect of full membership in 1992. In part, this was due to the fact that Carlsson's party was now in opposition. The SAP enjoyed greater flexibility in determining its EC policy. Yet, it also reflected that the party included a very sizable 'No' faction and, at the local party level, the majority of members were against Swedish accession. In effect, the SAP was split over the membership issue. In the Temo poll (April-May 1992), the spectrum of opinion on full membership was apparent.[109] SAP members expressed that only 24 percent favoured membership, with 47 percent against and 36 percent undecided. The SOM Institute however, suggested that the division within the Social Democrats was actually an elite-mass rank split. 'Firm' support for membership amongst party members fell from over 50 percent in 1990, to 25-27 percent in 1991 and to below 10 percent in

1992 - suggesting a clear majority of the SAP's mass ranks opposed full membership.[110]

As regards the Centre Party and the Christian Democrats, (which were coalition partners in the Bildt government from October 1991), 'No' groups were also prevalent at the local party levels, constituting a majority of party members. In the Temo poll, the Centre Party's figures were only 11 percent for, a resounding 61 percent against and 24 percent undecided. The Christian Democrats were similar to the Social Democrats' results with 26 percent for, 46 percent against and 28 percent undecided. The SOM Institute surveys also indicated an even worse picture for the pro-EC camp in general. 'Firm' support for full membership also fell amongst Centre Party members (from over 50 percent in 1990, 15-16 percent in 1991, to 13-14 percent in 1992) and the Christian Democrats (with figures of 54-55 percent, 10-12 percent and below 5 percent respectively).[111] Despite six of the eight major party leaders favouring membership, there was a dramatic shift against the EC within most of the political parties during 1991-92. Their leaderships were especially sensitive to their members' views and were cautious on full membership.

This had important implications for both the Left and Right of the political spectrum. In spite of the fact that in general, the parties on the Right of the spectrum (the Moderates, the Liberals and New Democracy) were mostly in favour, with 72 percent of Moderate party members, 58 percent of Liberals and 52 percent of New Democracy supporting full membership (Temo poll), the governing Centre-Right Bildt government was constrained by the less than enthusiastic support of the participating Centre Party and Christian Democrats. The Centre Party leadership, in order to quell discontent within its own ranks went to 'unprecedented lengths'. At its party congress in June 1992, it was agreed that non-alignment was an ideological and policy precondition for its support for EC membership, reaffirming its pressure on its coalition partners not to go for full membership at any cost.[112]

Although the Left was generally perceived to be against full membership, principally because it included the anti-EC Left Party and Greens (which according to the Temo poll, indicated that 71 percent and 71 percent of their party members respectively were against membership), the policy of the Social Democrats was also ambiguous. Even after the historic 1991 election defeat, the SAP's result of 37.7 percent was still more than 15 percentage points larger than any other party. The party would be central to the outcome of the forthcoming referendum on full membership. With a majority of party members against accession, Carlsson moved way from open support for full membership, without completely dropping it. Issues, such as the EC being identified with neo-liberal rather than Social Democratic economic solutions, fears of an interfering Brussels bureaucracy and that the full membership was an excuse for major changes in security policy were intermittently raised by Social Democrats.[113]

As Widfeldt notes, the internal debate within the SAP was, to a large extent, focused on the future of the welfare state. It incorporated the long-standing divide between 'welfare traditionalists' and 'modernisers'. With some simplification, the modernisers tended to favour accession and the traditionalists were split between those which perceived the Community as a threat to the welfare state, and those party members who saw full membership as a means to direct the Community towards a more extensive welfare state model.[114] Ironically, it was not until the 1994 party congress that the Social Democrats extensively debated the membership issue and only then once the accession negotiations were completed. In addition, the LO's conditional support for membership wavered during 1992. Its leadership moved to a policy of allowing its individual trade unions to adopt their own policies on the EC question. In effect, an elite LO leadership versus grass roots membership split was also apparent within the trade union movement as the EC became associated with measures aimed at cutting social provision.

Increasingly the case for full membership was linked to the Bildt government (especially as the Prime Minister was a long-standing champion of Swedish accession) creating problems for the Social Democrats and the LO. The EC issue became divulged within party politics. It was used by the Social Democrats as a baton to attack their Moderate and Liberal political opponents in particular. Yet the Social Democratic leadership faced a difficult dilemma. On the one hand, it could not afford to come out against full membership, even if the majority of its rank and file supported this policy. It would have been highly embarrassing to drop a policy Carlsson had spear-headed whilst in government less than twelve months before. On the other hand, the size of the 1991 general election defeat had re-prioritised Social Democratic targets. The re-gaining of political ground and effective attacks on the non-socialist government were now clearly number one. Bildt's policy on Europe was an obvious target because of its high profile.

By January 1992, the Social Democratic leadership had developed a strategy of trying to attack Bildt's vision of the Community and stress that a future SAP government would only pursue full membership on clearly defined Social Democratic principles. In effect, the Social Democrats still officially supported Swedish accession, but on policy grounds different to the non-socialists. On 19 March 1992, Carlsson announced that the party would not canvass for an unqualified acceptance of Swedish EC membership, but would instead illuminate both sides of the argument in what it called an 'educational campaign'. As Huldt aptly notes:

'Somehow there seemed to exist two European Communities to which membership applications could be made, that of the Bildt government and that of Social Democracy, and the Swedes would have to make the right choice'.[115]

In addition, the Centre Party, which had always been deeply divided over the membership question, decided to come clean. Its leader, Olof Johansson announced (27 March 1992), that it would adopt a 'neutral line'. Just because the party had previously backed Swedish accession during 1990-91, this did not mean that it would sanction any negotiated accession terms. In the same month, a poll of Centre Party activists showed the extent of their grass roots resistance to EC membership, when 58 percent expressed their opposition to Swedish accession, highlighting the real reason for Johansson's softened line on the Community. In contrast, the Christian Democrats remained committed to full membership since their July 1992 party conference. Yet, there was also a substantial majority within the party against full membership which made party coherence on the membership question difficult. In the same year, several 'anti-EC' groups were either formed or strengthened; the most notable being 'The Alternative to the EC' and the 'No to the EC' groups.

The net result of these actions on public opinion was negative. It only helped to complicate the debate, leaving the public even more confused and disheartened about EC membership in general. It seemed to the average Swede that at least two of the main political parties (including the largest) were backtracking on the membership issue, which hardly inspired confidence within the general public over the merit of Swedish accession. Overall, the prospect of the country becoming a full member of the Community looked far from certain by mid-1992. The events of 1992, in terms of the alterations to public and party opinion, reinforced the perception that Swedish politics was somehow changing and that the fragmentation of public and party loyalties to their respective political leaderships continued.

The Commission's Opinion on the Swedish Application

Given the relatively high degree of political instability on the EC issue, it could be argued that the EC's posture on the Swedish application would be critical. If the Commission's opinion was anything less than openly supportive, the pro-membership forces in Sweden would find the task of achieving accession even more difficult. It was with some trepidation and then relief that the Swedish political elite received the European Commission opinion on its application (31 July 1992).[116]

The July 1991 Swedish application compounded existing problems for the Community. Once a second EFTA state had followed Austria and applied for full membership, regardless of the outcome of the EEA negotiations, the Community was forced to address the likelihood that a new wave of applicant would be forthcoming from the EFTA sphere. The Community already faced applications from Mediterranean Europe (Turkey in 1987 and Cyprus and Malta in 1990) - none of which were likely to succeed in the near future - but the applications from Austria and now Sweden could not be ignored so easily. Consequently, the Council employed the Commission to outline a new strategy to shape the future enlargement of the Community, which was approved by the European Council's June 1992 Lisbon summit. The Commission's report entitled 'Europe and the Challenge of Enlargement', established a number of key criteria, which applicants must meet in order to join the EC:[117]

- under Article F of the Treaty on European Union (TEU), the applicant state must fulfill the three basic conditions of a European identity, democratic status and respect for human rights.

- the acceptance of the EU's political and economic system and the capacity to implement it. This pre-supposed a functioning and competitive market economy and adequate legal and administrative frameworks in the public/private sectors.

- compliance with the Community's existing 'acquis communautaire' including the contents, principles and political objectives of the Treaties.

- the acceptance by the applicant state of the more ambitious goals ('finalité politique') and policies outlined in the Treaty on European Union.[118]

In practice though, this Report was designed to provide a general platform that could be interpreted for all prospective applicants. In fact, they were shaped to exclude certain applicants mostly from the Mediterranean.

For Sweden, the report posed few difficulties. The country fulfilled all the major conditions. The Commission's report and the Lisbon Declaration noted that Sweden 'would not pose insurmountable problems' for the Community.[119] In reality, the Swedish application could not be superficially discounted, rejected or easily delayed on technical grounds, without incurring political embarrassment for the Community. After all, the Swedes had traditionally refused to join the Community for their own reasons rather than because they were totally unsuitable for full membership. Moreover, Carl Bildt had welcomed the agreement reached by the EC Heads of State on the TEU. He stated in December 1991 his government's willingness to first, participate actively as a future member in the field of foreign and security policy cooperation and second, its aspiration to join 'as soon as possible the work in view of the creation of the economic and monetary union, which would lay one of the main foundations for positive economic development in the decades ahead'.[120]

The Commission was generally keen to display a hard line towards the EFTA states during 1992.[121] In short the Commission wanted to make it clear that any of the EFTA states would have to accept the Union established by the 1992 TEU. In both the Commission's report and the Lisbon Conclusions, it was stipulated 'specific and binding assurances' would be sought from the EFTA states relating to their acceptance of the contents and principles of the TEU. The issue that was consistently identified as a problem, especially for the neutral EFTA states (including Sweden) was the definition and implementation of a Common Foreign and Security Policy as provided for under article J.1-10 (TEU). This would be an area of 'particular concern' for the Community.[122] Moreover, the EC Heads of State agreed at Lisbon that any accession negotiations could not begin until after the TEU had been fully ratified by the EP and the member states' legislatures and also after the Delors-II financial package to cover the costs of future policy developments had also been agreed. If this was to be the case and given the problems with the Danish rejection of the TEU and the difficulties of the Major government in steering the Maastricht Bill through Westminster, the chances of Sweden becoming a full member appeared slim.

Nevertheless, the Commission's opinion on the Swedish application was essentially positive and delivered relatively quickly. In all, it took the Commission only 13 months to deliver its opinion - highlighting the seriousness with which the Community considered Sweden as a viable and welcome future member. It contrasted sharply with the Commission's slow response to the Turkish application, which took 32 months.[123] In the conclusions of the Opinion, the Commission stated that 'the Union will on the whole benefit from the accession of Sweden' and even went as far as arguing that it 'would widen the circle of countries whose prospective economic, monetary and budgetary performance is likely to contribute to the development of the Economic and Monetary Union'.[124] In addition, the report suggested that there would be 'no insuperable problems of an economic nature' especially in the spheres of social and environmental policies and synergy effects in the field of research and development. Furthermore, the Commission believed that full membership would have benefits for Sweden. It could be 'expected to contribute to creating the conditions for strengthening the Swedish economy'.[125]

The report did identify a number of problematical areas associated with Swedish accession, but at the same time, 'the Commission considers that it should be possible to solve these problems satisfactorily during the accession negotiations'.[126] Swedish agriculture was mentioned. Although the country's agricultural policy had in the Commission's view been moving in the same direction as that of the EC's Common Agricultural Policy (CAP), 'accession would represent an important challenge for Swedish agriculture, resulting in lower prices, reduced support levels and increased competition'.[127] This was primarily due to the specific characteristics of Swedish agriculture, such as its short growing season, its Arctic and sub-Arctic nature, the country's low density of population, and the wider role of agricultural policy as a vehicle for maintaining people on the land in the Northern regions.

Changes would also be required in terms of regional subsidies and levels of competition in certain sectors. Swedish regional policies dealing with the particular difficulties of the country's northernmost regions 'would have to be implemented in forms compatible with the Community acquis'.[128] Swedish policies on alcohol were also especially mentioned. The country had traditionally maintained alcohol monopolies on the production of spirits, the marketing and importing of all types of alcohol and the exporting of spirits and strong beers on the grounds of combating alcoholism and protecting public health.[129] The Commission remained concerned over the compatibility of the alcohol monopolies with article 37 (EEC Treaty) dealing with state aids, which it regarded as 'particularly worrying'.[130]

Not surprisingly, the Commission identified security policy as a future area of concern. The report did recognise the change in Swedish perspectives. It expressed its approval for the Bildt government's renamed foreign and security policy with a European identity. However, the Commission still believed that the government's policy fell short of the objective of a common defence. There were 'reservations in the Swedish position relative to the eventual framing of a common defence policy and, in an even more marked way, regarding the possible establishment in time for a common defence'.[131] The Commission reiterated its view that during the forthcoming accession negotiations, specific and binding assurances from Sweden would be sought as regards her future commitment to fulfil any obligations under the defence and security pillar of the Union. In general, those areas that were identified were predictable. For the most part, the Commission openly favoured Swedish accession and as Frans Andreissen summarised at the publication of the Opinion 'Sweden will be able to sign up for the whole European Union lock, stock and barrel'.

The Aftermath of the Commission Opinion : A Complex Domestic Debate

The reaction among the main political parties (which were those already committed to membership) was generally favourable, especially as the Commission's opinion included no hidden surprises. Even the anti-EC Left Party and Greens found it difficult to criticise the report and focused upon traditional issues, such as the future of Swedish neutrality. Lars Werner, the leader of the Left Party argued that membership would mean relinquishing neutrality. Birger Schlaug of the Greens stressed that Sweden's international role as an independent country would be diluted by the membership of an emerging security arrangement. Interestingly, the Centre Party raised the same themes.[132] The Social Democrats also found the Opinion to be generally satisfactory. Yet, in line with the party's strategy of stressing its differences on Europe from that of the non-socialist government, Carlsson highlighted his concerns regarding Bildt's attempts to, at best dilute, and at worst, drop neutrality.[133] However, Carl Bildt in response argued that the government would continue to revise its security policy in line with the changing European situation.

What was clear from these reactions to the Commission's opinion was the lack of consensus amongst the main political parties over the implications of 'security' and 'a common defence'[134] - something that was not made any easier by the fact that the term is equally ambiguous in the rest of the Community and in the TEU. Certainly, the original (12 December 1991) consensus on the Swedish application had unfolded. The government now, at least in part, ignored the Riksdag's preconditions for EC accession - that membership would need to be compatible with the country's neutral status. Indeed, senior politicians such as Kjell-Olof Feldt called for a more honest debate on the future of neutrality in the light of the Commission's opinion.

On 9 August 1992, Sverker Åström re-entered the EC debate. He spoke out in favour of defence cooperation with the Community as a 'unique opportunity'. Interestingly, the former Under-Secretary of State for Foreign Affairs, who had long been regarded as the guru of neutrality commented that despite full membership being incompatible with previous concepts of neutrality, the post-1989 changes in Europe now made Sweden's strategic position different from the past. Therefore cooperation with the Community now offered new possibilities for Swedish security. Åström had come, albeit to a limited extent, to the aid of the Bildt government. His comments, which, after all, came from a person closely associated with Östen Undén and Olof Palme's foreign policies, reinforced the perception that Sweden was reaching a critical juncture in the future development of its security policy.[135]

By autumn 1992, the domestic debate on full membership was in full swing and still far from stable. Domestic public opinion was mostly negative and the main debate was directed along the lines of party politics. On the one side, the Bildt government stressed the progressive nature of accession and its implication for transforming Sweden. On the other side were the cautious Social Democrats, whose leadership favoured membership, but stressed the neutrality concerns and the lack of authority with which the non-socialist government was moving away from the Riksdag's original pre-conditions for membership.[136] In the middle, lay the aptly named Centre Party, which remained critical to debate. It held back the enthusiasm of two of its governmental coalition partners (the Moderates and Liberals) and was occasionally courted by the Social Democrats out to form a future government at the next general election in 1994. As Karvonen and Sundelius argue the Centre Party's political manoeuvring would be central to future political constellations and indeed, the outcome of the debate on full membership.[137]

At the same time, economic factors were hardly conducive to facilitating a calm and reasoned debate in Sweden. The recession was biting hard in 1992, with business confidence shaken to its core by the disastrous deregulation of financial services and the later virtual collapse of the Swedish property market and banking sector in 1991-92.[138] Moreover, there was also greater instability in international currency markets as doubts about the strength of Sweden's economy were commonplace. This led to the weak state of the Krona reaching crisis point in 1992. After several attempts at defending the Krona's pegging to the Exchange Rate Mechanism[139] during 1992 - even to the point of using drastic measures, (such as the raising of marginal interest rates from 13 percent on 21 August to 500 percent on 16 September 1992), the non-socialist government was finally forced to admit defeat. Inter-bank fund interest rates for example, rose dramatically within ten days during September - from 16 percent (7 September) to 70 percent (17 September). This consolidated pressures on a banking and financial system already experiencing difficulties and in addition, led to a major fiscal shortfall. Sweden tried to defend the currency by also borrowing heavily from the private sector markets. On 18 September, the country borrowed ECU 8 billion via a syndicated loan to replenish its currency reserves. However, on 19 November 1992, massive outflows of capital threatened to wipe out the Riksbank's reserves. The government abandoned the pegged ECU exchange rate in November and the Krona's value immediately sank by 11 percent against the Deutsche mark.

Between 1989-92, Sweden had experienced almost continual decline in market share. It fell by an average of 4-5 percent every year (4.4 percent alone in 1991 and 4.1 percent in 1992), indicating that Swedish export prices had become extremely uncompetitive. Exports declined to an historically low level in 1992.[140] Overall between the first quarter of 1990 and the first quarter of 1991, real GDP declined by a cumulative 7.5 percentage points. This was seen by many as a major defeat for the non-socialist government's strategy on Europe and resulted in an devaluation of the Krona by 25 percent in effective terms by October 1993. To the average Swede, the whole crusade towards full membership seemed to be unwinding. It raised concerns over whether the country would be able to withstand any economic transitional effects as a result of EC accession.

Given the Community's insistence on specific and binding assurances and its emphasis on the postponement of any forthcoming enlargement negotiations until after the ratification of the TEU at the very least, the likelihood of Swedish accession looked precarious. Neither the domestic factors within Sweden nor the Community's policy towards applicant states were ideal. The achievement of full membership by the Bildt government appeared to be an uphill task. Yet, by early 1993, accession negotiation between the two sides were in full swing and it is to this aspect that the next chapter will address.

Notes

[1] Wæver, O. (1992) Nordic Nostalgia: Northern Europe after the Cold War, *International Affairs*, 68, 1, pp. 77-102.

[2] This chapter will cover such issues as the impact of economic problems, the relative decline of the Swedish corporate model, greater political fragmentation and the changing nature of security policy. The EFTA and Nordic dynamics were covered in greater detail in Chapters Five and Six.

[3] The response was a study undertaken by the Swedish Institute of International Affairs - see Nordlof-Lagerkranz (eds.) (1990) *Svensk Neutralitet, Europa och EG*, MH Publishing/ Swedish Institute of International Affairs, Stockholm.

[4] Huldt, B. (1994) Sweden and European Community-building 1945-92, in Harden, S. (ed.) *Neutral States and the European Community*, Brassey's, London, p. 117.

[5] This event was given greater emphasis as the two leaders timed their announcements to coincide with a pro-EC speech in Stockholm by the Danish Foreign Minister, Ulf Ellemann-Jensen.

[6] For an examination of the non-socialist parties see Miles, L. & Widfeldt, A. (1995) The Swedish Non-Socialist Parties and the European Union, in Lovenduski, J. & Stanyer, J. (eds.) *Contemporary Political Studies 1995, Volume Three*, PSA/Short-Run Press, Exeter, pp. 1513-9.

[7] An appraisal of Sverker Åström's views on neutrality can be found in Åström, S. (1987) *Sweden's Policy of Neutrality*, Swedish Institute, Stockholm.

[8] See for example, Karvonen, L. & Sundelius, B. (1996) The Nordic Neutrals: Facing the European Union in Miles, L. (ed.) *The European Union and the Nordic Countries*, Routledge, London, pp. 245-59 or Miles, L. (1995) *Sweden, Security and Accession to the European Union*, Occasional Papers in Nordic Studies, No. 1, University of Humberside, Hull.

[9] See Johansson, O. 'You do not act responsibly on behalf of Sweden' *Dagens Nyheter*, 10 June 1990.

[10] Op. cit., Huldt (1994) p. 117.

[11] See the statement by Karl-Erik Sahlberg, spokesman for Federation of Swedish Industries in *Dagens Nyheter*, 6 June 1990.

[12] The LO's EC Committee was chaired by the pro-EC Gudmund Larsson, but included representatives from all 21 constituent trade unions (the majority were against Swedish

full membership) - Taken from an interview with G. Larsson on 6 February 1996 in Stockholm.

[13] Dølvik, J.-E. (1993) The Nordic Trade Unions and the Dilemmas of European Integration, in Fagerberg, J. & Lundberg, L. (eds.) *European Economic Integration: A Nordic Perspective,* Avebury, Aldershot, pp. 353-79.

[14] Taken from an interview with G. Larsson on 6 February 1996 in Stockholm.

[15] LO, (1990) *Trade Union Perspectives on European Integration - Europe, The Future and the Trade Unions,* LO, Stockholm, May, p. 25.

[16] Taken from an interview with G. Larsson on 6 February 1996 in Stockholm.

[17] Op. cit., Karvonen & Sundelius (1996) p. 247.

[18] For a more detailed discussion - see Widfeldt, A., (1996) Sweden and the European Union - Implications for the Swedish Party System in Miles, L. (ed.) *The European Union and the Nordic Countries,* Routledge, London, pp. 101-16.

[19] Taken from an interview with G. Larsson on 6 February 1996 in Stockholm.

[20] Op. cit., Huldt (1994) p. 118.

[21] Regeringsskrivelse, Riksdagen, Stockholm, 1990-91, p. 50.

[22] Taken from an interview with Viola Furubjelke, Chairperson of the Foreign Affairs Standing Committee on 8 February 1996 at the Riksdag, Stockholm.

[23] Miles, L. (1997) Sweden and Security in Redmond, J.(ed.) *The 1995 Enlargement of the European Union,* Dartmouth, Aldershot.

[24] See for example, Aylott, N. (1995) Why Sovereignty Matters: Swedish Social Democracy and European Integration in Lovenduski, J. & Stanyer, J. (eds.) *Contemporary Political Studies 1995, Volume Three,* PSA/Short-Run Press, Exeter, pp. 1180-7.

[25] Taken from an interview with Conny Fredriksson, International Secretary of the SAP on 16th September 1994 in Stockholm.

[26] Op. cit., Karvonen & Sundelius (1996) p. 248.

[27] Taken from an interview with Viola Furubjelke, Chairperson of the Foreign Affairs Standing Committee on 8 February 1996 at the Riksdag, Stockholm.

[28] Utrikesutskottets betänkande, *Swedish Security Policy,* 1991-92: UU19, ss 16 ff, Riksdagen, Stockholm, 1992, pp. 3-4.

[29] Sweden's experience with the pegging arrangeent was not a happy one. Most of the points raised here did prove to the case later and eventually forced Sweden to abandon its 'shadowing' of the ECU in November 1993.

[30] Gidlund, G. (1992) *Partiernas Europa,* Natur och kultur, Stockholm, p. 60.

[31] Royal Ministry of Foreign Affairs (1991), *Sweden, the EC and Security Policy Developments in Europe,* 2, UD, Stockholm, p. 14.

[32] Op. cit., Karvonen & Sundelius (1996) p. 248.

[33] Michalski, A. & Wallace, H. (1992) *The European Community: The Challenge of Enlargement,* Royal Institute of International Affairs, London, p. 100.

[34] For a survey of the 1991 general election see Widfeldt, A. (1992) The Swedish Parliamentary Election of 1991, *Election Studies,* 11, 1.

[35] New Democracy and the Christian Democrats both gained parliamentary representation in the Riksdag for the first time.

[36] Ibid., Miles & Widfeldt (1995) p. 1513.

[37] Taken from an interview with Jan Palmstierna, Assistant Under-Secretary of State, West European Integration Office, Ministry of Foreign Affairs in September 1994 in Stockholm.

[38] The Liberals and Moderates were conscious of the demands of the Christian Democrats, who had also been positive towards full membership, especially as their leadership sought a closer affinity with the larger continental Christian Democratic parties of the Community.

[39] Ibid., Miles & Widfeldt (1995) p. 1516.

[40] This was the start of a series of speeches outlining the new government's perspectives vis-à-vis European integration - most notably an address in Bonn on 13 November 1991 delivered to the Bonn office of the European Commission entitled *Schweden -vom zögernden zum begeisterten Europäer.*

[41] This commitment was at least partially maintained at the request of the Centre Party within the non-socialist coalition.

[42] The main aspects of official security policy doctrine is summarised in Goldmann, K. (1992) The Swedish Model of Security Policy' in Lane, J.-E., (ed.) *Understanding the Swedish Model,* Frank Cass & Co., London, p. 124.

[43] Op. cit., Huldt (1994) p. 122.

[44] Taken from an interview with Jan Palmstierna, Assistant Under-Secretary of State, West European Integration Office, Ministry of Foreign Affairs in September 1994 in Stockholm.

[45] Sundelius, B. (1994) Changing Course: When Neutral Sweden Chose To Join the European Community in Carlsnaes, W. & Smith, S. (eds.) *European Foreign Policy: The EC and Changing Perspectives in Europe,* Sage, London, p. 177.

[46] A useful summary of the changes to the support of the SAP is provided in Karvonen, L. & Sundberg, J. (eds.) (1991) *Social Democracy in Transition: Northern, Southern and Eastern Europe,* Dartmouth, Aldershot.

[47] Holmberg, S. & Weibull, L. (eds.) (1995) *Swedish Opinion,* SOM Institute, Göteborg, 1995, p. 2.

[48] Ibid., Holmberg & Weibull (1995) p. 4.

[49] Op. cit., Sundelius (1994) p. 194.

[50] Taken from an interview with Ninna Rösiö, Councillor at the Swedish Permanent Delegation to the European Communities in April 1995 in Brussels.

[51] Op. cit., Holmberg & Weibull (1995) p. 19.

[52] Mikko Mattila for example in his complex study of the relationship between economic factors and governmental popularity has argued that the 'economy matters'. It is however, not sufficient to rely on purely economic variables to explain whether there is a causal relationship between the two aspects - Mattila, M. (1996) Economic Changes and Government Popularity in the Scandinavian Countries, *British Journal of Political Science,* 25, July, pp. 583-600.

[53] Taken from Pedersen, T. (1994) *European Union and the EFTA Countries,* Pinter, London, p. 88.

[54] This view has been contested by Walter Korpi - see Korpi, W. (1996) Eurosclerosis and the Sclerosis of Objectivity: On the Role of Values Among Economic Policy Experts, *Economic Journal,* 106, November and Jonas Agell - Agell, J. (1996) Why Sweden's Welfare State Needed Reform, *Economic Journal,* 106, November.

[55] See for further details op. cit., Karvonen & Sundberg (1991).

[56] Jerneck, M. (1993) Sweden - the Reluctant European? in Tiilikainen, T. & Petersen, I. Damgaard, (eds.) *The Nordic Countries and the EC,* Copenhagen Political Studies Press, Copenhagen, p. 34 or see De Geer, H. (1992) *The Rise and Fall of the Swedish Model: The Swedish Employer's Confederation and Industrial Relations over Ten Decades,* Carden Publications, Chichester.

[57] In fact, from spring 1991, the Social Democratic government's official first priority of economic policy was no longer full employment but price stability.

[58] Olsson, A. S. (1990) *The Swedish Wage Negotiation System,* Dartmouth, Aldershot.

[59] Op. cit., Holmberg & Weibull (1995) p. 6.

[60] Op. cit., International Monetary Fund (1995) p. 12.

[61] Kokko, A. (1994) Sweden: Effects of EU Membership on Investment and Growth, *The World Economy,* 17, 5, September, p. 668.

[62] Lachman, D., Bennett, A., Green, J. H., Hagemann, R. & Ramaswarmy, R. (1995) *Challenges to the Swedish Welfare State,* International Monetary Fund, Washington D.C., September, p. 3.

[63] Henrekson, M. (1996) Sweden's Relative Economic Performance: Lagging Behind or Staying on Top?, *The Economic Journal,* 106, November, pp. 1747-59.

[64] Pontusson, J. & Swenson, P. (1996) Labor Markets, Production Strategies, and Wage Bargaining Institutions: The Swedish Employer Offensive in Comparative Perspective, *Comparative Political Studies,* 29, 2, April, p. 230.

[65] Iversen, T. (1996) Power, Flexibility, and the Breakdown of Centralized Wage Bargaining: Denmark and Sweden in Comparative Perspective, *Comparative Politics,* 28, 4, July, pp. 399-436.

[66] Iversen, Pontusson and Swenson have all expressed scepticism at the validity of such a link . They argue that decentralisation is difficult to reconcile with cost competitiveness as long as a government pursues full employment policies.

[67] The longer-term implications remain to be seen. In March 1997, the main employers and trade union organisations agreed a limited wage collaboration pact which has been hailed by some as a possible landmark in Swedish industrial relations.

[68] SOU, (1994) *Sverige och Europa: En samhällsekonomisk konsekvensanalys,* 6, Norstedts, Stockholm, p. 140.

[69] The first concerns over the high level of welfare spending were raised in the late 1970s - for example see Marklund, S. (1987) *Paradise Lost? The Nordic Welfare States and the Recession 1975-85,* Arkiv förlag, Lund.

[70] The reduction of welfare provision, the removal of the principle of solidarity and its replacement with the practice of means-testing and the privatising of public services was however, contested in certain quarters of the Left Party and the Social Democratic Party. For a survey of views in the SAP see Linton, M. (1993). Swedish Social Democrats and the Crisis of the Welfare State, *Renewal,* 1, 2, April, pp. 55-61.

[71] This assertion has been especially criticised by Jonas Agell. He argued that economic growth depends on many factors - 'unless one controls their influence in a systematic way it is not meaningful to attach value to partial correlations between growth and indicators of the size of the public sector' - op. cit., Agell (1996) p. 1764.

[72] Henrekson, M., Hultkrantz, L., Stahl, I., Söderström, H. T. & Söderström, L. (1994) *The Crisis of the Swedish Welfare State*, SNS, Stockholm, p. 4.

[73] According to this poll on the attitudes towards the public sector, 56 percent were in favour of a reduction in the public sector and welfare provision, although this was reduced to 50 percent in 1991 - a general election year - op. cit., Holmberg & Weibull (1995) pp. 10-11.

[74] The belief that the problems of the Swedish economy lie purely with the size of the public sector has been criticised. The McKinsey Global Institute has suggested that Sweden's uncompetitive private sector rather than an over large public sector constrained the country's growth - see Carnegy, H. (1995) Swedish Products Market Blamed for Ills, *Financial Times,* 8 September, p. 2.

[75] A good survey of the benefits of the Single European Market for Sweden is provided in relevant chapters of for example, Lyck, L. (ed.) (1990) *The Nordic Countries and the Internal Market of the EEC,* Handeshøjskolens Forlag, Denmark, 1990; Lundberg, L. & Fagerberg, J. (1993), *European Economic Integration - A Nordic Perspective,* Avebury, Aldershot or Baldwin, R. (1992) Is Bigger Better? The Economics of EC Enlargement, *Monitoring European Integration 3,* CEPR, London.

[76] EU Consequences Committee, (1994) *Sweden and Europe: Committee of Enquiry: Consequences of the EU for Sweden - the Economy,* SOU 1994: 6, UD, Stockholm, p. 20.

[77] Ibid., EU Consequences Committee (1994) p. 17.

[78] The numerical estimates presented in SOU 1994: 6, suggested an increase in the ratio of investment to GDP by about 1.1 percentage points as Sweden joins the EEA, with full membership raising the investment ratio a further 0.9-1.2 percentage points. Given tougher competition, a more advantageous investment structure and faster technology diffusion, it was proposed that annual Swedish GDP growth rates could be 0.4-0.5 percentage points higher if Sweden joins the Community instead of remaining just in the (then forthcoming) EEA - See Andersson, T. & Fredriksson, T. (1994), *Sveriges val, EG och direktinvesteringar,* Supplement 7 to SOU, *Sverige och Europa: En samhällsekonomisk konsekvensanalys,* 6, Norstedts, Stockholm.

[79] Sapir, A. (1994) Sweden: Effects of EU Membership on Investment and Growth: A Comment, *The World Economy,* 17, 5, September, p. 680.

[80] A study of Sweden and Security in the 1990s can be found in op. cit., Miles (1997).

[81] Kruzel argues that the growing importance of the northern military flank in Europe was one of the most serious challenges confronting Swedish neutrality in the 1980s - Kruzel, J. (1989) The Future of European Neutrality in Kruzel, J. & Haltzel, M. H. (eds.) *Between the Blocs,* Cambridge University Press, Cambridge, pp. 295-311.

[82] According to Kruzel, 'the marginality thesis argued that the greatest threat to international stability was a war between the superpowers; that in such a conflict, neither side could afford to use significant forces against a third party; and Sweden's

policy should therefore be to prepare to defend the country against marginal forces of the military blocs' - Kruzel, J. (1989) Sweden's Security Dilemma: Balancing Domestic Realities with the Obligations of Neutrality in Sundelius, B. (ed.) *The Committed Neutral - Sweden's Foreign Policy,* Westview Press, Boulder, p. 73.

[83] For an appraisal of the main tenets of neutrality see for instance, Åström, S. (1989) Swedish Neutrality: Credibility Through Commitment and Consistency in Sundelius, B. (ed.) *The Committed Neutral - Sweden's Foreign Policy,* Westview Press, Boulder, pp. 15-34. or Hakovirta, H. (1988) *East-West Conflict and European Neutrality,* Clarendon Press, Oxford.

[84] See Stern, E. (1990) *The U-137 Incident: A Study in Swedish Crisis Management,* International Graduate School, University of Stockholm, Stockholm or Hellberg, A. & Jörle, A. (1984) *Ubåt 137: Tio dagar som skakade Sverige,* Atlantis, Stockholm.

[85] According to these authors, 'an asymmetrical crisis' is in simple terms, a situation whereby a small state faces the awesome power of a neighbouring superpower. The case was useful because the smaller party (Sweden) lay outside the bloc division of Europe and free from intervening principles such as alliance commitments, superpower patronage or other types of security guarantees - Stern, E. & Sundelius, B. (1992) Managing Asymmetrical Crisis: Sweden, the USSR and *U-137, International Studies Quarterly,* 36, pp. 213-39.

[86] See for instance, Kjell Goldmann's article 'Blir neutraliteten omöjlig?' (Will neutrality become impossible?) *Svenska Dagbladet,* 1 June 1983.

[87] Vital, D. (1967) *The Inequality of States,* Clarendon Press, Oxford.

[88] Logue, J. (1989) The Legacy of Swedish Neutrality in Sundelius, B. (ed.) *The Committed Neutral - Sweden's Foreign Policy,* Westview Press, Boulder, p. 35.

[89] Sundelius, B. (1989) Committing Neutrality in an Antagonistic World in Sundelius, B. (ed.) *The Committed Neutral - Sweden's Foreign Policy,* Westview Press, Boulder, p. 12.

[90] See for example, Noreen, E. (1989) Perspectives on the Swedish Debate: With Particular Reference to the New Cold War Debate Between Social Democrats and Conservatives in the Early 1980s in Wæver, O., Lemaitre, P. & Tromer, E. (eds.) *European Polyphony: Perspectives Beyond East-West Confrontation,* Macmillan, London, pp. 250-68.

[91] Per Gyllenhammar in an article in *Dagens Nyheter* quoted from Nordic Council, Slopa neutraliteten *Nordisk Kontakt,* 10/11/1990, p. 73.

[92] Taken from op. cit., Pedersen (1994) p. 88.

[93] Royal Ministry of Foreign Affairs, (1991) *Sweden, the EC and Security Policy in Europe - Statement to the Riksdag on June 14 1991 on Sweden's Application for Membership of the European Community,* 1991:2, UD, Stockholm, p. 8.

[94] Ibid., Royal Ministry of Foreign Affairs (1991) pp. 10-11.

[95] Ibid., Royal Ministry of Foreign Affairs (1991) p. 13.

[96] On 19 June 1992, for instance, the Swedish Supreme Commander, Bengt Gustafsson, was quoted in *Svenska Dagbladet* as suggesting that Sweden would have to add an Atlantic dimension to its defence policy as well as expand to its military cooperation in Europe (as long as the EU's defence policy was not better developed).

[97] Taken from an interview with Jan Palmstierna, Assistant Under-Secretary of State, West European Integration Office, Ministry of Foreign Affairs in September 1994 in Stockholm.

[98] Arter, D. (1993) *The Politics of European Integration in the Twentieth Century*, Dartmouth, Aldershot, p. 225.

[99] Op. cit., Huldt (1994) p. 123.

[100] These general observations were made in a survey of public opinion in *Svenska Dagbladet*, 30 March 1992.

[101] Quoted in op. cit., Arter (1993) p. 225 and taken from the Nordic Council (1991), Många osäkra i EG-Frågan, *Nordisk Kontakt*, 12, pp. 92-3.

[102] Op. cit., Arter (1993) p. 225.

[103] Nordic Council, (1992) Risk för partisplittring efter växande EG-motstånd, *Nordisk Kontakt*, 3, pp. 82-3.

[104] Nordic Council, Ruotsalaiset vastustvat EY-jäsenyyttä, *Kristityn Vastuu*, 14 May 1992.

[105] This survey covered the period from September 1989 to June 1991, but its conclusions on the EC debate in Sweden remained generally correct for late 1991 and most of 1992 as well - see Wallin, U. (1992) *EG hot eller löfte?*, Department of Journalism and Media Communication, University of Göteborg, Göteborg.

[106] Hallgren, M. (1993) Sweden's Rocky Road to EC Membership, *Current Sweden*, No. 400, Swedish Institute, Stockholm, October, p. 3.

[107] This survey was published in *Göteborgs-Posten* in the 14 June edition and summarised in the SIP, Newsletter from Sweden, 29 June 1992.

[108] This survey by the SIFO Institute and *Göteborgs-Posten* was conducted exactly one year after a similar assessment had been carried out by this institutional combination. At that time the results had been 48 percent in favour and only 24 percent against.

[109] The Temo Institute and the newspaper *Dagens Nyheter* conducted this survey (21 April to 20 May 1992). Its general figures on public opinion support for full membership was 39 percent in favour, 38 percent opposed and 21 percent undecided.

[110] Figures supplied by the SOM Institute - op. cit., Holmberg & Weibull (1995) p. 21.

[111] Figures supplied by the SOM Institute - op. cit., Holmberg & Weibull (1995) p. 21.

[112] Op. cit., Huldt (1994) p. 124.

[113] Taken from an interview with Conny Fredriksson, International Secretary of the SAP on 16th September 1994 in Stockholm.

[114] Op. cit., Widfeldt (1996) p. 110.

[115] Op. cit., Huldt (1994) pp. 125.

[116] Taken from an interview with Ninna Rösiö, Councillor at the Swedish Permanent Delegation to the European Communities in April 1995 in Brussels.

[117] An appraisal of the criteria is provided in for example, Pinder, J. (1993) The Future of the European Community: A Strategy for Enlargement, *Government and Opposition*, 27, 4, or Michalski, A. & Wallace, H. (1992) *The European Community: the Challenge of Enlargement*, European Programme Special Paper, Royal Institute of International Affairs, London, or Miles, L. (1993) *Scandinavia and European Community*

Enlargement: Prospects and Problems for Sweden, Finland and Norway, Centre For European Union Studies, Paper 1/93, University of Hull, Hull.
[118] Taken from Commission of the EC (1992) *Europe and the Challenge of Enlargement,* Bulletin of the EC, Supplement 3/92, Commission of the EC, Brussels, p. 11.
[119] European Council, (1992) *European Council in Lisbon, 26-27 June 1992, Conclusions of the Presidency,* SN 3321/1/92, European Council, Brussels, p. 3.
[120] Bildt, C. quoted in Commission of the EC (1992), *Sweden's Application for Membership: Opinion of the Commission,* SEC (92) 1582 final/2, 7 August 1992, Commission of the EC, Brussels, p. 3.
[121] Taken from an interview with Leon Gordon of the European Commission's Enlargement Task Force in April 1995 in Brussels.
[122] Ibid., European Council (1992) p. 18.
[123] For the Turkish case see for example, Redmond, J. (1993) *The Next Mediterranean Enlargement of the European Community -Turkey, Cyprus or Malta?,* Dartmouth, Aldershot, or for a comparison of differing enlargement phases see Miles, L. (1995) *Enlargement of the European Union,* Dossier No. 36, University of North London Press, London.
[124] Op. cit., Commission of the EC (1992) SEC (92) 1582 final/2 p. 28.
[125] Op. cit., Commission of the EC (1992) SEC (92) 1582 final/2 p. 28.
[126] Op. cit., Commission of the EC (1992) SEC (92) 1582 final/2 p. 28.
[127] Op. cit., Commission of the EC (1992) SEC (92) 1582 final/2 p. 28.
[128] Op. cit., Commission of the EC (1992) SEC (92) 1582 final/2 p. 28.
[129] Op. cit., Commission of the EC (1992) SEC (92) 1582 final/2 p. 30.
[130] Op. cit., Commission of the EC (1992) SEC (92) 1582 final/2 p. 19.
[131] Op. cit., Commission of the EC (1992) SEC (92) 1582 final/2 p. 29.
[132] Reactions to the Swedish debate can be found in the Swedish newspapers of the 1 August 1992 (*Svenska Dagbladet, Expressen, Dagens Nyheter, Skånska Dagbladet, Arbetet and Aftonbladet*).
[133] For more details see op. cit., Miles (1995).
[134] Op. cit., Huldt (1994) p. 130.
[135] Åström, S. (1992) EC Defence Cooperation is to Sweden's Advantage, *Svenska Dagbladet,* 9 August.
[136] Taken from an interview with Conny Fredriksson, International Secretary of the SAP on 16th September 1994 in Stockholm.
[136] Op. cit., Karvonen & Sundelius (1996).
[137] Op. cit., Karvonen, L & B. Sundelius (1996) pp. 245-59.
[138] Certain Swedish banks even reached the point of technical insolvency. Nordbanken, for example, - the result of a merger in 1989 between PKBanken and Nordbanken and retaining the latter's name - made losses of $1536 million in 1991 and $733 million in 1992 with technical insolvency being declared in 1991. The financial crisis which engulfed Sweden was however, a Scandinavian phenomenon. For an assessment of the extent of the Swedish banking collapse see Pygott, J. & Kilmister, A. (1995) *The*

Financial Crisis in Scandinavia 1990-1992, Occasional Papers in Nordic Studies, No. 3, University of Humberside, Hull.

[139] The Krona was formally pegged to the ECU on a band of 1.5 per cent either side of the ECU in May 1991 in order to demonstrate the Swedish government's commitment to full membership and to establish its economic credentials. For a detailed evaluation of monetary policy see Barnes, I. (1996) Monetary Integration and the 1995 Nordic Enlargement in Miles, L. (ed.) *The European Union and the Nordic Countries,* Routledge, London, pp. 169-85.

[140] Op. cit., International Monetary Fund (1995) p. 54.

8 Approving Accession 1993-95

On 1 February 1993, accession negotiations between the European Community (EC)[1] and the four EFTA applicants - Austria, Finland, Norway and of course, Sweden began. At this time, the official goal was that the enlargement process should be completed quickly and efficiently in order to allow the four applicants to join the Community *en bloc*, just under two years later (1 January 1995). To many observers and given the events of the previous year both within the Community and Sweden, the fact that accession negotiations had begun at all was astonishing. Moreover, many viewed the timetable for eventual accession as optimistic. Nevertheless, Sweden, along with Austria and Finland (but not Norway) went on to become full members of the (now) European Union (EU) on schedule on the 1 January 1995.

The objectives of this chapter are twofold; to examine the government's role within the accession negotiations - in other words in negotiating membership terms - and also to evaluate the domestic process of approving full membership. In order to fulfil these twin objectives, the chapter will first, analyse why the accession negotiations began so quickly. Second, the government's declared priorities for the accession negotiations and the eventual accession terms will be evaluated. It will be argued that the Swedish negotiators, for the most part, gained a generous agreement from the Community and this was primarily due to the concerns of both sides at the size of domestic opposition to the country becoming a full member. Finally domestic reactions to full membership and the ensuing referendum (13 November 1994) will be analysed. By taking this approach, it will be evident that domestic approval for full membership was far from resounding and this will have implications for Swedish governments in the post-1995 period.

Prioritising Accession

Given the fact that the European Council at its Lisbon Summit (June 1992) had steadfastly declared that the (then) Community would not open accession negotiations until it had completed its initial plans for deepening - in other words the complete ratification of the TEU and final agreement between the existing member states on the EU financing through the Delors-II budgetary package - the prospect of Swedish full membership looked to be more likely in the distant rather than near future.[2] Ultimately and as Miles notes elsewhere, Sweden's full membership would be delayed by and tied to the solving of several internal EC problems.[3] In particular, dealing with, amongst other things, the implications of Denmark's rejection of the TEU (in the June 1992 public referendum), the problems of the Major government in steering the TEU through the British Parliament and finally, the eventual judgment of the German Constitutional Court on the compatibility of the Treaty with the country's Basic Law.[4]

Swedish accession was put back on track by the cumulative effect of a number of internal dynamics operating within the Community in late 1992. From June-December 1992, the British government held the European Council's Presidency and like most preceding Presidencies, tried to impose a specific set of priorities on the Community's agenda. In June of that year, the Major government announced its five point-plan for steering the Community during this unstable period in its history. One of the objectives was the speeding up of the enlargement process and opening of accession negotiations with the EFTA applicants. Apart from the UK's Conservative government's belief that the incorporation of four (perceived) like-minded ex-EFTAns would bolster British future influence in the Community, the Major government argued that prioritising the enlargement would, albeit to a limited extent, direct the Community's attention away from the completion of the ambitious TEU based policies and in particular, Economic and Monetary Union (EMU). Sweden, along with the three other EFTA applicants, gained a powerful champion inside the Community - one which at this time held the Council Presidency and influenced its immediate agenda.[5]

At the European Council's Edinburgh Summit (December 1992), the British made their consent on other pressing elements of the Community's business - especially final agreement on the Delors-II package - conditional upon the other member states agreeing to start accession negotiations in early 1993 and thus, even before the Community had officially transformed itself into the European Union. Undoubtedly though, the position of the EFTA applicants was also helped by the solving of some problems associated with TEU ratification at Edinburgh. At the Summit, the member states agreed to the Danish government's demands for a specialised 'historic compromise' and consequently, the Danes likewise committed themselves to holding a second referendum on the TEU.

At Edinburgh then, it was decided to open accession negotiations in 1993 regardless which marked a major change by the Community and a reversal of the Lisbon declaration. Yet, it could be argued that some of the main preconditions of Lisbon had, to some extent, been dealt with at Edinburgh anyway. The budgetary agreement precondition had been solved and the most notable problem for TEU ratification - that of dealing with Danish opposition - had been addressed. For the majority of member states, speeding up the enlargement process was also a limited tactical manoeuvre. It placed additional pressure on Danish voters to approve the TEU in the second referendum and was a positive move on the part of the Community.

Furthermore, there was a general feeling within the Commission that its existing policy on enlargement was untenable by December 1992.[6] External pressure on the Community was mounting not just from Eastern Europe, but also from within EFTA - something which the July 1991 Swedish application reinforced. The Community was no longer confronted by just two applicants from EFTA, but had also received them from Finland (March 1992) and Norway (1992)[7] forcing the Community to consider an immediate response. This pressure was reflected in the speed with which the Commission delivered its opinions on the three outstanding Nordic applicants with the opinion on Sweden being delivered in August 1992, Finland in November 1992 and Norway in March 1993. Indeed, the time period from the application to the opening of accession negotiations was record-breaking (at least in terms of the Community's history). For Sweden it took just 19 months, for Finland, 11 months and for Norway an amazing 4 months. In most quarters, and including the Commission, there was a realisation that EC enlargement policy was fast approaching obsolescence as regards Sweden and its EFTA partners.[8]

However, the Edinburgh agreement on the terms of Denmark's participation in the Union did, as Pedersen argues, include some elements of 'variable geometry, which 'might be used by applicant states in their negotiations with the Union. There was a clear risk that the Danish model might create a precedent'.[9] The Commission therefore highlighted that this courtesy would not be extended to the accession negotiations. New member states would only be eligible for temporary derogations from EU rules or transitional arrangements.[10] It is unclear to what extent that this was taken as read either by the Swedish negotiators or domestic actors.

Swedish Perspectives on the Accession Negotiations

Within Sweden, it was generally agreed amongst the political elite that given the negativity of public opinion and the political parties' internal disunity the quicker the accession negotiations were begun the better.[11] At least then, the issue would definitely be resolved through a relatively speedy process and would limit the level of division with Swedish society. One of the first summaries of the government's ongoing revision of EC policy was made by Prime Minister Carl Bildt in a famous speech in Brussels to the Foundation Paul-Henri Spaak (16

September 1992).[12] Bildt highlighted that enlargement would, contrary to many views, actually reinforce the Union's emerging CFSP. Sweden would as an EC member, be able to make 'a decisive contribution' to the stability of the Northern fringes of the Union and especially within the Baltic Republics. He also suggested that the distinction between being a member of military alliance or not was increasingly artificial. Sweden was despite its 'non-participation in military alliances' one of the leading contributors to peace-keeping operations. Commenting on the Western European Union (WEU), which is, after all, an important link to the CFSP, the Prime Minister argued that given this line of reasoning Sweden's relationship with the WEU would be decided once the country had become a full EC member. Sweden's position as regards the CFSP would also need to be carefully defined in the accession negotiations. Bildt also stressed the sensitivity of Swedish public opinion on, for example, alcohol monopolies, which would be critical to any future accession negotiations.

Another notable résumé of governmental thinking was given in a speech by the (then) Minister for Foreign Affairs, Margaretha af Ugglas at Chatham House in London (November 1992). According to Pedersen, the speech gave the impression that Sweden 'would be a fully committed member of the European Union'. The Minister highlighted that cooperation could be possible at the supranational level for economic, defence, migration and communications issues.[13] Ulf Dinkelspiel, the Minister for European Affairs and Foreign Trade had also stated in late 1992 that the government 'would not put a brake on future progress towards the goals which are formulated in the Maastricht Treaty in the area of security policy ... no additional commitments will be required by Sweden beyond those which were agreed by the member countries at Maastricht'.[14]

In addition, the non-socialist government formally summarised its priorities for the forthcoming talks in the opening statement by Ulf Dinkelspiel, in his capacity as Swedish chief negotiator, at the start of the accession negotiations (1 February 1993). In his statement, Dinkespiel drew attention to the fact that the negotiations would 'not be starting from scratch' given the previous 1972 Free Trade Agreement and the 1992 European Economic Area (EEA) accord.[15] He also alluded to the common challenges confronting both the existing Community and Sweden in the shape of the reforming of the Central and Eastern European Countries (CEECs), 'our common task of combating unemployment and stimulating economic recovery' and limiting ecological degradation.[16] The linkage between Nordic cooperation and Community membership was also mentioned at several points. Most importantly for this discussion, Dinkelspiel outlined those principles and policies that would be regarded as critical in determining whether Sweden would go to become a full EC member. These included:

- *openness and transparency.* Dinkelspiel stressed that Sweden had 'important experiences to share' with the EC as regards public accountability. Attention was drawn to the principles of open government (*offentlighetsprincipen*), free public access to official records and protection afforded to those who give information to the media (*meddelarfriheten*), which, he alleged, 'are fundamental principles laid down in the Swedish constitution which guarantee citizen's access to information on public matters'.[17]

- *the principle of subsidiarity.* The chief negotiator specifically highlighted 'respect for the national identities of member states and safeguards on the powers of national and local authorities'. He suggested that the transfer of sovereignty would be limited. The Swedes shared the view 'that the Community should only take actions where an objective can better be attained at the Community level than at the level of the individual states'.[18]

- *the social dimension.* This was, in Dinkelspiel's view, 'a crucial corollary to economic integration'. The Bildt government looked forward 'to actively contributing to the further development of ... the working environment and the dialogue between the social partners'. In particular, it welcomed the TEU's Social Protocol and 'the elaboration and implementation of common measures in the labour market field'.[19] In the opening remarks, the promotion of sexual equality was also mentioned.

- *Regional Policy.* The Swedish negotiators emphasised the 'permanent geographical features and difficulties' of the country and that these must be incorporated within the EC's current regional policy. In particular, the right of the Bildt government to 'pursue an active and ambitious national policy for regional development' (to maintain the rural populations in Sweden's arctic and sub-arctic northern regions) would need to be safeguarded.

- *Environmental Protection.* This area was highlighted in Dinkelspiel's opening remarks as being of significance to Swedish perspectives - 'we expect the highest level of ambition will apply in the environmental area and thus that there will be no lowering of standards'.[20] Environmental issues are given a high-profile by the public, especially by those concerned that full membership would not lead to a deterioration in Sweden's strict environmental laws.

- *Agricultural Policy.* Whilst the Swedish delegation stressed the commonalties between the post-1990 reformed agricultural policy and the CAP, Dinkelspiel also stated that his government expected that 'consideration must be given to the specific conditions for agricultural production in Sweden' and especially the country's low population density, its short growing season and the problems for farmers enduring Arctic and sub-Arctic conditions. The north of Sweden (including the Sami peoples), the forest areas of the South and on the islands of Öland and Gotland were specifically mentioned.

- *Common Commercial Policy and the Customs Union.* The Bildt government deemed the continuation of Sweden's free trade agreement with the Baltic States as being of central importance in order to support their reform programmes.[21]

- *Commercial Monopolies.* Although the Swedish government accepted the 'acquis' as regards commercial monopolies, Dinkelspiel declared that it was essential that the government maintained its alcohol monopolies which 'are based on important health and social policy considerations'.[22] This was important for domestic reasons as the public favoured restrictions on alcohol consumption.

The Swedish delegation also sought to calm the Community's nerves as regards the government's acceptance of the TEU's flagship policies and to, albeit to a limited degree, address the issue of 'specific and binding assurances'. Dinkelspiel reiterated that the government accepted the TEU's 'finalité politique' and the Community's 'acquis communautaire'. In particular, he addressed the security policy question. He argued that the Bildt government 'wished to participate fully in the Common Foreign and Security Policy (CFSP) within the framework of the Union' and wanted to 'to participate in the emerging Economic and Monetary Union (EMU),[23] especially as joint action to achieve monetary stability was an important prerequisite for facilitating growth and employment. However, provisos were also included on both counts, which whilst being moderate in tone, would not have completely satisfied the Commission. A final position on EMU would be left until 1998 and as regards the CFSP, Dinkelspiel noted that:

> 'Sweden's policy of non-participation in military alliances remains unchanged. At the same time, we recognise that the eventual framing of a common defence policy, which might in time lead to a common defence, is one of the CFSP goals, which is to be further discussed in the context of the 1996 review conference. We will not hamper the development of the European Union as it moves towards this goal'.[24]

The Swedish delegation also suggested that some areas of negotiation would be difficult, most notably on the size of the country's budgetary contribution which 'may constitute a problem'.[25] In general though, Dinkelspiel's tone was positive. He stressed that both sides should 'be able to find mutually acceptable solutions for the many important issues on our agenda'.[26] Indeed, some areas of concern for the Bildt government were intentionally omitted in order to ensure that the negotiations would get off to a good start.[27]

The Accession Negotiations

The accession negotiations began relatively quickly on the 1 February 1993[28] with the ambitious schedule of finalising the enlargement negotiations by January 1994 and full ratification to be completed in time for full accession on 1 January 1995. Although the four applicant states were often viewed as a cohesive group by the Union with the inter-linking of issues, the negotiations were principally on a bilateral basis between the Union and the respective applicant with coordination appearing intermittently between them on such issues as agricultural subsidies and environmental standards.[29] Nevertheless, there was considerable 'spill-over' between the differing sets of bilateral negotiations with EU concessions given to one applicant usually being extended to all or at least used as a basis for further negotiation with other applicants.

The Bildt government adhered to the traditional Swedish consultative approach to policy making - with the delegation receiving specialist support on individual policy areas from the respective ministries back home.[30] The Cabinet Office for instance, assigned the Swedish Board of Agriculture the task of producing the necessary documentation on agricultural issues for the delegation prior to the negotiations. The Board set up a specific EC Secretariat to correlate the studies and documents produced to prepare the way for the transition to full membership.[31]

The negotiations were unlike any previous accession negotiations and fell into four phases. The first spanned February-June 1993 and covered uncontroversial and background issues. At this stage, the general mood was of optimism. After all, unlike previous accession rounds, these accession negotiations were different in having a substantial foundation already constructed due to the previous European Economic Area (EEA) agreement. The Bildt government had already accepted the principles of the Single European Market and nearly 12,000 pages of the 'acquis'.[32] Moreover, in May 1993, the Danes finally approved the Maastricht Treaty in their second referenda. This boosted the enlargement negotiations by cementing the EU's negotiating position on the Treaty.[33] The Union appeared to have the upper hand, displaying a relatively hard negotiating line with the applicants.

This period proceeded relatively quickly as the negotiations were preliminary and concerned with establishing common positions between the Union and the applicants. Significantly, the phase did not touch upon the larger and more difficult areas of divergence between the applicants and the Union. It was more concerned with the details of the accession agenda and the technical issues deriving from the SEM and the EEA agreement, such as common positions on safety-belt legislation.

The second phase from June 1993 and culminating with a crucial series of meetings in December 1993, was dominated by a sense of increasing frustration as the negotiations became more protracted. This was not surprising as this was the first time the negotiations tackled sensitive issues. There was considerable posturing by the applicants (including Sweden) and the Union. At this point, it became evident why these accession negotiations would be unlike previous ones. Unlike prior enlargements, the four applicants were advanced liberal democracies with traditions of democracy and consultation through referenda. Sweden, along with its EFTA compatriots, introduced an extra, visible dimension to the negotiations. They would have to constantly consider the impact of any accession deal on the subsequent referenda in each state.

This additional dimension was influential for several reasons. First, the EU's most recent experience with public referenda had not been a positive one. The Union had experienced damaging challenges to its competence and credibility at the hands of the domestic populations during the previous year when it had been put to public judgment. The Danish rejection of the TEU (May 1992) and the close vote in the later French referendum on the Treaty showed that there was a distinct difference of perception between governmental and public views on the EU. In addition, the Swiss rejection of the EEA in their December 1992 plebiscite further illustrated that the EFTA populations were not convinced of the merits of the EU. The three Nordic applicants - most notably in Sweden and Norway - also included substantial domestic opposition to their respective countries' full membership. The inclusion of Norway was psychologically important, as the country had previously completed accession negotiations in an earlier application and had fallen at the final hurdle when its population rejected EU membership in 1972 in a referendum by 53 percent.[34] Much of the blame for the EU's only previous rejection was placed at the doors of the accession negotiators and their insensitivity to Norwegian fisheries demands.

In short, approval for full membership by referenda could not be taken for granted in Sweden. In 1993, the negotiations and especially the Union were constantly aware that there was considerable domestic opposition in the Nordic applicant states.[35] The level of benevolence conceded in the details of the agreement would become critically important both in terms of presentation and argument against the anti-EU domestic lobbies in applicant states. This phase of negotiations had to deal with the more sensitive areas, such as agriculture, regional policy and the CFSP, at a time when Swedish opinion polls took a further turn for the worse. Between March 1993-March 1994, opinion polls showed a consistent majority against full membership, with, for example, 44 percent of Swedes opposed in September 1993.

Several issues illustrated both the sensitivities of the Swedish domestic situation regarding EU accession and the importance of presentation. The issue of *'snus'* or wet snuff tobacco, for instance, was portrayed as both a sensitive issue for Sweden and an area where the EU was taking a hard line. It was claimed by the EU that *'snus'* would be illegal under an EU health directive in force since July 1993. It was also argued that the public would never agree to EU membership unless this cultural issue was solved by an exemption.[36] Sweden gained the exemption it required and consequently, the Bildt government's prestige rose with domestic voters.

It was during this period, that the negotiating 'balance of power' swung towards the applicants. The four states increasingly dictated the parameters of the negotiations as domestic and vocal opposition to full membership become increasingly evident. In late 1993, there was considerable concern expressed by individual EU member states such as Germany, that the negotiations were too protracted and needed to be more flexible. From October 1993, the first signs of progress on the more sensitive larger issues were beginning to be seen (see Table 8.1). Agreement on the EU customs union was completed (October) and the EU outlined its proposals on the transition of Nordic and Alpine agriculture (November). Nevertheless, even in November 1993, the Danish Council presidency and Belgium issued warnings that the negotiations would have to be accelerated if they were to stand any chance of completion by March 1993. In essence, the priority for the EU negotiators subtly altered from one initially based on ensuring that the applicants subscribe to the Union's parameters to one guaranteeing that the negotiations could be realistically finalised and therefore would not be seen as failure for the European Union.

The enlargement negotiations were in reality as important to the European Union as to the applicants. From the wider perspective, the accession negotiations could be seen as a new beacon of achievement for the Union providing a new sense of success in a period of 'consolidation' after the problems of ratifying the Maastricht Treaty.[37] In practice, the European Union could not afford to fail. The detail of the negotiations become more centred around the needs of the applicants than of the European Union. The eventual ratification of the TEU (1 November 1993) gave the Union a boost of energy and a redirection of focus on the most pressing issue of the enlargement negotiations. The Danish tenure as Council Presidency was coming to an end in December and this provided an additional greater zest for agreement given Danish sympathies for the Nordic applicants.

The Turning Point - The December 1993 Preliminary Agreements

A final set of negotiations leading up to Christmas 1993 proved crucial to the process. These negotiations began on 9 November 1993 and continued intermittently until the 23 December. The December agreements on environmental and social policy, alcohol monopolies, the CFSP and regional initiatives were critical to the eventual outcome. They allowed for further agreement to be sought and at least a partial belief that the negotiations would finish in time (for the revised deadline of 1 March 1994). By 22 December 1993, out of a total of 29 chapters, 18 were agreed with Sweden. It gave the negotiations a sporting chance of completion on time (see Table 8.1).

At the 'fifth round' December 1993 accession meetings, the first agreements on regional aid were finalised, and the 'Maastricht Chapters' were dealt with. Common positions on EMU and the CFSP were achieved with the Bildt government agreeing to an ambiguous statement on CFSP commitments. Interestingly, the special declaration on the CFSP - which was specifically designed to reassure the Commission and the member states that this enlargement would not slow down its future development - included a number of important aspects. The declaration stated that the parties agreed that the accession 'should strengthen the internal coherence of the Union and its capacity to act effectively in foreign and security policy' and that the new member states 'will from the time of their accession, be ready and able to participate fully and actively in the CFSP as defined in the TEU'.[38] It also included a special reference to the new member states' willingness on accession to 'take on in their entirety and without reservation all the objectives of the TEU' and the provisions of Title V.

Environmental standards were also generally agreed. The applicants gained four-year transitional periods, during which they could maintain their high standards at present levels, whilst the EU would endeavour to raise its own environmental standards. During the period, a 'consultation procedure' would enter force. This issue was positively presented with the Commission showing a conciliatory tone for Nordic domestic consumption giving the impression that this was a victory for the applicants and that the EU recognised their superiority in this respect. However, this was mainly for presentational purposes. In reality the agreement on environmental standards provides no guarantees that after four years, Sweden will not have to lower its standards to conform with the EU.

On the issue of alcohol monopolies an interesting compromise was found. Alcohol monopolies were sensitive in Sweden as they were maintained on the grounds of public health and thus were an area where the government could not be perceived to concede on for domestic reasons. Equally, the issue of liberalising monopolies is at the heart of the SEM programme and could not be seen easily solved. The Swedish position paper on alcohol monopolies issue was forthright, arguing that 'if the Swedish alcohol monopolies were to be dismantled, Sweden would soon be faced with increased consumption of alcohol and a very significant increase in the harmful effects'. It estimated a rise in premature deaths as a result of rising alcohol consumption 'by at least 1,200 per annum in the case of a 25 percent increase in consumption and by 2,500 per annum in the case of a 50 percent increase'.[39] In fact, the Bildt government agreed to abolish the state monopolies for the import, production and wholesale distribution of alcohol, but maintained the monopoly on retail sales of alcohol. This issue proved to be a classic example of the compromise between the EU and the Swedish government. Although the Swedish delegation did indeed, concede ground, the intention was to present it either as a fair deal or as a victory for Sweden to sustain domestic support for the EU application.[40] At face value, little would seem to have changed in the eyes of the Swedish public as the monopoly on retail outlets remained intact, even though liberalisation would have partially occurred.

Agreement on the exemption of the *'snus'* trade from EC health directives was also made in November 1993. This was regarded by the Swedish delegation as a sensitive issue back home (given the number of domestic users - around 800,000 - and the symbolic implications its proposed outlawing under EU rules would have on the traditional way of life of the mostly anti-EU Swedes). Indeed, for strategic reasons, the Bildt government talked up its position on *'snus'* and delayed announcing its preliminary agreement with the EU until December in order that its impact on public opinion would be maximised.

The third phase (January to March 1994) marked the transformation of the accession process. A sense of urgency entered the negotiations. There was considerable posturing by the Union with the down-playing of the possibilities of agreement by the 1 March 1994. The chances of concluding the negotiations were at best only reasonable, given that certain key issues, such as agriculture, regional policy, alpine transit, budgetary contributions and Norwegian fisheries remained unresolved. A new institutional dimension also strengthened the resolve of both sides to reach agreement. The European Parliament's (EP) consent for the Accession Treaties was needed under Rome Treaty (article 238). However, the postponing of the enlargement deadline from January to March 1994 introduced a new problem as the negotiations coincided with the same year as the EP's direct elections. If the EP was to approve the accession deal before its dissolution in May 1994 (which was essential if the January 1995 deadline was to be observed), then the negotiations would have to be concluded on time. Only then could the EP approve the accession treaty between 10 March-4 May 1994.

Table 8.1   **A Chronology of the Swedish-EU Accession Negotiations**

1993	Decision Taken
1 Feb	Dinkelspiel's Speech and the Opening of Accession Negotiations.
11 March	Chs. 3 (Workers), 4 (Capital), 8-12 (Education - Company Law) declared 'non-problematic'.
28 May	Unable to agree to common positions under Chs. 1 (Goods), 2 (Establishment) and 13 (Environment).
8 June	Chs. 3, 5 (Transport), 7-11 closed.
28 July	Agree to common positions on third life assurance directive (Ch. 2). Ch. 21 (Industrial Policy) declared 'non-problematic'.
23 Sept	Agree to common positions on energy (Ch. 14). Ch. 17 (Customs Union) declared 'non-problematic'.
4 Nov	Ch. 2 declared 'non-problematic'.
9 Nov	TEU Chapters now included in negotiations.
21 Dec	Chs. 6 (Competition Policy), 13, 24-26 (CFSP, JHA chapters) closed.
1994	
8 Feb	Ch. 17 closed.
17 Feb	Joint Declaration on Nordic Cooperation agreed (Ch. 29).
22 Feb	Agreement between three Nordic applicants on rights of Sami people (Ch. 29).
1 March	Agreement on agriculture (Ch. 15), regional (Ch. 20) and budgetary questions and agricultural quotas.
30 March	Final Agreement on Chs. 23 (EMU) and 28 (Institutions).
11-12 Apr	Acceptance of Accession Treaty and beginning of ratification process.
24 June	Signing of Accession treaty at Corfu.

The EP dimension was one of the greatest catalysts for meeting the March deadline. Failure threatened the enlargement timetable - something neither the EU nor the Bildt government could afford. Agreement was only concluded due to the flexibility of the Union negotiators, who often conceded on the key issues. The Swedish delegation was (along with the Norwegians) accused of being blatantly stubborn and of achieving 'highway robbery' on the issues of agriculture and budgetary contributions. Consistently, when the choice for the Union was between financial concessions or matters of principle, the EU's solution was to opt for monetary persuasion.

The Terms of the March 1994 Agreement

On the 1 March 1994, the European Union managed to secure final agreement with Sweden, Finland and Austria on the final detail of their accession packages, after marathon negotiating sessions.[41] Indeed, Sweden was first to reach a conclusive deal on the morning of 1 March. Agreement was finally struck on the last outstanding issue of budgetary contributions and the related EU financial compensation for farmers for their transition to CAP prices from the first day of accession. In the final hours, the Commission conjured up an extra ECU 750 million (£840 million) to cushion the immediate impact of EU entry, raising the value of its sweeteners to all four applicants from ECU 2.8 billion to ECU 3.6 billion (£2.8 billion) over four years. Under the formula, Sweden was allocated ECU 375 million to be used as a temporary EU budgetary rebate.[42] The money is to be officially used to bolster farmers' incomes over four years as farm prices were brought into line on the first day of EU membership.[43]

Not until the end of the transitional period (1999) would the (then) four applicants have contributed the net ECU 1.7 billion to the EU budget. The issue of budgetary contributions proved a prickly one and was related to other aspects of the accession negotiations. Sweden faced no wrenching adjustment of its agricultural regime. Previous reforms since 1990 have brought their farm prices close to EU levels. However, the country gained a budgetary rebate worth up to ECU 2 billion in the first three years as a farm adjustment payment. The Swedish purse contributed only ECU 50 million net to the EU budget in its first year of membership and the bulk of the savings will be during the country's first two years of membership. The full net contribution of ECU 750 million will not be due until Sweden's fifth year of membership.[44] As one of the Swedish negotiators glibly noted 'it pays to be stubborn' and the delegation returned home with the country's wallet relatively intact.[45]

The general features of the budgetary agreement were that the Swedish contribution to the Union's budget would be phased in over four years, which meant an estimated total reduction of approximately SEK 9.2 billion. Overall, the budgetary cost for 1995 was estimated to be SEK 9 billion and SEK 11-12 billion in 1996. This tangible reduction would help reduce the strain on the government's domestic budget commitments in the first two years, although there would be gradual increases in the two following years.[46] According to the Foreign Ministry, this solution 'satisfactorily reflects Sweden's negotiation requirements'.[47] However, as Merriden argues, 'Stockholm will still end up as a very large contributor to the EU budget' and from a pessimistic (if in practice rather unlikely) view, the Swedish government could be forced to re-negotiate the country's budgetary contribution in the light of growing anti-EU public opinion.[48]

On the 7 April, the Ministry of Foreign Affairs issued an overview on the outcome of Sweden's negotiations with the Union. In general, the Swedish negotiating team had made the prospect of full membership as viable as possible.[49] The delegation achieved its underlying objective that as a result of full membership, 'Sweden will participate fully in the Union's decision-making since it will be represented in all the EU institutions'.[50] As regards policy areas, the various positions were given. Some areas were presented as clear victories for Sweden - most notably on the budgetary contribution, agriculture, regional support to the country's Northern areas, the exception of *'snus'* tobacco from EU public health laws and the continuation of Sweden's free trade agreement with the three Baltic states.

On agricultural matters, Sweden would participate in the CAP from its first day of membership, but would maintain existing levels of production of cereals, milk, sugar and beef and receive compensation for the transition. As a result, Sweden was guaranteed a base area of 1.8 million hectares, a sugar quota of 370,000 tonnes and a milk quota of 3.3 million. Headage payments would also be made for a maximum number of animals of different types, but this would correspond to current totals before membership. Most importantly, support for agriculture in Northern Sweden would stay at current levels or would be even higher as a result of full membership. During the negotiations, the government ensured that EU support would be paid out to Less Favoured Areas (LFA).[51] In practice, elements of the 1990 agricultural reforms were reversed and some of the areas previously deregulated were re-regulated under the CAP.[52] The inclusion of a new Objective 6 within EU regional policy criteria (based upon low density of population) also meant that Swedish traditional criteria for supporting sparse populations, long distances, small local markets, short growing seasons and a cold climate were incorporated within EU policy.[53] The government estimated in 1994 that this provided SEK 900 per inhabitant for regional and structural development in Sweden.

In other high profile areas, the Swedish delegation was less successful. The Bildt government stressed that the accession agreement would 'safeguard the foundations of Sweden's alcohol policy'.[54] The agreement, which took the form of an exchange of letters between the Commission and the government allowed for the fact that whilst, the National Monopoly for the Retail Sale of Alcoholic Beverages (*Systembolaget*) was retained under the terms of the agreement (with non-discriminatory treatment of suppliers), the import, export, wholesale and production monopolies would be, none the less, phased out. The government rationalised this agreement by stating that it achieved the best of both worlds. On the one hand, it ensured that sales of alcohol would still be controlled and on the other, there would be greater competition between suppliers and more product choice for consumers.[55]

Sweden's requirement of retaining standards of environmental protection which are more stringent than those currently applicable in the EU was observed under the so-called 'third option' agreement. Total EU financial support for environmental protection in Sweden was also likely to amount to ECU 165 million. It was interesting to note that during the ensuing press conferences on the agreement, there were divergent opinions between the Swedish delegation and the Commission Enlargement Task Force over the extent to which and for how long Swedish higher environmental standards could be maintained. In short, the Bildt government did not gain cast-iron guarantees from the Commission that either EU environmental laws would be improved to Swedish levels or that some areas of Swedish standards would not have to be eventually downgraded.

In the two flagship areas of EMU and the CFSP, open-ended agreements were also made. Although the Swedish government agreed, for instance, to fully and actively participating in the EU's emerging CFSP, it also stipulated a number of provisos. As the Foreign Ministry noted in its April policy statement,

> 'There are no legal impediments to participation in cooperation on the same terms as existing members of the Union. Sweden will not prevent other countries from developing a common defence policy if they so wish, but we will decide ourselves whether or not we want to participate in such a policy in the future. Sweden's non-participation in military alliances continues to apply'.[56]

As regards the two high-profile issues of social policy and openness/transparency, the government achieved very little, apart from statements of intent or unilateral declarations on the Swedish side. In a letter from Commissioner Padraig Flynn to the Swedish Minister of Labour, Mr Börje Hörnlund, it was recognised that full membership would have no negative implications for the functioning of the Swedish labour market and that 'collective agreements are a perfectly satisfactory instrument for the implementation of EC directives in the labour market area'.[57] This was in any case, always likely to be the case and was more a symbolic gesture than any concession on the part of the Union. Sweden also resorted to unilateral declarations being incorporated into the conference's documents on the 'principle of publicity' and greater transparency in EU decision-making.[58]

At face value, the Swedish delegation seemed pleased with the outcome and had at least gained agreement in many of the crucial areas.[59] Despite being a publicised event, its effect on the domestic debate was difficult to gauge for as Widfeldt notes elsewhere, 'in many ways the accession agreement raised as many questions as it answered. Many of the specific agreements on controversial areas, such as defence cooperation, would still be subject to later decisions after Swedish accession'.[60] In general though, the Union's strategy of appeasing the Swedish public was, at least initially, successful. The accession agreements were, for the most part, regarded by the Swedish public as fair. Carl Bildt celebrated the accession deal as the country's 'most important international agreement of the century'.[61] This was reflected in opinion polls, showing previously strong 'No' support shrinking to 42 percent and the 'Yes' vote sharply rising to 35 percent in March 1994.

Overall, the fact that the accession terms would be put to public judgment in a referendum proved to be a persuasive factor which influenced the nature of the accession negotiations, strengthening the Swedish government's hand and changing the orientation of the European Union's negotiating position. The Norwegian rejection of 1972 proved to be a useful example which the negotiators sought not to repeat. Yet, there was consternation on the part of the Bildt government that the good work of the accession agreement would be undermined by the internal EU disunity as soon as the negotiations were concluded.[62] The statement by the Greek Foreign Minister and chairman of the last sessions of the accession negotiations, Theodoros Pangalos, was especially disliked when he declared at the conclusion of the negotiations,

> 'Now that this is done, now that I have done my duty ... I honestly want to say that this decision is wrong ... the EU should not have undertaken new responsibilities before the Community structure deepens'.[63]

The fourth phase of the accession negotiations ironically did not directly include the applicant states at all. This small period (March 1993) was dominated by internal wrangling within the EU over the impact of enlargement on its institutional structure. It illustrated that the accession negotiations are multi-faceted and do not just have implications at either the EU-applicant level or at the applicant domestic level, but also had profound implications for consensus within the existing EU itself. As early as May 1992, the Commission recognised that the redistribution of power among Union institutions and member states to accommodate the new members would be sensitive. In a confidential document drawn up by the Commission's Enlargement Task Force, it was suggested that this should be determined at the 1996 IGC.[64] Nevertheless, the issue of voting rights in the Council of Ministers would have to solved before then, given the practical need for the enlarged EU to make decisions before the review took place.

In short, there were political problems between the Twelve over competing technical scenarios for voting rights in the enlarged Council of Ministers. The 'blocking minority' stood at 23 votes or roughly 30 percent under Qualified Majority Voting - something which the British and Spanish governments initially resisted changing. They argued that it should remain unaltered as 23 votes allowed a combination of two large states and one small state to veto Euro-legislation. The majority of member states and the EP proposed that the percentage should be maintained with an enlarged Council of Ministers needing 27 votes for a 'blocking minority'. The voting rights issue struck at the very core of the European Union's institutional principles, yet challenged the roles of existing member states and their perceived national interests within the EU, rather than questioned the EU's general flexible attitude towards the applicants.

The hasty solution - the Ioannina compromise (30 March) - was an obvious fudge by the Union. It allowed for the number of votes needed to block Union legislation to rise from 23 out of 76 to 27 out of 90 from the day of accession. However, where a minority of between 23 and 26 votes opposes a new law, the matter should be discussed for a 'reasonable period'. The UK also gained assurances from the Commission that this new qualified majority ruling would not be used on social legislation.[65] Ioannina was presented as a transition measure as institutional aspects would be reviewed at the 1996 IGC. However, from the Swedish perspective, Bildt found it hard to hide his exasperation with the events and that this would neutralise any positive effects stemming from the completion of the accession agreements. His government sought to play down the issue as an EU internal problem and nothing to do with Sweden, but this only helped to confuse an already cautious public.

The initial fears about the possibility of the European Parliament rejecting the accession treaties proved unfounded. The EP - keen to show that it would be responsible with its new powers under the assent procedure - approved the accession treaty with Sweden on time and with a resounding majority. In its vote on the admission of Sweden (May 1994), the country's accession was approved by 380 votes for, 21 against and with 60 abstentions (out of 461 total votes cast).[66]

The Domestic Setting

The cumulative impact of the disharmony within the Twelve was, to some degree, to reinforce existing public attitudes on the question of full membership. Public opinion remained stable from late 1992 onwards with a consistent majority against full membership present in almost every poll taken by the SIFO Institute (see Chapter Seven). In October 1992 under the influence of the first Danish rejection of the TEU (in June 1992) as many as 53 percent of Swedes stipulated that they would vote against EU membership, with only 30 percent in favour and 17 percent undecided. In December 1992, the 'No' vote had reduced slightly to 50 percent, with the 'Yes' camp improving to 33 percent, but again with 17 percent undecided.

By February 1993 after the start of the accession negotiations and in the aftermath of what is generally perceived to be the successful Edinburgh Summit, the 'No' vote had declined to 43 percent. However, this did not translate into 'Yes' votes. Their segment of the vote remained at 32 percent, but with more undecided (26 percent). As Pedersen notes, the transfer of opponents to the undecided camp reflected the belief that it may be possible to negotiate Danish style 'opt-outs',[67] although the Commission had stated that this would not be the case for any of the four EFTA applicants.

By May 1993 and with the 'accession negotiations honeymoon' fading, public opinion again hardened against membership. Those opposed to full membership rose again to 46 percent, with 33 percent in favour and the undecided segment dropped to 21 percent.[68] Yet, positive approval in the second Danish referendum on the TEU (18 May 1993) did lead to a growing belief that in spite of opinion polls the outcome of a Swedish referendum on full membership would be favourable. A *Svenska Dagbladet* (1 June 1993) survey, for example, indicated that a majority (55 percent) thought that any future referendum would approve membership with 31 percent believing in a prevailing 'No' vote. The overall picture remained confused with opinion polls unable to explain why a Swedish public predominantly against membership, for the most part, still believed that any future referendum would deliver a positive outcome.

The non-socialist government embarked on a two-pronged strategy to deal with the dilemma of negotiating accession terms and at the same time trying to legitimise full membership amongst an unconvinced Swedish public. First, the government and the mainstream political parties argued that full membership was not a foregone conclusion and would be conditional upon the accession terms. As Dinkelspiel noted (August 1993), 'the devil is in the detail' and the most difficult phase of the negotiations had still not been dealt with.[69] Second, a lengthy, consultative process was enacted to disseminate information on full membership and to examine its merits. A series of high-profile *ad-hoc* Commissions were established, which were to indirectly persuade elite opponents and the mass public of the benefits of Swedish accession.

On 10 December 1992, the government appointed a commission of independent academics - the so-called Lindbeck or Economic Commission (*Ekonomikommissionen*) - to examine the country's economic crisis and possible solutions. The Commission, whilst not directly dealing with the arguments of full membership, did have to 'deal with short-term, as well as medium term problems' of which the transition of the economy to accommodate EU membership was considered. In its final 200 page report (published 9 March 1993) entitled *Nya Villikor för Ekonomi och Politik, Ekonomikommissionens förslag,*[70] the Commission mentioned three areas of transition for the economy arising out of future EU membership - competition policy, changes to the agricultural sector and the budgetary costs of full membership. It estimated that the net cost associated with membership would be in the range of SEK 10-20 billion per year and that because of certain Swedish tax rates, such as on alcoholic beverages needing to be cut, there would be a direct loss of tax revenues in the SEK 5-10 billion range.[71]

Interestingly, the Lindbeck Commission also highlighted than any antidote to Sweden's economic problems would also require a degree of political and institutional reform. The Commission for example, stressed the fact that governmental terms were reduced to three years, affecting the continuity of government policy; that the power of the Riksdag was too large undermining the Finance Ministry in 'an excessively protracted budgetary process' and enabling the country's fragmented party system to limit the influence of governments.[72] In effect, the Commission was arguing that the country's consensual democracy (the first point of the Diamond) had become unbalanced. Moreover, the Commission also pointed to the fact that the traditional view of interest groups 'constructively represented in the decision process and leading to efficient consensual expression of the public interest' had become diluted. Interest groups were no longer as active and 'the division of responsibilities between the government authorities and organised special interest is blurred. ... In practice, state and society are regarded as almost synonymous because non-governmental organisations are so closely interwoven with the political process'.[73] In other words, the Lindbeck Commission also indicated that the second point of the 'Swedish Diamond' - the corporate system - would need further reform. It envisaged, 'a more explicitly pluralist society ... and the political system, in particular, the Riksdag, is left squarely with the responsibility for preserving the public interest'.[74] To some extent, the Lindbeck Commission advocated further changes to the 'Swedish Diamond' and reinforced the domestic debate over whether that fundamental reform was essential (of which full membership could be a part).[75]

In the same month as the Lindbeck Commission presented its final report and 20 months after the membership application, the government appointed a parliamentary committee to prepare a comprehensive assessment of the economic effects of EU membership. The objective was to provide a 'Swedish Impact Assessment', a common point of departure for the public debate during the forthcoming campaigns of the November 1994 referendum, and as a complement to the information presented by amongst others, the media and political parties.

The 10-member committee, which included representatives from industry, the trade unions and interest organisations, was instructed to 'analyse the economic consequences for Sweden of various forms of participation in the process of European integration'.[76] Specific aspects needed special consideration by the EU Consequences Committee including for example, the effects on economic growth, labour market policies, employment, consumer welfare, regional development, environment and equality, which, albeit to a limited extent, tentatively touched on the ground partially covered by the previous Lindbeck Commission. The remit of the Committee also included an investigation of the potential alternatives to full membership from a 'medium-term perspective' covering the next 5-10 years.

In short, the EU Consequences Committee was to provide 'a very comprehensive discussion of the economic effects of integration'.[77] Under the chairmanship of Björn Molin, it began its operation in March 1993, met nine times. It delivered its final 480 page report (summarising its findings) plus nine separate chapter supplements (examining specific issues) in January 1994.[78] As requested, the final report identified three alternative scenarios for Swedish-EU relations:

- *Sweden and the EEA Agreement* - the Committee's 'reference alternative'.

- *Full membership.* Sweden would participate fully in the activities of the SEM. The membership scenario differed in two important respects - by adding 'stability to the conditions' that apply to the SEM and by increasing the country's influence in EU decision-making.

- *Sweden outside the Single European Market.* This assumed that the country maintained its 1972 Free Trade Agreement.

The Committee in particular concentrated on two main themes to gauge the effect that each of the alternatives would have - namely the impact of the three scenarios on levels of economic growth when Sweden became part of the SEM and the implications for policy areas once they became subject to common EU decision-making as part of the obligations of full membership.[79] However, in practice, this was not an easy task and subject to a degree of speculation. The difficulty for the Committee was two-fold. Not only was the Community and indeed Sweden, in transition, but the Committee was in fact comparing processes and not conditions. As the itnoted in its final conclusions,

> 'There is no *status quo*, no alternative in which everything would remain as it is today. Reality is changing. Forecasts turn out to be wrong. When comparing processes - which are unpredictable - it is practically impossible to quantify the results'.[80]

In many ways, its original remit was virtually impossible to fulfil in 1994 even given the Committee's requirements of considering the medium-term. It could be argued, albeit to a limited extent, that as a result of these provisos the Committee's role did not necessarily educate the public but merely raised the spectre of full membership.

What was clear from the Committee's conclusions was that it believed that full membership was the most attractive option.[81] The deficiencies of the EEA were stressed, whilst the third option was dismissed. It involved the greatest measure of uncertainty and which in the long term would require the harshest level of adjustment from an isolated Sweden. For the most part, the Committee indirectly argued in favour of the full membership option on a number of grounds. The maximisation of Swedish influence in EU decision-making was emphasised; as was 'the very tangible psychological effect' of being a member for promoting Swedish business and exports. In particular, the Committee highlighted that the economic effects of full membership would make Swedish participation in the SEM permanent, lead to a corresponding increase in levels of investment within Sweden and stem the flow of capital leaving the country. As the Committee itself noted:

> 'EU membership will not automatically solve the problems the Swedish economy has to overcome, but we believe that the chances of overcoming them will be better with higher investments and the more favourable productivity trend that this could lead to. ... Higher investment speeds up the restructuring process, which brings about higher productivity and higher value added. This in turn means a stronger international competitive position and the ability to achieve a higher level of real wages in the economy'.[82]

In many ways, it is difficult to gauge the extent to which these elite bodies influenced either public opinion or the general debate on full membership. Public opinion on the EU question remained static and mostly anti-EU throughout 1993.

What the Lindbeck Commission and EU Consequences Committee did was in fact to provide a barrage of data and expert opinion which the 'Yes' and 'No' campaigns could fight over. When it came to raising the level of debate without necessarily changing many peoples' actual minds, the bodies were successful. However, they tended to reinforce the governmental perspectives and provide extra legitimacy for the original decision to apply for membership status, even if the political parties and domestic public opinion remained as divided as ever.

Certainly, the first main debate to appear after the agreeing of the accession terms concerned the nature of the domestic ratification and in particular, the nature and timing of the future public referendum on the full membership question. Although not constitutionally required or binding on the government, the main political parties agreed that a referendum approving full membership was essential and the outcome of which would in practice, be respected by the government. As Widfeldt argues two factors were influential in the debate on the timing of the referendum.[83] First, the opinion polls of the time indicated that any referendum in the near future would most probably result in a Swedish rejection. Secondly, there was to be a general election scheduled for September 1994.

The Social Democrats and the Centre Party were still deeply divided on the EU issue. Both parties wished to avoid a referendum in the near future before the Riksdag election as this would risk them entering (for them the more important) election campaigns hurt by damaging internal splits inflicted in any previous referendum discussion. It was decided (18 March 1994) that the referendum on full membership would in fact take place after the September election on the 13 November 1994. To some extent, wider strategic considerations were also significant as the timing of the referendum meant that the Swedes would be aware of the results of the Austrian and Finnish referendum outcomes. This 'East to West' referendum process was criticised by the anti-EC camp as being designed to maximise the chances of a 'domino effect' and a 'Yes' majority in the Swedish case, as Austrian and Finnish approval for full membership was expected.[84] The decision on the date of the referendum in practice marked the start of the campaigns, although to a large extent, attention was diverted before September towards the Riksdag election. The intensity of campaigning on the EU issue dramatically increased after the general election.

On 24 August 1994, the Bildt government submitted its bill concerning full membership to the Parliament. The Bill proposed that Parliament should approve the agreement reached during the accession negotiations and allow Sweden to become a full member. It did however, stipulate that a decision on this matter would not be taken until after a consultative referendum had taken place. As Ulf Dinkelspiel in his role as Minister for European Affairs stated in his address to the Riksdag:

'The referendum which is to be held on 13 November will determine the historic decision which is currently facing Sweden. A "No" vote will mean "No", and "Yes" will mean "Yes". All political parties have declared that the result of the referendum will be respected. If the outcome is "No", the Government will withdraw the Bill'.

However, the Minister did none the less, recommend full membership:

'EU membership will mean that Sweden can achieve major national goals more easily than if we choose to remain outside the Union'. ... Membership of the EU will give us greater opportunities to safeguard Sweden's interests and to influence development in other countries. This will give Sweden a place and a voice in the EU, thus entitling us to vote in Europe'.[85]

The bill consisted of four main sections - the government's reasons for joining the EU, a description of the historical development of European integration, an examination of the results of the negotiations and the consequences for membership and a final section summarising the legislation and 'constitutional pre-requisites' for full membership.[86] Crucially, the bill stated that the government 'had arrived at a satisfactory agreement - with the broad consensus amongst the political parties - and that, in all important respects, this agreement meets the requirements established prior to the negotiations'.[87]

Approving Accession: Towards the Referendum

The accession negotiations did not represent the end of the accession process. The real battle for accession has just begun and was in many ways, between the Swedish government and the domestic population. The delay in gaining final agreement had a negative effect on the domestic public opinion making the EU less attractive due to its own disunity. The initial progress evident in Swedish opinion polls towards a favourable referendum outcome at the time of the March accession agreement noticeably dissipated during the EU voting rights dispute. Domestic party and public opinion was now sensitive to the changing perceptions of EU unity.

The Legacy of the September 1994 General Election

The referendum was preceded by the September general election and formed the backdrop against which the referendum was fought. This was influential in three ways. First, there was a general consensus amongst the major political parties that this was to be an election conducted solely on domestic issues. The election was fought on the issues of the budgetary deficit, levels of national debt and rising unemployment. In particular, by the time of the election, the national debt level stood at SEK 1,300 billion, only slightly short of Sweden's entire GDP for 1993 of SEK 1,450 billion.[88] The issue of EU membership was divorced from the election and left for debate in the future referendum.

Second, the SAP won a resounding victory. It turned in its best performance since 1982, capturing 45.3 percent of the votes and 161 of the 349 parliamentary seats. Ingvar Carlsson returned as Prime Minister leading a minority administration. This result had major implications as regards the EU debate. In the first place, the return of a Social Democratic administration actually increased the chances of a positive vote in the later referendum. This seemed somewhat ironic given that the SAP remained split on the issue and that the previous Bildt government had been enthusiastically in favour of full membership. It was argued that given the fact that the Social Democrats were split on the EU issue, there was a greater chance of a 'Yes' vote with a Carlsson government. Dissident Social Democrats would be less inclined to vote negatively in the referendum and against a Social Democratic government, than if a non-socialist administration had led Sweden into the referendum campaign.

To some extent, this was immediately reflected in SIFO public opinion polls. September 1994 was the first month since spring 1992 that showed a tiny majority in favour of membership. With the fall of the Bildt government, the changing constellation of political forces now worked in favour of full membership. As Bjørklund argues,

> 'The opposition to full membership had interfered with opposition to the Conservative Prime Minister Carl Bildt. It was partly an opposition to the form of membership which Bildt was agitating for. When the Social Democrats were in charge and therefore responsible for taking the decisive step into the EU the membership alternative would appear more acceptable'.[89]

This was also partly the reason why Carlsson cited the EU issue as one of the reasons for refusing to consider a coalition with the pro-EU Liberal Party after the election. He claimed that a coalition with the Liberals would trigger negative reactions among the trade union movement and active party workers. It was suggested that only a Social Democratic government could guarantee a majority of voters in favour of membership, especially once Ingvar Carlsson pledged to campaign for EU membership after the SAP's June 1994 conference approved this policy by 2-1. A Social Democratic government would also slow the Bildt administration's shift away from neutrality. Carlsson, after all, had criticised Bildt for his statements concerning Sweden's role in the Baltic region. However, in the Social Democratic government's first foreign policy declaration in 1994,

Carlsson maintained that the security of the Baltic states was important to Sweden and cooperation would be intensified.[90]

Third, those parties which opposed full membership did well in the election and those parties identified as being pro-EU generally suffered. The pro-EU Liberal Party saw its share of the vote drop from 9.1 percent (1991 general election) to 7.2 percent (1994). In contrast, the anti-EU Greens and the Left Party increased their share of the vote from 3.4 percent (1991) to 4.5 percent and from 4.5 percent (1991) to 6.2 percent respectively. The election increased the number of anti-EU MPs from around 20 to between 60-65. The Left Party which had prior to the 1994 election been the only anti-EU party with representation in the Riksdag, was joined by the small Green Party which regained its seats in the September general election and in the last eight weeks of the referendum campaign joined the anti-EU parliamentary opposition. Aside from the Greens and the Left Party, 17 prominent Social Democrats were also in the anti-EU camp. This partly explains why two well known EU opponents were included in the Social Democratic Cabinet (Margareta Winberg as Minister for Agriculture and Marita Ulvskog as Minister for the Interior).

To some extent, the aftermath of the September election created a lull in the debate on full membership. In part this was due to a shift in public attention away from the EU issue to the tragic sinking of the ferry *Estonia* (28 September 1994), with the loss of some 900 lives. The country went into mourning for several weeks over the loss of many Swedes. Moreover, the Social Democratic government's immediate priorities were essentially economic. In Ingvar Carlsson's statement of policy to the Riksdag (7 October 1994), the Prime Minister highlighted the new government's five main tasks - to restore public finances and to reduce unemployment; to safeguard prosperity, to increase Sweden's international commitment (especially in the UN and the Baltic); to establish closer cooperation with other European countries and to achieve an ecologically sustainable industrial society. The speech was not EU focused, but rather dealt with the more pressing issues of economic revival.

The Referendum Campaign

The legacy of the 1994 general election created an unusual situation for the party campaigners. On the one hand, the central role of the Social Democrats was confirmed. Yet, the divisions within the Social Democratic Party (in which it was estimated that up to 45 percent of members were anti-EU)[91] and the appointment of prominent anti-EU campaigners to the new Cabinet meant that Carlsson's ability to provide strong leadership in favour of full membership was weakened.[92] Opinion polls indicated that there were strong anti-EU inclinations among voters who usually supported the Social Democrats. In addition, the success of the anti-EU parties in the election also meant that the Carlsson government was reliant upon their support in the Riksdag. The government therefore took a cautious line on the EU issue.

Public opinion polls also suggested that the electorate remained evenly split on the membership issue in 1994 and that the party campaigns would be instrumental in determining the referendum's outcome. Up until the last week of the referendum campaign, the 'No' side still maintained a slim lead. It was only in the last week of the campaign that the 'Yes' campaign was in the ascendancy. Even then a series of negative opinion polls appeared on 11 November.[93] It was so close that if the referendum had taken place ten days before, then a 'No' vote would have been the probable outcome.

At the risk of seeming slow and indecisive, Carlsson adopted a low key approach. Carlsson allowed the Social Democratic party to fund and run two campaigns, one of which was led by the two anti-EU campaigners in his Cabinet. However, for the most part, the 'No to the EU Movement' lacked a strong enough profile and effective organisation to attract the large number of vulnerable grass-roots Social Democrats. It was only in the last week, when the vote was looking too close to call that Carlsson became more assertive and galvanised the 'Yes' campaign. As Lindström notes, 'as the referendum day neared the campaign of the Social Democratic party focused on the personal confidence in its own leadership' with the SAP leaders stressing that full membership was right for the future of the party and for the country.[94] On 8 November, Carlsson and his Finance Minister, Göran Persson, for instance, warned that a negative vote would damage the government's efforts to control the budget deficit and lead to a run on the Swedish currency.[95]

The Centre Party showed similar divisions. It had decided to recommend to its voters to approve full membership only after an extra party congress had been held after the conclusion of the accession negotiations in May 1994. Although the decision was approved by a convincing majority (194 votes against 92), it was be no means clear if the party could convince its grass-roots party members and voters to support such a decision. During the campaign, the most prominent Centre Party representative was Hans Lindqvist for the 'No' side. He had been elected male chairperson of the 'People's Movement against the European Union', but he did not enjoy a leading position in the party. In terms of party strategy, the Centre Party conducted a lower profile campaign, doing little to deal with the issue of internal party division. The party's leader (Johansson) was almost completely absent from the media spotlight. In fact, as Miles and Widfeldt note elsewhere remarkably few from the party were seen in the media advocating a 'Yes' vote despite the party's official position. On the face of it, the Social Democratic strategy seems to have worked better.[96]

It was economic arguments, such as providing new sources of employment, injecting liberalisation into an overly regulated economy and consolidating governmental policies dealing with the budgetary deficit that were the main themes of the 'Yes' campaign. The pro-EU campaign linked together the Union as an international solution for domestic economic problems with the argument that Sweden must fully participate in EU decision-making if its long-term future was to be secured.

The 'No' campaign was centred around the Greens, the Left Party and the anti-EU Social Democrats.[97] Its campaign issues were more political and emotional. They ranged from the argument that membership would undermine Swedish democracy, that it would reduce social provision and environmental standards, to being an attack on 'Swedishness', women's rights and Nordic co-operation. The 'No' campaign found that concerns over open government and consensual democracy were especially influential with sceptical voters. However, to a large extent, the issue of security policy remained overshadowed by the economic priorities.[98] Non-alignment played only a relatively minor role in the debate, reflecting perhaps its declining importance on the political agenda. The severe recession of 1990-93 meant that ultimately the electorate placed economic recovery above all else.

The referendum campaign was perceived as a battle between the established government, parties and industrial lobbies and the more fringe elements of Swedish society. In the later stages of the campaign, Swedish industry mobilised itself and entered the debate on a large scale. On 22 October, the four executives of the country's largest forestry firms, Stora, SAC, Mood and Assidoman - issued a joint statement calling for a 'Yes' vote in order to secure Swedish exports.[99] In a much noted *Dagens Nyheter* interview on the eve of the referendum, Percy Barnevik, head of the multinational company ABB (Asea Brown Boveri) and one of the country's best known business leaders argued that Sweden should join the Union in order to allow it to participate in the historic task of integrating Western and Eastern Europe. The leadership of the trade union movement also exerted pressure on its members. In order to influence the vote of public employees, for instance, the local government employees union leader, Ms Lillemor Arvidsson, appeared on national television three days before the referendum to announce that she had decided to vote 'Yes', with two more public employee union leaders declaring in favour of membership the next day.

Indeed, the day before the vote Carlsson and Bildt joined forces in a rare show of unity and appealed for a positive outcome in a final television debate. They jointly argued that EU membership was now vital to the Swedish economy and hardly mentioned security issues at all.[100] As Bjørklund notes, the strength of opposition to the EU among the population seemed remarkable compared to the meagre corresponding opposition within the elite establishment and illustrated how divisive the EU issue was within Swedish society.[101]

A Brief Survey of the Referendum Results

On 13 November 1994, Sweden voted by 52.27 percent against 46.83 percent (with 0.9 percent blank votes) in favour of joining the EU (see Table 8.2). Turnout averaged 83.32 percent across 29 regional constituencies. Although the vote was positive, it was hardly an overwhelming endorsement of full membership. 2,833 million people voted for EU membership (with 2,539 million voting against) out of a total voting population of 6,510 million people.

Table 8.2   Overall Results of the 13 November 1994 Referendum on EU Membership

	Absolute Numbers	Percentage
'Yes'	2,833,721	52.27
'No'	2,539,132	26.83
Blank Ballots	48,937	0.9
Valid Votes	5,421,790	
Invalid Votes	2,297	
Total Votes	5,424,087	
Electorate	6,510,055	
Turnout	5,424,087	83.3

Source: Embassy of Sweden, London (1994).

In reality though, the vote was carried on a regional constituency basis, with seventeen regional constituencies approving membership and twelve voting against. More importantly, the more populous, southern and urban regions, such as Stockholms Kommun (522,805 voters) and Stockholms Iän (694,000 voters) voted decisively in favour - by 61 percent in both cases. These two constituencies alone accounted for 623,000 of the 2.8 million voters who approved of EU membership in the referendum. The three constituencies of Malmö represented another 310,000. In total, the seven combined constituencies of Stockholm, Malmö and Gothenburg accounted for 1.1 million of the 2.8 million 'Yes' votes (see Table 8.3). Ultimately, the 'Yes' vote was carried by the southern, urban areas and in particular, the three main cities of Stockholm, Malmö and Gothenburg (61.9 percent, 66.9 percent and 56.5 percent respectively in favour).

Table 8.3   Voting Outcomes of the 1994 Referendum by Constituency
(Percentage)

Name of Constituency	Yes	No	Blank	Turnout
Stockholms kommun	61.50	37.58	0.92	82.11
Stockholms län	61.44	37.66	0.90	84.36
Uppsala län	53.38	45.55	1.07	83.97
Södermanlands län	53.79	45.26	1.96	83.76
Östergötlands län	53.90	45.02	1.08	83.78
Jönköpings län	48.45	50.71	0.84	84.94
Kronobergs län	51.35	47.64	1.01	83.99
Kalmar län	48.29	50.79	0.92	82.06
Gotlands län	50.87	48.10	1.03	80.68
Blekinge län	46.46	52.61	0.93	83.29
Kristianstads län	56.74	42.39	0.87	81.24
Malmö kommun	66.47	32.70	0.84	80.00
Malmöhus läns norra	61.28	37.91	0.80	81.54
Malmöhus läns södra	66.45	32.56	0.99	86.04
Hallands län	57.82	41.12	1.06	85.08
Göteborgs kommun	56.33	42.77	0.90	82.03
Bohuslän	51.08	48.06	0.86	85.42
Alvsbörgs län norra	46.46	52.63	0.91	84.04
Alvsbörgs län södra	50.96	48.03	1.01	83.48
Skaraborgs län	49.52	49.41	1.08	83.53
Värmlands län	47.07	52.11	0.82	82.83
Örebro län	47.01	52.03	0.96	83.24
Västmanlands län	54.30	44.77	0.93	83.03
Kopparbergs län	38.73	60.42	0.84	83.60
Gävleborgs län	41.33	57.82	0.85	81.24
Västernorrlands län	41.67	57.63	0.70	82.96
Jämtlands län	27.74	71.53	0.73	85.04
Västerbottens län	36.97	62.34	0.69	84.05
Norrbottens län	34.75	64.63	0.62	83.02
Overall Result	**52.27**	**46.83**	**0.90**	**83.32**

Source: Embassy of Sweden, London (1994).

Note: The Table does not include 'Void' votes as these were too minimal to be of significance. They are however included in the overall figures for turnout.

In contrast, Northern Sweden voted overwhelmingly against EU membership. Nine out of the ten most Northern provinces (from Norbotten in the far North down to Örebro) voted against and in most cases, with large majorities, Jämtlands, for instance, voted with a huge majority of 71 percent against membership (the largest majority either way in all of Sweden).[102] However, the main problem for the 'No' campaign was that the areas that voted against EU membership with sizable majorities (six having anti-EU majorities of over 57 percent), also tended to be those with low population density. Their votes were easily offset by the more populous and 'Yes' voting constituencies of the South. For example, the combined Northern constituencies of Norbotten, Västerbotten, Jämtlands and Västernorrlands (which incidentally were those with the largest majorities against membership) were only equal in population size to the one of the 'Yes' voting constituencies of Stockholm (Stockholms Kommun). In terms of regional constituencies, the referendum was numerically won in the marginals of Sweden's South East and South West. For example, the regions of Kalmar (48.2 percent-50.7 percent against), Jönköping (48.5 percent-50.7 percent against), Alvebörgs läns södra, (50.9 percent-48.1 percent for) and Skaraborgs län (49.5 percent-49.4 percent for).

The Lessons of the Swedish EU Membership Referendum

Geography, class and political sympathies were deciding factors in how people voted. Factors such as sex, age and employment played less of a role. In geographic terms, there were clear North-South, urban-rural divides on the EU membership issue. The large anti-EU majorities in the North will mean that although the Social Democratic government won the referendum, it will be constrained by the large amount of domestic opposition.

As a rule, the class vote was strong. In general, those in paid employment and students voted 'Yes' to the EU, whereas the unemployed and those working from home voted against in large numbers. In short, it is the educated and the better off which expected to gain from membership. Civil servants and entrepreneurs proved to be two of the strongest groups in favour and voted in large numbers for membership (see Table 8.4). In complete contrast to their Finnish counterparts, there was a heavy preponderance of 'Yes' votes amongst Swedish farmers, especially in the South. This suggests that the large geographical 'No' vote in the North was not entirely due to the areas' reliance on farming, but indicates a wider rural and even provincial-based opposition to membership. The general rule was the higher the income and educational level of the voter, the stronger the support for full membership.[103]

**Table 8.4   Voting Outcome of the 1994 Referendum by Class/
Professional Group (Percentage)**

Class/Professional Group	'Yes'	'No'	Blank
Paid Employment	53	46	1
Unemployed	39	61	0
Early Retirement	48	51	1
Working From Home	39	61	0
Students	55	44	1

Source: Embassy of Sweden, London (1994).

In terms of political allegiance, members and sympathisers tended to follow party lines (see Tables 8.5a and 8.5b). Those voters who sympathised with the parties on the Left, generally voted against, such as the Greens and Left Party voters. There was also a large majority of non-socialist party supporters who voted for membership. Some 86 percent of Moderates, for example, voted in favour. Those who voted 'Yes' were mainly higher income supporters of the right-of-centre parties. The centre ground was far more splintered. About half of the SAP supporters voted 'No' (49 percent - see Table 8.5a), especially those in blue-collar work. Of the Centre's supporters, the majority voted against membership. The dividing line was presumably between the large farmers in the South (who voted 'Yes') and the small farmers in the North, who voted against.

**Table 8.5a   Voting Outcome of the 1994 Referendum by Party
(Percentage)**

Political Party	'Yes'	'No'	Blank
Moderate Party	86	13	1
Liberal Party	81	18	1
Social Democratic Party	50	49	1
Centre Party	45	54	1
Christian Democrats	41	59	0
New Democracy	34	62	4
Green Party	15	84	1
Left Party	10	90	0

Source: Embassy of Sweden, London (1994).

Table 8.5b   Voting Outcome of the 1994 Referendum by Political Stance (Percentage)

Left/Right	'Yes'	'No'	Blank
Far Right	31	69	0
Centre Right	40	59	1
Centre	46	53	1
Centre Left	75	24	1
Far Left	86	13	1

Source: Embassy of Sweden, London (1994).

In terms of age, opposition among first time voters (18-21 age group) was higher than expected. This may have reflected their general insecurity about Sweden's future, given its recent economic troubles. However, all the age groups over the age of 21 voted in favour (see Table 8.6). Most women however, voted against (by 52 percent - see Table 8.7). This can be at least partially attributed to their heavy reliance on the public sector for employment and services and reflected their concern that EU membership would undermine their social rights. In particular, women between 22-64 voted against and this was reversed in the same groups for Swedish men (see Table 8.8). Despite the government's arguments about reforming the system through full membership, many women feared that the welfare system would be under threat from EU membership. Bjørklund argues that this was the prevailing factor and determined why Sweden joined and Norway chose not to. In Sweden, the majority of men outweighed the majority of women and therefore, reduced the impact of the large numbers of anti-EU women.[104]

Table 8.6   Voting Outcome of the 1994 Referendum by Age (Percentage)

Age	'Yes'	'No'	Blank
18-21	40	59	1
22-30	52	47	1
31-64	53	46	1
64-	58	41	1

Source: Embassy of Sweden, London (1994).

Table 8.7   Voting Outcome of the 1994 Referendum by Gender (Percentage)

Gender	'Yes'	'No'	Blank
Female	47	52	1
Male	57	42	1

Source: Embassy of Sweden, London (1994).

Given the large number of women working in the public sector and their anti-EU tendencies, it is not surprising that if gauged systematically, public sector employees were more likely opponents of the EU than private sector employees. In terms of the public sector, 48 percent of employees voted 'Yes' to membership. When gauged along gender lines within the public sector, the related figures were 53 percent of men voting in favour compared to only 46 percent of women in the public sector. The corresponding figures for the private sector were 59 percent of private sector employees voting 'Yes' (the respective figures for men in the private sector was 59 percent and 58 percent of women in favour). However, as the Swedish public sector is far larger than the average in EU countries, the outcome of voting within the public sector was more important in terms of affecting the referendum result.

Table 8.8   Voting Outcome of the 1994 Referendum by Age and Gender (Percentage)

Age Group	Female - 'Yes'	Males - 'Yes'
18-21	34	46
22-30	47	57
31-64	49	58
64-	54	64

Source: Embassy of Sweden, London (1994).

Overall, those elements that might be described as the most characteristically 'Nordic' part of the electorate, such as those dependent on the welfare system and those outside the large cities, rejected membership. The most common argument against membership was the defence of national sovereignty linked with concern for Swedish democracy - 'the people's right to decide'. To an extent, this argument seemed to be countered by the 'Yes' camp which consistently argued that national sovereignty had become an illusion.[105] In terms of policy areas, the 'No' camp focused on specific areas that were sensitive and emotional to the public, such as, the future of the country's alcohol monopolies, the survival of *'snus'*-taking, the maintenance of stringent environmental standards and the size of Sweden's EU budgetary contribution. For the most part, full membership was interwoven with the general concerns of the public over the country's future and more specifically, whether by joining the EU, the public was in some way, surrendering its long-standing social democracy. As Lindström succinctly put it,

> 'Some said the referendum was ultimately about people choosing values. Be that as it may. First and foremost, membership was about choosing arenas'.[106]

What is clear is that the referendum result openly exposed the regional, class and gender division within Swedish society. Although the main political parties were, albeit to a limited degree, responsible for convincing the public and must retain some level of legitimacy, several of the mainstream parties will also be continually conscious of their internal divisions on the EU issue. The Social Democrats, the Centre Party and the Christian Democrats still suffer from friction between their respective leadership and the mass party membership, whilst the two anti-EU parties - the Left Party and the Greens - have taken heart from their renewed popularity as a reservoir for disgruntled Social Democrats and anti-EU supporters. Certainly, it will take a considerable time to alter domestic political attitudes towards the European Union. This inhibited the freedom of manoeuvre of governments even after the country has become a full EU member. The one perhaps positive outcome (apart from approving full membership) was that the usage of consultative referendum as a means of legitimising key governmental decisions was a success and redressed criticism arising from the previous experiences of 1955 and 1980.

The Social Democratic government's problems with maintaining public support for EU membership look far from over. To some extent, this was recognised by Carlsson on the night of the 'Yes' campaign's victory in the referendum, for instead of stressing the triumph of the pre-EC supporters, the Prime Minister highlighted the slim margin of the victory and that a substantial minority of Swedes had registered their discontent. The next few years he argued would be a time of healing. The strong views of the EU sceptics would not or could not be ignored. In his address to the Riksdag some ten days after the referendum victory, Carlsson confidently stated that:

'This is a historic step for Sweden as a nation - for the entire Swedish people. However, ... we must not forget that this is taking place against the background of an evenly balanced referendum. It is important that, notwithstanding our views on the referendum, we all endeavour to achieve a national consensus on Sweden's special interests in the European Union'.[107]

Given the fact that there was relatively little time left if Sweden was to accede to the Union on schedule (1 January 1995), the November debate marked the critical point in finalising the last aspects of full membership. Despite the original bill on accession being introduced in August, there was an agreed need for a further constitutional amendment which identified the constitutional terms on which the country accepted EU obligations. A new paragraph was inserted into article 5 of Chapter 10 of the Constitution Act which stipulated that,

'Parliament can transfer its right to make decision to the European Communities as long as these maintain a protection of freedoms and rights which is equal to the one granted in this Constitutional Act and in the European Convention on Human Rights and Fundamental freedoms. Parliament decides on such a transfer with a three-fourths majority. The decision can also be made by the procedure that applies for the passing of constitutional laws'.[108]

As Luif notes, Sweden imposed formal limits for the transfer of law-making power to the EU.[109] It transferred this power to the European Communities and not the EU on the grounds that only the three Communities can generate supranational law.[110] In reality, this reflected the continuing sensitivity of the EU issue and the uncertainty surrounding the compatibility of parliamentary sovereignty with future EU obligations. Crucially, the constitutional amendment was none the less passed by the Rikdag (23 November). It allowed for the Parliament to formally approve the Law Concerning Sweden's Accession to the European Union (on the basis of the constitutional amendment) on 15 December 1994. The last constitutional requirement for full membership was henceforth completed on time and with relatively little fuss.[111] Furthermore, by the end of the year, there seemed to be a growing optimism in the state of the economy. In the National Institute of Economic Research (*Konjunkturinstitutet*) autumn report, it was estimated that the country's GDP had risen by almost 2.5 percent in 1994 with an expected further increase of 2.75 percent in both 1995 and 1996. This was attributed to the Krona's depreciation, coupled with low wage increases, strong productivity growth and reduced payroll taxes, which had led to a 'spectacular improvement' in international competitiveness. For the first time in several years, there was a growing feeling of optimism that full membership would not be that painful for the country's economy.

Conclusion

Overall, the accession negotiations maintained a dynamism of their own in which the balance of power shifted away from the European Union towards the applicant states. The internal dynamics of the negotiations became overtaken by external influences. The EU did not gain the specific and binding assurances which it had optimistically called for at the Lisbon Summit in 1992. Instead it gained the image of a successful outcome, which was a triumph for the Union at a time of dwindling confidence.

There was also a growing asymmetry of perspectives between the EU and Sweden as the accession negotiations progressed. For the Union, the concept that the negotiations could not be seen to fail became more important than negotiating the fine details of the agreement. Whereas, for the Swedish government, the details of the accession deal became increasingly significant, if it was to be successfully defended in the following referendum. The government needed to be perceived domestically as 'winning' or at least as gaining a comprehensive agreement, especially as public opinion hardened against EU membership during the period of the negotiations. When the negotiations came down to brinkmanship in March 1994, most external observers judged that Sweden had won generous terms on the major issues. This was partly presentation as can be seen from the environmental standards issue. Yet, Sweden did for the most part gain a comprehensive accession deal, which compared to previous enlargement negotiations was generous on the part of the Union.

The November 1994 referendum also illustrated that the priorities of the Swedish political agenda have altered. The long-standing domestic consensus on security policy amongst the main political parties has disappeared and the 1994 referendum also suggests that the importance of security policy has also correspondingly declined. Differences in policy are now possible between the parties as the issue was no longer the main priority. Economic issues were more dominant during the referendum campaigns. In effect. the change in emphasis from the fourth (neutrality) to third point (economic interdependence) of the 'Swedish Diamond' was almost complete.

Notes

[1] It was not until the 1 November 1993 that the TEU's ratification process was completed and the EC was officially incorporated into the European Union (EU).

[2] The Lisbon Conclusions also stated that in its view the EEA agreement paved the way for negotiations on enlargement which could be finalised quickly with those EFTA countries seeking EU membership. The Presidency called for preparatory work including the Commission's negotiating position to be finished in time for the

European Council in Edinburgh. The Council also agreed that an enlargement to
incorporate the EFTA countries was possible without the need for institutional reform -
European Council, (1992) *European Council in Lisbon, 26-27 June 1992, Conclusions
of the Presidency,* SN 3321/1/92, European Council, Brussels.

[3] These views were first articulated in Miles, L. (1996) The Nordic Countries and the
Fourth EU Enlargement, in Miles, L. (ed.) *The European Union and the Nordic
Countries,* Routledge, London, pp. 63-78.

[4] In fact, although the EFTAns were to be put on a fast track, there was a dispute
between the UK, Germany and Denmark on the one side, who wanted a speedy start to
accession negotiations and the Mediterranean member states (led by Spain) who
insisted that the issue of resources (the TEU and the Delors II package) must be agreed
first - see Cameron, F. (1995) The EU and the Fourth Enlargement in N. Nugent (ed.)
*The European Union 1994 Annual Review of Activities (Journal of Common Market
Studies),* Blackwell, pp. 17-34.

[5] Cameron has also argued that a wider second political reason was also persuasive. The
post-1989 changes in Eastern Europe effectively reduced the Commission's concerns
regarding the EFTA neutrals and their compatibility with full membership - ibid.,
Cameron (1995) p. 19.

[6] Taken from an interview with Francisco Granell of the European Commission's
Enlargement Task Force in Brussels in April 1995.

[7] Switzerland had also applied in June 1992 but its application was by this time
suspended due to the rejection by public referendum of the EEA agreement (6
December 1992) by 50.3 percent and 18 of its 26 cantons - see Schwok, R. (1994)
Switzerland: The European Union's Self-Appointed Pariah in Redmond, J. (ed.)
Prospective Europeans, Harvester-Wheatsheaf, Hemel Hempstead, pp. 21-39.

[8] Taken from an interview with Leon Gordon of the European Commission's
Enlargement Task Force in Brussels in May 1995.

[9] Pedersen, T. (1994) *European Union and the EFTA Countries,* Pinter, London, p. 136.

[10] In other words, the 1995 accession negotiations were to follow what Preston calls the
'classical Community method' for dealing with enlargements - Preston, C. (1995)
Obstacles to EU Enlargement: The Classical Community Method and the Prospects for
a Wider Europe, *Journal of Common Market Studies,* 33, 3, September, pp. 451-63.

[11] Taken from an interview with Jan Palmstierna, Assistant Under-Secretary of State,
West European Integration Office, Ministry of Foreign Affairs in September 1994 in
Stockholm.

[12] Bildt, C. (1993) *Address to 'La Fondation Paul-Henri Spaak',* Palais des Academies,
Brussels, 16 September.

[13] Ibid., Pedersen (1994) p. 91.

[14] Dinkelspiel, U. (1992) *Information to Parliament concerning Sweden and the
European Community,* UD, Stockholm, 8 October, p. 1.

[15] Dinkelspiel, U. (1993), *Opening Statement at the Start of the Accession Negotiations
between Sweden and the European Communities,* UD, Stockholm, p. 1.

[16] Ibid., Dinkelspiel (1993) p. 3.

[17] Ibid., Dinkelspiel (1993) p. 4.

[18] Ibid., Dinkelspiel (1993) p. 4.

[19] Ibid., Dinkelspiel (1993) p. 5.

[20] Ibid., Dinkelspiel (1993) p. 7.

[21] The Community had not finalised its own free trade agreements with the Baltic states at this time.

[22] Ibid., Dinkelspiel (1993) p. 10.

[23] Ibid., Dinkelspiel (1993) p. 6.

[24] Ibid., Dinkelspiel (1993) p. 6.

[25] Ibid., Dinkelspiel (1993) p. 11.

[26] Ibid., Dinkelspiel (1993) p. 12.

[27] A report by the Commerce department in the Ministry of Foreign Affairs in 1991 mentioned other problems that did not find their way into Dinkelspiel's opening remarks. These included for example, some Swedish excise duties such as package duty and the tax on commercials, which would need to be abolished, and that the government's relatively generous trade policy towards the Third World may be compromised by participation in the Lomé Conventions. The report also argued that full membership would inevitably lead to trade disputes with key non-member states - most notably with the United States and Japan - see Ministry of Foreign Affairs (1991), *Konsekvenser av ett svensk EG-medlemskap*, UD, Stockholm, May.

[28] Norway's accession negotiations began slightly later in April 1993 as the Commission's Opinion on the Norwegian full membership application of 25 November 1992 was not delivered until 24 March 1993 - see Commission of the EC (1992), *Norway's Application for Membership: Opinion of the EC*, COM (93) 142 FINAL, 24 March 1992, Commission of the EC, Brussels.

[29] The applicants generally preferred to negotiate bilaterally because each feared that its accession might be delayed by difficulties in the negotiations with the others. Nordic solidarity was seldom much in evidence - For an 'insiders' assessment see Avery, G. (1994) The European Union's Enlargement Negotiations, *Oxford International Review*, Summer.

[30] Taken from an interview with Jan Palmstierna, Assistant Under-Secretary of State, West European Integration Office, Ministry of Foreign Affairs in September 1994 in Stockholm.

[31] Swedish Board of Agriculture, (1995) *The Swedish Board of Agriculture*, Jordbruks Verket, Jönköping, p. 3.

[32] European Free Trade Association, (1992) *The European Economic Area*, paper 2/92, EFTA, Geneva, p. 2

[33] The Danish Second Referendum was held in May 1993 and approved the TEU by a majority of 59 percent - see Worre, T. (1995) First No, then Yes: The Danish Referendums on the Maastricht Treaty 1992 and 1993, *Journal of Common Market Studies*, 33, 2, pp. 235-58.

[34] For a comprehensive discussion of the previous Norwegian application see for instance, Allen, H. (1979) *Norway and Europe in the 1970s*, Universitetsforlaget, Oslo, 1979 and for a comparison of the 1972 and 1994 experiences see Sæter, M. (1996)

Norway and the EU Domestic Debate Versus External Reality, in Miles, L. (ed.) *The European Union and the Nordic Countries,* Routledge, London, pp. 133-49.

[35] Taken from an interview with Francisco Granell of the European Commission's Enlargement Task Force in Brussels in April 1995.

[36] Taken from an interview with Ninna Rösiö, Councillor at the Swedish Permanent Delegation to the European Communities in Brussels in April 1995.

[37] Taken from an interview with Leon Gordon of the European Commission's Enlargement Task Force in Brussels in May 1995.

[38] Commission of the European Communities, (1994) *Documents concerning the accession of the Republic of Austria, the Kingdom of Sweden, the Republic of Finland and the Kingdom of Norway to the European Union,* Official Journal of the European Communities C241 29.8.1994, Commission of the ECs, Brussels, p. 381.

[39] Ministry of Foreign Affairs (1993), *Position Paper of Sweden on Alcohol Policy and Related Issues,* CONF-S 22/93, 8 April 1993, UD, Stockholm, p. 4.

[40] A similar solution was found to Swedish concerns in the energy field and the implications of membership of EURATOM (i.e. the competence of the EURATOM Supply Agency in the field of trade in nuclear materials and the role of the Commission as regards safeguard measures). In the end, Sweden bowed to EU competence. However, a joint declaration recognised Sweden's right to decide whether or not to produce nuclear energy. It resolved the popular fear that EURATOM would somehow require the country to remain nuclear. This was especially sensitive as regards Swedish public opinion due to the 1980 referendum on the future of Swedish civil nuclear power.

[41] Agreement with Norway took longer being finally reached 15 March due to problems over Norwegian fisheries and the CFP.

[42] Common Ideal Triumphs Over Niceties, *The European,* 4-10 March 1994, p. 3.

[43] This ingenious deal solved what had been identified by the Commission since February as the 'green hole'. With Sweden the essential problem for the Union was how to resolve the last remaining problems whilst avoiding (or limiting concessions on) the Swedish delegation's demands for a 'phasing in' of its budgetary contribution. The Commission recognised that it would have to 'co-finance' compensatory aids to Swedish farmers from the common budget if they were to agree to align immediately with CAP agricultural prices, but this was resisted by the British and Germans concerned about its implications for the EU budget. In effect, the 'green hole' was the phenomenon whereby the new member states during the first year of membership would receive much less than their normal payments from the common agricultural fund because reimbursement under financial accounting rules are made only in the year that were incurred. As the new members would not have contributed to the EU budget in 1994, there was no eligible national expenditure (in 1994) to be reimbursed in 1995. The Commission's solution was to devise a 'lump-sum' payment to each new member state from the agricultural section of the budget - an 'agro-budgetary package' over the first four years of membership. In other words, Sweden was compensated for the adjustment of prices which it had effected before accession - an unexpected concession on the part of the Union. It solved the problems of agricultural transition and Sweden's

budgetary request and allowed the payment of the Swedish budgetary contribution under normal rules from the outset, since the adjustment of its net contribution would be effected by means of temporary higher receipts of EU funding -Avery, G. (1995) *The Commission's Perspective on the EFTA Accession Negotiations*, Working Papers in Contemporary European Studies, No. 12, Sussex European Institute, Sussex, pp. 6-7.

[44] Cash Carries the Day in Enlargement Talks, *Financial Times*, 2 April 1994, p. 2.

[45] Persson, L. Expanded EC Poses Problems for Britain, *The Sunday Times*, 6 March 1994, p. 18.

[46] Ministry of Foreign Affairs, (1994) *Sweden's Negotiations on Membership of the EU*, UD, Stockholm, 7 April, p. 9.

[47] Ibid., Ministry of Foreign Affairs (1994) p. 9.

[48] Merriden, T.(1994) How will the EFTA Four affect the EU Twelve? *European Trends*, 2nd quarter 1994, Economist Intelligence Unit, pp. 54-5.

[49] Taken from an interview with Ninna Rösiö, Councillor at the Swedish Permanent Delegation to the European Communities in Brussels in April 1995.

[50] Op. cit., Ministry of Foreign Affairs (1994) p. 2.

[51] Op. cit., Ministry of Foreign Affairs (1994) p. 8.

[52] Swedish Board of Agriculture (1993), *The Swedish Agricultural Reform*, Jordbruks Verket, Jönköping.

[53] The global amount allocated from the EU's Structural Funds (after adjustment for Norway's rejection of membership) for the period 1995-99 is ECU 1,420 million for Sweden - Commission of the ECs, (1994) *Impact of the Three New Member States on the European Union*, Background Report, B/06/95, Commission of the ECs, Brussels, pp. 3-4.

[54] Op. cit., Ministry of Foreign Affairs (1994) p. 4.

[55] The reality has been somewhat different and the agreement has been proved to amount too little in practice. Due to its status as an exchange of letters, the agreement is open to legal challenge in the European Court of Justice. Indeed, a case doing just that was being heard by the Court in 1997. Harry Franzén, a grocer from southern Sweden challenged the monopoly status of *Systembolaget* as regards retail sales by selling bottles of wine in his village store, resulting in his prosecution by the authorities. His case has been referred to the European Court by the district court in Landskrona, In the preliminary ruling delivered in March 1997, the monopoly was judged to be at odds with EC law by Advocate-General Micheal Elmer and the Court was expected to give a similar ruling in late 1997. The preliminary decision was a shock for the Swedish government which had been confident of winning the case.

[56] Op. cit., Ministry of Foreign Affairs (1994) p. 4.

[57] Op. cit., Ministry of Foreign Affairs (1994) p. 9.

[58] Swedish Institute, (1995) *Sweden in the European Union*, Fact Sheets on Sweden, January, p. 1.

[59] Taken from an interview with Ninna Rösiö, Councillor at the Swedish Permanent Delegation to the European Communities in Brussels in April 1995.

[60] Widfeldt, A. (1996) Sweden and the European Union Implications for the Swedish Party System in Miles, L. (ed.) *The European Union and the Nordic Countries,* Routledge, London, p. 107.

[61] Swedish and Finnish PMs Set For Battles on the Home Front, *Financial Times,* 2/4/1994, p. 2.

[62] Taken from an interview with Jan Palmstierna, Assistant Under-Secretary of State, West European Integration Office, Ministry of Foreign Affairs in September 1994 in Stockholm.

[63] Granell, F. (1995) The European Union's Enlargement Negotiations with Austria, Finland, Norway and Sweden, *Journal of Common Market Studies,* 33, 1, pp. 117-42.

[64] Taken from an interview with Leon Gordon of the European Commission's Enlargement Task Force in Brussels in May 1995.

[65] Major Forced Into Corner on Europe, *The Times,* 28/4/1994, p. 1.

[66] For a review of the EP voting on the four applicants - see Miles, L. (1995) *Enlargement of the European Union,* European Dossier, No. 36, University of North London, London, p. 27.

[67] Op. cit., Pedersen (1994) p. 93.

[68] A summary of these polls can be found in the *Göteborgs-Posten,* 22 May 1993.

[69] Dinkelspiel, U. Det svåraste återstå EG-förhandlingarna, *Svenska Dagbladet,* 18 August 1993.

[70] The report was translated into English and printed as Lindbeck, A., Molander, P., Persson, T., Petersson, O., Sandmo, A., Swedenborg, B. & Thygesen, N. (1994) *Turning Sweden Around,* MIT Press, Cambridge, MA.

[71] Taken from Ibid., Lindbeck et al. (1994) p. 133.

[72] Lindbeck, A., Molander, P., Persson, T., Petersson, O., Sandmo, A, Swedenborg, B. & Thygesen, N. (1993) Sweden, *Economic Policy,* 8, 17, October, pp. 219-63.

[73] Ibid., Lindbeck et al. (1993) p. 244.

[74] Ibid., Lindbeck et al. (1993) p. 244.

[75] Most of the Lindbeck Commission's conclusions were contested recently by Jonas Agell and Walter Korpi. Korpi, for instance, recently refuted the Commission's conclusion that 'Sweden's problems are largely due to distorted markets, aging institutions and ossified decision-making outcomes' as 'careless analysis with systematic errors'. Korpi disliked the Commission's reliance on the 'biased evidence' of cross-national productivity increases and OECD rankings based on GDP per capita adjusted by purchasing power parities - Korpi, W. (1996) Eurosclerosis and the Sclerosis of Objectivity: On the Role of Values Among Economic Policy Experts, *The Economic Journal,* 106, pp. 1727-46. This remains a minority view and the Commission's conclusions have been universally accepted.

[76] EU Consequences Committee, (1994) *Sweden and Europe Committee of Enquiry: Consequences of the EU for Sweden - The Economy Summary and Conclusions,* SOU 1994: 6, EU Consequences Committee, Stockholm, p. 9.

[77] Kokko, A. (1994) Sweden: Effects of EU Membership on Investment and Growth, *The World Economy,* 17, 5, September, pp. 667-77.

[78] The supplements took the form of background papers on the effects of integration on particular sectors - textiles, agriculture, the public sector - and on broader issues, such as labour markets, foreign investment, monetary policy and social welfare.

[79] Op. cit., EU Consequences Committee (1994) p. 34.

[80] Op. cit., EU Consequences Committee (1994) p. 34.

[81] The Committee's conclusions have been reiterated in other independent studies - see Baldwin, R. (1992) Is Bigger Better? The Economics of EC Enlargement, *Monitoring European Integration 3*, CEPR, London; Baldwin, R. (1994) *Towards an Integrating Europe*, CEPR, London and Baldwin, R., Haaparanta, P. & Klander, J. (eds.) (1995) *Expanding Membership of the European Union*, Cambridge University Press, Cambridge.

[82] Op. cit., EU Consequences Committee (1994) p. 40.

[83] Op. cit., Widfeldt (1996) p. 107.

[84] Bjørklund, T. (1996) The Three Nordic 1994 Referenda Concerning Membership in the EU, *Cooperation and Conflict*, 31, 1, March, pp. 11-36.

[85] Quotations from Ministry of Foreign Affairs, (1994) *Press Release EU Bill Submitted to Parliament*, 24 August 1994, UD, Stockholm, p. 1.

[86] Ibid., Ministry of Foreign Affairs (1994) p. 3.

[87] Ibid., Ministry of Foreign Affairs (1994) p. 3.

[88] Svensson, S. (1994) Social Democrats Return To Power, *Current Sweden*, No. 404, Swedish Institute, Stockholm, p. 5.

[89] Op. cit., Bjørklund (1996) p. 14.

[90] Carlsson, I., (1994) *Statement of Government Policy by the Prime Minister to the Swedish Parliament*, 7 October, UD, p. 3.

[91] According to Statistics Sweden, 54 percent of Social Democrats voted against membership on the day of the referendum.

[92] Taken from an interview with Conny Fredriksson, International Secretary of the SAP on 16th September 1994 in Stockholm.

[93] Carnegy, H. Swedes Reminded That Quisling was Pro-Europe, *Financial Times*, 11 November 1994, p. 3.

[94] Lindström, U. (1995) *Scandinavia and the European Union: the Referenda in Denmark, Finland, Norway and Sweden, 1992-94*, unpublished monograph, University of Bergen, Bergen, p. 31.

[95] Carnegy, H. Swedish Leaders Plead EU Cause, *Financial Times*, 8 November 1994, p. 2.

[96] Miles, L. & Widfeldt, A.(1995) The Swedish Non-Socialist Parties and the European Union, in Lovenduski, J. & Stanyer, J. (eds.) *Contemporary Political Studies 1995 Volume III*, PSA/Short-Run Press, Exeter, p. 1517.

[97] The Liberals and the Moderates also included their own vocal opponents to full membership in the shape of Björn von Esch for the Moderates and Ingela Mårtensson for the Liberals. By the time of the actual referendum their influence was negligible. The parties were recovering from electoral defeat at the 1994 general election and both opponents were no longer representatives in the Riksdag after the election - reducing

their impact on the debate. Von der Esch even went on to form a new but totally unsuccessful anti-EU political party.

[98] Op. cit., Kokko (1994) pp. 667-77.

[99] Carnegy, H. Swedish Forestry Companies Join Forces to Urge EU Membership, *Financial Times,* 22 October 1994, p. 2.

[100] Carnegy, H. Swedish Political Rivals Unite to Call for Yes Vote on EU, *Financial Times,* 12 November 1994, p. 1.

[101] Op. cit., Bjørklund (1996) p. 15.

[102] Jämtlands has been included within the Northern counties, even if in fact it is geographically in mid-country and represented the border between the South-North axis of voting majorities.

[103] For more details see Lindahl, R. (1994) Svensk debatt och opinion i EG/EU-frågan in J. Bingen and R. Lindahl, *Nordiske skjebnevalg?* Europaprogrammet, Oslo.

[104] Op. cit., Bjørklund (1996) p. 27.

[105] Op. cit., Bjørklund (1996) p. 33.

[106] Op. cit., Lindström (1995) p. 81.

[107] Ministry of Foreign Affairs, (1994) *Speech to the Swedish Parliament on 23 November 1994 by the Prime Minister, Ingvar Carlsson, with reference to the outcome of the referendum on membership of the European Union,* UD, Stockholm, 2 December, p. 1.

[108] Taken from Luif, P, (1995) *On the Road to Brussels,* Austrian Institute of International Affairs, Laxenburg, p. 340 and translated from the Constitutional Act published in SFS 1994, p. 1483.

[109] Ibid., Luif (1995) p. 340.

[110] Riksdagen, *Sveriges medlenskap in europeiska unionen,* Regeringens proposition 1994-95: 19, Del 1, Stockholm, gotab, 1994, p. 497.

[111] Only the Greens abstained during the 23 November vote on the constitutional amendment. The 15 December approval was done without any formal vote since no party had demanded a 'No' to the ratification of the Treaty. The Speaker of the Riksdag did not even allow for the Greens to register the abstention they had planned, giving the superficial impression of a virtually universal consensus on full membership in the Parliament - see Ljungberg, D. (1994), Historiskt beslut utan större dramatik, *Dagens Nyheter,* 16 December 1994, p. A8.

9   EU Member 1995-96

Compared to the public attention surrounding the November referendum and the close margin of victory in favour of membership, the actual event of becoming a full member (1 January 1995) was a relatively low-key affair.[1] Ingvar Carlsson, for example, refrained from making any major public address and was satisfied with merely stating that this would become a fact during radio and television interviews on New Years Eve. There were no special festivities and the occasion was marked only by the Swedish flag being raised at the EU Headquarters in Brussels. None the less, the country's transition to becoming an EU member was now complete; closing one era of Swedish history and opening another. As His Majesty King Carl XVI Gustaf stated 'We Swedes wish to help promote peace and harmonious development in the new Europe. With the European Union as our framework, the prospects are singularly bright'.[2]

At face value then, much of the uncertainty surrounding Sweden's future role in the EU should have dissipated now that the country had finally completed the tenuous road to full membership. The clear message from the Swedish elite was one of simultaneous relief and fragile confidence - that the country should from now on concentrate on defining the future obligations of being a full member rather than whether or not to be one. After all, Sweden, along with Austria and Finland, joined the Union during an introspective phase and just before the EU was to further define its objectives, policies and structure for the next millennium.

However, Sweden's first year of membership was a mixed success and was marked by public discontent and disappointment with the immediate impact of full membership. Far from proving to be a year of stability and healing, a degree of uncertainty prevailed within domestic discussions on Sweden's participation in the Union. The main objective of this chapter will be to examine Sweden's experiences of full membership in its first year. Particular attention will be paid to the country's first direct election to the European Parliament (EP) and to governmental perspectives towards the 1996 Intergovernmental Conference (IGC). The chapter will argue that the public's disillusionment is the net result of exaggerated expectations (before joining) of the economic benefits of being a full EU member.

264

Governmental Ambitions

In his first statement of government policy (23 November 1994) since the referendum, Ingvar Carlsson outlined the priorities that the Social Democratic government would push for as an EU member in 1995. In particular, the (then) Prime Minister highlighted two important influences on government policy. First, the need for the Swedish government to maximise its direct democratic influence on the Union and 'if this to be possible, continued lively political debate is needed throughout the country'.[3] In other words, a debate on the future of the EU (and Sweden's role within it) was deemed to be essential. Second, that 1995 marked the year of important preparation for the Intergovernmental Conference starting in 1996 when the future of the EU will be determined. In effect, the EU debate entered a new phase. As Carlsson himself noted,

> 'The dividing line is no longer between "Yes" or "No". It is now a question of discussing the whole gamut of political issues and here the different parties have a responsibility to their voters to represent the political programme they campaigned for in the election'.[4]

Yet, despite the parameters of the EU debate altering from one focused on the merits of membership to one concerned with maximising Swedish influence as an EU member, the government's official priorities remained much the same. In his speech (23 November), the Prime Minister reiterated many of the issues that Ulf Dinkelspiel (as the country's chief negotiator and Minister for European Affairs in the non-socialist government) had highlighted several times in the previous year. Carlsson drew attention to the government's desire 'to achieve a vigorously democratic Europe' and a Union based on the principles of transparency and public access to official records; that the Riksdag was given 'proper opportunities to follow the work of the Swedish government in the Council of Ministers'. He argued that the country's security policy of non-participation in alliances remained unchanged and that the government would prioritise 'additional measures to fight unemployment'.[5] Carlsson also stressed that the credibility of its economic policy would increase as a member of the Union and that international cooperation over tightening up environmental standards, especially in the Baltic and Eastern European regions would be advantageous.[6]

What was most striking about Carlsson's statement was the lack of clear references to any kind of vision of the future EU or Europe in general. An essentially practical picture of Sweden's role within the Union was presented, which no doubt helped to reinforce the public's perceptions that the benefits of accession were basically economic and quantitatively based. This was, in part, a governmental reflection of the domestic public's caution on EU matters. It also represented an acknowledgment that not all of the main priorities, such as the transparency and environmental standards issues, had either been dealt with completely or to the satisfaction of the Social Democratic government as part of the previous accession agreements.

Nevertheless, if Carlsson's statement of the two essential elements of Swedish participation is used as the basis of analysis then some useful comments can be made regarding the country's initial experiences of full membership in 1995. As regards the former and the promotion of a lively debate on the EU, then three aspects seem important - the performance of the Swedish economy, the development and nature of public opinion as a full member and the outcome of the country's first direct election to the European Parliament in September 1995.

An Improving, Yet Fragile Economy

At virtually the same time as the Riksdag was completing the last constitutional requirements for accession to the Union, the Parliament approved further spending cuts in December 1994 aimed at improving the country's public finances in the Fiscal Policy Bill. It allowed for SEK 20.1 billion of spending cuts. In the eyes of the Swedish public, EU accession and the performance of the country's economy were still inter-linked and economic-based.

The economy grew favourably during 1995. Exports continued to increase strongly and foreign investment in Sweden rose to almost SEK 100 million in 1995 - behind only France and the UK in Europe - acting as two good indicators of growing market confidence in the performance of the economy.[7] GDP growth amounted to some 3 percent (exceeding the EU average for 1995) and resulted in a small decline in registered unemployment. The unemployment figure of 8 percent, although unacceptable amongst domestic circles, was actually comparable to most other EU countries.[8] Inflationary pressure diminished and the increase of the consumer price index remained at 2.6 percent during the year. By 1995 for example, relative unit labour costs were now bearable and proportionate to levels of productivity. Over the period 1991-95, relative unit labour costs had fallen by 27 percent.[9] At the same time, real economic growth benefited from a decrease in both short-term and long-term interest rates during the latter part of 1995 and a simultaneous strengthening of the Krona. The turnaround in the economy was also reflected in the improved state of fiscal policy. The surplus in the current account balance grew to over 2 percent of GDP - the highest figure since 1973. The government's sector's financial deficit reduced by 3 percentage points of GDP and the gross debt ratio virtually ceased to increase.[10] None the less, despite the increased prosperity, this did not translate into a strong 'feel good' factor amongst the populace. The legacy of severe recession had left a cautious attitude within the country's households. Private consumption rose very moderately due to stagnant real income.

On 1 October 1995, the government in its Budget bill to the Riksdag proposed a further SEK 4.6 billion in spending cuts in order, it claimed, to finance its contribution to the Union. The government argued that this period of austerity, was 'laying the foundation for a new period of economic growth, increased employment and sound government finance'.[11] In effect, the proposals would supposedly lead to the central government financial deficit being cut by half from 13 percent of GDP in 1994 to an envisaged 7 percent in 1996.[12] The bill was given a mixed reception - with the financial markets cautiously supporting the need for cuts and the trade unions critical that the majority of the cuts would come from the Ministry of Health and Social Affairs and amounted to SEK 8.4 billion by 1998. The reforms included tougher rules for those out of work with, for instance, the pre-benefit waiting period of 20 days for those who voluntarily quit their jobs extended to 40 days.[13] Göran Persson, the (then) Finance Minister was placed in the unenviable position of having the reforms criticised from both sides - 'by some as too small, and by others as too great, depending on whose ox is being gored'.[14]

What was clear from the revival of the economy was that the divisions within Swedish society remained relatively wide with a corresponding rise in strike action throughout the country demonstrating against cuts in welfare, and job losses. From January 1995, for example, there were numerous strike actions by the public sector unions - *Kommunal* and SKTF - protesting at the loss of services in the country's 288 municipalities, including kindergartens, refuse collection, dental surgeries and sports clubs.[15]

Hostile Public Opinion

1995 was a difficult year for the governing Social Democrats. To a certain extent, this was a reflection of the declining popularity of the Carlsson government. The ruling Social Democrats were to some extent suffering from declining popularity as a result of Carlsson's announcement to step down as Prime Minister at the March 1996 SAP congress (which created uncertainty over the government's future direction) and in response to the cuts in welfare provision. The SAP government was also affected by the turmoil within the party. A credit card scandal surrounding the Deputy Prime Minister and (then) widely regarded as Prime Minster elect, Mona Sahlin, led to widespread public criticism. Sahlin was fighting for her political life throughout 1995 following disclosures that she misused an official credit card and failed to pay her individual bills on time.[16] With Sahlin out of the running, the party then spent a fraught few months searching for its new leader, which was made more difficult as each of the leading candidates - Finance Minister Göran Persson, Coordination Minister Jan Nygren and Agriculture Minister Margareta Winberg - declined to be nominated for the leadership. During winter 1995, the Social Democratic government appeared to be a 'lame-duck' with no-one seeming to want the job as the new premier.

Yet, this fluid time for the Carlsson government was reinforced by negative public opinion polls on whether EU membership for the country was 'a good thing'. In many ways, the narrow margin of victory by the 'Yes' camp in the referendum compounded the problems of convincing the electorate of the merits of full membership. The 5 percent margin of victory meant that in practice, the populace was almost immediately seized by doubts. The picture was made worse by the apparent disillusionment with the benefits of membership. Although difficult to quantify, the general impression amongst the public had been that full membership would help to deal with some of the country's most pressing economic problems. This impression was at least partially promoted by the leading pro-EU political elite during the referendum. Economic issues, such as increasing economic growth, greater inward investment, rising international trade, and ultimately, tackling unemployment and deteriorating public finances were seen as the key aspects of the pro-EU campaign (see Chapter Eight). The statements of the various elite leadership had, albeit to a limited extent, suggested that full membership would be instrumental to the economy's initial revival, be essential to its longer-term survival and would in any case have immediate benefits for the Swedish consumer. In practice, full membership was not going to immediately, nor single-handedly, solve these problems. As Luif notes, the dynamic effects of full membership had been preceded and dissipated by previous EEA membership, whilst factors like exchange rate variations could compound the EU effects.[17] In psychological terms, full membership suffered from the problem of rising domestic expectations. It had been set an artificially high target to fulfil by the population.

Unfortunately, there was no immediate reduction either in food prices or in consumer prices of alcoholic beverages - two of the immediate benefits that the 'Yes' camp had pushed. Agricultural prices in Sweden before membership were in fact, more or less in line with those of the CAP and thus did not lead to major reductions in prices (as in the case of Finland), whilst the liberalisation of the alcoholic monopolies had been limited by the original accession agreement. Moreover, in spite of the improvement in the economy, most households were pessimistic. They were wary of the fragility of the economy pointing especially to the fact that the unemployment rate remained stubbornly high. Job security for the average Swede remained far from ideal or secure. For the public, the benefits of full membership had been initially disappointing and in direct contrast to the hype of the referendum campaigns.

According to Eurobarometer figures, Sweden continued throughout 1995 to have the smallest proportion of citizens which viewed the EU as 'a good thing' hovering at less than 40 percent of all those consulted. As regards the more specific question of continued EU membership, then a similar trend within public opinion was evident. By May 1995, public opinion had hardened dramatically - with a mere 28.6 percent being in favour of EU membership. In July 1995, 61 percent of Swedes stated that they would vote against membership, if the referendum on approving accession had been conducted then.[18] By November 1995, some 12 months after the original referendum, the picture was even worse. Domestic support for full membership dropped to the lowest ever officially recorded figure. Opinion polls (mainly published in *Dagens Nyheter*) showed that only 26 percent of Swedes were now in favour of full membership compared to 52 percent a year earlier. However, the 'anti-EU' segment of public opinion remained solid. In May 1995, 61.9 percent declared that they would vote 'No' in another EU referendum; in November the proportion was still 60.5 percent.[19]

The division between elite and public opinion on the merits of full membership also remained as strong as ever. Whilst the Liberals and Moderates were clearly in favour of full membership (60 percent of their respective supporters supporting this policy), this was not the case for the Social Democrats, Centre Party and Christian Democrats. All these parties maintained official policies supporting full membership, but in each case the majority of their respective supporters were negative to the EU.[20] The strength of this elite versus grass-roots division was clearly demonstrated in the first direct election to the European Parliament (18 September 1995).

The Direct Election to the European Parliament[21]

a) The Symbolism of the Election

In many ways, the election was symbolic for both Sweden and the European Union. From the Swedish perspective, it was the first direct election to the European Parliament to take place since accession. It provided an early official test of public opinion regarding membership since accession, and to a lesser extent, awareness of the role of the European Parliament itself. To a limited degree, the election also attracted interest given the narrow approval of full membership in its 1994 referendum. It was hoped by the pro-EU forces that there would be a significant increase in support for the European Union now that the country was a full member. It represented the first national election in which a new electoral procedure had been comprehensively used in Sweden and acted as a *de facto* constitutional test-bed. Finally, the election was conducted almost exactly twelve months after Ingvar Carlsson's minority government had been elected to power in September 1994. It provided a timely opportunity for the people to voice their opinions on the performance of the Social Democratic government and their austerity programmes.

For the European Union, the Swedish election was also of significance. In one sense, the election was unusual in that it did not take place simultaneously with EP elections in other member states. The EP had already been through its five-yearly cycle of direct elections in June 1994 before Sweden had joined the European Union. For the political scientist, the election provided a useful occasion to consider the potential for 'opinion transfers' between member states and whether, there are any implications for public opinion formation due to external influences of direct elections in other member states.[22] Indeed, it could also be argued that the Swedish direct election would present a more accurate picture of public opinion. This election, unlike the referendum, was free from any kind of 'Domino strategy' whereby results in other countries would affect the way the average Swedish voter acted. The election also represented the first of the three direct elections to take place in the new member states since the enlargement of the Union to fifteen. It was argued that the election provided some rather tentative indicators of the success of full membership and to a lesser extent, the European Parliament in the new member states. From this perspective, the Swedish example seemed to be relevant given that public opinion had been consistently the least enthusiastic about the merits of full membership and according to opinion polls, was solidly against it. In theory then, the direct election should have attracted substantial interest from within Sweden and from outside observers.

Certainly, for the Swedes, the direct election was the first time that a personal vote system had been used. The new electoral system had, to a limited extent, been tried previously in the 1994 local elections and would, if successful this time, be used for the 1998 general election. The electoral procedure used was a modified version of the party list system which had previously operated in Sweden. However, voters were permitted in this election to also express a preference for specific party list candidates on their voting forms. The electoral rules stipulated that if any candidates gained a 'personal vote' of more than 5 percent of that party's overall national vote, then they would rank in ascending order of popularity (according to the size of their 'personal' vote) above all others on the national party lists.

The new procedure introduced some interesting and at least for the Swedes, new aspects to elections. Personal as well as party campaigns became more apparent as candidates sought to raise public awareness of their personal attributes in order to differentiate themselves more from other candidates. For example, Cecilia Mälmstrom, a liberal, ran a personal campaign in Göteborg. This new option seemed to be popular with voters as 55 percent of those who voted indicated a preference for individual candidates, even though this was not compulsory. At the same time, the new procedure may have also deterred some voters, although this remains to be proven.

Despite all the symbolism associated with the election, the actual event was rather low-key. It can be argued, albeit to a limited degree, that voters were suffering from the dual problem of electoral fatigue and rising disillusionment with the EU issue. The government had only completed the long process of negotiating and ratifying accession a year earlier and, for the most part, full membership had been a dominant political issue for most of 1994 due to the referendum. To the average Swede, the EU issue was exhausted. This, in part, explained the growing hostility towards the EU in public opinion polls in 1995.

The party campaigns during the election were also lack-lustre. They revolved mainly around domestic issues. Where EU aspects did appear they focused on Sweden's role in the future Union and did not revert back to the question of full membership.[23] The campaigns were roughly split into two types - those of the pro and anti-EU parties. For the most part, the pro-EU parties concentrated on themes which centred on how they intended to influence the future development of Europe. One of the main campaign slogans of the Social Democrats was '*Sätt Europa i arbete*' (Put Europe to Work), whilst the Liberals' (People's Party) main party slogan was '*Se möjligheterna*' (See the Opportunities). However, the pro-EU parties did not refrain from criticising each other's positions even though they all followed a pro-EU membership line. The Moderates, for example, led their campaign with the slogan '*Man måste veta vad man vill*' (One Must Know What One Wants), which was targeted at the governing Social Democrats and alluded to their limited success in revitalising public finances and took a swipe at their internal party division over full membership. Indeed, the Centre Party and the Social Democrats maintained two differing party lists from both the 'Yes' and 'No' factions of their respective parties. This helped to complicate the choices of voters, who were also confronted with the voting for personalities as well as parties in the election.[24]

In contrast, the two main anti-EU parties - the Greens and the Left Party - emphasised that they were pro-Europe, but against full membership. The Greens focused on the theme of '*Mot Europa*' (which in Swedish is actually a pun as 'Mot' can mean 'against', yet also 'towards'). The Left Party also tended to follow this line and with the Greens, stressed the threats of EU membership to social and environmental policy, women's rights, the welfare state and democracy under the banner '*Mer demokrati - mindre union*' (More Democracy -Less Union).

However, the campaign that attracted the most criticism came from the Centre Party. The party based its campaign around the slogan, '*Nja till Europa*' (which translates in English as both 'Yes' and 'No' to Europe at the same time).

It argued that their party undetook the most 'honest' campaign of all the parties by taking a moderate stand. In theory, the Centre Party claimed that there were both positive and negative benefits to Europe and that this should be seen as the most pragmatic and realistic approach. However, in practice, the campaign was tailored to cater for intra-party opposition, especially within the country's rural heartland where the Party is popular. Yet the Centre Party was, for the most part, criticised as indecisive and vague.

What was also noticeable was not just the poor standard of the various campaigns but also the low commitment amongst party workers. In this respect, the Social Democratic campaign was a case in point. The SAP party machine had great difficulty in motivating its members and had similar problems in engaging the similar minded trade union members in the campaign.[25] In part, this was due to a number of factors. The party had won an historic election victory only twelve months before and was therefore somewhat immune to the concerns of the public. Moreover, despite the campaign being fought on mostly domestic issues, SAP-trade union cooperation had been damaged by the government's austerity programmes and its party cooperation with the Centre Party. Finally, internal unity was prioritised above the external credibility of the direct election campaign.[26] To offset long-term, damaging internal disunity, the SAP bore the political costs of running two differing and simultaneous 'pro' and 'anti' EU campaigns, which complicated the role of party campaigners. Ironically, the Social Democrats were not helped either by the fact that the most notable opposition leader, Carl Bildt, was away in Bosnia (as a high-profile EU peace-negotiator) which made it difficult - both politically and logistically - to counteract the criticisms of the non-socialists.

b) Election Outcome

The results of the direct election were striking (see Table 9.1). In general, the pro-EU parties did badly and the anti-EU parties benefited. The Social Democratic Party (SAP) was the main loser, registering only 28.1 percent of the vote, compared to 45.3 percent in the 1994 general election some twelve months earlier. However, this disastrous result for the Social Democrats cannot be entirely attributed to their pro-EU stance. It did in fact, also reflect their open division on the issue and that they were in government, following unpopular austerity policies, which were unlikely to be vote-winners. Although the pro-EU Liberals also suffered (seeing their share of the vote reduced to 4.8 percent in 1995 from 7.2 percent in 1994), Carl Bildt's Moderates (which were widely regarded as the most pro-EU party in Swedish politics) slightly improved its share of the vote to 23.2 percent in 1995 from 22.4 percent in 1994). However, in contrast, the clearly anti-EU parties, the Greens and Left Party did exceedingly well. The

Greens, for instance, more than trebled their share of the vote (17.2 percent compared to 5 percent in 1994). The Left Party also doubled its share (12.9 percent instead of 6.2 percent). In sum, the results indicate that the electorate was not enthusiastic neither about full membership nor the role of the European Parliament.

Table 9.1 **Results of the Election to the European Parliament (18 September 1995)**

Party	Votes	Percentage	EP Seats
Moderate Party	621,568	23.2	5
Liberal Party	129,376	4.8	1
Centre Party	192,077	7.2	2
Social Democrats	752,817	28.1	7
Left Party	346,764	12.9	3
Greens	462,092	17.2	4
Christian Democrats	105,173	3.9	0
New Democracy	2,841	0.1	0
Others	70,443	2.6	0
Valid Votes	2,683,151	Turnout	41.63 percent
Blank and Invalid Votes	44,166		
Total Votes	7,727,317		
Electorate	6,551,591		

Furthermore, there were regional variations between the performances of the individual parties, which albeit to a limited degree, reflected their positions on the EU question. The pro-EU Moderates performed better in their traditionally strong geographical areas of cosmopolitan Stockholm, Göteborg and Malmö (scoring for example 32.2 percent and 33.2 percent for the two Stockholm, and 29 percent and 33.7 percent for the two Malmö electoral districts). However, these areas also contain elements of the electorate that are most pro-EU and therefore their voting patterns were in line with their thinking on the EU. Equally, the anti-EU Greens and Left Party did most well in the Northern areas, which are also the most sceptical about full membership. The Greens for instance, gained 20.5 percent of the Jämtlands län EU constituency (roughly twice the votes of the Moderates). The Left Party also did exceedingly well in three Northern regions registering for example, 21.1 percent of the votes in Jämtlands län, 23.9 percent in Västerbottens län and 27.8 percent in Norrbottens län (on average three times as many votes as for the Moderates) - which incidentally were also three of the constituencies that voted against EU membership with large majorities in the 1994 referendum. Indeed, the performance of the Left Party in these regions was roughly two-three times better than their national average for the election (12.9 percent). Thus, to a limited degree, the North-South division on the EU question continued to be reflected in the election results.

There are problems with this analysis and the analogy should not be stressed too much. The case of the Social Democrats does confuse the picture. Although suffering a decline in electoral popularity across the country, they tended to do better in the Northern regions (their vote spanned between 29.7-38.5 percent in the six northernmost (and essentially anti-EU) constituencies than in the cosmopolitan South (where their vote in the three largest cities was between 22.3 (Stockholms Kommun) and 33.9 percent (Malmö Kommun)). However, in the Southern areas the Social Democrats generally lost votes to all parties due to their status as the governing party.

Probably the most indicative variable in the election result was not the levels of party support, but the very poor turnout amongst voters. The overall turnout, including invalid votes amounted to a mere 41.63 percent and represented less than half of the entire electorate. For Sweden, this turnout figure was unusual. The country has a tradition of high turnouts in elections. The turnout for the previous September 1994 general election, for instance, was 86.8 percent.

In many ways, the first Swedish direct election displayed similar characteristics to those in other member states. The fact that this was a secondary election to a mostly unpopular European institution had a dual effect. On the one hand, the electorate suffered from the problems of electoral fatigue and growing disillusionment regarding the membership issue. Moreover, the fact that a new electoral procedure was also introduced could have also deterred voters. On the other hand, the election also provided a chance for the electorate to register a 'protest' vote at the progress of the minority Social Democratic government, especially as it had introduced numerous cost-saving reforms aimed at cutting the large budgetary deficit and national debt. To some extent, the poor performance of the Social Democrats was exaggerated by the fact that they were in government, cutting back public expenditure and trimming welfare state provision, which were all unpopular among their traditional voters. Traditional Social Democratic voters could afford to take a swipe at the SAP as there was no chance of the election result leading to a change of government.

Similarly, the exceedingly good performance of the Left Party and the Greens can in part, be explained by the transfer of disillusioned Social Democratic voters to these parties. It has been estimated that, for example, eight of ten traditional Social Democratic sympathisers refrained from casting their vote in this election and, of those that did, they tended to be of the 'anti-EU' persuasion and there to make a political protest.[27] The success of the Greens and the Left Party was also due to the fact that these two parties were the two main anti-EU parties. In particular, as the Social Democrats were internally divided on the issue, these parties acted not only as a reservoir for disillusioned voters, protesting at the national performance of the Social Democratic government, but also for voters across the political spectrum who vehemently oppose full membership. In sum, the Greens and the Left Party benefited from 'protest' votes aimed at the national government and from those focused at EU membership.[28]

c) Lessons Arising from the Direct Election

The outcome of the direct election does have ramifications for both the Swedish political scene and the European Parliament. As regards domestic politics, the Left Party and the Greens were quick to call for a national referendum on whether the country should stay in the European Union and for the wider principle of using referenda to approve any further extensions of EU competencies. Although the former demand is unlikely to succeed and Sweden will continue to remain a full member, the principle of using referenda to approve any future TEU-based reforms will be more difficult to ignore.

The result of the election also had implications for the composition of the European Parliament. Prior to the September 1995 election, all of the Swedish MEPs were appointed by the Riksdag, based on the proportion of seats each party held in the national legislature. However, since the direct election, Swedish Social Democratic representation in the Parliament has been reduced from eleven to only seven MEPs, which will severely inhibit its influence on the Socialist Group. Pauline Green, leader of the Parliament's Socialist Group, claimed the poor Social Democratic performance illustrates that,

> 'Europe has to deal with issues that affect people's lives. We need to take action on issues, like the Employment Union which the Swedish Social Democrats have been trying to pursue in the Council of Ministers. When the Swedish people see the result of that sort of policy, they will reassess the way they vote'.

The Moderates retained their five seats in the European Parliament, the Centre Party its two and the Liberals their single seat, although the Christian Democrats lost their only seat as a result of a fall in their vote to below the 4 percent threshold for seats (their vote fell from 4.1 percent in 1994 to 3.9 percent in 1995). All these parties retain their limited influence on their various party groups in the European Parliament. Nevertheless, whereas the Left Party only had one Euro-MP (and the Greens none) before the election, the Left Party now has three and the Greens four. This will have two effects. First, roughly half of the twenty-two Swedish MEPs have been elected on anti-EU platforms and could be seen as comparable to Danish 'anti-marketeers'. Second, the inclusion of four anti-EU Swedish Greens will create some tension with the Parliament's Green Group. The Swedish Greens will join a Group that is by no means anti-European.

In general, the 1995 direct election resulted in resounding victory for the anti-EU forces. Overall, they (the Greens and Left Party) captured 30.1 percent of overall vote. In comparison, the pro-EU forces seemed in disarray. The Social Democrats were divided; even to the point of offering two lists of candidates - one headed by a pro-EU campaigner and another by an anti-EU figure. In reality each list contained a mixture of pro and anti-EU supporters; just the proportion was different and much to the consternation of voters. Consequently, their party took just 28.1 percent; their worst electoral result since 1911.

The most likely implication arising from the election result is that the anti-EU parties have not relinquished the idea of possible withdrawal from the Union. The 'Yes' or 'No' debate has 'thus assumed a dominant role in opinion moulding, overshadowing other key European issues, such as enlarging the European Union to include the countries of the former Eastern Europe'.[29] In November 1995, barely two months after the direct election, another opinion poll published in *Dagens Nyheter,* indicated that 42 percent of the Swedish people now supported their country's withdrawal from the Union, whilst 35 percent wanted to remain a member and the rest were undecided. Moreover, despite the up-turn in the economy, reaching nearly 4 percent growth in 1995, this has not been equated with the benefits of full membership. The government continued to stress the need for further economic belt-tightening as part of the drive towards EMU. The public perceived that the severe austerity packages of the Social Democratic government were in part forced upon them because of its desire to allow Sweden to eventually participate in Economic and Monetary Union (EMU).

Rather the psychological legacy of the pre-accession campaigns led the public to expect relatively immediate benefits from full membership - something that was always unlikely. Despite the symbolism of the 1995 direct election, the country is far from being reconciled with its new role as a full member. The public are only just beginning to realise that the benefits of EU membership are political and considerably more long-term. Certainly successive governments will continue to enjoy lively debates on the EU question - some perhaps more livelier than they would at face value, prefer. Thus, the struggle between pro and anti-EU forces over membership is not over, although the forum for political battle seems to be shifting towards the shape of EU cooperation and of how Sweden should contribute towards it.

Swedish Influences on the European Union

Given this rather tenuous domestic scene in which the Carlsson government found itself on the EU issue - enduring internal party disunity and hostile public opinion simultaneously - it is not surprising that the government quickly launched a number of policy initiatives aimed at making full membership more attractive to the domestic population.

a) Initiating Policy

In terms of EU policy development, the Carlsson government was relatively quick to act in a number of areas - transparency, the social dimension and the Common Foreign and Security Policy (CFSP). By April 1995 for example, the government had reached broad agreement with its Danish and Finnish counterparts to promote greater transparency in EU decision-making and in the same month jointly proposed to the Council of Ministers that its minutes and voting outcomes should be published for public consumption.[30] To some extent, this was a defensive strategy. The Swedish media were already beginning to bring court actions over the compatibility of EU decision-making procedures with the rights of citizens under constitutional arrangements.[31]

However, the possibilities for a dynamic Swedish response were reinforced by the fact that the country joined the Union just as it was about to embark on its next phase of development. Consequently, the government found itself in the demanding position of having to raise the EU question again in order to develop its position in time for the IGC starting in March 1996.

In effect, Swedish preparations for the IGC were in progress from autumn 1994. They principally took place in two phases and at two levels. The first phase was essentially domestic-orientated, during which the Social Democratic government sought to identify and articulate the important questions to be raised at the conference. This in practice meant wider domestic discussion and in particular, greater promotion of the fact that an important conference affecting Sweden would take place in the coming year. The second phase was the transfer of Swedish priorities to the EU level though the working of the Reflection Group and the opening of the conference itself.

The first major summary of governmental priorities regarding the future IGC were presented to the Riksdag by the Minister for European Affairs, Mats Hellström (1 June 1995).[32] The speech formed the backbone of the government's initial position and outlined in its (later) publication 'Sweden's fundamental interests prior to the 1996 Intergovernmental Conference'.[33] During the first phase of domestic consultation, the work of the government was also reported to the Riksdag's Advisory Committee on European Affairs and the Standing Committee on the Constitution. Consultations on the IGC took place for example, soon after the delivery of Hellström's speech (22 June 1995).

In Hellström's address to the Parliament and the government's initial report, the Minister recognised that the forthcoming IGC 'is an important opportunity for Sweden to influence and further the objectives to which we give priority in EU cooperation'.[34] In short this was the time for important consultations between the government and the Riksdag. The Minister especially outlined Sweden's three foremost goals in view of the conference: to promote initiatives aimed at strengthening the EU's democratic legitimacy, to support the process of further EU enlargement and to bolster EU cooperation especially in areas associated with high rates of growth and employment and the improvement of the environment. Interestingly, the speech included references to a number of key policy areas. The most prominent being Hellström's first goal - the promotion of the Union's democratic legitimacy - which has become the common theme of Swedish membership. As the Minister noted,

> 'Popular support is crucial. This was made particularly clear when the Maastricht Treaty was to be ratified, which proved to be a difficult political process in some member countries. It is a challenge to the EU and to Sweden as a member state, to make the integration of Europe into the concern of every citizen and to strengthen democratic influence'.[35]

Perhaps the next most important was the Minister's second goal - that of further EU enlargement - but here the government's emphasis is more specific and revolves around ensuring 'that the Baltic states are treated ... in the same manner as the other Central and Eastern European countries'.[36] Further enlargement would also provide the opportunity for institutional reform aimed at promoting greater transparency in EU decision-making. The emerging CFSP and EMU were also acknowledged as important, although the government wished to ensure that the CFSP remained closely tied to the so-called Petersberg tasks of peace-keeping operation, humanitarian contributions and conflict management. The Social Democratic Minister also stressed that the promotion of 'a lasting high rate of employment is a central goal for Sweden in EU cooperation, a goal which should also be promoted within the framework of the intergovernmental conference'.[37]

In many ways, the speech and accompanying documentation incorporated few surprises. The Carlsson government was, in effect, reiterating the issues which had been previously highlighted as part of the accession process. The speech was essentially pragmatic, containing no references to the government's vision of what kind of EU it would like to see develop in the longer-term - although the Minister did briefly refer to the Union he did not want to see emerge. The general tone was one of cautious optimism, As Hellström indicated, the government's initial preference was for a flexible and mostly intergovernmental Union,

> 'We do not want the EU to develop in a federalist direction. A well balanced application of the principle of subsidiarity will lead to a more effective cooperation in that decisions will be taken at the level where they belong'.[38]

Yet, he did not dismiss the development of a Europe of variable geometry and that in some policy areas, it was acceptable that countries could approach an agreed goal at different speeds, provided that this did not undermine the balance between large and small member states of the Union. To some extent, the government displayed its long-standing intergovernmental tendencies (indicating that the legacy of the 'Swedish Diamond' was prevalent) and the country's status as a small peripheral player in the expanded EU.

The government was not slow however, in developing some of its ideas. On top of various statements about the potential development of the Union's CFSP, the government also submitted a draft version of its Convergence Programme for facilitating future Swedish membership of EMU as early as June 1995. After consideration by the Advisory Committee on EU Affairs in the Parliament, the government decided to present the programme to the EU for approval in July 1995. The Convergence Programme was of course based upon the economic policy adopted by the government in the 1994-95 parliamentary session. In the Programme, the government argued that the prospects of Sweden being able to meet the TEU's convergence criteria were 'good' - although according to the schedule, public finance needed to be further reinforced by approximately SEK 8 billion in both 1997 and 1998 (i.e. a total of SEK 16 billion by 1998). This would be needed in order to meet the convergence criteria's reference value on the deficit of public finance - 3 percent of GDP - by 1997 and to eliminate it entirely by 1998.[39] However, the Social Democratic government, conscious of public hostility, was careful to stress that the Programme was significant for domestic reasons and that it did not automatically mean that Sweden would participate in EMU. As the (then) Finance Minister Göran Persson noted when he unveiled the Programme,

> 'This programme shows that within a few years Sweden will have a good chance of fulfilling the requirements for full participation in the EU's Economic and Monetary Union. But Sweden may also choose to remain outside, in which case the need for a strong Swedish economy is at least as great as if we want to be members. The convergence programme thus fulfils an important purpose, regardless of whether we choose to join EMU or not'.

On this dual basis, the plan attracted broad political backing, including official endorsements from the Centre Party (which was not surprising given that the party has informally supported the minority Social Democratic government in a 'Red-Green' alliance since April 1995), the Christian Democrats and the Green Party. As Haag succinctly commented, the programme 'is thus somewhat of a paradoxical plan for simultaneously making it possible for Sweden either to join the EU currency union or to remain outside it. Its most important point is that Sweden must strengthen its economy in various ways in order to regain its freedom of action and be able to choose its own future economic path'.[40] The entire parliamentary support added up to nearly two-thirds of the Riksdag's seats, giving the initial impression of a consensus on EMU. In reality, neither the public nor the financial markets shared the government's optimism about the possibilities of being ready to join the third stage of EMU in 1999.[41]

In addition, the government also continued with the idea of developing a more structured approach to fighting unemployment in Europe, even to the point of proposing the incorporation of an employment chapter in any revision of the TEU at the 1996 IGC. On 1 September 1995, for example, the government formally stated that, 'the persistent, very high level of unemployment in Europe constitutes the biggest internal problem which the EU and its member states are faced with today'.[42] Of course, the government was, to some extent, harping on an issue that the Union had already agreed was a rising priority and at its two summits at Essen and Cannes. The Union had already recognised that there needed to be increased coordination of economic and employment policies, especially to promote future stability as the Union moved towards EMU.

The employment issue was attractive to the government for several reasons at both the national and supranational level. As a minority Social Democratic regime suffering from the constraints of internal SAP division on the EU issue, the promotion of the fight against unemployment would promote greater unity by stressing a common theme for all Social Democrats. It was hoped that the anti-EU grass roots would be appeased. It was also argued that the unemployment issue would make the benefits of EU membership more real to a hostile Swedish public. In other words, it would help to satisfy the high domestic expectations of the benefits of membership and, at least partially, neutralise the 'legacy of pre-accession'. At the EU level, the fight against unemployment had the dual advantage of highlighting the continuity in Swedish ideas in the post-accession period and at face value, the government championed an issue which other member states seemed to support. In other words, the government might be able to achieve results on this issue.

Consequently, in its September paper, the government initially proposed that the future IGC should 'consider the introduction into the treaty of a new chapter, entitled Employment Policy', which would set out the general aims, procedures and 'a common commitment to certain principles of employment policy'.[43] In many ways, the chapter was more about principles and commitment than real positive results, but would contain an article stating that the member states regard the attainment of a high level of employment as a matter of common concern. It would further state that the aim of their policies would be to attain a rate of employment sufficient to meet the common economic, social and environmental goals laid out in article 2 of the Treaty and to contribute 'to the achievement of an improved balance in public finances'.[44]

The proposals were well developed. The chapter would include, for example, procedures for formulating, implementing and monitoring coordinated employment strategies. The Social Affairs and Ecofin Councils would devise annual draft guidelines for the EU and/or member states' employment policies. Each member state would adopt a multi-annual programme in accordance with the Treaty's employment policies and an EU Employment Committee would be established to advise on employment trends.[45] Finally, the chapter would also incorporate a 'common employment strategy' including provisions on equal opportunities, improving real wages and profits, additional training for workers, active labour market policies and to overcome regional variations in employment.[46] Most of all, the Swedish proposals insisted on 'a strengthening of the Social Dialogue in order to enhance the contribution that the social partners are able to make to dynamic and efficient local labour markets'.[47]

Ironically, the employment chapter proposals did not (initially) prove as attractive as first appears either at the domestic or supranational level. For the most part, the proposals received a domestic lukewarm response as they became the vehicle for a traditional Left-Right political dogfight on the nature of economic policy. They were widely criticised for not amounting to much in practice and would be difficult to translate into a coherent strategy at the EU level. In December 1995, for example, the government's plans for an employment union failed to win the backing of any of the opposition parties. The leaders of the six opposing parties universally rejected the government's blueprint at a party leader conference on the IGC on the grounds of being 'intangible and unrelated to economic reality'.[48] The Left Party and the Greens criticised the proposals for undermining the national economic policy and for being too puny to protect Swedish workers. On the other hand, the Centre and Right parties questioned the viability of such a policy and the economic reasoning behind it - harping that this would be a return to the interventionist economic style that had got Sweden into an economic mess in the first place.

Similarly, among the other member states, there was a mixed response. The British maintained their resistance to any EU development in the social policy area, whilst other governments (principally Germany, France and the Mediterranean member states) questioned the cost of such a policy on the EU international competitiveness. From the end of 1995, the government had, to some extent, prioritised transparency question above the employment chapter amongst its IGC priorities. However, this has not meant that the Swedes have dropped the plan. There is a good chance that the employment chapter will be incorporated in some form into the new treaty negotiated at the IGC.[49]

One of the other main priorities of the government was Swedish input into the Reflection Group which was formed on the instruction of the European Council at its meeting in Corfu in June 1994. The Heads of State and Governments decided to establish a group (the Reflection Group) as a potential 'think-tank' to prepare for the IGC and headed by the Spaniard Carlos Westendorp. What was initially striking about the Reflection Group was the various backgrounds of its members. Some representatives were drawn from independent bodies and did not hold governmental office, some were merely diplomats (for instance, from Italy, Luxembourg and Austria), and others were of ministerial status (such as France, Ireland, the UK and the Netherlands). Although this ensured that the Reflection Group was not merely another COREPER as it consisted of a mixture of ministers and independent thinkers, it did result in the Group's agenda being more limited than first anticipated. It created the further problem of first and second-class members as the ministers dominated proceedings as they were closer to the government's own work.

Sweden's representative came from the latter grouping (Mr. Gunnar Lund from the Ministry of Foreign Affairs was appointed). This illustrated the seriousness with which the Social Democratic government took the EU's development and their simultaneous wish to ensure that any initiatives of the Group were not too ambitious or forward thinking - which would threaten key Swedish interests, such as the evolution of the CFSP. Gunnar Lund was also required to consult with the Riksdag's Advisory Committee on European Union Affairs on a continuous basis, which helped to provide cross-party support for any Swedish initiatives in the Group.

In accordance with the Corfu mandate, the Reflection Group tentatively examined ideas in connection with the TEU's provisions which were to be reviewed at the 1996 IGC. It necessitated considerations of institutional matters covered in the European Council's Brussels conclusions (1993) and the later March 1994 Ioannina compromise. The Group was also given the additional mandate by the European Council in Cannes (June 1995) to focus on questions of direct interest to EU citizens, with an emphasis on employment, the environment, internal and external security and subsidiarity questions. To some extent, the inclusion of employment, transparency and environmental questions was as a direct result of Swedish and wider Nordic pressure.[50] The first meeting of the Reflection Group took place in Taormina in Sicily (2 June 1995) with the final report completed on time for European Council meeting in Madrid (15-16 December 1995).

In general, the Carlsson government welcomed the Group's final report especially as the report and the Madrid conclusions included a number of welcome signs for the Swedes. References were made to, amongst other things, maintaining solidarity between member states who may be 'in' or 'out' of the future third stage of EMU (which at this time, it was most likely that Sweden would remain outside), and the European Council reaffirmed its commitment to 'the fight against unemployment and for equal opportunities' as a priority task of the Union. The Council also approved the translation of the previous Essen recommendations into multiannual employment programmes by the member states and the further development of an EU wide job-creation strategy.[51] To some extent, the Swedish government was able to keep the pressure on the employment issue at the supranational level. It was also encouraged by the European Council's acceptance of the continued importance of enlargement. In particular, reference was made in the conclusions to its interest 'in promoting political stability and economic development in that region'. In many ways, the Reflection Group and the Madrid summit proved to be a success for Swedish policy-makers. Both the Group and the summit refrained from any comments on any future vision of Europe and remained essentially pragmatic.

b) Mobilising for the IGC

The IGC Committee

It was widely recognised by the government that the main challenge facing it was to mobilise a wider party and public consensus on the EU. It was hoped in elite circles that a more open and consultative process regarding the IGC would help to neutralise any myths about full membership and at the same time, help to revive the fortunes of the Carlsson government. In both cases, the Social Democratic government was keen to ensure that the process on the IGC was open and in the traditional Swedish manner, consensus-building. Part of this strategy required greater mobilisation and information amongst the political elite and especially within the Riksdag. This dissemination of information was to be coordinated through a specialised parliamentary committee - the Swedish Parliamentary IGC 96 Committee. In planning from the 1 February 1995, Hellström appointed the committee (9 March) and assigned it to carry out several tasks. According to the Committee's terms of reference,[52] these included:

- conducting studies of major specific issues which may be discussed at the 1996 IGC.

- encouraging public debate on the key issues to be considered by the IGC and 'to give the advocates of various views an opportunity to argue their case'.

In practice, this dual strategy would (according to the terms of reference) provide 'the best way in which Sweden can promote its EU objectives when it takes part in the Conference'.[53] This made sense as it would require the political elite and public to focus upon the key objectives for the forthcoming conference and neutralise the unusual circumstance in which the country found itself. To some extent, Sweden (along with Austria and Finland) differed from the other EU members since unlike them, the country had not taken part in the specific debate on the original TEU and yet, had just conducted an extensive public debate on the full range of EU cooperation as part of the November 1994 referendum. The danger for the government with this strategy was that it would set up a specific stall against which the public would judge its performance in the IGC.

Interestingly, the Committee's terms of reference included a number of specific objectives for it to examine - namely the effects of enlargement, especially on the balance between large and small member countries; any potential or necessary modifications of EU decision-making to allow for further EU enlargement; any possible changes to the institutional balance of power between the EU institutions and finally, the future of the subsidiarity principle. Most of all and in many ways, summarisiing the internal friction within Swedish policy towards the EU, the Committee was instructed to conduct 'an analysis of the balance between, on the one hand, intergovernmental cooperation and, on the other hand, the need for more coordinated forms of decision-making in EU cooperation'. This would be 'of particular interest'.[54]

As a reflection of the seriousness with which the IGC Committee was held as part of the government's strategy, the Committee was given a relatively high-profile. The Committee was chaired by the well-respected political scientist and Social Democratic M.P., Björn von Sydow, and consisted of 10 additional members. In terms of its composition, the Committee followed the usual parliamentary procedure of appointing informally in proportion to their overall representation in the Riksdag.[55] Consequently, it was made up of four Social Democrats, two Moderates, with the rest of the parliamentary parties receiving one representative each. Given its dual task - of investigating IGC issues and encouraging a wider public debate - the Committee was also assigned a budget of SEK 11 million and a five person supporting secretariat. The majority of this finance was directed at promoting wider public discussion.

As regards its first objective (of investigating the key IGC issues), the Committee was quickly able to organise itself. At the end of the day it produced an extensive array of government reports on the key policy issues. A comprehensive version was submitted to the Riksdag (9 February 1996) and a government report followed in March.[56] The Committee adopted several approaches. First, the key areas for analysis were identified and a list of various questions to be answered drawn up. Ten problem areas were initially identified, including the CFSP, transparency, the consequences of enlargement to include the CEECs, subsidiarity, future democratic control in the EU, further measures to increase the Union's legitimacy, citizenship, EMU, environmental policy and JHA aspects.[57] Second, a number of experts were commissioned by the Committee to write specialised reports.[58] Third, a series of hearings and seminars on various themes and issues relating to the IGC were held and included regional debates all over the country from November 1995. The hearings covered the key areas, such as a seminar (July 1995) on 'The Road to the 1996 IGC', a hearing on the further EU enlargement (August 1995) and a seminar on transparency (September 1995).

Turning to the objective of encouraging public debate, the Committee also adopted a comprehensive strategy. In addition to organising a series of public hearings, the dissemination of information on the IGC was also helped by the Committee's publishing activities. In effect, the Committee attempted not just to focus attention on the conference, but also to develop the public's appreciation of longer-term EU development, which it considered to be essential since Sweden was a new member state and 'European issues should have their natural place in the Swedish political and public debate.[59] It directed its funds at three levels in the public domain - that of adult education through a programme of informing the wider public (*folkbildning*); the development of young people at the upper secondary school level and finally through a discussion of Sweden's policies towards the IGC. This strategy was vital if the Committee was to fulfill its second task and its own goal of ensuring that 50 percent of the population would come into contact with the IGC debate. This was an ambitious task given that by February 1996, opinion polls indicated that barely 40 percent of the public had even heard of the IGC.

Overall, by the time of its winding up (May 1996), the IGC Committee was widely regarded as a limited success story. The Committee was certainly more successful as regards its first objective of investigating the main issues surrounding the IGC. The Committee eventually produced 21 specialist reports on the IGC (including four on EU enlargement).[60] In general, the mixture of practitioners, administrators and academics as a forum of experts proved to be beneficial. The fact that the expert reports were mostly conducted by independent specialists helped to dismantle political party and public mistrust of the process and added weight to future government policy on the IGC. Indeed, for the Social Democrats and the Centre Party, the IGC Committee helped to reduce the degree of internal disunity. It could be used as a basis for informed internal party discussion and as a valve to relieve tension. According to Björn von Sydow, the Committee facilitated a more open debate on the IGC and ensured at the parliamentary level, that Riksdag members would be able to conduct informed debates on EU issues.

In effect, the IGC Committee was successful at the elite level, even though there was still not universal coverage.[61] The main political parties and interest groups, such as the SAF, TCO or the Farmers' Association (LRF) only put 'an occasional direct emphasis on the IGC discussion.[62] This was partly due to the fact that the other major EU-related issue, EMU, intermittently erupted on to the domestic stage and became one of the main political issues during 1996. Interestingly, the anti-EU parties and the 'No to the EU' movement also argued that the government should initiate debates on both the IGC and EMU and that if either was rejected in any future referendum then full membership should be terminated. The EMU question tended to have a dual effect. On the one hand, it stole the limelight away from the IGC. On the other, the two issues were perceived as interlinked (in the public's eyes) and therefore the promotion of the IGC was undermined by the unpopularity of EMU amongst the public.

The Committee was perhaps less effective at encouraging public debate on the IGC. Whilst it welcomed the broad spectrum of non-governmental organisations' and public authorities' participation in the seminars and hearings and most were able to express their views to the Committee, it is more doubtful whether it fulfilled its goal of reaching over 50 percent of the population. Given the substantial level of electoral fatigue and public hostility to the EU, the Committee set itself a difficult task. To a large degree, the public opinion polls have not altered on the EU with a large majority still opposing it, whilst levels of public debate are still superficial regardless of the IGC Committee. Even though public knowledge of the IGC was high when compared to other member states (and may have been the result of the direct election campaigns) at 42 percent in summer 1995, this percentage had actually reduced in later opinion polls in February 1996 to 39 percent. As Lindahl noted many of the reports emanating from the IGC Committee were published very late 'and had only a marginal effect on the pre-IGC debate'.[63] However, if the task of the Committee was to inform rather than necessarily persuade the public on the benefits of full membership, then the benefits of the Committee's activities will also be felt during the later stages of the conference. It is more likely that the Committee's most important effect will be that it promoted a wider dissemination of information generally on the EU.

ii) *The Government's Report to the Riksdag*

By the time that the government submitted its report to the Parliament (30 November 1995), much of the work on Swedish preparations for the IGC had been completed.[64] The report contained very few surprises. Yet, it was useful for a number of reasons. First, it included a public résumé of the government's preparations for 1996, Second, it outlined overall Swedish objectives and finally, it specified the government's position on particular policy areas. In general, the report became the benchmark for governmental and opposition parties' spokesmen on the IGC issue.

Taking the report's sections on overall objectives, what was striking was the continued lack of reference to a Swedish vision of a developing EU and/or governmental preferences for further integration, be it 'multi-speed, multi-tier, variable geometry or "Europe á la carte"'. In other words, the Social Democratic government's priorities on the EU remained, as Gunnar Lund (Under-Secretary for Foreign Affairs) noted 'typically Swedish and pragmatic'.[65] To some extent, the omission of reference to the kind of EU the government would like to see emerge was strange in a report on a conference whose initial mandate had been to do just that. In practice, the government's IGC preparations were clouded by the domestic constraints of a hostile public and a split SAP. If there was any kind of coherent Social Democratic policy towards the EU, it was one that essentially stressed the economic benefits of membership in the domestic arena.

As in the previous governmental documents published in July 1995, the November report concentrated on Swedish attitudes towards specific policy areas. Once again, the report highlighted the same issues - greater democracy, access to public information and transparency in EU decision-making; equality between men and women; support for further enlargement (in particular to include the Baltic states); a larger commitment on the part of the EU to fighting unemployment; the realisation of the SEM and EMU; environmental protection; workers' rights, the CFSP and reform of decision-making arrangements. However, there were also some noticeable differences in emphasis between issues within the report. The democracy and transparency issues were mentioned foremost - highlighting the government's decision to champion these aspects at the IGC and the language used within the report was forthright. The report, for example, specifically mentioned that Swedish-style arrangements would be the most appropriate and the government wished 'to ensure that there is a permanent guarantee that the public have insight into the activities of EU institutions'.[66] Provisions concerning public access and transparency principles should be incorporated into the Treaty[67] and the right of non-governmental organisations (NGOs) to facilitate cooperation should be more explicit in the Treaty.[68] Moreover the government also alleged that it had sought to promote greater sexual equality in the Union and that it would press for progress in this area at the IGC as it had done so successfully at the 1995 Cannes Summit. In general, the transparency issue attracted broad political support from all parties and the domestic debate was restricted to universal condemnation of its absence at the EU level.

As regards the inclusion of an employment chapter in the Treaty, the government remained officially committed to its incorporation at the IGC. In reality the government was cautious about its chances at the IGC, but was pleased that Mr. Lund had ensured that the government's proposals were at least partially discussed and conditionally accepted within the preceding Reflection Group as part of the IGC preparations. To court other member states' support, the government continued to stress that its twin objectives in the employment area were essentially about creating common conditions and ambitions and to formulate the institutional mechanics, rather than dealing with specific policy.[69] In particular, the government continued to assert that the objectives of EMU and an employment chapter were compatible. EMU would maintain the low price stability necessary for creative efforts at tackling rising unemployment.[70]

Interestingly, in the report, the SAP government stressed the need to complete and expand the Single Market and included a specific section on consumer interests. The government argued that an effective European consumer policy with high levels of consumer protection was still absent. It proposed the establishment of a supranational European consumer policy and that 'it should be stated more clearly that the promotion of consumer interests is a major goal of the Union'.[71] In part, this was for domestic reasons and tried to deal with public disappointment with the impact of the SEM and the benefits of lower pricing and greater choice for Swedish consumers.

Environmental protection was also given a relatively high profile in the report for similar reasons. The report explicitly mentioned that one overall objective was that 'Sweden should not be obliged to reduce environmental standards and also we should be an active force in EC environmental policy so that new environmental rules are set at the highest possible level of protection'.[72] In effect, the government was advocating that it would like to see the EU set minimum standards and allow member states to decide individually on still higher ones. To a large degree, this reflected the weaknesses of the accession agreement's 'third option' solution, which left a number of important questions for the Swedes unanswered and which the government sought to redress at the IGC. This also meant the government would push for an environmental goal for the CAP (to be included in Article 39 of the EEC Treaty). The government's emphasis on environmental questions was also popular amongst the domestic public. Opinion polls regularly placed the environment as one of the most important in any EC-related survey. Even the anti-EU parties argued for more extensive EU decision-making when dealing with environmental legislation.[73]

Ironically, the issues which were given by far the greatest attention in the November document were the CFSP, cooperation in Justice and Home Affairs (JHA) and changes in decision-making arrangements. In part, this reflected the wider agenda of the IGC, but also indicated the continued (if declining) sensitivities of the government in these policy areas.[74] Turning to the JHA aspects, the government tentatively stated they would join the Schengen agreement (in order to deflect problems arising from full membership for the Nordic Passport Union and Common Labour Market).[75] What the government was clear upon was, first, the need for a simplification of EU procedures in the JHA area - calling for greater coordination at committee level - and second, the transfer of some areas from the intergovernmental third pillar (JHA) to the supranational first pillar (EC). Whilst the former could be seen as consistent with the Carlsson government's themes of simple and transparent EU decision-making; the latter was surprising given the intergovernmental preference of the Social Democrats and the domestic public concerns over the EU impinging national sovereignty.[76]

In terms of EU institutional questions, traditional Swedish concerns remained pre-eminent. The report specifically recognised that these questions would figure prominently in the IGC. Institutional adaptation was essential if the EU was to further enlarge in accordance with the European Council's declarations in Copenhagen (June 1993) and that consequently, EU decision-making procedures would need to be simplified.[77] Most importantly though, the government would be unwilling to consider any major initiatives that would undermine national sovereignty and 'as far as Sweden is concerned, it is vital that our influence is not reduced. In addition, the balance between large and small member states shall not be undermined'.[78] Whilst in certain areas, the Carlsson government accepted the wider application of Council qualified majority voting (QMV), any major proposals challenging the powers of smaller member states would be resisted by Sweden, such as the weighting of votes in the Council to reflect population size to a greater extent or the loss of Commissioners and judges for small states.

Although the government paid deference to its intergovernmental preferences of the past, the Swedish position 'cannot be classified as either purely integrationist or purely intergovernmentalist. It contains elements of both schools of thought'.[79] Interestingly, intergovernmental tendencies were evident in its approaches towards the European Parliament and the CFSP, but not for example, in the area of environmental policy. Hence, Sweden showed a cautious and almost opportunistic attitude towards the EU's development combined with a fair degree of pragmatic ambiguity. This is clearly embodied in its attitude towards QMV and the role of small states, where the issue for the government was to ensure that the weighting of votes reflects a careful balance between the two. It is also evident in its general support for increased powers for the Commission - which it sees as an ally of small states - and its cautious attitude towards reforming the more federally inclined EP. Although the Swedes, for example, were willing to see a limited extension of the EP's powers, they also wanted to reinforce the role of the national parliaments in the decision process in order to consolidate democratic legitimacy. It is unclear in the report as to what degree any friction between the expanded roles of the EP and the national parliaments would be reconciled.

Whilst most of the main political parties in the Riksdag took exception to various and differing aspects of the report, its cautious and pragmatic style was acceptable to almost everyone. In the interest of maintaining at least, the appearance of parliamentary unity behind the government's future negotiating strategy, the report was unanimously approved by the Riksdag. No formal vote was taken. In effect, the government's hands on negotiating the future IGC were not tied. Unlike the accession negotiations no pre-conditions were placed on the government. This was, in many ways, a wise move given the changing agenda and the nature of intergovernmental negotiations during the IGC process.

Conclusion

By the time of the formal resignation of Ingvar Carlsson as Prime Minister and party leader of the Social Democrats in March 1996,[80] the government's position on the EU and IGC was therefore well advanced. This, to some extent, helped to ensure a relatively high degree of continuity of policy when Carlsson handed over the running of the country's executive at a critical time to his successor, Göran Persson. In addition, the country's economic policy was also not subject to major rupture as Persson served as Carlsson's Finance Minister and architect of most of the government's austerity packages. Indeed, the new Prime Minister received a reasonably warm welcome from Swedish business and industry elements precisely because of his 'good housekeeping' background.

His ascendancy was aided by the fact that Persson was guaranteed to take over the leadership of the SAP and the government in advance. He was the only candidate and was thus easily elected at the SAP's extraordinary conference (15 March 1996). Moreover, in anticipation for the changeover in leadership, Persson, when still Finance Minister had announced new pledges to fight unemployment and a limited restoration of social insurance benefits in January 1996 as 'a sop' to the influential LO and the more left-wing elements of the party faithful.[81] In addition, the new premier took over at a time when the economy had, whilst still fragile, partially revived. The budget deficit had rapidly reduced and central government debt was at this time, being estimated to stabilise relative to GDP by the end of 1996.

Yet, this did not mean that Carlsson had left office during a period of unity on the issue of European integration. The premier was openly criticised for his handling of, amongst other things, the repatriation of Kurdish asylum seekers in January 1995, the de-commissioning of nuclear power plants and the long-standing Øresund bridge project. Carlsson was also challenged for his outspoken comments in February 1996 that Sweden may be ready to join NATO at the turn of the millennium.[82] The Social Democratic government was also vulnerable to criticism on its views on future Swedish participation in EMU. On the one hand, the government faced pressure from organisations such as the Federation of Swedish Industries, which called for the government to 'redouble its efforts to fulfil the conditions for participation in EMU'[83] and on the other, growing internal pressure from within the SAP for a referendum on any future move to join a single currency. Dozens of motions for example, demanding a plebiscite on the issue of joining a single currency were submitted to the extraordinary congress.[84] In an effort to pre-empt and quell these fears, Persson was forced to claim in January 1996 that the EMU could be delayed as a result of any future downturn in the country's or the European economy.[85] Furthermore, there was also disquiet from several industrial quarters about the possibilities of a dip in the fortunes of the fragile Swedish economy in early 1996.

It was not surprising then that in the first statement of government policy presented by the new Prime Minster, Göran Persson, to the Parliament (22 March 1996), the European Union issue played a relatively backseat role. The main priority of the new government was the economy and the halving of unemployment 'to 4 per cent by the year 2000'.[86] According to Persson, this policy combating unemployment rested on four corner-stones - stable and sustainable finances, the provision of favourable conditions for companies and enterprise, life long learning and new contracts of cooperation between interest groups. It was only in the latter parts that the importance of the IGC and the future of Swedish security policy was mentioned. Yet it is the debate on the EMU that attracts the public's attention rather then the IGC and is where, most likely, Persson's attention on EU matters will be most directed. [87] None the less, if the first year of full membership is anything to go by, the Persson government will face many of the same constraints as the previous Carlsson administration. Continued problems with public opinion and disunity between and within the main political parties on the EU issue will mean that the next few years for the Persson government will not be easy when dealing with the EU's future development.

Notes

[1] For convenience, the author has decided to end the book with the resignation of the Carlsson administration in March 1996. This cut-off point is appropriate for three reasons. It allows for Sweden's first year of membership to be analysed. It is symbolic in that the period ends with the retirement of Ingvar Carlsson, the Social Democratic Prime Minister responsible for the submission of the 1991 application and for eventually steering the country to membership. Finally, the book ends just before the

Intergovernmental Conference (IGC) reviewing the future of the Union started and thus, will prove to be a juncture in the development of the European Union itself.

[2] Ibid., Swedish Institute (1996) p. 5.

[3] Ministry of Foreign Affairs (1994), *Speech to the Swedish Parliament on 23 November by the Prime Minister, Mr. Ingvar Carlsson, with reference to the outcome of the referendum on membership of the European Union,* UD, Stockholm, 2 December, p. 2.

[4] Ibid., Ministry of Foreign Affairs (1994) p. 2.

[5] Ibid., Ministry of Foreign Affairs (1994) p. 4.

[6] Ibid., Ministry of Foreign Affairs (1994) pp. 4-5.

[7] Figures supplied by the Invest in Sweden Agency, (1996) *Invest in Sweden Report 1996,* Invest in Sweden Agency, Stockholm, p. 6.

[8] If people on government training and employment programmes are included within the unemployment figure, the actual rate is close to 13 percent. In fact, the unemployment issue still forms the mainstay of the debate between the mainstream political parties. In February 1997, the government announced that total unemployment had risen slightly from 8.1 percent in January to 8.8 percent in February, casting doubt on the Persson government's commitment to reduce unemployment by half by 2000. In response, the Social Democrats launched a SEK 66 billion four year programme aimed specifically at reducing mass unemployment in April 1997.

[9] Ibid., Invest in Sweden (1996) p. 7.

[10] Figures supplied from Ministry of Finance (1996), *Sweden's Economy 1996,* Ministry of Finance, Stockholm, p. 1.

[11] Ministry of Finance, (1995) *Press Release 1.10.1995,* Ministry of Finance, Stockholm, p. 1

[12] This budget represented the first budget bill to cover an extended 18-month period from July 1995 to December 1996 as the Parliament had decided that from 1997 onwards, the fiscal year would coincide with the calendar year.

[13] Taken from Swedish Institute, Persson optimistic on growth prospects but union and employers voice doubts, *Faxed From Sweden,* 3, Swedish Institute, Stockholm, 10 November 1995, p. 1.

[14] Board, J. B. (1995) Sweden: A Model Crisis, *Current Sweden,* No. 410, September, p. 5.

[15] Swedish Institute, Strike Action hits municipalities as union and employers lock horns, *Faxed From Sweden,* 1, Swedish Institute, Stockholm, 1995, p. 2.

[16] Sahlin was accused by the Stockholm tabloid, *Expressen,* for example, of being approached by bailiffs for not paying her income tax arrears, television licence fee and 19 parking offences. After several defences on national television, Sahlin was none the less forced to retire from the leadership contest to succeed Ingvar Carlsson in March 1996 and eventually to resign from the government in the following November.

[17] Luif, P. (1995) *On The Road To Brussels,* Austrian Institute of International Affairs, Laxenburg, p. 350.

[18] Carnegy, H. Nordic States March to Different EU Tunes, *Financial Times,* 5 July 1995, p. 3.

[19] See Jahn, J. & Widfeldt, A. (1996) European Union Accession and its Aftermath in Sweden: Are the Swedes Fed Up with European Union Membership? in Hampsher-Monk, I. & Stanyer, J. (eds.) *Contemporary Political Studies 1996 Volume Two,* Political Studies Association/Short-Run Press, Exeter, pp. 417-23.

[20] For the Social Democrats, EU opposition was as high as 63.3 percent of supporters; for the Christian Democrats, it was 66.4 percent and for the Centre Party, it was a whopping 72.7 percent against.

[21] For a review of the direct election see Miles, L. (1996) The 1995 Swedish European Parliamentary Election: Is Sweden Turning its back on the European Union? in I. Hampsher-Monk, I. & Stanyer, J. (eds.) *Contemporary Political Studies 1996 Volume Two,* Political Studies Association/Short-Run Press, Exeter, pp. 1007-12 or Miles, L. & Kintis, A. (1995) The New Members: Sweden, Austria and Finland in Lodge, J. (ed.) *The 1994 Elections To The European Parliament,* Pinter, London, pp. 227-36.

[22] For example, whether the Swedish result influenced the voting patterns in the other new member states and in particular, the Finnish direct election (20 October 1996).

[23] For a more detailed account see Widfeldt, A. (1996) The Swedish European Election of 1995, *Election Studies,* 1.

[24] Interestingly, the other party suffering from internal disunity on the membership issue - the Christian Democrats - ran a single campaign and offered only one party list. They incidentally failed to get any candidates elected providing a strong indication that there are strong links between the EU issue, its management by the respective party leadership and the levels of discontent within the respective party organisations.

[25] Taken from an interview with Wrede, H. at the International Department of the Social Democratic Party, Stockholm, 2 February 1996.

[26] Taken from an interview with Wrede, H. at the International Department of the Social Democratic Party, Stockholm, 2 February 1996.

[27] Taken from an interview with Wrede, H. at the International Department of the Social Democratic Party, Stockholm, 2 February 1996.

[28] Taken from Agence Europe, 19 September 1995, p. 3.

[29] Taken from Swedish Institute (1996), *Sweden in the European Union,* Fact Sheets on Sweden, Swedish Institute, Stockholm, March, p. 2.

[30] These proposals were successful. A Code of Conduct for access to EC documentation was adopted by the Council (December 1993) and by the Commission (February 1994) - Preston, M. (1996) Openness and the European Union Institutions, *European Access,* 4, pp. 7-10.

[31] The Swedish Union of Journalists were by 1995 pursuing clarification on the principle of public access at the EU level and the status of the special declaration attached to accession treaty. It emphasised the notion that the public access rules were fundamental to 'Sweden's constitutional, political and cultural heritage'. The equivalent EU declaration noted the Swedish position, but drew attention to its obligations as a member state to follow EC law - see Axberger, H.-G. (1996) Public Access To Official Documents, *Current Sweden,* No. 414, Swedish Institute, Stockholm.

[32] See Riksdagen, Minutes, 1994-95: 113.

[33] A pamphlet using the title 'Sweden's Principle Interests in View of the 1996 IGC was published in July 1995 which detailed the high-priority issues at the IGC. The text was aimed at the general public and as means of stimulating public debate.

[34] Ministry of Foreign Affairs (1996), *Sweden's Principle Interests in View of the 1996 EU Intergovernmental Conference,* Cabinet Office, UD, Stockholm, July, p. 1.

[35] Ibid., UD (1996) p. 2.

[36] Ibid., UD (1996) p. 3.

[37] Ibid., UD (1996) p. 6.

[38] Ibid., UD (1996) p. 5.

[39] Ministry of Finance, (1995) *Press Release 12 June 1995*, Ministry of Finance, Stockholm, p. 2.

[40] Haag, M., (1995) EMU Membership an Open Issue as Economy Rebounds, *Current Sweden,* No. 411, September, p. 1.

[41] There has been a notable turnaround in the Swedish economic position in 1997. The April 1997 review of the Convergence Programme was very positive in tone. The public deficit for example had been reduced 'at an unexpectedly fast rate'. It amounted by the end of 1996 to SEK 42 billion or 2.5 percent of GDP (well ahead of third review's forecast of 4 percent) and would move into surplus in 1998. In addition, GDP growth for 1997 was estimated to be 2.3 percent, with inflation remaining at around 2 percent in 1997. The national debt level was also estimated to continue to fall to around 74 percent by the end of 1998. According to estimates by the European Commission, Sweden would now qualify as one of the first wave of EMU members. The country was showing good progress on the debt ratio which remains the only major economic question mark on EMU participation. It could qualify on the debt ratio criteria under article 130c.

[42] Ministry of Finance, (1996) *Strengthening the Fight Against Unemployment - An Issue for the Intergovernmental Conference,* UD, Stockholm, 1 September, p. 1.

[43] Ibid., UD (1996) p. 2.

[44] Ibid., UD (1996) p. 2.

[45] Ibid., UD (1996) p. 2.

[46] Ibid., UD (1996) p. 3.

[47] Ibid., UD (1996) p. 3.

[48] Swedish Institute, European Jobs Programme Hitch, *Faxed From Sweden,* No. 5, 8 Swedish Institute, Stockholm, 8 December 1995, p. 3.

[49] The later Persson government achieved a number of notable successes in negotiating the inclusion of Swedish proposals on the employment chapter, peace initiatives, equality issues, the environment and transparency into the Irish Presidency's Draft Treaty in December 1995. Their incorporation into the final position could, according to chief negotiator Gunnar Lund, be regarded as 'a great victory for Sweden' - see Sverige mycket nöjt med utkast till EU-fördrag, *Svenska Dagbladet,* 12 December 1995, p. 2. Indeed, opposition from France and Germany to the Swedish proposals became more muted in 1997, whilst the change of government in the UK in May effectively ended to substantial British opposition. The incorporation of an employment chapter into the IGC treaty now looks a certain.

[50] Taken from an interview with Mr. Gunnar Lund, Under-Secretary of State, Ministry of Foreign Affairs, Stockholm, 7 February 1996.

[51] Taken from the Conclusions of the Presidency reprinted in a special edition of Agence Europe, on the Madrid Summit 15-16 December 1995, No. 6629, Agence Europe, Brussels, 17 December 1995, p. 6.

[52] Swedish Parliamentary IGC 96 Committee (1995), *Committee Terms of Reference*, Dir 1995: 15, Swedish Parliamentary IGC 96 Committee, Stockholm, p. 1.

[53] Ibid., Swedish Parliamentary IGC 96 Committee (1995) p. 2.

[54] Ibid., Swedish Parliamentary IGC 96 Committee (1995) p. 4.

[55] Taken from an Interview with Mr. Björn von Sydow at the Riksdag, Stockholm, 8 February 1996.

[56] The Review was entitled *Sverige, EU och framtiden, EU 96-Kommitténs bedömningar inför regeringskonferensen (Sweden, the EU and the Future: The EU 1996 Committee's Review at the IGC)*, and published by the SOU 1996: 19, Stockholm, Fritzes.

[57] Swedish Parliamentary IGC 96 Committee, (1995) *Sweden Prepares for the Intergovernmental Conference in 1996*, Swedish Parliamentary IGC 96 Committee, Stockholm, p. 5.

[58] The expert contributors incorporated practitioners and academics from all disciplines. The process included prominent figures from Swedish academia, such as Magnus Jerneck (The Principle of Subsidiarity in the European Union) and Bengt Sundelius (From Small State Identity to Smart State Profile in the European Union).

[59] Taken from an Interview with Mr. Björn von Sydow at the Riksdag, Stockholm, 8 February 1996.

[60] See for example, Swedish Parliamentary IGC 96 Committee, (1995) *Abstracts of Expert Reports to the Committee*, Swedish Parliamentary IGC 96 Committee, Stockholm.

[61] According to Mr. von Sydow, the only problem concerning the commissioning of expert reports was regarding the employment chapter, for example - Taken from an interview with Mr. Björn von Sydow at the Riksdag, Stockholm, 8 February 1996.

[62] Lindahl, R. (1996) The Swedish Debate in Janning, J., Algieri, F., Rodrigo, F., Lindahl, R., Grabbe, H. & Hughes, K. *The 1996 IGC - National Debates (2) -Germany, Spain, Sweden and the UK*, Discussion Paper 67, Royal Institute of International Affairs, London. p. 40.

[63] Ibid., Lindahl (1996) p. 39.

[64] Ministry of Foreign Affairs, (1995) *The EU Intergovernmental Conference 1996*, Report 1995/1996: 30, UD, Stockholm, 30 November. This report can also be found as *Skrivelse till riksdagen (Address to the Parliament)* 1995-96: 30.

[65] Taken from an interview with Mr. Gunnar Lund, Under-Secretary of State, Ministry of Foreign Affairs, Stockholm, 7 February 1996.

[66] Op. cit., UD (1995) p. 16.

[67] The Swedes actually went on to propose three new articles be included in the revised Rome Treaty. These articles would be made applicable to the second and third pillar by amendments of the TEU. Article 192a would allow any natural or legal person to have

a right of access to documents held by a Community institution. Article 192b empowers the Council to adopt regulations (under the procedure for article 189b) concerning the registering and open access to documents. Article 192c would also introduce the idea of a new form of legal action (under the article 173 procedures) - Taken from a speech by Dan Eliasson, Advisor to the Ministry of Justice at a UACES conference, University of Wales, Cardiff, 4 December 1996.

[68] The government officially tabled a working document for the IGC in 1996 which called for the general principle of access to be incorporated into any post-IGC Treaty and that 'the most efficient way to increase openness in the European Institutions is to ensure that citizens have access to documents that form the basis of the discussions and decisions'. The Working Document was published in *European Access,* August 1996, 4, pp. 11-2.

[69] Taken from an interview with Mr. Gunnar Lund, Under-Secretary of State, Ministry of Foreign Affairs, Stockholm, 7 February 1996.

[70] In late 1996, the chances of the government forcing the incorporation of an employment chapter into a post-IGC Treaty greatly improved. Gunnar Lund was able to negotiate its inclusion into the Irish Draft treaty (which cited the Swedish proposals almost verbatim). Lund had equal success with equality issues, the environment and transparency. This, he claimed in December 1996, was 'a great victory for Sweden' see Sverige mycket nöjt med utkast till EU-fördrag, *Dagens Nyheter,* 13 December 1996.

[71] Op. cit., UD (1995) p. 23.

[72] Op. cit., UD (1995) p. 23.

[73] Op. cit., Lindahl (1996) p. 45.

[74] Swedish Attitudes towards the CFSP (as detailed in the report) will be fully addressed in Chapter Ten.

[75] Sweden did in fact go on to agree to join Schengen in December 1996.

[76] Of course, in reality, these concerns may be more perceived than real and in any case, have not been picked upon greatly by either the Swedish press or the anti-EU political parties.

[77] At the meeting of the European Council at Copenhagen (June 1993), the member states agreed explicitly that the Central and Eastern European countries which so wished should become EU members. Further EU enlargement to incorporate the CEECs was now inevitable.

[78] Op. cit., UD (1996) p. 34.

[79] Op. cit., Lindahl (1996) p. 43.

[80] Ingvar Carlsson retired from active politics for personal reasons and according to him, so that he could spend more time with his family.

[81] Persson announced for instance, that unemployment would be halved by the year 2000, Social insurance benefits were also to be increased to 80 percent of full income. This was less than a year after the same Finance Minister had cut such payments to 75 percent of full income in order to reduce the large state budgetary deficit - Swedish Institute, Persson pledges to cut unemployment and restore social benefits, *Faxed From Sweden,* No. 2, Swedish Institute, Stockholm, 26 January 1996, p. 1.

[82] For further details see Chapter Ten.

[83] Swedish Institute, Industry bosses rally behind EMU, *Faxed From Sweden,* No. 4, Swedish Institute, Stockholm, 23 February 1996, p. 3.

[84] Swedish Institute, SDP members urge EMU referendum, *Faxed from Sweden,* No. 1, Swedish Institute, Stockholm, 12 January 1996, p. 4.

[85] Swedish Institute, Economic and Monetary Union could be delayed - Persson, No. 2, Swedish Institute, Stockholm, 26 January 1996, p. 3.

[86] Ministry of Foreign Affairs, (1996) *Statement of Government Policy presented by the Prime Minister to Parliament, Friday 22 March 1996,* UD, Stockholm, p. 1.

[87] For brief summary of events in 1996 see Miles, L. (1997) Swedish Priorities Towards the IGC, *Current Sweden,* No. 415, Swedish Institute, Stockholm.

10 The 'Membership Diamond' and Post-1995 Sweden

The retirement of Ingvar Carlsson brought the first phase of Swedish full membership to a temporary close. Carlsson after all, was responsible for submitting the 1991 application, for steering the country to full membership in late 1994 and in spearheading governmental preparations for the 1996 IGC. Yet, the country's relationship to and attitudes towards the European Union remains in a transitional stage (see Chapter Nine). This chapter argues that whilst the 'Swedish Diamond' is of significant use in explaining the country's transition to full membership, the country is now confronted with a differing set of options as a result of becoming a full EU member. Consequently, the 'Swedish Diamond' also needs to be revised in light of these developments. In effect, a revised 'Membership Diamond' is now more useful as a conceptual framework to evaluate future Swedish perspectives towards European integration.

The 'Membership Diamond'

The 'Membership Diamond' builds upon the concept of the 'Swedish Diamond'. Its four 'points' derive from much the same assumptions and relate to a variety of domestic/internal and international/external factors. However, the 'Membership Diamond' reflects the changes in emphasis within and between the four points and the nature of domestic, rather than necessarily international constraints on Swedish policy-makers (see Table 10.1). The most notable differences include:

- the overwhelming dominance of economic factors in determining Swedish attitudes, which has driven changes within the 'Membership Diamond'.

- that the 'third point' of the 'Membership Diamond' is therefore dominant, has influenced major change on the other three points and led to growing challenges to and instability in, the first and second points.

- that there has been a growing domestic debate over these economic factors.

- that domestic factors are now critical in defining Swedish perspectives on European integration rather than international security dimensions (and in particular non-alignment and neutrality).

- that the greatest transformation has occurred within the 'Membership Diamond' fourth point. It has been reduced both in influence and in nature. In effect, Sweden's security doctrines of the 1990s are much more flexible than those of the 1950-80s.

Table 10.1   The 'Membership Diamond'

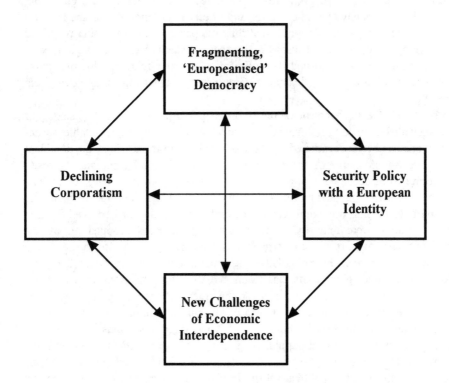

a) Point 1: A Fragmenting, 'Europeanised' Consensual Democracy?

i) Fragmentation

It can be argued that the traditional view of Sweden as a stable consensual democracy is now less convincing. Fragmentation and dissension have started to appear at various levels within the Swedish polity. To some extent, this has been due to a twin phenomenon - first, the rising level of confrontation within day-to-day politics and second, the 'Europeanisation' of the Swedish political system. Yet, allegations that the Swedish version of consensual democracy has been eroded is far from new. As evident from previous chapters, elements were unstable from the 1970s onwards. Sannerstedt and Sjölin have argued that Swedish cabinets have become weaker and briefer in duration during the last two decades.[1] The two authors suggest that this was partly due to the rising workload and complexity of the Riksdag's business (which has presented greater opportunities for division) and the polarisation of party relations. Internal party cohesion and looser voter allegiances were, amongst other things, apparent from the late 1980s.

Yet, the replacement of the traditional five party system (consisting of two socialist and three non-socialist parties) with a more unpredictable seven-party one has been accentuated by the EU membership issue.[2] First, the dominant and most stable party of the post-war era - the Social Democrats - already suffering from declining support as a result of less resilient voter allegiances - have been further plagued by internal disunity on the EU issue. This difficulty for the party leadership was reinforced by the fact that both the Carlsson and Persson administration were minority governments; in both cases propped up by the parliamentary support of the Centre Party from early 1995. Although the SAP's parliamentary size is healthy (due to its impressive performance at the 1994 Riksdag election), grass roots dissension and worsening relations with its trade union partners are evident as the governing Social Democrats grapple with the poor state of public finances.[3] Government cuts in public welfare received widespread condemnation by both the SAP and trade union mass membership. Second, the rise in electoral popularity of 'fringe' parties, such as the Greens, the Christian Democrats and the rejuvenated Left Party introduced new and serious forces into the Swedish political rubric. In two of the three cases (the Greens and the Left Party) their rise in electoral support has, at least in part, derived from their status as Sweden's anti-EU parties.

Without doubt, the expansion of the party system was the result of declining voter allegiances which, especially on the Swedish Left, are now less firm than in the past.[4] To some extent, the greater number of floating (and usually ex-Social Democrat supporters) emanates from the SAP's official pro-membership status, which is unpopular with its traditional voters. In contrast, on the Right, the electoral popularity of Bildt's Moderates has steadily risen in the 1990s. The increase in support for the Moderates likewise derived (albeit to a limited extent) from its status as the most pro-EU Swedish party, as a reservoir for enthusiastic pro-EU voters and that as premier, Bildt headed the government that negotiated accession terms. The Right, whilst seemingly more united than the Swedish Left has been split into the ardent pro-EU Liberals and Moderates and the cautious Christian Democrats. Overall, the political spectrum seems to be presently dominated by two large parties representing the Centre-Left (Social Democrats) and Centre-Right (Moderates) separated by a disunited centre and surrounded on the fringes by the electoral popularity of the anti-EU Greens and Left Party.

Political scientists, such as Vedung and Jahn, have argued that the exclusive dominance of a Left-Right dimension in Swedish politics is now questionable. New issues, such as the environment and nuclear power, have created additional cleavages that cut across traditional ideological divides and have facilitated instability within the party system.[5] Indeed, rising party fragmentation reflects the fact that traditional areas of consensus have become politicised. It is easy to place the membership question within Vedung and Jahn's category of 'new issues', especially as the EU issue has 'turned out to be particularly painful' for the main political parties and their levels of public support.[6] The popular conflict over the issue reflects the divisive nature of European integration and reinforced existing internal divisions present within the parties. The situation was complicated by the fact that there are important differences between the party elite and their mass membership and that official party policy supporting EU membership was not shared by large parts of the electorates:

> 'In party terms, the EU issue was as much a question of elite versus grass roots within parties as it was a struggle between parties. The struggle between pro- and anti-EU forces was a struggle between coalitions where each side of the issue was made up of strange bedfellows. In other words, the EU issue was different from most other issues'.[7]

With some simplification, EU supporters were more united primarily because it contained the majority of the political establishment. In contrast, the anti-EU camp tended to be a nebulous coalition of fringe elements. Yet, Esaiasson and Homsberg's conclusions that political representation in Sweden still remains more elitist than populist helps explain why the country joined the EU in the end. These authors argue that the country is essentially run through 'representation from above' with 'a top-down process of opinion formation'.[8] The inherent (if declining) deference of the populace towards their political leaders enabled the political elite to carry the day in the 1994 referendum and persuade the wider population of the benefits of membership. None the less, the degree to which elite opinion differed from the rank and file of society was evident immediately after the referendum, when anti-EU campaigners 'more or less openly accused the 'Yes' campaign of scare mongering and manipulation'.[9] Even in 1996, only the Moderates and the Liberal party can claim to have the majority of their mass party membership in favour of full membership. The fear that full membership requires major concessions of national sovereignty and policy-making will move even further away from local people ensures that the issue will keep open traditional divisions within Swedish society - North versus South, rural against urban, and conservative versus liberal.

This explains why for instance, the Social Democrats barely managed to scrape together a majority of their own followers to vote in favour of membership in the November 1994 referendum. Yet, to some extent, the EU issue highlighted the wider dilemma for the SAP in reconciling its grass roots social democracy ideology with the EU's promotion of freer market mechanisms and trade liberalisation. The problem for SAP is that full membership may further dilute its ideology and the process of transition into an essentially white-collar, Centre-Left 'catch-all' party.[10] As Thomson succinctly puts it, 'The social democratic problem is that advanced capitalism is leading to the breakdown of the institutions necessary to implement a social democratic strategy'.[11] Without alternative policies emanating from the EU, and with its value system being undermined, this could accelerate SAP disunity and eventual electoral decline. Ironically, it could be argued that the EU issue reinforces the process by which the SAP becomes progressively less social democratic and increasingly classless in orientation through each stage of revisionism.

Full membership contributed to the polarisation that undermines the country's consensual democracy - creating a formal division between the mainstream pro-EU and the peripheral anti-EU political parties. Although this does not completely correspond to a Left-Right division in Swedish politics (and was more accurately a Left versus Centre-Left, Centre-Right split), the anti-EU Left Party and Greens have acted as a reservoir for those members of the society wishing to keep the anti-EU voice alive. Ironically, the new cleavage created by the EU issue ensures that the main beneficiaries are the more extreme parts of the political spectrum. On the one side, the anti-EU Left Party and Greens and to a lesser extent, the pro-EU Moderates on the Centre-Right. The parties of the Swedish Centre are more vulnerable to internal disunity on the EU issue and are the main losers from the new cleavage. Overall, this means that the centre of Swedish politics - in terms of ideological and elite versus grass roots division - will be turbulent. As this is usually fertile ground and the foundation of any successful attempts at consensus-building by government, consensual policy-making on the EU affairs will be difficult in the near future.

ii) Europeanisation

At the same time as the party picture remained confused, the political system incorporated changes aimed at encouraging policy-making by consensus on EU-related matters. Some of the temporary measures, such as the IGC Committee, were evaluated in Chapter Nine and this section will examine the permanent structural changes to decision-making. At the executive level, this process is well-advanced. Governmental ministries were formulating Swedish perspectives on the EU for years prior to full membership as a result of the EEA and the accession negotiations. However, membership has facilitated the creation of permanent structures to promote closer contact between the executive and legislature and within the Parliament on EU matters. The most striking example was the establishment of the Riksdag's Advisory Committee on European Union Affairs.

The package implementing full membership included an amendment to the Parliament Act which introduced the Riksdag's formal participation into EU decision-making. This amendment created the Advisory Committee as the main parliamentary instrument for consultations with the government on EU issues. Consequently, the Committee was established when the country joined the Union and was modelled on its Danish counterpart in the Folketing.[12] It consists of 17 members, the same number as the other Riksdag's committees. However, as Luif notes, the term 'Advisory Committee' indicates that the its tasks differ from other parliamentary committees, for unlike the usual committees of the Riksdag, it does not deal with bills or motions introduced by individual M.P.s or the government.[13] Its main task is to act as a consultative body for discussing EU matters and presenting the 'parliamentary view' with representatives of the government.[14] In practice then, the Advisory Committee is not as powerful as its Danish counterpart and remains more aloof from the respective parliament's legislative functions.[15] Gustavsson, for example, suggests that the Swedish committee is a 'semi-Danish model' due to the fact that its decisions are not binding as in the Danish case.[16]

The Committee is designed so that it 'deals with all the Union's areas of cooperation. At one meeting, a diversity of issues, such as foreign policy, agricultural policy or police cooperation, may be discussed'.[17] The government is required to inform the Committee on all questions to be dealt with by the European Council, before it takes important decisions concerning its conduct in Council negotiations. According to the Parliament Act (Chapter 8, article 15(1)), the government must also discuss topics that the Committee itself deems significant. This is an important right for the Committee if it is to be an effective instrument 'since the possibilities to influence the outcome of an issue are greater at an early stage of proceedings within the EU'.[18] It is intended therefore, that the Committee is not just reactive, but is also pro-active. Provided at least five of the Committee members ask for consultations, then a meeting must be held with government representatives. The only exception to this rule is where such a meeting would harm Swedish interests (Parliament Act, Chapter 15(2)), although it is unclear as to how this would be decided and by whom in practice. The most likely scenario is that this provides a disclaimer for the government of the time.

In addition, the government is required to provide written background information to its members in preparation for its sessions and the Committee can demand information and discuss issues that may have not yet reached the level of the EU's Council of Ministers. The Committee has similar powers when it comes to information from regional authorities. Yet the government does have the right to decide on the dissemination of information for authorities not under the Riksdag's control (Parliament Act, Chapter 8, article 16(1)). The Committee's procedures are also of significance. It convenes on a Friday in order to discuss topics forthcoming at the next week's EU Council meetings and is usually attended by the relevant Minister or Under-Secretary of State who will be participating at the next EU Council meeting.[19] Nor is the focus of the discussion restricted to just the EU's first pillar (EC). The Committee is free to discuss issues arising from the second and third pillars created by the TEU. The discussion can lead to changes or additions to governmental viewpoints provided that a majority of the Committee are so inclined and it appears on the record as part of chairperson's summing up.

However, the crucial point is that the Committee's role is 'advisory'. The government, whilst perhaps not always politically or morally correct, is not legally bound to follow the Committee's opinions. Moreover, Hegeland and Mattson have argued that the Swedish committee is much weaker in terms of influence than its Danish counterpart for several reasons. First, Sweden has a tradition of strong government and that given the relative stability of governments, ministers 'appear to regard themselves as being less constrained by decisions in the European Committee than their Danish colleagues'.[20] Second, the Committee normally gets involved in the decision-making process at a very late stage and government decisions have already been influenced by actors apart from the Advisory Committee. Third, given the Committee's large remit to cover all EU matters, it suffers from a heavy workload and a lack of issue-specific knowledge which 'sometimes render the consideration of some matters quite superficial'.[21] Indeed, the Committee did not reject any of the government's proposals in 1995 illustrating the subsequent difficulties of the opposition parties in uniting to reject a government proposal. However, to a certain extent, this also reflects the relative immaturity of the Committee and that the majority of committee members are supporters of full membership. Given the delicate domestic situation of the issue, they are unwilling to stir up controversies on individual EU matters so soon after the completion of the accession process.

Interestingly, the meetings are not open to public (Parliament Act, Chapter 8, article 17), although minutes (which are open to public inspection) are kept. However, either the government or the Committee can declare any information discussed in the proceedings as secret if there are the usual important reasons, such as for national security or if it has implications for foreign relations with other countries.

In general, the Advisory Committee whilst including some constitutional deficiencies, has been regarded initially as a useful vehicle for promoting parliamentary consensus and ensuring governmental accountability. In the report of the Riksdag's Standing Committee on the Constitution for example, the role of the Advisory Committee was portrayed in a positive light arguing that through it, the Parliament obtains, 'real influence on Sweden's positions in the meetings of the European Union's Council. ... It can be assumed that the government will not take a position which contravenes the view that the Advisory Committee expressed during the consultations'.[22]

Despite the Advisory Committee acting as the main vehicle for presenting the parliament's views on the EU to the executive, the Riksdag's 'Europeanisation' was not been solely restricted to this body. Just as the ministries have dealt with the domestic implications of the EU policies (and vice-versa), then so has the work of the existing standing committees. Dialogue between government and the Riksdag also takes place through the standing committees relating to their specific policy remits. Hence, the establishment of the Advisory Committee does not formally affect the handling of the normal work of the standing committees.[23] If a bill or motion concerns EU cooperation, it is dealt with by the standing committee responsible for the subject area concerned.[24]

The government is required to inform the parliament of all new proposals put forward by the Union. Important proposals must also be accompanied by a written statement on the significance for the Swedish legal system. This information will eventually end up not only with the Advisory Committee but also with the relevant standing committee(s) dealing with that policy area and leading to consultation between the Advisory Committee and the respective standing committee(s). Indeed, the standing committees can influence government thinking on EU matters through consultations with the various ministries or through reports presented to the parliament's plenary session. They can also take up questions in reports put to the plenary on their own initiative, request governmental statements of opinion and submit reports to the Advisory Committee so that the EU Council can take these points of view into account when it consults with government.[25] This is in addition to the rights of individual

MPs, such as, to require the government to answer questions on EU matters[26] and that the government must annually submit a written report about EU cooperation for plenary debate.

The Parliament is slowly reforming to coordinate its efforts on EU matters more effectively and 'should be seen in the light of the increasing internationalisation of politics'.[27] The government's IGC preparations, for instance, were reported not just to the Advisory Committee on EU Affairs (22 June 1995), but also to the Standing Committees on Foreign Affairs and on the Constitution.[28] This 'Europeanisation' of the Riksdag has led to more effective cross-party and inter-committee contact. However, the Advisory Committee acts as a vital filter. It allows the Riksdag to speak to the government on EU matters with a clearer voice. The Committee was designed to be the primary parliamentary body dealing with EU matters, providing an overall coordination role. Its composition includes a large number of senior politicians, such as party leaders and standing committee chairpersons, giving it substantial influences inside and outside the Parliament.[29] Indeed, the government's IGC report (30 November 1995) included a commitment to consult the Advisory Committee on continuous basis.

Yet, 'Europeanising' the Riksdag is still at an early stage. The high-profile composition of the Advisory Committee has the advantage of improving the dissemination of information throughout the Parliament, but has led to some tension between the various standing committees and the Advisory Committee over its competencies.[30] Although the Standing Committee on the Constitution issued several statements to the effect that the authority of the specialised parliamentary committees was in no way affected, a *de facto* distinction has been drawn in terms of approach - with the Advisory Committee acting as a general policy forum and the Standing Committee(s) being restricted to policy details.[31] Relations between the Advisory Committee and the *ad-hoc* parliamentary IGC 96 Committee also remained unclear. The possibilities for lobbying the Advisory Committee, whilst at first sight seeming large have also been restricted by its wide policy remit, even though it includes influential parliamentarians.

None the less, the new procedures illustrate the seriousness with which the Riksdag considers the obligations of full membership and the desire to promote consensual policy-making. The Advisory Committee, for instance, provides a direct channel for opposition parties to influence government action and encourage parliamentary support for government policies during future EU negotiations. It remains to be seen whether the procedures will be effective in coping with the growing fragmentation of party politics and the hostility of public opinion towards the Union.

b) Point 2: Declining Corporatism

The full membership question was also influenced by the wider trends concerning Swedish industrial relations. The fragmentation of party politics has to some degree been reinforced by the growing complexity of industrial relations, wage bargaining and the changing influences of key interest groups on government. Certainly, the long-standing system of centralised collective bargaining of wage agreement has all but disappeared within Sweden. It was replaced by a mixture of sectoral and locally negotiated wage agreements by 1995, accelerated by the experience of recession in the early 1990s.[32] Despite the attainment of the Rehnberg measures, which effectively amounted to centrally set wage increases for 1991 and 1993, this did not stop the SAF announcing in 1991 that it would no longer participate in central negotiations with the LO or the PTK (*Privattjänstemannakartellen* - the Federation of Salaried Employees in Industry and Services) when the measures expired (1992). In 1993, the Association of Swedish Engineering Industries, VF (*Sveriges Verkstadsindustrier*) also stipulated that it will no longer negotiate a sector agreement, but would shift further to the company level. In response, the main trade union organisations, (LO, TCO and SACO) formed a platform to force employers to negotiate sectorally, and eventually persuaded the VF to sign a two-year sectoral agreement (which expired in March 1995).

Indeed, the process of change has intensified. Between March-May 1995, several sectoral agreements were concluded. The paper and pulp industry, for instance - which is dominated by the Wallenberg group - led the way with a two-year agreement incorporating a 3.8 percent pay rise for 1995 and 1996 (of which 2.3 percent was guaranteed to all workers and 1.5 percent was divided on the basis of local negotiations). The agreement was criticised by the VF, but since the SAF had given up central bargaining, each sector can decide for itself. The VF went on to sign a three-year agreement with the Metall Union (23 May 1995) after mediation which awarded a 3.5 percent rise per year and a limited reduction in working hours for the 300,000 employees in the engineering industry. In short, there have been major reforms affecting the entire Swedish system of industrial relations. A 'low cost flexibility coalition' (spearheaded by the larger employers) has emerged, prompting major changes.[33] The country experienced a period of substantial institutional revision (between 1990-96) because of greater pressures to decentralise, liberalise and as a response to further internationalisation (see Chapter Seven).

Overall, a number of trends have developed within Swedish industrial relations which has made economic planning more complex. First, the balance of power between the trade unions and the employers' organisations has altered in the 1990s. With some simplification, the trade unions which were influential in the 1970s-80s have been usurped by the power of the employers' associations. As a result, there has been a growing gap between the trade unions and the employers' federations leading to an increased number of strikes in 1995. On the one side, the trade unions are on the defensive as they face attacks on their negotiating influence from employers and try to restrict the scope of the government's austerity packages affecting the welfare state.[34] In general, the trade unions are trying to ensure that negotiations return to the national level and/or if this is not an option, at least remain within sectoral agreements.

On the other side, the SAF-led employers' groups are keen to promote greater flexibility in and productivity of the work force in order to increase international competitiveness. Provoked by the LO's political activism (in part as means of deflecting pressure for welfare cuts), the SAF has increased its lobbying activities. It stepped up its campaigns to amongst other issues, reduce welfare spending, limit subsidies to unemployment insurance funds, shorten the length of unemployment benefits and measures aimed at reducing trade union influence; bringing it into direct confrontations with the LO in particular. Overall, the 'Swedish Employer Offensive' continues in the late 1990s.

In addition, there has been a greater level of disunity between the various components on the trade union movement and employers' federations respectively. Taking the former, the general movement from a primarily blue-collar based to an essentially white-collar workforce, has made it increasingly difficult for the trade union movement to speak with one voice. The blue-collar LO for instance, has faced the dual challenge of attracting new members from white-collar industries and growing rivalry with the white-collar TCO (Central Organisation for Salaried Employees - *Tjänstemännens Centralorganisation*) and SACO (Swedish Confederation of Academics - *Sveriges Akademikers Centralorganisation*). Although both the TCO and SACO have tended to follow the path set by the LO, it is undeniable that the balance of power is altering between them.[35] By 1992, for instance, the LO's share of total trade union membership had fallen to 57.5 percent (from 78.9 percent in 1945) compared to the doubling of the TCO's share (from 13.3 percent in 1945 to 33.7 percent in 1992.[36] Confronted by internal rivalry within the trade union movement and the simultaneous decline in the central negotiating role, the unity of the movement has been under threat.

At the same time, the onset of more localised bargaining has, albeit to a lesser extent, affected the influence of the over-arching Employers' Federation, the SAF. Certain employer groupings, such as the large export orientated firms and industrial giants, such as the Wallenberg group have been more inclined to 'go it alone'. This has been reflected at a sectoral level, such as through the more independent line of the VF. With some simplification, there has been internal friction within the SAF between the federations representing export-orientated and domestic industries, and between large and small firms, reflecting, to some extent, the fortunes of the respective businesses in the early 1990s. In effect, Sweden has endured a dual economy since 1993 with a prosperous exporting sector benefiting from the Krona's devaluation contrasting sharply with the fragile state of the domestic market in the aftermath of the 1990-93 recession. Most noticeably, there was a high degree of tension between the VF and the overarching SAF executive throughout 1995 on the future of company agreements. This internal disunity was further compounded by the SAF's merger with the Swedish Federation of Industries, changing its structure into a nebulous business association.

The flux of industrial relations has also impacted on the Swedish political scene. Relations between the main political parties and the interest groups has become more complex in recent years. Tensions between the Social Democratic government and the LO loomed larger; leading to poor relations between the main two traditional components of the labour movement. At the 1995 and 1996 traditional May Day rallies of the trade union movement, for instance, the Social Democrat government received virtually unprecedented harsh criticism of its austerity packages and calls from some quarters of the LO to cut its formal ties with the SAP. In addition, the 1996 LO congress virtually 'turned into a demonstration of discontent with government policies'.[37] The decline of the corporatism was partly to blame for rising grass roots disloyalty within the mainstream parties and especially the Social Democrats. The party leaderships are now confronted with dealing with an arena of interest groups that is overcrowded and multifaceted and without any sole interest organisations to rely wholeheartedly upon. This was especially appropriate when it came to the EU issue, for 'there was not one single special interest that could not find a good reason to call upon their supporters to vote "No" to EU membership'.[38] Worse still for the Social Democrats, the LO refused to risk internal conflict and thus robbed the SAP of its usual ally in mobilising the rank and file on policy issues. The resulting 'disorder' has changed the role of the state. As Jelle Visser succinctly comments,

> 'Dragged into the conflict, the state became much less effective as the insurer and gate-keeper of the corporatist arena. We may today think of Swedish industrial relations as an example of bargained corporatism, but not as a *model* case. It is no longer the land of self-sustained corporatism, high productivity and high wages, as it used to be twenty years ago'.[39]

Overall, it can be argued that confronted with such an array of opinions from the main interest group actors - on the configuration of industrial relations, the various antidotes to the economy's fragility and the nature of the austerity packages - the ruling Social Democrats refrained from developing a coherent or new industrial relations strategy.[40] As Wilks notes, the virtual re-structuring of industrial relations has not only reduced dramatically the ability of national government to manage the economy, but more significantly, signalled the end of the domestic investment strategy based on class compromise originally embodied in the 'spirit of Saltsjöbaden'.[41] After all, the SAF was sticking to its cautious opposition to centralised bargaining, whilst the trade union remained officially in favour of re-imposing it in 1995-96. The most likely scenario is the maintenance of sectoral bargaining. Whilst the Social Democratic government has ruled out income policies and appealed to both parties to return to central agreements, a comprehensive return to centralised bargaining is unlikely. Yet, the Krona's instability during the 1990s and governmental preparations for possible participation in EMU cannot dismiss completely the imposition of future income policy to promote stability, although it does seem at this point unlikely.[42]

However, what is clear is that the traditional corporate framework has now significantly altered from that of the 1970s. A localised and sectoral based bargaining structure is here to stay. Indeed, the trade unions are in a period of intellectual limbo (having no coherent strategy or philosophy for the future of industrial relations) and consolidation as they deal with internal rivalry between the main union confederations. The ramifications of this revised corporate framework - which, after all, influenced governmental and public opinion on European integration - is that the policy outcomes will be as complex as ever. Most of all, the consensus between the two main branches of industrial relations in Sweden has disintegrated. This crucial aspect which was instrumental in leading to the Swedish application way back in 1990, will be a major problem for future Swedish EU policy. Certain trade unions have become the main interest group opposition to full membership, whilst the SAF has fully embraced the Union (and even future Swedish membership of EMU). Without doubt, the divisions within and between the main corporate actors on the EU issue will make the development and wider popularity of government policy on EMU and the IGC more difficult.

c) Point 3: The New Challenges of Economic Interdependence - FDI and EMU

It can also be argued that since accession Sweden has been confronted with a slightly different set of variables governing the third point of the revised 'Membership Diamond'. In reality, the challenges facing the Swedish government (in terms of its economic interdependence with the rest of Europe) has altered in nature. They no longer derive from the ambitions of securing quantitative terms of trade, such as access to EU markets for Swedish goods or increased trade liberalisation. These goals have been achieved through the EEA and later full membership.[43] Rather the main aspirations for Swedish trade policy arise from two areas. As regards the existing EU member states, it is the achievement of qualitative economic breakthroughs, such as gaining better allocation of scarce resources through the removal of Non-Tariff Barriers (NTBs) that are now the priority. With some simplification, it is no longer merely access to EU policies that is important, but rather securing the fullest utilisation of benefits for Sweden from those policies. In short, the new challenges of economic interdependence originate from, firstly, such issues as gaining greater Foreign Direct Investment (FDI) from EU companies and whether or not the country should participate in Economic and Monetary Union (EMU). The second area of challenge lies within the realms of EU external relations and Sweden's influence upon it. In this respect, the government was keen to ensure that the Baltic states are at the forefront of EU aid programmes to non-member states and in any future EU enlargement in the next century.[44]

Turning to the internal EU issues, Swedish perspectives on European integration will at least in the early years of full membership, be clouded by the priorities of securing the greatest level of economic benefits from the Union and making the country an attractive centre for future investment. Much of the thinking behind this lies from three sources. First, that full participation in EU policy areas will dampen the harsh economic experience of the 1990-93 recession. Fears that there may be a revived capital drain (with rising outward investment and the relocation of production facilities abroad as happened during the recession) remain prevalent. A constant argument used in the domestic debate on European integration has centred upon whether the country can afford to be too peripheral to EU policy developments. As Agell comments 'Sweden is a small fish in a big pond of investment opportunities'.[45] Second, that as Sweden fully participates in the SEM it will become a larger recipient of FDI, leading to improved international competitiveness, higher levels of employment and guaranteeing the future of generous welfare provision. FDI will be at least one way of bridging the gap between the two segments of the dual economy and revive the country's sluggish domestic market. Third, that the largest question in the near future concerning the attractiveness of Sweden for investment will depend on the governmental policy towards EMU.

To some extent, levels of FDI into Sweden from outside companies will be used as a barometer of the success of full membership. After all, increases in FDI was one of the main arguments articulated by the 'Yes' campaign during the 1994 referendum. Indeed, levels of inward investment will rise in the short-term regardless and depend on factors such as the starting of large infrastructure projects like the Øresund bridge project in 1996. Yet, FDI has noticeably increased reaching the highest figure for Sweden since the 1960s at SEK 100 million in 1995 and double the figure for 1994.[46] Overall, it has been estimated that total gross investment will increase by 10 percent in 1996 and by more than 2 percent in 1997, with the investment ratio (which has been at a low level) rising from 17 percent in 1997 to 20 percent in 2001.[47] Part of the investment increase will be as a result of the benefits of full membership and are illustrated in other ways, for despite generally weak growth in Western Europe, exports of goods and services continued to grow by 4 percent in 1996 allowing for a small surplus in Sweden's current trade account.[48]

This has positive benefits but has also sparked a political debate concerning the ownership of Swedish industry, which had already come to a head during the ill-fated merger debate between Renault and Volvo car companies in 1993-94.[49] Although the government has abolished most restrictions on the foreign ownership of Swedish companies' shares, this has not prevented the issue from being used in the political battle over the benefits of full membership. In 1994, for example, there were approximately 3,762 foreign-owned companies in Sweden, accounting for 10 percent of private employment and 16 percent of the work force in manufacturing. In 1995 alone, foreign net purchases of Swedish shares amounted to an impressive SEK 14 billion. Yet, the FDI issue permeates debates on full membership and acts as a gauge of its success for all sides of the political spectrum. Concern has been expressed by the anti-EU forces about whether the Social Democratic government through membership has allowed too much of the country's 'family silver' to be sold off too cheaply. Certainly, foreign ownership has risen corresponding to just over 30 percent of the market value of shares on the Stockholm Stock Exchange in late 1995.[50]

However, by far the biggest consideration for Swedish government will be the development of a coherent policy towards the evolution of EMU. This, in many ways, will be the primary new challenge confronting the country in the near future. It will form the mainstay of the third point of the revised 'Membership Diamond'. The importance of the EMU programme in shaping the country's perspectives on European integration was recognised early on by the Swedish government. As long ago as 1991, the (then) Bildt government stipulated that the country would accept the TEU's entire contents and consequently, the objective of EMU. More or less as soon as the country became a full member, the Carlsson government turned its attention to placing the country in a position where it would be able to meet the TEU's convergence criteria and to decide on whether to join third stage or not. The Riksbank for example, along with the other central banks participated in numerous committees of the European Monetary Institute (EMI) almost from the first day of membership.[51]

In June 1995 - barely six months after joining - the government presented its convergence programme for economic policy with the declared intention that 'Sweden meets the convergence criteria in the Maastricht Treaty, as well as goals related to employment and environmental objectives' (see Chapter Nine).[52] The programme contained budget policy goals aimed at the stabilisation of central government debt in relation to GDP by 1996 and for the deficit measured as the consolidated general government financial balance to be eliminated by 1998. The programme was based on the assessment of economic trends made in the revised national budget in April 1995. It also incorporated a consolidation programme including measures leading to the reinforcement of public finances by SEK 118 billion by 1998.[53] The programme was accepted by a broad majority of the Riksdag, with provision being made for reviews of the success of the programme at six-monthly intervals. It was also approved by the European Council at a subsequent EU meeting. Although reviews of the programme are needed for economic reasons they will also serve the dual political purpose of ensuring that the Riksdag remains informed and that Swedish EMU policy is continuously on the political agenda. Indeed, the first review of the programme took place in November 1995 with the second following in April 1996.[54] The focusing of domestic attention on EMU will also be facilitated by the establishment of an expert parliamentary committee under the chairmanship of Assar Lindbeck (known as the EMU Committee) in October 1995 to examine the merits of EMU and the implications that Swedish participation would have for domestic policy-making and the economy.[55]

The influence of the 'Membership Diamond' third point will be further strengthened by economic developments that have greatly improved the chances of meeting most of the convergence criteria by 1998. The reinforcement of public finances in 1996 was for example, greater than expected and better than the programme's estimates.[56] Indeed, later estimates predicted that government finances would be in surplus by 1998 to the sum of SEK 126 billion.[57] The government's consolidated debt was also estimated to have fallen to 77.7 percent at the end of 1996. This is a markedly lower debt ratio than that estimated in the original programme. Overall, GDP was gauged to have increased by around 3 percent in 1995 and 1.6 percent in 1996. It raised expectations that Sweden, in spite of initial pessimistic predictions, might qualify for participation in the third stage of EMU after all. The government's consolidation measures were increased to SEK 126 billion, equivalent of 8 percent of GDP, (from SEK 118 billion and 7.5 percent of GDP) in the Spring Budget Bill in April 1996 - signalling the government's commitment to continue getting the country's finances in order. The economic situation in early 1996 remained, however, unclear. There was a slackening in economic activity in late 1995, which led to a downward adjustment of government forecasts for 1996-97. Yet despite the economic slowdown in late 1995, this did not prevent the Ministry of Finance predicting in its April 1996 (and later April 1997) reviews that as a result of the programme the consolidated government deficit would be further reduced.[58] In short, Sweden now stands a good chance of being eligible for stage three as it will, most probably, meet TEU's convergence criteria on budget deficits (which must not exceed 3 percent of GDP). The changes in Swedenís economic fortunes have enabled the country to be considered as a serious future EMU candidate.[59]

In general, the slackening of the country's economy in late 1995 was relatively short-lived. Growth in Europe and the USA increased in 1996 leading to a rise in Swedish exports, which provided a larger contribution to GDP growth in 1996 and 1997. At the same time, the Ministry of Finance considered that it was likely that there would be no major discernible increase in inflation. It remained low (1.7 percent in March 1996) and would increase only slightly in 1997 to around 2 percent. The country would most probably meet the convergence criteria on inflation rates in 1998.

At face value, the main problems regarding the country's ability to meet the convergence criteria, however, remains the size of government debt and to a lesser extent, the Social Democratic government's refusal to join the Exchange Rate Mechanism (ERM).[60] Although falling, the consolidated governmental gross debt (according to the TEU's definition) was a staggering SEK 1,300 billion equivalent to 79.6 percent of GDP in 1995 (falling to 77.7 per cent in 1996) and way above the 60 percent criteria in the TEU. Nor is Sweden likely to meet this criteria in the near future. Gross debt is still expected to be over 70 percent of GDP at the end of the decade. The most optimistic figure is that if further budgetary reinforcement measures are included, the estimated gross debt will be slightly over 65 percent and outside the convergence criteria's values. The attitude of the European Commission on this issue will be critical. However, the Commission's attitude seemed to be softening in 1996. It argued that the country would qualify under the debt criteria after all, as the government had shown 'good progress' in reducing it by 5 percentage points from its highest peak of 1974.

The government and the Riksbank have also ruled out Swedish entry into the ERM on the grounds that this was no longer mandatory as an EMU pre-condition because the Mechanism is not the same as it was at the time of the TEU's signing. A strict interpretation of the membership criterion stipulating that any country participating in EMU must previously have been an ERM participant for two years was therefore no longer valid. However, given the changes to the ERM in 1993, the Commission has also taken a more flexible view when interpreting this criterion as well. This change in the Commission's perspective may also remove this problem for Sweden. Ultimately, the decision on who participates in the EMU is based as much on political considerations as economic ones. Nevertheless, Mr. Lars Heikensten, Deputy Governor of the Riksbank also claimed that the Riksbank does not consider membership of a new exchange rate system should be mandatory for countries that remained outside EMU either.[61]

However, by far the largest problem for the government revolves around the lack of party and public support for EMU. In May 1996 - barely two months into Persson's premiership - the division within the ranks of the Social Democrats was demonstrated when four key figures (in the daily newspaper, *Dagens Nyheter*) jointly urged the party to commit itself to a plebiscite before any decision on Swedish EMU participation. The four which included Kenth Pettersson (the prominent anti-EU head of the powerful retail industry union, *Handels*), and Sören Wibe, (an EU sceptic deputy of the European Parliament) claimed that the SAP was heading for disaster at the 1998 general election if it denied the Swedish people a say on EMU.[62] There is even an undercurrent of political tension within the SAP Cabinet on the single currency issue.[63]

Nor is the government safe on the EMU issue in terms of gaining a majority in the Riksdag. Four of the seven parliamentary parties - the Left Party, Greens, Christian Democrats and the Centre Party (which remains the key parliamentary ally of the Social Democratic government) have declared against Swedish involvement in EMU. Together they control 83 of the 349 Riksdag seats and, along with dissident Social Democrat MPs) would form a parliamentary lobby that the minority Persson government would find difficult to ignore.[64] In particular, the EMU issue has created major tensions between the already split Social Democrats and their Centre Party allies in the Riksdag.[65] The EMU issue has also created further problems for the government as regards other political actors. It endures opposing pressures from main influential interest groups. The Riksbank and the SAF have informally urged the government to be among the first batch of countries to form a single currency.[66] In contrast, Sweden's most powerful trade union congress, the LO, has been more cautious on the question.[67] In addition, public opinion polls on the EMU question indicated throughout 1995 that only 20-30 percent of the populace favoured future Swedish participation.

It is not surprising that the Social Democratic government refused to commit itself on the EMU issue - stressing that a decision on EMU does not have to be taken until 1998 at the earliest and will be made by consensus. In the Carlsson government's IGC report (30 November 1995), it was careful to highlight that an eventual position on the country's participation in the third stage of EMU would 'be adopted in the light of future events' and that the final decision on EMU 'rests with the Swedish Parliament'. This policy was continued under Prime Minister Persson, although for domestic reasons, governmental statements in early 1996 continued to play down the possibilities of joining a single currency. In May 1996, for example, Persson recognised that a parliamentary vote on EMU membership would probably be lost, whilst the new Finance Minister, Erik Åsbrink appeared to leave the option of referendum on EMU open when he stated in Brussels that a decision on EMU would require 'a broad foundation' of Swedish public opinion.[68]

Without reservation, the Membership Diamond's third point in now one based on securing the best economic deal for Sweden through full membership. It is perhaps the most influential point in driving the country's attitudes on European integration. The key areas of FDI and EMU will, to a large extent, dictate how the public perceives full membership and levels of domestic resistance to further European integration.

d) Point 4: Swedish Security Policy with a European Identity

The fourth point of the revised 'Membership Diamond' remains within the sphere of Swedish security policy. However, since security policy has been reduced to simply 'non-participation in military alliances' and has undergone fundamental change since 1989, it now reflects little of previous pre-1989 doctrine of neutrality. Most importantly, since 1991 and the statements of (then) Prime Minister Carl Bildt, it has now been re-labelled to incorporate a substantial European identity. During the accession negotiations, Sweden agreed to becoming 'a full and active member of the CFSP'. With this in mind, the country's participation in an emerging Common Foreign and Security Policy (CFSP) will, along with EMU, be some of the key aspects affecting domestic perspectives on European integration in the late 1990s.

The basic dilemma is that the Union's CFSP still remains immature and simultaneously accompanies the transitional phase of Swedish security policy. In reality, it is not difficult for the government to accept the principles and content of the EU's CFSP as it remains at this point, mostly undeveloped. The CFSP as (established by Title V of the TEU) promises more than it actually delivers. Certainly, in terms of the CFSP's basic principles, Sweden has little to object to. Article J.1 is careful to refer to 'the Union and its member states' in defining and implementing a CFSP, signalling its intergovernmental nature. However, the foreign commitments outlined in article J.1, such as to safeguard common values and fundamental interests, strengthening the security of the Union and its member states and preserving peace and international security in accordance with the UN, are mostly practised by Sweden. In 1994, for instance, Sweden committed a stand-by brigade to UN peacekeeping forces. In June 1995, Carl Bildt was appointed as the European Union's chief mediator for the former Yugoslavia.

Nor is the concept of systematic cooperation objectionable to the Swedes, as long as the Council remains the body responsible for deciding 'joint actions' and will continue to do so by unanimity. It is only on procedural questions and in adopting joint actions that qualified majority voting can then be used. Thus Sweden's national security interests can be protected. The fact that neutral Ireland, Finland and Austria are part of the CFSP is also perceived as a welcome sign that the CFSP's ambitions will remain limited. The IGC is further perceived as a chance for the Swedes to influence the revision of the CFSP's provisions, especially as the 1948 Brussels Treaty expires in 1998.

i) Areas of Swedish Concern

Recently, Sweden has followed the EU lead and was willing to concede some of its autonomy. For example, Sweden followed the EU when recognising new European states. When the EU was prevented from recognising Macedonia due to Greek objections, Sweden also delayed its decision. Nevertheless, there are three areas of concern for the Swedish government. Two of which arise from article J.4 of the TEU, which stipulates that the CFSP will incorporate 'all questions related to the security of the Union, including the eventual framing of a common defence policy, which might in time lead to a common defence'.

First, the CFSP envisages the eventual framing of a common defence policy. According to Carlsson, this could be problematical as 'Sweden's non-participation in military alliances, with the aim of making it possible to be neutral in the event of war in our vicinity remains unchanged'.[69] However, the country already became involved in coordinated actions. In September 1994, the government declared that it would participate in NATO's 'Partnership For Peace' (PfP) initiative on the grounds that it was a confidence building measure and included the Central and Eastern European states. Since then, Swedish governments have argued that the 'Petersberg tasks' provides the new framework on which to judge the merits of assistance to joint projects and military intervention. The definition of non-participation in military alliances has been interpreted flexibly. If Sweden can participate in a future EU defence policy will depend on whether it will require collective security guarantees. This will be difficult for the government to adhere to given the problems that it faces in maintaining domestic support. Consequently, in May 1995, it rejected the possibility that the CFSP should include a 'Mutual Assistance' clause.

Second, the CFSP also foresees the creation of an eventual common defence. This is open to many interpretations, from limited collective security guarantees to a fully fledged, integrated European defence forces. However, for the most part, an EU common defence is still too ambitious for the incremental nature of Swedish security policy. According to Mrs. Lena Hjelm-Wallén in January 1995, the Social Democratic government's security policy has three elements. First, that the Minister believed that decisive steps towards a common defence would not be taken at the 1996 IGC. Second, if such steps were taken then Sweden would not participate in binding defence cooperation. Third, that the government would not obstruct other EU members from seeking common defence.[70] Implicit within governmental thinking is the assumption that a multi-tier development of the CFSP is likely and acceptable.

The third concern revolves around the CFSP's institutional arrangements. Under TEU's article J.4.4 of the TEU, the EU has virtually subcontracted 'decisions and actions of the Union which have defence implications' to the Western European Union (WEU).[71] Consequently, the government argued that any common defence will be developed through the WEU and it is WEU membership and not CFSP participation that is problematical for security policy. Sweden only took up observer status of the WEU (January 1995) to allow the government to participate in discussions on humanitarian operations and peace-keeping, but did not involve any Swedish military obligations.

In practice, the problem for the Swedish government lies in the fact that the WEU fulfils three roles. On the one hand, it represents the CFSP's embryonic defence organ. On the other, it includes a territorial defence guarantee (article V WEU Treaty), as well as acting as the 'European pillar' within NATO. For the government, full WEU membership includes a collective defence commitment and the acceptance of an associated role within NATO - something that contravenes the country's 'non-participation in military alliances'. In April 1995, the government reaffirmed that it had no plans to either become full WEU or NATO members for the foreseeable future.[72]

There are numerous problems with the Swedish position and there is still a high level of ambiguity regarding governmental policy towards the CFSP. This partly reflects the declining domestic consensus between the main political parties on the future of security policy. In response to criticisms by the Centre Party, the Carlsson government during the February 1995 parliamentary debate seemed to be moving back towards a stricter policy of non-alignment, underscoring its reluctance to be part of a European defence force. In its governmental statement (22 February), Carlsson was careful to state that 'we must not lead other states to expect a Swedish military involvement in the event of an armed conflict. Sweden neither needs or wishes to impose restrictions on itself'.[73] Indeed, there were terse exchanges between Bildt and the Social Democrats as he argued that the new government seemed to be moving away from the former non-socialist government's position that Sweden would intervene in any Baltic armed conflict.

However, the government seemed to again soften its position regarding the CFSP in May 1995. Foreign Minister Lena Hjelm-Wallén suggested that the EU's CFSP should be strengthened at the 1996 IGC and that there was a need to 'take a long, hard look at the consensus requirement' for CFSP action.[74] Otherwise, further enlargement would undermine the EU's capacity to deal with external problems. The government qualified this by declaring that it would not agree to being outvoted where a vital national security interest was at stake, but would consider modifications to the CFSP if the interests were not of a vital national security nature. The real problem for the EU and Sweden is determining who decides whether the issues are of vital or only of minor national interest.

Nor has it prevented there being a softening of Swedish attitudes towards the participation of troops in transnational security cooperation. The government has been more amenable to what it regards as military collaboration with other European countries in peacekeeping operations and humanitarian relief. The Swedes have increasingly rationalised cooperation under the remit of the 'Petersberg tasks'. In December 1995, for instance, Lena Heljm-Wallén declared that Sweden would participate in the Implementation Force (IFOR) authorised by the UN Security Council Resolution to implement the Dayton/Paris Peace Agreement in Bosnia-Herzegovina, even though it was under NATO leadership. At first glance, this seemed to be at odds, or at least blur, the existing commitment to non-participation in military alliances. Indeed, 870 Swedish troops formed part of the Nordic Brigade assembled for IFOR - though they are not equipped for attack operations.[75] As Lindahl has identified, although the Swedish government (during both the Carlsson and Bildt eras) acted cautiously as regards the CFSP as public opinion is deemed to be sensitive to moves away from abandoning Swedish neutrality, the steps taken during the 1990s 'must be regarded as substantial'.[76] Indeed, the crises affecting the former Yugoslavia has indirectly acted as accelerator to changes in security policy as the government has been progressively drawn into closer military cooperation with the WEU and NATO powers through IFOR and the wider PfP.

The gradual change to Swedish thinking on security policy is no better illustrated than by the Joint Report of the Riksdag's Foreign Affairs and Defence Standing Committees (November 1995). It stated that military non-alignment, aiming at the possibility of being neutral in the event of war remained unaltered. However, this no longer meant that the country would restrict its cooperation in European security matters with other countries. On the contrary, the Joint Report argued that Sweden be an active contributor to future peace and stability in Europe, although the longer term development of security policy would also depend on global development as well. Most importantly and in contrast to the pre-1989 doctrine of Swedish neutrality, the Joint Report rejected an immutable binding of the country's foreign policy for every conceivable situation in an unpredictable world.[77]

This thinking was also apparent in the IGC report to the Riksdag. The government's overall strategy was that whilst it recognised that the CFSP's instruments 'must extend to broad area, ranging from preventive diplomacy to peace-keeping forces' and that it also wanted 'to make the CFSP more effective', there should be no major changes to the decision-making machinery of the CFSP.[78] The report confirmed the previous statements of the Foreign Minister and categorically stated that,

'There is no question of abolishing the right of veto for foreign and security policy decisions. In questions which involve vital foreign and security policy interests, Sweden cannot allow herself to be outvoted by a majority of EU members'.[79]

Once again the government was willing to concede some ground in that 'it might be possible to modify the principle of unanimity in questions of more limited scope'.[80] In effect, the report subtly indicated that the government, whilst acknowledging that there is a lack of sufficiently comprehensive joint structures within the second pillar, was unwilling to sanction little more than relatively superficial changes. It proposed limited improvements, such as better systems for 'early warning' information gathering and the country will continue to remain a WEU observer. In effect, Sweden 'is not prepared to accept or issue any military security guarantees. As a result, participation in common defence is not an option as far as Sweden is concerned'.[81]

If the ambiguities in the Swedish position are to be removed, then the EU must also take action. The EU must further define its security responsibilities and needs to clarify the relationship between the 'Atlanticist' defence of NATO and the CFSP's future common defence. Thus, the position, despite being somewhat ambiguous will remain until the relationship between the CFSP, WEU and NATO is more clearly defined. Officially, Sweden will remain for the most part, an aloof observer, while at the practical level it will cooperate as part of the CFSP on a selective basis. For domestic reasons, the government will continue to refer to the 'Petersberg tasks' as a way of explaining any cooperation. For example, in May 1995, the Swedish government took the decision to participate in the WEU police force in Mostar.

None the less, the Swedish government faced continued pressure to further re-orientate its security policy.[82] In response to wider lobbying for a more effective CFSP from other EU member countries internationally and at the same time, having decided to reduce its armed forces as part of budgetary cuts, Swedish military strategy is essentially based on cooperation with Western Europe and the EU in particular. The government continues to stress a note of caution on plans to merge the WEU into the EC pillar at the IGC, highlighting that it must not undermine Sweden's existing security policy or the Union's enlargement eastwards to incorporate the Baltic states.[83] In addition, it remains concerned that attempts by the Baltic states to join NATO would not serve Swedish security interests. There is little public support for Swedish participation in NATO for instance. A survey by the University of Göteborg for instance, in June 1996 found that over 70 percent of those polled wished to preserve the country's military non-alignment and barely 17 percent favoured Sweden joining NATO.[84] The Foreign Minister again felt obliged in the Riksdag in June 1996 to rule out Swedish NATO membership. Clearly in the security sphere, Swedish elite preferences are for an intergovernmental framework. Sweden will seek to maintain some kind of right of veto within the CFSP structure.[85]

Whilst the general governmental and party consensus is that the CFSP must become more effective, 'opinions differ on how this goal is to be achieved'.[86] The traditional domestic consensus on security policy amongst the main political parties has disappeared, with the Social Democrats preferring to maintain non-alignment and the Moderates wishing to abandon it.[87] The role of the Centre Party is also of relevance especially given its parliamentary alliance with the governing Social Democrats. At the moment, it favours a nominal non-aligned position for Sweden. This will make comprehensive party consensus difficult and increases domestic friction over and within security policy. Certainly proposals such as establishing a CFSP figurehead/senior post whilst not universally rejected is widely regarded as rather ineffective and impractical. However, there is a minimal level of consensus that future cooperation should be based on the 'Petersberg tasks' and is therefore compatible with the country's non-alignment. For these reasons, the Swedish government proposed that they be formally incorporated within the CFSP at the IGC with the general support of the main political parties.

Differences in policy are now possible between the parties as the issue is no longer the main priority. Economic issues are presently more dominant than security aspects. If there are any major issues in the domestic debate relating to security aspects, they are primarily concerned with defining the best way of assisting the development of the Baltic Republics and security in the region. On this issue, public opinion remains firmly against military guarantees and tends to emphasise economic aid to the Baltic states as a means of guaranteeing Swedish security interests. Yet, given its lower profile and greater flexibility, opinion polls have shown a greater tendency amongst the populace to at least, consider future European defence cooperation more flexibly, especially as regards conflict prevention and peacekeeping missions.

Security policy is still in a period of transition and will affect Swedish attitudes towards European integration for many years to come. The question is no longer whether neutrality is compatible with full membership (as was the case in the pre-1989 period), but rather to what extent security policy will be tied to the wider security structures in Europe.[88] To a large degree, the mutual security interests that Sweden shares with the other Western European powers as regards Eastern Europe (and especially the Baltic region) will act as a catalyst for future cooperation. In a keynote speech to the Riksdag by Foreign Minister, Lena Hjelm-Wallén (12 February 1997), she made the clearest statement yet that the government is keen to strengthen links with NATO, short of full membership of the defence alliance.[89] The Minister stated that the government supported NATO enlargement to the East as a means of promoting stability in Europe. She also suggested that Sweden's 'non-alignment line is not a goal but a means' and that the country was keen to make its opinions known to NATO 'even if we are not party to the decisions'. The challenge of Sweden's future role in the emerging CFSP (and even NATO) will ensure that security issues remain problematical for the Social Democratic government in the short-term and will not be removed from the political agenda.

Conclusion

It can be argued that the revised 'Membership Diamond' provides a conceptual framework to consider the guiding factors that will influence Swedish policy on European integration throughout the 1990s. Now that the country has finally become an EU full member, however tentatively, the process of domestic 'Europeanisation' will continue. Swedish governments will continue to grapple with the EU's ambitious policy portfolio.

It seems more than likely that the Diamond's third (economic interdependence) and fourth (security) points - like those of its 'Swedish Diamond' predecessor, will be dominant in shaping elite views on European integration. However, rather than acting as separate competing dimensions - with economic interdependence pushing forward European integration and security concerns constraining it - the two latter points of the 'Membership Diamond' are now more complimentary. None the less, there will remain a degree of tension between these two points as illustrated by the mixed policy approach taken by Social Democratic governments on EU issues. For some policies, the government stresses intergovernmental perspectives, such as on the CFSP, and in other areas, such as the SEM and environmental policy, pushes for supranational action. To a degree, the friction has become 'internalised' by Swedish full membership. The government will no doubt continue to adopt this typically Swedish, essentially pragmatic and rather opportunistic, 'mixed' approach to European integration.

Whatever the outcome, Sweden's future is intrinsically tied to developments led by the larger states of Western Europe. The country has finally accepted that it can no longer afford to be politically aloof from Europe on security grounds alone. It therefore seems that Sweden in the 1990s will be, more than likely, transformed from Miljan's 'reluctant European' to a more active, but still 'cautious EU full member'. The constraint on successive governments in the 1990s remains the domestic picture and more specifically, how to convince a sceptical population of the merits of the European Union. Until the benefits of full membership become apparent and the political parties can deal with their internal disunity and the hostility of their mass membership on the EU question - in other words, the Diamond's first and second points are revised - then the country's transition to full membership will be painful and will restrict the government's effectiveness in EU negotiations.

Notes

[1] Sannerstedt, A. & Sjölin, M. (1992) Sweden: Changing Party Relations in a More Active Parliament in E. Damgaard (ed.) *Parliamentary Change in the Nordic Countries*, Scandinavian University Press, Norway, pp. 99-149.

[2] If New Democracy are included then it could be argued that there would be an eight party system. However, given the poor performance of New Democracy at the 1994 election and its defunct status as a political force, the re-emergence of New Democracy looks unlikely in the near future.

[3] This point has been made in a much wider context. Pontusson, for example, has argued that why the Social Democrats experience dramatic reductions in support at particular points in time is related to their failure to manage the economy - Pontusson, J. (1995) Explaining the Decline in European Social Democracy, *World Politics*, 47, pp. 495-533.

[4] For a more detailed assessment of the changes to the party system and in the party organisations see Pierre, J. & Widfeldt, A. (1994) Party Organizations in Sweden: Colossuses with Feet of Clay or Flexible Pillars of Government? in Katz, R. & Mair, P. (eds.) *How Parties Organize: Change and Adaptation in Party Organizations in Western Democracies*, Sage, London, pp. 332-56.

[5] Vedung, E. (1988) The Swedish Five-Party Syndrome and the Environmentalists in Lawson, K. & Merkl, P. H. (eds.) *When Parties Fail: Emerging Alternative Organizations*, Princeton University Press, Princeton; or Jahn, J. (1992) Nuclear Power, Energy Policy and New Politics in Sweden and Germany, *Environmental Politics*, 1, 3.

[6] Svåsand, L. & Lindström, U. (1996), Scandinavian Political Parties and the European Union, in Gaffney, J. (ed.) *Political Parties and the European Union*, Routledge, London, pp. 205-19.

[7] Ibid., Svåsand & Lindström (1996) p. 209.

[8] These authors argue that in Sweden 'it is the voters, in the main, who have adapted themselves to the politicians' way of seeing things, rather than the other way round' - Esaiasson, P. & Holmberg, S. (1996) *Representation From Above: Members of Parliament and Representative Democracy in Sweden*, Dartmouth, Aldershot, pp. 310-11.

[9] Jahn, D. & Widfeldt, A. (1996), European Union Accession and its Aftermath in Sweden: Are the Swedes fed up with European Union Membership? in Hampsher-Monk, I. & Stanyer, J. (eds.) *Contemporary Political Studies 1996, Volume One*, PSA/Short-Run Press, Exeter, p. 417.

[10] A good summary can be found in Wilks-Heeg, S. (1996) *The Political Economy of Social Democracy: The Swedish Collapse, the Danish Mystery, the British Mirage and the German Dilemma*, South Bank European Papers, 2/96.

[11] Thomson, S. W. J. (1996) The Social Democratic Dilemma in Hampsher-Monk, I. & Stanyer, J. (eds.) *Contemporary Political Studies 1996, Volume Three*, PSA/Short-Run Press, Exeter, p. 1461.

[12] Taken from an interview with Mr. Hans Regner, Advisory Committee on European Union Affairs, in the Riksdag, 7 February 1996.

[13] Luif, P. (1995) *On The Road To Brussels*, Austrian Institute of International Affairs, Laxenburg, p. 341.

[14] The Swedish Advisory Committee differs 'in a fundamental sense from traditional parliamentary committees. Instead of its task (as with traditional parliamentary committees) being to prepare the ground on issues that will be later decided upon by the parliamentary body as a whole (and making no final decisions of their own, but merely offering recommendations on how Parliament should decide), the Advisory Committee's main function is 'to serve as an advisor to the government rather than to Parliament, and to represent Parliament in its relations with government'. - Hegeland, H. & Mattson, I. (1996) To Have a Voice in the Matter: A Comparative Study of the Swedish and Danish European Committees, *Journal of Legislative Studies*, 2, 3, Autumn, pp. 198-215.

[15] Taken from an interview with Mr. Hans Regner, Advisory Committee on European Union Affairs, in the Riksdag, 7 February 1996.

[16] Gustavsson, S. (1996) Preserve or Abolish the Democratic Deficit? in Smith, E. (ed.) *National Parliaments as Cornerstones of European Integration*, Kluwer, Dordrecht, pp. 113-40.

[17] Secretariat of the Advisory Committee on EU Affairs, (1995) *The Swedish Parliament and the European Union*, Fact Sheet on the Riksdag, No. 15, Riksdagen, Stockholm, June, p. 2.

[18] Ibid., Secretariat of the Advisory Committee on EU Affairs (1995) p. 2.

[19] However, it should be noted that the complaisant attitude of ministers towards the Committee has, albeit to limited degree, undermined this power. Swedish ministers on many occasions fail to show up in person at the committee meetings and instead send an administrative officer. This has been the case in roughly 20 percent of pre-Council consultation meetings of the Committee - Taken from an interview with Mr. Hans Regner, Advisory Committee on European Union Affairs, in the Riksdag, 7 February 1996.

[20] Op. cit., Hegeland & Mattson (1996) p. 203.

[21] Op. cit., Hegeland & Mattson (1996) p. 203.

[22] Konstitutionsutskottets betänkande, *Samverkan mellan riksdag-regering med anledning av Sveriges anslutning till Europeiska unionen*, Konstitutionsutskottets betänkande 1994-95:KU 22, Riksdag, Stockholm, 7 December 1994, p. 15.

[23] However, it has been argued that the establishment of the Advisory Committee has led to a centralisation and a deviation from the established committee structure of the Parliament. In an evaluation by the University of Uppsala the Committee is said to entail a deparliamentarisation in that important segments of domestic politics are subsumed under the domain of foreign policy and the Advisory Committee's remit. In other words, the positions of the leaderships of the various parties has been

strengthened at the expense of the politicians active on the standing committees - Remissyttrande (1994) Dnr. 1024/94, 27 April, Uppsala, Uppsala University.

[24] In the Riksdag, consideration of EU matters 'is not the prerogative of any one particular committee'. The Advisory Committee does not prepare matters for parliamentary consideration, or issue recommendations which are subject to parliamentary votes and do not require a vote in plenary sessions. All this remains within the remits of the existing Standing Committees.

[25] Op. cit., Secretariat of the Advisory Committee on EU Affairs (1995) p. 3.

[26] Op. cit., Secretariat of the Advisory Committee on EU Affairs (1995) p. 3.

[27] Op. cit., Hegeland & Mattson (1996) p. 200.

[28] Ministry of Foreign Affairs (1995) *The EU Intergovernmental Conference,* Report 1995/96: 30, UD, Stockholm, 30 November, p. 5.

[29] Taken from an interview with Mr. Hans Regner, Advisory Committee on European Union Affairs, in the Riksdag, 7 February 1996.

[30] The government has redirected its attention away from the Riksdag's Standing Committee on Foreign Affairs (which up until 1995 dealt with EU related issues) and towards the Advisory Committee on European Union Affairs. The Standing Committee on Foreign Affairs may not have as much access to government ministries on EU matters, but has however, retained its ability to initiate reports on the CFSP - Taken from an interview from Miss Viola Furubjelke, MP and Chairperson, Standing Committee on Foreign Affairs, Riksdag, Stockholm, 8 February 1996.

[31] However, it does also illustrate the wider dilemma facing the Riksdag on EU matters. The usage of the Standing Committees allows expertise in specific EU policy areas to be developed and used and yet, at the same time, the need for consistency requires that the parliament consult with government with a single voice and through one parliamentary body, which could allow some members to function as spokesman for their parties on these issues - Taken from an interview with Mr. Hans Regner, Advisory Committee on European Union Affairs, in the Riksdag, 7 February 1996.

[32] This may not mean the end of some kind of partnership between the various arms of Sweden's industrial relations. In March 1997, a new consensus between employers and trade unions (representing 800,000 manufacturing workers) was found. The background of mass unemployment in Sweden in the 1990s has led to a growing pressure for a new rapprochement. The two sides agreed to appoint an industrial committee charged with overseeing labour market stability and arbitrating conflicts with the power to impose a two-week cooling off period in the event of a threatened strike. In addition, the government has pressured both the LO and the SAF to find a new arrangement for organising wage bargaining.

[33] The term was coined by Iversen in Iversen, T. (1996) Power, Flexibility, and the Breakdown of Centralised Wage Bargaining: Denmark and Sweden in Comparative Perspective, *Comparative Politics,* 28, 4, July, pp. 399-436.

[34] The challenge facing the Swedish trade unions are quite large. A recent study of trade unions have concluded that in general 'it is a difficult process for trade unions to adopt elements of new politics. ... By and large, Swedish trade unions are not very responsive to new politics'. This has meant that they have been slow to react to international

economic pressures in particular - see Jahn, D. (1993) *New Politics in Trade Unions,* Dartmouth, Aldershot, pp. 192.

[35] See for example, Ahlen, K. (1989) Swedish Collective Bargaining Under Pressure: Inter-Union Rivalry and Incomes Policies, *British Journal of Industrial Relations* 27, 3.

[36] Visser, J. (1996), Corporatism Beyond Repair? Industrial Relations in Sweden in Ruysseveldt, J. V. & Visser, J. (eds.) *Industrial Relations in Europe Traditions and Transitions* Sage, London, p. 185.

[37] Hadenius, S. (1997) *Swedish Politics in the 20th Century: Conflict and Consensus,* Swedish Institute, Stockholm, p. 169.

[38] Op. cit., Svåsand & Lindström (1996) p. 214.

[39] Op. cit., Visser (1996) p. 200.

[40] The degree of pressure that the governing Social Democrats find themselves under was illustrated in February 1997. An acrimonious row broke out between the main industrial leaders (led by Peter Wallenberg) and the government after the country's leading industrialists launched a blistering attack on the Social Democratic administration. In a half-page article in *Dagens Nyheter* which was signed by 101 top industrialists, the authors accused the government of failing to safeguard the interests of the country's business sector. They especially drew attention to the government's recent announcement of public spending increases and the decision to start closing down the country's nuclear power plants. The criticisms were widely condemned by government ministers.

[41] Wilks, S. (1996) Class Compromise and the International Economy: the Rise and Fall of Swedish Social Democracy, *Capital & Class,* 58, pp. 91-113.

[42] Op. cit., Visser (1996) p. 202.

[43] Of course, the degree of trade interdependence between Sweden and the EU remains of central importance and is still the fundamental foundation of Swedish-EU relations. In 1995, for instance, 49.6 percent of Swedish exports went to the Union and 54.7 percent of imports came from the EU. Indeed, Germany (11.1 percent of exports and 16.1 percent of imports), the UK (8.5 percent of exports and 8.4 percent of imports) and Norway (6.8 percent and 5.3 percent respectively) continue to be the country's foremost trading partners.

[44] The Swedish governmental strategy as regards the Baltic states is to build bridges among EU member states in support of the three Baltic Republics applications for full membership and to promote closer regional cooperation through the Baltic Sea Cooperation Council - see Chapter Six or Crona, E. (1996) The New Baltic Sea, *Current Sweden,* No. 413, April, Swedish Institute, Stockholm.

[45] Agell, J. (1996) Why Sweden's Welfare State Needed Reform, *The Economic Journal,* 106, November, p. 1768.

[46] Invest in Sweden Agency (1996), *Invest in Sweden Report 1996,* Invest in Sweden Agency, Stockholm, p. 11.

[47] Ministry of Finance (1996), *Sweden's Economy April 1996,* Ministry of Finance, Stockholm, pp. 53-4.

[48] Konjunkturinstitutet, *Press Release June 1996,* Konjunkturinstitutet, Stockholm, 25 June 1996, p. 2.

[49] For a more detailed discussion of the Volvo-Renault Merger episode see Miles, L. & Gray, D. (1994) The Volvo-Renault Merger - A Case Study of a European Multinational Merger, *Journal of Industrial Affairs*, 3,2, Autumn, pp. 43-89

[50] Op. cit., Invest in Sweden Agency (1996) p. 11.

[51] Ingves S. & Brandimarti, A. (1995), EMU's Final Objective - A Single Currency, published in the Quarterly Review of the Riksbank, 4, Riksbank, Stockholm, p. 33.

[52] Ministry of Finance, (1995) *Press Release 12 June 1995*, Ministry of Finance, Stockholm, p. 1.

[53] Ibid., Ministry of Finance (1995) pp. 1-2.

[54] The fourth review of the convergence programme was completed in April 1997.

[55] The EMU Committee released its first reports in late 1996 recommending that Sweden would not and should not join the third stage of the EMU timetable in the first tranch of EU members. Instead, the government should, in typical Swedish fashion 'wait and see' what progress on the timetable is made in the late 1990s.

[56] The consolidated general government financial deficit for 1995 was estimated to be SEK 146 billion, equivalent to 9 percent of GDP, in the June 1995 Convergence Programme. According to April 1996 review, the deficit was actually SEK 132 billion, equivalent to 8.1 percent of GDP - see Ministry of Finance, (1996) *Review of the Swedish Convergence Programme*, Ministry of Finance, Stockholm, April, p. 1. Progress has continued at an impressive rate. According to the later April 1997 review, the deficit had fallen by 1996 to SEK 42 billion or 2.5 percent of GDP - an improvement of 8 percentage points since 1994 and much better than initial forecast of 5.2 percent for that year in the original programme. In accordance with the accounting rules of the EU, the deficit amounted to an equivalent of 3.6 percent of GDP in 1996.

[57] Ministry of Finance (1997) *Review of the Swedish Convergence Programme*, Ministry of Finance, Stockholm, April, p. 1.

[58] The corresponding figure for 1995 was estimated by the Ministry of Finance to have been a deficit of SEK 132 billion or 8.1 percent of GDP.

[59] Indeed, in a report published by the Commission in April 1997, Sweden was included as one of the country's likely to be eligible for the first wave of EMU membership. In spite of problems over the level of Sweden national debt, the Commission argued that the country had showed good progress towards meeting the criteria and could therefore qualify.

[60] This still remains the case even after the Finnish government's decision to allow the marrkka to join the looser ERM in late 1996.

[61] Mr. Lars Heikensten (1996), Deputy Governor of the Riksbank speaking at Unibank's Investment Seminar, Copenhagen 8-10 May, Sveriges Riksbank, *Address by Mr. Lars Heikensten, Deputy Governor, Sveriges Riksbank, at Unibank's Investment Seminar, Copenhagen, 8-10 May 1996*, Sveriges Riksbank, Stockholm, p. 9.

[62] Taken from Swedish Institute, Divisions grow over EMU as leading Social Democrats demand referendum on Swedish entry, *Faxed From Sweden*, No. 10, Swedish Institute, Stockholm, 24 May 1996, p. 1.

[63] The Taxation Minister, Thomas Östros, for instance, warned of 'the perils of Euro-federalism'. He voiced concern that Swedish membership of a single currency could lead to a loss of power over national taxation policy in February 1997.

[64] Ibid., Swedish Institute (1996) p. 1.

[65] The controversy over EMU has further increased. In April 1997, the Centre Party, which forms part of an alliance supporting the minority Social Democrats in the Parliament, threatened to stop cooperating if the government entered any future EMU arrangement. Taken from *The European*, 24-30 April 1997, p. 9.

[66] Later the Riksbank and the SAF officially announced in February their support for Swedish participation in the single currency as part of the first group of EMU members.

[67] In response to the statements by the central bank and the SAF and as means of influencing the Social Democrats who hope to make a decision on the single currency at their 1997 party congress, the LO officially announced in April 1997 that it opposed Swedish participation in EMU (at least in the short-term). The LO's chairman, Bertil Jonsson, argued that a vital precondition for EMU would be that Swedish wages did not rise above those of other comparable member states.

[68] Op. cit., Swedish Institute, (1996) p. 1.

[69] Ministry of Foreign Affairs (1994), *Statement of Government Policy Presented by the Prime Minister to the Swedish Parliament,* 7 October, UD, Stockholm, p. 13.

[70] Ministry of Foreign Affairs, (1995), *Address by the Minister For Foreign Affairs at the National Conference of the "People and Defence" Federation,* 31 January, UD, Stockholm, p. 2.

[71] For a detailed assessment see Salmon, T (1995), *The Common Foreign and Security Policy and Defence,* Discussion Paper of the Jean Monnet Group of Experts, CEUS, Hull.

[72] However, a major domestic debate was sparked shortly after by Carlsson's comments (February 1996) that Sweden might be ready to join NATO at the turn of the century. Carlsson was speaking at a conference of civil and military personnel in the skiing resort of Sälen and his comments were in response to claims by several prominent international security experts that the time was now ripe for the country to join NATO. However, his references were to rule out NATO membership in the immediate future. His reference to a 'more flexible and pragmatic' approach to Swedish defence matters was universally interpreted in a converse manner by the press and thus indicated that in the medium term the government would be willing to abandon 'non-alignment in military alliances'. Carlsson was especially criticised by the Centre Party leader, Olof Johansson, the Left Party and the Greens for signalling the relinquishing of Swedish independence in military affairs and vindicating their suspicions on EU membership.

[73] Ministry of Foreign Affairs, (1995) *Statement of Government Policy Presented at the Parliamentary Debate on Foreign Affairs,* 22 February, UD, Stockholm, p. 3.

[74] Ministry of Foreign Affairs, (1995), *Towards a New European Security Order - A Swedish View,* 30 May, UD, Stockholm, p. 10.

[75] Taken from op. cit., Luif (1995) p. 369.

[76] Lindahl, R. (1996) The Swedish Debate in Janning, J., Algieri, F., Rodrigo, F., Lindahl, R., Grabbe, H. & Hughes, K. *The 1996 IGC - National Debates (2)*, Royal Institute of International Affairs, London, p. 46.

[77] Sveriges säkerhetspolitik, Sammansatta utrikes och försvarsutskottets betänkande, 1995-96: UFöU1, 23/11/1995, Gotab, Stockholm, 1995, p. 38.

[78] Op. cit., Ministry of Foreign Affairs (30 November 1996) pp. 26-7.

[79] Op. cit., Ministry of Foreign Affairs (30 November 1996) p. 27.

[80] Op. cit., Ministry of Foreign Affairs (30 November 1996) p. 27.

[81] Op. cit., Ministry of Foreign Affairs (30 November 1996) p. 30.

[82] Prime Minister Persson was forced in September 1996 to stoutly defend the country's continued non-alignment during a brief visit by the US Defence Secretary William Perry. The US representative claimed during a TV interview that he failed to understand Sweden's non-alignment and that it no longer carried any meaning. In response, Persson pointed to the Defence Secretary's 'far too close-sighted perspective'. However, he did suggest that there were greater opportunities for Swedish foreign policy cooperation with its western partners.

[83] The Swedes, for instance, resisted French-led proposals in March 1997 for a much-enhanced role for the WEU, including troop-raising for EU peace-keeping projects. They feared this may lead to the EU being interpreted in Moscow as a military organisation, which could then scotch the chances of the Baltic Republics joining the Union at a later date.

[84] Swedish Institute, Sweden stands clear of NATO debate as public gives backing to neutrality, Faxed from Sweden, No. 11, Swedish Institute, Stockholm, 14 June 1996, p. 2.

[85] Although Swedish governmental policy towards the CFSP will remain essentially intergovernmental and 'minimalist', it will be difficult for the government to maintain a static policy in the security area either towards the EU or NATO. As Sæter notes Swedish policy-makers soon realised that the real issue is not whether or not to participate in defence and other security arrangements and actions of a military kind. The question for these countries is rather how such a participation should take place in the future. Thus, despite Sweden's minimalist policy it will inevitably find itself drawn into an ever closer relationship with NATO and the WEU. Indeed, this was more or less acknowledged in the joint Finnish-Swedish memorandum (25 April 1996) to the IGC Presidency advocating 'an enhanced EU role in crisis management' covering all military aspects. In particular, the memorandum called for the CFSP to have a stronger act of 'empowerment' in which 'all the contributing member states will participate on an equal footing in planning and decision-making relating to operations enacted by the EU' - Sæter, M. (1996) *The Nordic Countries and the Perspective of a 'Core' Europe*, NUPI Working Papers, No. 558, September, NUPI, Oslo.

[86] Op. cit., Lindahl (1996) p. 47.

[87] The Moderates for example, have opnely canvassed for Swedish NATO membership. Indeed, the party's secretary, Gunnar Hökmark, also proposed in March 1997 that Sweden develop a military partnership with its Nordic neighbours in readiness for the country's eventual entry into NATO.

[88] Mouritzen has argued that Swedish EU membership therefore presents a whole new series of 'new autonomy dangers' which governments will have to grapple with - Mouritzen, H. (1997) *External Danger and Democracy: Old Nordic Lessons and New European Challenges,* Dartmouth, Aldershot.

[89] Ministry of Foreign Affairs (1997) *Declaration by the Foreign Minister in the Foreign Affair's Debate in the Riksdag (12 February 1997),* UD, Stockholm.

Index

N.B. (1) Unless otherwise specified, references are to Sweden.
N.B. (2) The Swedish letters Å, Ä and Ö are classed as A and O in this index.